BLUEPRINTS

for Achievement

In the Cooperative Classroom

3rd Edition

James Bellanca & Robin Fogarty

Foreword by Arthur L. Costa

CORWIN PRESS
A SAGE Publications Company
Thousand Oaks, California

For information:

Corwin Press
A Sage Publications Company
2455 Teller Road
Thousand Oaks, California 91320
www.corwinpress.com

Sage Publications Ltd.
1 Oliver's Yard
55 City Road
London EC1Y 1SP
United Kingdom

Sage Publications India Pvt. Ltd.
B-42, Panchsheel Enclave
New Delhi 110 017 India

Printed in the United States of America

LCCN 2002116928
ISBN 1-57517-548-7

This book is printed on acid-free paper.

05   06   07   08   09   10   9   8   7   6   5   4   3   2   1

Mary Beth Brumagin

CONTENTS

ABSTRACT

Based on the most comprehensive and current research in the areas of cooperative learning and cognitive instruction, *Blueprints for Achievement in the Cooperative Classroom* presents the best instructional practices for the K–12 classroom teacher. Beginning with the nitty-gritties of forming cooperative learning groups, *Blueprints* takes you step by step from the forming (introductory) phase to the subsequent phases of norming, conforming, storming, and performing. Each chapter is introduced with a background piece that defines and explains its basic concept. This descriptive section is followed by specific and necessary input for the three fully developed lessons—elementary, middle, and high school models—featured in each chapter.

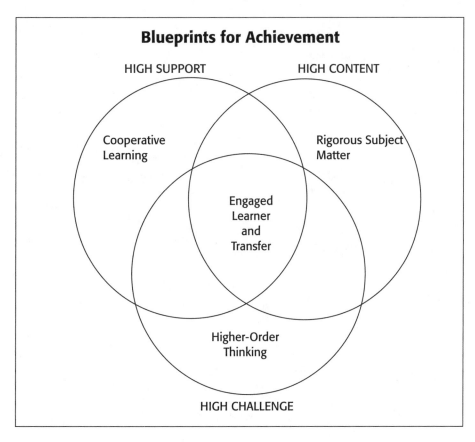

Blueprints for Achievement

HIGH SUPPORT HIGH CONTENT

Cooperative Learning

Rigorous Subject Matter

Engaged Learner and Transfer

Higher-Order Thinking

HIGH CHALLENGE

The lessons are filled with practical ideas and in-depth examples that integrate what research has proven to increase student achievement. For the novice or for the experienced teacher already using cooperative learning, *Blueprints* verbally and graphically displays the elements that promote high-content, high-support, high-challenge lessons for all students. "High content" refers to rigorous academic subject matter with conceptual learning as its base. "High support" targets positively structured peer interactions for intense student engagement. "High challenge" means that learning tasks promote higher-order thinking and require intense engagement by students.

FOREWORD

When I was young, my childhood chums—Charlie, Ronnie, Junior—and I would work for days digging gigantic pits in a nearby vacant field. We constructed a fort where we could hide from the world, fantasize about soldiers, cowboys, and distant lands, and do all those magical things little boys so fervently do. Now if our mothers had told us to go out and dig a hole that large, we would have resisted the task, resented having to do it, and procrastinated as long as possible. Why is it that humans devote so much energy and time to enjoying a difficult task when we do it with others, but are reluctant to go it alone? The answer lies in our human passion for interconnectedness.

We learn myriad intellectual skills and dispositions through our interactions with others. Empathy is enhanced when we listen to others, value one another's unique contributions, take another person's point of view, achieve consensus, and resolve conflicts. We learn to persist by keeping our ideas in the mix, to think flexibly by combining ideas with others or even abandoning our own ideas as we evaluate other's ideas, and to analyze by dividing up the work—one person is responsible for one part and another person is responsible for the other part. We serve as critical friends providing checks and feedback about one another's thinking. Such discourse enhances metacognition as we must articulate our thoughts to communicate and make our patterns of thinking more explicit and subject to analysis by other group members. As we plan, discuss, and report, we meld our information, experiences, and ideas to synthesize a richer product. The result of this cooperative development of thinking—"co-cognition"—produces a collective process of thought more potent than any one contributor's thinking.

Learning in cooperative groups facilitates thinking about systems in which many variables are constantly interacting. Each variable affects another which affects another and so on. Families, weather systems, and national economies are examples of dynamic systems where tiny inputs can reverberate, producing dramatically large consequences. Thus, collaborative thinkers realize the potential to significantly influence the direction of the community of which they are a part.

As individuals develop collaborative abilities, they are characterized by altruism, collegiality, and the giving of self to group goals and needs. Interdependent persons contribute to a common good and they also draw on the resources of others. They value dialogue and are able to hold their own beliefs and actions in abeyance in order to lend their energies to the achievement of the group's goals. They envision the expanding capacities of the group and its members, and value and draw upon the resources of others.

Students learn to become self-directed in collaborative groups; they learn to be self-managing, self-monitoring and self-modifying. As students perfect their performance in groups, they develop operational indicators of what they do or say as they solve problems, make decisions, reason, and create. These indicators serve as criteria by which to evaluate their own and others' performance. Through this collaborative process, students develop a set of criteria, internalize those criteria, and keep in the mind the criteria as they work together. As they reflect on the group's performance, they rate their own performance according to these criteria. When these criteria are developed collaboratively, students derive a common definition and vision of what effective group problem solving is and how it is enacted. In turn, the collaboratively developed concepts, visions, and operational definitions are used to guide, reflect upon, and evaluate one's own performance while in groups or alone.

As persons become more interdependent, they may experience a sense of kinship that comes from a unity of being, a sense of sharing a common habitat (class, school, neighborhood), and a mutual bonding to common goals and shared values. Interdependent individuals enlarge their sense of self from a conception of "me" to a sense of "we." They understand that "as we transcend the self and become part of the whole we do not lose our individuality but rather our egocentricity" (Sergiovanni 1994).

Vygotsky (1962) lends psychological support for cooperative learning as a way of developing intellectual capacities. He states, "Every function in cultural development appears twice: first on the social level, and later on the individual level; first between people and then inside." This applies equally to attention, to memory, and to the formation of concepts. All the higher functions originate as actual relationships between individuals.

Others have repeatedly supported this principle with research. Their findings suggest that there is a strong positive relationship between the ability to perform higher-order thinking and to think more critically and creatively when learning occurs in group settings. These "higher" functions have been viewed as beneficial by-products of cooperative learning (Johnson and Johnson 2001; Perkins 2001).

The teacher's role is critical as a stimulator and mediator of this process. The skillful teacher structures the cooperative classroom, presents or surfaces problems to resolve, mediates each group's work with questions and nonjudgmental feedback, monitors and assesses individual and group progress, and invites reflection on and meaning making from the cooperative learning process. Of most importance, the teacher models thinking and cooperating in all they do.

Blueprints for Achievement in the Cooperative Classroom includes a wealth of student activities with explicit guidelines for teachers and effective research on which they are based. In *Blueprints,* thinking is not only a by-product, but is also an intention of cooperative learning—one of the goals and desired outcomes of the collaborative efforts of students and teachers. And, *Blueprints* goes several steps beyond. It gives critical help in extending thinking into every corner of every classroom in a cooperative school. It guides the transfer of cooperating and thinking beyond the school walls and provides a blueprint for a new look at how students, teachers, and the entire staff can benefit from quality cooperative learning experiences.

Arthur L. Costa
Granite Bay, California
2002

ACKNOWLEDGMENTS

There are a number of dedicated colleagues scattered across this country (and over the Canadian border) who sparked us with the inspiration, ideas, and real-life illustrations to move us from thinking to inking. As noted within the pages of the book itself, the extensive work of David and Roger Johnson in the field of cooperative learning undergirds the entirety of *Blueprints.*

Paralleling the Johnsons' influence, Art Costa's work in cognitive instruction is evident throughout the book. In addition to these special educators, we would like to acknowledge the work of Frank Lyman and Jay McTighe for their ideas on thinking tools; Beau Fly Jones for her work with cognitive organizers; Ann Brown, David Perkins, and Robert Swartz for extending our understanding of the metacognitive level of thinking; and David Perkins, Gavriel Salomon, and John Barell for their latest thoughts on transfer.

For fear of forgetting the "somebodies" who perhaps deserve our thanks most, we extend our heartfelt gratitude to the many school practitioners who led the way with us toward this rich synthesis of the best research and the best practice; your blueprints became our *Blueprints.*

At SkyLight, we would like to thank the production and editorial staff . . . David Stockman for the cover design and inside illustrations, Bruce Leckie for the book and page layouts, Jean Ward for her editorial guidance, Donna Ramirez for coordinating the project and for the revision input, and Dara Lee Howard and Heidi Ray for editing. Without their efforts, this publication would not be.

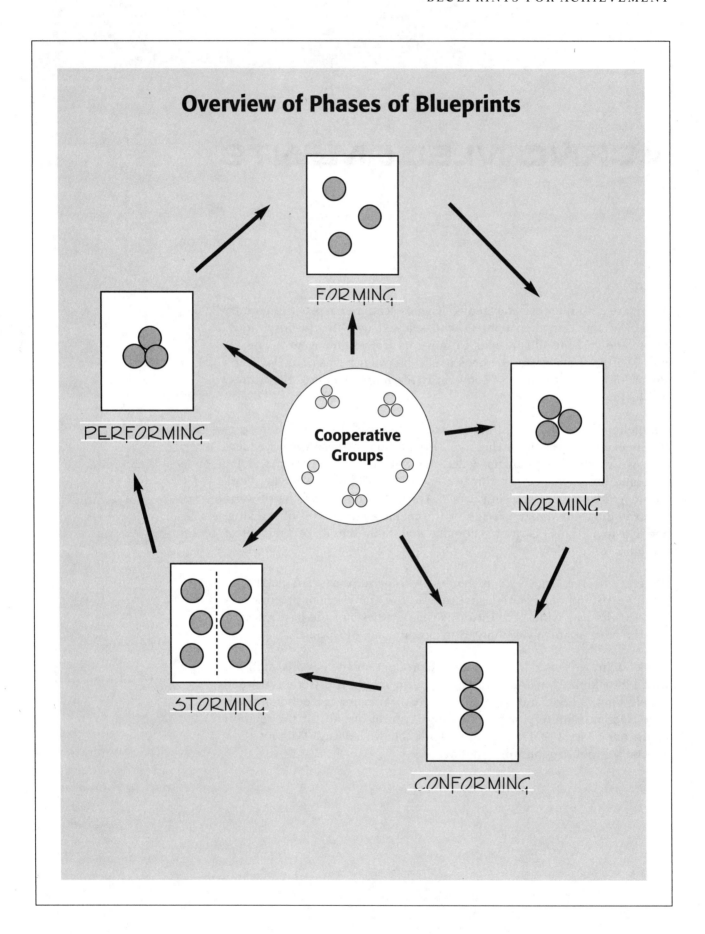

Overview of Phases of Blueprints

FORMING

PERFORMING

Cooperative
Groups

NORMING

STORMING

CONFORMING

INTRODUCTION

A NEW BLUEPRINT FOR TEACHING AND LEARNING

Blueprints for Achievement in the Cooperative Classroom is more than just another book about cooperation in the classroom. It is a guide for those creative and seasoned teachers who see the cooperative classroom as a community of students eager to learn, not just for higher scores on standardized tests, but for transferring what they learn beyond the schoolhouse walls. It is also a "must read" for those novice teachers who want to start their careers with the best foot forward.

The blueprint concept is more than a simple metaphor for organizing a book. The blueprint metaphor challenges the factory metaphor that has dominated the American concept of schooling for sixty years. For too many decades, Henry Ford's assembly line has served as the model for American education. The end result? Millions of students, the products of "teacher-proof" curriculum and instruction, roll off the school assembly line and are given evermore easily earned stamps of approval. Supervisors, newly trained with bland checklists, watch as each teacher follows step-by-step instructions. At the end of the line, students are tested, checked, and measured to ensure they meet minimal educational standards.

By the turn of the twentieth century, Ford, Chrysler, and General Motors had recognized the limits of their assembly lines. It is time for American schools to do the same. In the blueprints metaphor, the schoolhouse is not a factory but rather an artisan's workshop where the master nourishes and enriches the apprentices' talents. The apprentices learn not for a one-size-fits-all test; they learn to develop knowledge, skill, and talent that will serve them well when they step into their own world of work.

The blueprints metaphor of the artisan's shop advocates subtle shifts in the nature of the schoolhouse. In place of learning for a test, it advocates learning for a lifetime. In place of the teacher as dispenser of bits of factual knowledge, it advocates the teacher as master artist. In place of the teacher as giver of information, it advocates the teacher as architect of the intellect.

SHIFTING TO THE BLUEPRINTS METAPHOR

Such a shift sounds like an awesome task. In one sense, it is; in another, the shift allows teachers to do what most dreamed that teaching would allow them to do—develop each child's unique capabilities to the fullest. It allows them not to punch out copycat products, but rather to create talented students who are ready and able to transfer learning to a multitude of changing challenges.

The shift has already begun in some classrooms. Aided by supportive professional development, emerging research on how the brain works, and encouraging supervisors, thousands of teachers are applying the tools of cooperative learning, thinking, problem-based learning, and problem solving in their classrooms. National professional organizations—American Federation of Teachers, National Council of Mathematics Teachers, National Science Teachers, Association for Supervision and Curriculum Development, National Boards for Professional Teaching, National Education Association, and National Staff Development Council—have called for major instructional reforms that use these methods.

Three Levels of Learning

Just what is needed to engage all teachers in this shift? *Blueprints* is organized to give teachers a three-level framework that enables them to redirect their instructional goals. It introduces practical steps for establishing a cooperative climate (level 1), for initiating deep understanding (level 2), and for preparing students for transfer (level 3). (See Figure 0.1.) Certainly, the instructional tools are available to shift from a recall curriculum to a three-level transfer curriculum.

Three-Level Framework for Instruction

3 Transfer
2 Deep Understanding
1 Cooperative Climate

Figure 0.1

At the first level, cooperative learning establishes positive, collaborative relationships among students and teachers. These relationships are essential building blocks in a community of learners with high-level cognitive goals. Cooperative learning encourages internal motivation and collaborative inquiry instead of resorting to coercive discipline practices that rely on external motivation. Cooperative learning replaces self-centered individualism with communities of learners who support and enhance each other's growth and development.

After expanding students' willingness to learn together (level 1), teachers who are committed to teaching for understanding move to a second, higher level of instruction—teaching students how to use their brains more creatively and critically (level 2). As students increase their abilities to reason, solve problems, and make decisions while using a more rigorous curricular content, the teacher quickly perceives student readiness to look beyond the limits of any lesson and begins teaching for transfer (level 3).

The three levels of learning advocated by *Blueprints* are built around the words of the American jurist Oliver Wendell Holmes, Jr.: "There are one-story [intellects], two-story [intellects], and three-story [intellects] with skylights. All fact collectors, who have no aim beyond their facts, are one-story [minds]. Two-story [minds] compare, reason, generalize, using the labors of the fact collectors as well as their own. Three-story [minds] idealize, imagine, predict—their best illumination comes from above, through the skylight."

Blueprints combines Holmes' words and Bloom's taxonomy (Bloom et al. 1956) to form a three-story intellect. The three-story intellect uses Bloom's taxonomy to describe thinking processes at each of the three levels: analyzing, predicting, and evaluating. Rather than memorizing the taxonomy for a graduate school test—as has been the experience of thousands of classroom teachers—teachers now give top priority to using the taxonomy. Teachers and students who center daily teaching and learning practices around these processes move most quickly and successfully through a curriculum that imbeds higher-order thinking in every nook and cranny of the curriculum.

Instructional Methods

The methods selected for this book are drawn from a variety of resources. Johnson and Johnson's (1974, 1978a, 1978b, 1979, 1982, 1984, 1986, 1987, 1999a, 1999b) conceptual cooperative learning model is the starting point for Level 1 instruction; it is supplemented with more practical structures, strategies, and curriculum models from Kagan (1977, 1992), Sharan and Sharan (1976), Slavin (1977a, 1977b, 1979, 1980, 1983a, 1983b), Cohen (1986), and Gibbs (1987). *Blueprints* includes only those methods that have passed the test of time in a variety of classrooms. These strategies have proven adaptable across the curriculum as the best tools both for creating a cooperative classroom culture and for developing collaborative work habits so that they may become more productive learners in the classroom and in life beyond the classroom. Most important, the methods selected have a successful track record in classrooms with low-performing students at high risk of failing in school.

However, these methods will not succeed unless educational conditions in the classroom and at the school site encourage the deep changes that *Blueprints* advocates. Change is a challenge—a tough challenge. When students and teachers have become accustomed to low expectations for learning and teaching, shifting to new, higher expectations for cooperating, thinking, and transferring is sometimes difficult. These shifts take time and effort, not because the methods themselves are difficult or inappropriate, but because beliefs held for "what is" are easier to hold than beliefs for "what might be." Students' and teachers' expectations for learning must be changed. If a teacher puts her best effort into using ineffective practices and her students fail, she can more easily blame failure on the students' deficiencies and will find little reason to believe that any other approaches could possibly produce better results. Thus, the challenge to change becomes a challenge not only of methods, but also of belief in the possibility of what might be. Thus, the secret of raising student scores in a school is not in having one teacher try one or two cooperative methods (that's a start); rather, it is in spending the time and energy to make every teacher and student in the school shift their beliefs as well as change their expectations and their methods for teaching and learning. Educators must question and change their mental model. *Blueprints* is designed to encourage the faculty in a school to work together toward this goal, starting with simple methods and advancing to more complex, higher-order strategies in the context of an increasingly collaborative community.

As will be explained in chapter 1, research shows that nine strategies have major influence on student achievement. Of these nine, cooperative learning is the strategy that researchers describe as the most powerful tool. And, as teachers will discover in this book, cooperative learning can be fully integrated with the other strategies. The teacher who makes regular and consistent use of the *Blueprints* framework not only brings the achievement advantage of cooperative learning to the classroom, but also brings the benefits of the other eight strategies coupled with many emerging insights about how the brain works. (See chapter 4.) Fully implementing this research—the blueprint for achievement—in each and every classroom at a school is the starting point for teachers who want to bring the most effective instruction to their students as well as the starting point for educators who want meaningful, schoolwide change that results in noticeable and measurable student achievement gains.

CREATING COOPERATIVE CLASSROOMS IN FIVE PHASES

Teachers who want to effectively implement the blueprint for achievement must use strategies within the context of a cooperative classroom culture. In essence, this means the teacher will spend the school year molding her class into a single cooperative group. This group will pass through five predictable phases of development: forming, norming, conforming, storming, and performing (see Figure 0.2). As the class passes through these steps (and sometimes regresses), behaviors and attitudes change and a more easily managed focus on collaboration and achievement blossoms.

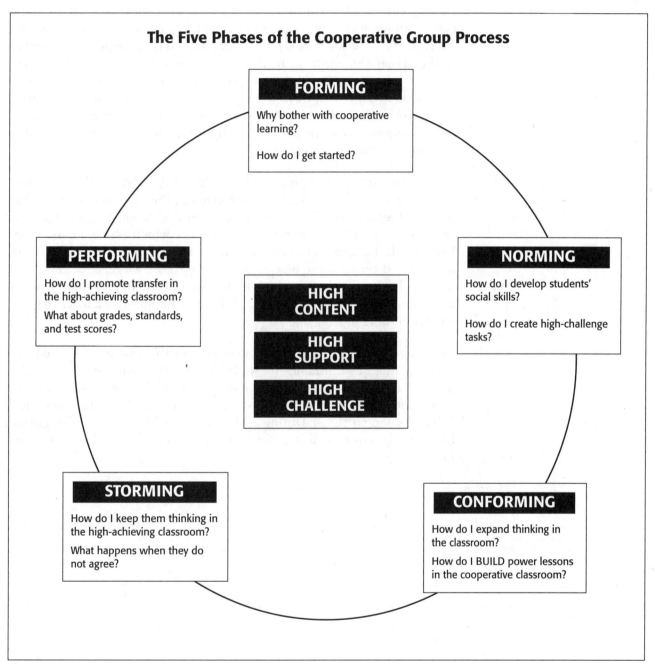

Figure 0.2

In the first phase, forming, teachers teach students how to cooperate. They select instructional strategies that enable them to organize the students and to BUILD new lessons within the *Blueprints* framework. (BUILD is explained in chapters 2 and 6). At this point, teachers are forming new expectations that will help students adjust to behaving cooperatively and prepare for the challenges of the following phases.

As teachers focus on creating cooperative classrooms, they must remember that students are highly individualistic. Most students are more comfortable learning alone—their past experience has assured them they can "make their mark" in the classroom. For some, making a mark has meant earning good grades. For others, it has meant grabbing peer attention by being anti-grades or by being "the bad kid." In the beginning, some students, and even some parents, may react adversely to cooperative learning in the classroom. Most likely, the A students will raise loud objections. Some will want to take over their groups and do all the work, and keep their grade. Others will ask their parents to speak against cooperative group work. Similarly, some F students will rebel by acting out to avoid their new group responsibilities. On the other hand, others will show a new and surprising interest in schoolwork.

Each phase brings out predictable student behaviors. If the behaviors most associated with a phase are not evident, the class is not yet in that phase. *Blueprints* highlights the specific strategies most appropriate for each phase in order to help teachers identify which phase a class is in. Because all students do not march to the same drumbeat, all students will not proceed through the phases in lock step. Nor will classes enter and leave a phase on the same schedule. In some cases, an individual student or a whole class may fall out of a phase and require more teacher guidance to resume moving ahead.

The class' success in any phase depends on the teacher. As a teacher becomes more comfortable and skilled in selecting appropriate strategies not only for a lesson, but also for the class' development as a cooperative unit, students learn the benefits of working together and adopt new behaviors and attitudes. During each phase, teachers can look for a number of road signs to expected behaviors that occur during that phase (see Figure 0.3).

Expected Behaviors for Each Stage

Forming
- Students say, "I want to do it myself."
- Teacher is confused about small group instructions, roles and responsibilities, and expectations. Teacher wonders, "Am I doing this right?"
- Inappropriate behaviors disrupt the small group.
- One student does it all.
- Groups form slowly.
- Noise abounds.
- Teacher shows an inability to assess group work or process.
- Students need detailed instructions for the task.

Norming
- Students learn the social skills, but apply them inconsistently (e.g., not always listening or sometimes using put downs).
- Students complain about each other.
- Fewer disruptive misbehaviors occur in the group.
- Students begin to do their jobs in the group.
- Teacher increases in her ability to report on content and cooperation in the group.
- Groups begin to focus on their goals, but more "I" than "we" behaviors occur.
- Students show increased tolerance of individual differences.
- Students accept one another more.

Conforming
- Group shows increased readiness to think.
- More students volunteer to share group thinking.
- Off-group task behaviors occur only occasionally.
- Tasks take less time.
- Students do jobs in small groups.
- Students use social skills to solve problems in the group.
- Higher-order thinking becomes the norm.

Storming
- Students in groups propose best thinking strategy (e.g., brainstorming, evaluating) or visual tool (e.g., Web, T-chart).
- Students use strategies without procedural instructions.
- Students check own thinking and cooperating.
- Students share roles equally.
- Students engage in problem solving.
- Students assess their own social skills and thinking behaviors.
- "We" behaviors dominate.
- Students provide lengthy assessments of the ideas in a lesson.
- Students assert their own opinions, yet look for compromise.

Performing
- Students require minimal instruction on small-group procedures.
- Students spend minimal time off task.
- Teachers mediate student understanding and transfer of content.
- More students volunteer for all-class discussions than time allows.
- Students show an increase in understanding of the content in small-group and class-wide discussions.
- Students show interest in the cooperative climate.
- Students express concern about individuals who need to be included more.
- Students plan ways to improve the cooperative climate.
- Students' products show a high level of quality.

Figure 0.3

CONNECTION WITH PRIOR KNOWLEDGE OF BEST INSTRUCTIONAL PRACTICES

How does *Blueprints* fit with what teachers already know about the best approaches to instruction—direct instruction; learning styles; multiple intelligences; Teacher Expectations, Student Achievement (TESA); inquiry models; integrated curriculum; and models of teaching? *Blueprints* assumes that good instruction is not limited to a single method or approach, but rather is a robust repertoire of teaching strategies.

Blueprints shows how teachers' knowledge about TESA (wait time, equal distribution of questions, teacher mobility, etc.), McCarthy's 4MAT (learning styles), Gardner's multiple intelligences theory and framework, brain research, and other best practices can fit within and enhance the *Blueprints* framework. In addition, *Blueprints* integrates more complex models of inquiry (problem-based learning, case studies, project and service learning, and performance learning) and other integrated curriculum models with more complex cooperative learning processes. *Blueprints* provides a path to cooperative learning, teacher by teacher, school by school.

The Teacher

Each teacher's move into the cooperative-cognitive model is a process of change. The process starts with the teacher's commitment to integrate the principles and practices for creating a high-challenge, high-support, high-content classroom. The teacher can start by duplicating an informal approach of simple engagement activities such as think-pair-share, explain why, or we-bags to initiate lessons (see chapter 2). Or, they may scatter provocative group strategies throughout a unit: a graphic organizer to compare characters in a novel, a project to research and make a collage of the author's life, and a group portfolio of book reports on other works by the author. These informal approaches introduce students to more thought-provoking lessons and increase student interest in the curricular content.

However, to make a significant and measurable impact on student achievement, the teacher must advance from the informal use of strategies to a formal approach. In the formal approach, she transforms her entire instructional format by infusing cooperative and cognitive learning throughout all elements of daily instruction and assessment. Her units create a cooperative culture that moves every lesson through the three-story intellect model (see chapter 4) with the goal of making each student a thoughtful problem solver and team player.

The School

If the school wants to show schoolwide gains in achievement, all teachers in the school must work together, not alone, to infuse this approach throughout the entire school day. The principal and the school team need to target student achievement in one or more subjects with cognitive skill development and cooperative behavior as the schoolwide goal. Working as a collaborative schoolwide team, they must dedicate one to three years to attain a measurable achievement goal with mandated standardized tests. They must carry out a plan to infuse cooperative learning and thinking across the curriculum. Each teacher must integrate the principles and practices in his or her daily lessons and meet weekly with grade-level or subject-area peers to review and polish classroom practices in cooperative learning and thinking.

Quarterly, grade-level teams can present a history of their activities, student materials, and observations to the entire school team. Using a variety of measures, including standardized test scores, surveys, observation records, and other assessment tools, these teams can record progress to their goal. At least once a year, they can report formally to the district administration to document progress toward the achievement goal.

The *Blueprints* approach cannot be implemented with a quickie workshop or two. Successful implementation requires teachers to invest thirty to forty hours in classroom instruction, paying careful attention to assessment and reflection as they try out techniques. Teachers participating in a schoolwide implementation guided by a committed instructional leader must add another thirty or forty hours dedicated to peer team and school-wide meetings. These meetings focus on the quality of applications over a two- to three-year time span.

When it comes to raising student academic performance, it is important that serious users of this approach consider the *high* in high expectations. The words, *high expectations for all,* are easy to say. What is difficult is to align actions that connect these words to classroom instruction that has *high challenge, high support,* and *high content* intertwined in every activity. High challenge relates to the way higher-order thinking strategies (chapter 4) are used to move students above and beyond rote memory tasks, filling in the blanks, or other low cognitive tasks. High support relates to the way the teacher creates a climate of mutual respect and trust among the students—for each other and for the teacher. High support is marked by encouragement (in place of put downs), peer support teams, and the mastery of complex social skills (chapter 3). High content relates to a curriculum of rigor. In mathematics, this means focusing on core concepts of algebra and geometry, not on the memorization of procedures; in science, it means focusing on science concepts, not fun activities; in reading, it means reading for understanding and complex comprehension across the curriculum. In all content areas, high content relates to how well students understand and transfer the principles as well as the practices of that curriculum.

FACILITATING THE FIVE PHASES OF COOPERATIVE LEARNING

Designing for the high-content, high-cooperation, and high-challenge classroom requires blueprints and specifications that guide the various phases of the construction process.

How this Book Is Organized

Blueprints is divided into parts, one for each of the five phases—forming, norming, conforming, storming, and performing. Each part is divided into two chapters. The first chapter in each part introduces basic concepts and strategies for the beginner. The second chapter in each part elaborates on the cooperative learning model for more experienced teachers.

How the Chapters Are Organized

Each chapter is designed as a blueprint and includes three components—draft, specs, and blueprint.

Draft

In the Draft section, the chapter's concept is developed with definitions, descriptions, explanations, rationale, and research. The Draft section provides the research and background for the specific high-content, high-support, and high-challenge elements designed into each lesson included in the chapter. By reading the Draft prior to using the lessons, teachers gain a grounding in the philosophy behind the lesson's strategy.

Specs

Specifications for the lessons are given in the Specs section. Input needed by students prior to the lesson, background material, tools, cooperative group structures, thinking skills focus, and pertinent notes to the teacher are all found in the Specs section.

Blueprints

Separate model blueprints (lessons) for elementary, middle, and secondary levels of instruction appear at the end of each chapter. Each lesson is age- and content-appropriate to a specific grade. Although the lessons are ready to use in the classroom, teachers may adapt the lessons to fit their situation and their students' needs.

Lessons are divided into three sections—Setting Up the Scaffolding, Working the Crew, and Reflecting on the Design—and each section is designated by a different icon.

Prior to the Lesson: Setting Up the Scaffolding

All preparation, input, handouts, and materials needed prior to the activity are included in Setting Up the Scaffolding. Typical elements in this section might include a focus activity, instructions, and identification of the cooperative social skill and targeted thinking skill. This is the preparation teachers do as they begin to plan the lesson.

During the Lesson: Working the Crew

This section of each lesson centers on the interactivity that occurs during the actual lesson. This activity includes the cooperative interaction structure and the graphic organizer with which the students' work is outlined in practical, ready-to-use classroom procedures.

After the Lesson: Reflecting on the Design

This section focuses on the processing procedures conducted after the cooperative thinking activity. Metacognitive discussion questions, log entries, follow-up strategies, practice, transfer, and closure activities might be included in Reflecting on the Design. This piece pulls the lesson toward closure.

Three appendices follow the final chapter. Appendix A comprises the glossary. Appendix B answers the most frequently asked questions about *Blueprints* and cooperative learning. Appendix C provides a set of blackline masters arranged by chapter.

SUMMARY

Given the large amount of research that demonstrates the powerful effects that well-implemented cooperative learning can have on achievement and behavior, we have a number of hopes for the future:

- We hope there will be an end to those two-hour inservice training sessions that only give superficial glances at cooperative learning or the latest thinking strategy. Conversely, we hope that a concerted effort be made to create graduate courses and professional development programs that allow time for teachers to develop the abilities required to facilitate the cooperative-cognitive model.
- We hope that teachers schedule time each week to synthesize the best practices identified by research into lessons that focus on student achievement.
- Finally, we hope teachers have regular, scheduled opportunities throughout the year to build their school's collaborative learning community with a focus on planning how to use best research to promote even higher student achievement. For those who are willing to take the time and the effort to perfect the art and the craft of this approach, the reward will be seeing that all children, given the best of instruction, learn more, learn faster, and learn better.

By itself, cooperative learning has proven over the years to be the most powerful tool for raising student achievement. When thinking challenges are woven throughout cooperative lessons, the combination of complex thinking and collaborative performance provides the impetus for shifting the curriculum from a superficial recall of selected facts to a transfer curriculum that empowers students to be lifelong learners.

In this context, any discussion of the notion that "all students can learn" must include classroom implementation of high content, high challenge, and high support into all classrooms, most especially those classrooms with high-risk, low-performing students that are most denied access to cooperative learning and higher-order thinking. Some advocates of reform—who are sure that many teachers have neither the skill nor the motivation to learn how to structure such lessons—look to the simplicity of more "teacher-proof" recipes as the only way to increase student achievement. With one broad stroke, these so called advocates sweep away all opportunity for students to become the high achievers and thoughtful learners that the *Blueprints* model has so successfully facilitated.

The path to successful implementation of this way of teaching is not easy. However, two decades of research, as highlighted in this new edition, shows that the difficult is possible. Schools that have used *Blueprints*— Chicago, Rockford (IL), Peoria (IL), San Francisco, Cleveland, Indianapolis, New York, and thousands of classrooms in other rural and suburban schools—also show that this way of teaching works. In a multitude of classrooms, improved achievement scores are attributable to the hard and skilled work of teachers, who are well-trained, supported, and facilitated by strong site leaders and guided by knowledgeable and dedicated district leaders. As a result, their students have scored better on their standardized tests and have discovered the powerful benefits of learning. Moreover, these students have learned to behave better, think more skillfully, and gain a deeper understanding of more difficult curricula.

In this new edition of *Blueprints*, seasoned veterans and novice teachers will find many practical and tested tools for creating mindful teachers. In addition to these tools, they will find an attitude and belief about teaching and learning that takes very seriously those words of Oliver Wendell Holmes, which form the framework for *Blueprints*. May every teacher-learner who studies the contents of this book open the skylight to each and every student who enters her classroom and climbs the *Blueprints'* stairway.

Blueprints for Achievement

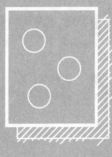

FORMING

PERFORMING

NORMING

CHAPTER 1

Phase 1

FORMING

Level 1
Why Bother with
Cooperative Learning?

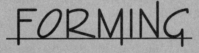

STORMING

CONFORMING

in the Cooperative Classroom

1

WHY BOTHER WITH COOPERATIVE LEARNING?

Ours is a time of pioneering . . . The foundations of the new building of humankind are deepening . . . The vitality of youth and the inspiration of teachers will help to create educational forums for public service."

—M. C. Richards

Draft

Q **What goal in Goals 2000 does cooperative learning support?**

A Cooperative learning directly supports creating literate Americans who work successfully in a global economy and who competently exercise their citizenship rights and responsibilities.

The twenty-first century educational agenda appears overwhelming. Schools are involved in major initiatives, ranging from implementing standards-based curricula to preparing students for high-stakes tests and from mentoring quality teachers to differentiating instruction for diverse learners. The saga of this burgeoning agenda began with a bold initiative called Goals 2000 (see Figure 1.1) and journeys through the standards movement to results-driven, performance-based curriculum, data-driven accountability, and state-managed testing agendas. In the early 2000s, the focus is squarely on state tests and the high stakes they carry for schools.

The path from the intended, high expectations of Goals 2000 and efforts to establish standards-based and performance-based curricula to the focus on high-stakes testing agenda sounds like a biblical tale: The 1989 Education Summit convened by George H. W. Bush and the nation's governors, begot Goals 2000 (see US Department of Education 1996). Goals 2000 begot the standards movement. Standards begot results-driven accountability, performance tasks, and scoring rubrics. Accountability begot high-stakes state testing to measure student achievement.

So, where does cooperative learning fit in this milieu of reform movements? What is so compelling about a cooperative learning approach to instruction? What supports its use in the nation's classrooms? Can't students learn more from the expert—the teacher—than they can from other students? Is this much ado about nothing?

Goals 2000

(These goals were created at the 1989 Charlottesville Education Summit.)

By the year 2000:

- All children in America will start school ready to learn.
- The high school graduation rate will increase to at least 90 percent.
- All students will leave grades 4, 8, and 12 having demonstrated competency over challenging subject matter in the core academic areas.
- US students will be first in the world in mathematics and science achievement.
- Every adult American will be literate and will possess the knowledge and skills necessary to compete in a global economy and exercise the rights and responsibilities of the citizenship.
- Every school in the U.S. will be free of drugs, violence, and the unauthorized presence of firearms and alcohol and will offer a disciplined environment conducive to learning.
- The nation's teaching force will have access to programs for the continued improvement of their professional skills and the opportunity to acquire the knowledge and skills needed to instruct and prepare all American students for the next century.
- Every school will promote partnerships that will increase parental involvement and participation in promoting the social, emotional and academic growth of children.

(From US Department of Education 1996.)

Figure 1.1

A LOOK BACK AT COOPERATIVE LEARNING

The naysayer who asserts that cooperative learning is just a fad or another new wrinkle may find the following bit of history interesting. Pioneer families knew the benefits of tutoring their children in groups. In their schools, several families gathered their children into one room. Very often, older students paired with younger students "to cipher the slates," read stories, and review bible lessons. The young teacher, very often one of the oldest students, relied heavily on the children to help each other with lessons. Well into the twentieth century in rural America, the one-room schoolhouse with cross-age tutors, cooperative learning groups, and group investigations were the norm. Not until the urban school emerged and the modern factory arrived did schools adopt the assembly line model of teaching and learning. Even at that time, educational leaders, such as Parker, Dewey, Washborne, and Deutsch, were strong advocates of the cooperative learning model. As early as 1889, Pepitone, Twiner, and Triplett were conducting the first formal studies of cooperative learning. Today, numerous studies by Johnson and Johnson (1986, 1999b), Slavin (1983a), and others document the powerful effects of cooperative learning and specify the elements needed to make cooperation work in the classroom. No other instructional method used today can claim the quantity or quality of research highlighting its success.

In the 1970s, two major school issues gave birth to a concentrated focus on cooperative learning: mainstreaming and integration.

Public Law 94-142, passed by the US Congress in the 1970s, required schools to restructure classrooms to include students with physical, behavioral, and learning challenges. Many students previously segregated from regular classrooms were mainstreamed now into those classrooms. Many teachers, not knowing how to handle the "special" students, were concerned about how the "regular" and the "special" students would get along. Many mainstreamed students lacked social skills and antagonized their peers; many regular students also lacked social skills and estranged their new classmates.

Following the integration directions established by the US Supreme Court in Brown v. Board of Education in 1954, schools across the nation were challenged to restructure student assignment patterns. "Separate but equal" schools were out. As students from different racial groups mixed in desegregated schools and classrooms, teachers were concerned with how these young people would get along.

Contributions by Practitioners

Roger and David Johnson (1974), two brothers at the University of Minnesota, proposed a solution that applied to both challenges—direct instruction of social skills with guided classroom practice. They theorized that if students were taught to work cooperatively in small groups, they would develop positive social skills. This in turn, they speculated, would speed the integration of students who saw each other as different.

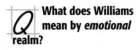
What does Williams mean by *emotional* realm?

Williams (2001) considers the emotional realm to encompass not only the emotional bonds between classroom inhabitants but also the acknowledgement of emotion-laden topics in the curriculum.

To everyone's pleasant surprise, the data gathered in these early programs showed that Johnson and Johnson's methods not only improved student-to-student interaction but also had an unpredicted dramatic side effect—increased students' academic achievement and self-esteem.

From this early research sprang more than 600 studies by Johnson and Johnson and others. Over and over, with a consistency and reliability remarkable for a school methodology, the studies have demonstrated how and why cooperative learning is one of the most powerful teaching and learning tools available. In their meta-study of research on the various models of teaching, Joyce, Weil, and Calhoun wrote: "Cooperative learning procedures facilitate learning across all curriculum areas and ages, improving self-esteem, social skill and solidarity and academic learning goals ranging from the acquisition of information and skill through the modes of inquiry of academic disciplines" (2000, p. 15).

No instructional tool has held the researchers' attention more than the cooperative model. Johnson and Johnson (1999b) point out that the results hold true across age, subject matter, race, nationality, sex, and every other discriminator.

Williams (2001) reframes the conceptual model with the addition of the emotional realm. Although based firmly in Johnson and Johnson's conceptual framework, the idea of emotions (Goleman 1995) is interwoven into the elements of the cooperative group interactions.

Major Findings

There are a number of major findings that frame the cooperative learning model:

- Students who learn in the cooperative model perform better academically than students who learn in the individualistic or competitive models. Johnson and Johnson's (1999b) meta-analysis of 122 studies showed that cooperative learning tended to give higher achievement results than either individualistic or competitive models, especially in high-level tasks such as problem solving, concept attainment, and predicting. Further studies indicated why this superior success occurs.

- Because of the quantity of cognitive rehearsal in cooperative learning groups, all students of all ability levels enhance their short- and long-term memory as well as their critical thinking skills (Johnson and Johnson 1999b).

Ah-ha!

- Cooperative experiences promote positive self-acceptance; therefore, students' learning, self-esteem, enjoyment of school, and motivation improve (Johnson and Johnson 1999b).

- Cooperative learning leads to positive interaction among students; therefore, students' intrinsic motivation and emotional involvement in learning are developed to a high degree (Johnson and Johnson 1999b).

- Cooperative learning nurtures positive peer relationships and structures positive interactions; therefore, students develop stronger scholastic aspirations, more pro-social behavior, and more positive peer relationships (Johnson and Johnson 1979; Johnson and Matross 1977).

- Cooperative learning may be the most flexible and powerful of all the classroom grouping strategies (Marzano, Pickering, and Pollock 2001, p. 91)

- Considerable evidence shows that partnerships in learning have a positive effect on learning by students of all ages and in most content areas (Joyce, Weil, and Calhoun 2000).

- Cooperative learning not only increases academic achievement, but also it teaches students how to work in teams, how to give and receive criticism, and how to plan, monitor, and evaluate individual and joint activities (Cawalti 1995).

APPROACHES TO COOPERATIVE LEARNING

There are a variety of successful approaches to cooperative learning. Although it is clear to researchers that classrooms organized for cooperative learning produce superior academic, social, and personal results, they do debate on which is the *best* approach—at least, best as measured by research standards. Most classroom teachers adopt a single approach or a combination of approaches that works best with their own teaching style and their students. Research shows that the most effective practitioners pull the best ideas from each approach to create their own approaches.

A brief look at five major models (see Figure 1.2) clarifies their pluses and minuses and helps teachers understand how many successful cooperative tools are available.

Cooperative Learning: Five Models

MODEL	CREATOR	DESCRIPTION	PLUSES	MINUSES
The Conceptual Approach	Johnson and Johnson	Theories of cooperation, competition, and expectation-state theory	+ creative teachers create + can easily enhance what experienced teacher already does	- extra planning time - not step-by-step - requires full commitment - sometimes used only as filler - time away from content
The Curriculum Approach	Slavin	Curriculum packages that have cooperative learning structured into the materials	+ easy to train + daily plans + pretested strategies + instructional variety + higher-order thinking + critical attributes of cooperative learning included + improves self-esteem and achievement	- no direct teaching of social skill - discourages transfer - few curriculum packages available
The Structural Approach	Kagan	A repertoire of interactive strategies	+ simple structures + easy for students + builds repertoire of strategies + problem solving and higher-order thinking	- cutesy - assumes transfer - ineffective if restricted to low-level tasks
The Group Investigation Model	Sharan and Sharan	The ultimate classroom jigsaw	+ improves students' inquiry, social skills, creative problem solving + improves teacher's facilitation skills + give depth to content	- not good for curriculum coverage - ineffective if students have poor social skills - won't work if parents want same assignment for all
Blueprints for Achievement	Bellanca and Fogarty	A synthesis of the four cooperative learning approaches with higher-order thinking focus	+ transfer + extend thinking + creative application + unifying curriculum	- needs time - requires training - needs commitment from school and district - difficult to test experientially

Figure 1.2

Model 1: The Conceptual Approach

Roger Johnson, a science educator, and his brother, David Johnson, a social psychology researcher, used their early studies of cooperative learning to frame the conceptual approach. They argue that all effective cooperative learning is marked by five critical characteristics: face-to-face interaction, individual accountability, cooperative social skills, positive interdependence, and group processing (see Figure 1.3). If all five are present, students are engaged in cooperative learning; if any one attribute is missing, students may be doing group work, but they are not involved in cooperative learning.

Johnson and Johnson's
Five Elements of Cooperative Groups

1. **Face-to-Face Interaction.** The physical arrangement of students in small, heterogeneous groups encourages students to help, share, and support each other's learning.

2. **Individual Accountability.** Each student is responsible for the success and collaboration of the group and for mastering the assigned task.

3. **Cooperative Social Skills.** Students are taught, coached, and monitored in the use of cooperative social skills, which enhance the group work.

4. **Positive Interdependence.** Students are guided by a common goal, group rewards, role assignments, and other means in completing the learning task.

5. **Group Processing.** Students reflect on how well they work as a group to complete the task and how they can improve their teamwork.

Figure 1.3

In any cooperative lesson, these characteristics overlap. However, if all five are not present, students are not engaged in true cooperative learning. The characteristics operate as mental hooks to provide a framework for designing strong and effective cooperative learning tasks. They also provide an umbrella under which a large variety of cooperative strategies, structures, and activities may be gathered and as a checklist for the teacher designing for cooperative learning.

Pluses of the Conceptual Model

For teachers who dislike recipe and workbook teaching, the conceptual model is a delight. Experienced teachers can use the characteristics to measure what they already do with groups and make quick, positive adjustments that result in greater student-to-student teamwork. For the teacher who has never used groups, the approach provides definite standards that point to sure ways to start. Johnson and Johnson recognize—as do researchers of adult learning such as Fullan (1982), Knowles (1978) and Krupp (1981, 1982)—that teachers are most likely to add to their personal repertoire of skills and strategies when they have beacons to guide their progress.

Minuses of the Conceptual Model

There are several definite minuses to the conceptual model. First, it requires teachers to spend extra time planning lessons. Even when teachers use this approach only to guide lesson planning, they must take time to restructure lesson plans. When teachers take a bolder step and prepare an inquiry or group investigation, they must take even more time to prepare the lesson.

Second, the conceptual approach does not work well for teachers who want a step-by-step procedure manual. Teachers using this approach must be comfortable creating lessons around required concepts and skills. The teacher who cannot tolerate ambiguity or does not want to take a chance that a lesson might flop without a step-by-step process may be uncomfortable starting here.

Third, the conceptual model requires a full commitment to learning and transfer. The teacher needs time to learn the model; to develop the skills, strategies, and structures; and to redesign the classroom. As Joyce, Weil, and Calhoun (2000) have pointed out, this instructional change process requires well-taught demonstrations, solid peer coaching programs, and administrative support for implementing the changes.

Fourth, because it does not use prepared day-to-day cooperative learning curriculum, the conceptual model sometimes is used only as filler (e.g., What do we do on Friday afternoons? or Let's play a cooperative game).

Finally, the conceptual approach bumps against the "coverage" curriculum. It does take more time in the crowded day to teach lessons in the conceptual model of cooperative learning. Where does the social skill instruction fit in? Where is the time for group processing? The conceptual approach demands time away from content coverage to ensure successful learning by all students.

Model 2: The Curriculum Approach

Slavin's research focuses on cooperative learning and basic skill instruction (1977a, 1977b, 1979, 1980, 1983a, 1983b). Slavin and his colleagues at the Johns Hopkins University Center for Research on Elementary and Middle Schools (Slavin and Hansell 1983; Slavin and Oickle 1981) have developed a series of cooperative curriculum programs in mathematics and language arts. To promote workable alternatives to tracking and ability grouping practices, especially where those practices are detrimental to poor and minority children, they have pre-scribed specific cooperative strategies to promote heterogeneous cooper-ation. They stress four packages that all teachers can learn and use easi-ly (see Figure 1.4).

Slavin's Curriculum Packages

1. Team Accelerated Instruction (TAI)

2. Cooperative Integrated Reading and Composition (CIRC)

3. Teams, Games, Tournaments (TGT)

4. Student Teams, Achievement Division (STAD)

Figure 1.4

Team Accelerated Instruction (TAI) is a mathematics program that com-bines cooperative learning with individualized instruction in a heteroge-neous classroom. Designed for grades 3–6, TAI asks students to tutor each other, to encourage accurate work, to produce positive social effects, and to handle the record-keeping logistics of individualized instruction or programmed learning. Teams of high, middle, and low achievers take achievement tests at eight-week intervals for placement in the individual-ized program. In the teams, students help each other through the materi-al. Each day, the teacher pulls students from the heterogeneous groups for focused instruction. Students work within teams and across teams to progress through the material. Each week, progress scores are established for each team. Criteria are established in advance for the degrees of recognition each team may receive.

TAI is most notable for dispelling the myth that mathematics instruction must be done by track or ability grouping. One look at the results clearly shows that TAI students of all abilities increase their skills and under-standing in computation, concepts, and applications as well as improve their self-concept, enjoyment of mathematics, behavior, relationships, and acceptance of others' differences.

Cooperative Integrated Reading and Composition (CIRC) is a cooperative curriculum for language arts, grades 3–4. Students are divided into read-ing groups (8–15 students) and reading teams (2–3 students). As students work in their teams, they earn points for their groups. Students earn cer-tificates based on accumulated points from their scores on quizzes, essays, and book reports. The teacher monitors the progress of teams using a variety of strategies or instructs other teams in comprehension strategies (e.g., predicting, comparing, drawing conclusions). Included in the strategies are partner reading, story prediction, words aloud practice, spelling review, partner checking, and team comprehension games. At times, students work individually, doing independent reading, basal work, or book reports.

Research on CIRC shows that it particularly benefits mainstreamed handicapped students without detriment to the highest-performing students. High, medium, and low performers showed equal gains, although the mainstreamed handicapped gains were most impressive.

Teams, Games, Tournaments (TGT) is perhaps the most widely known of Slavin's curricular approaches. The TGT package is adaptable to any curricular area, K–12. In this format, students work in groups to master content provided by the teacher. After practicing on worksheets, students demonstrate mastery of the content in weekly tournaments. Students compete in teams against other teams of equal ability (e.g., top achievers vs. top achievers).

Student Teams, Achievement Division (STAD), designed by Slavin and the Hopkins Group in 1982, uses heterogeneous groups (4–5 students of mixed ability, ethnic background, and gender). The groups use worksheets that have the answers provided. The common goal is to understand the answers, not to fill in the blanks. The teams quiz each other until all members understand the answers. The task is completed when the teacher gives an individual quiz to each member. The team score is the sum of the improvement points earned by each individual. Special recognition is given to the teams with the greatest improvement.

Pluses of the Curriculum Approach

There are seven pluses for the curriculum approach:

- It is easy to train teachers in this approach. The lessons and strategies are preset for a beginning level training program and show how to use the set curriculum.
- The approach builds in daily cooperative learning that needs little preplanning on the teacher's part. Providing daily lesson plans increases the probability that teachers will use them.
- The strategies are pretested for appropriateness to each content area. The teacher can worry less about "doing the right thing."
- The curriculum has built-in instructional variety. Small-group, large-group, and individual activities are balanced with direct instruction by the teacher.
- The programs take a higher-order thinking approach to direct instruction and guided practice of content.
- Most of the critical attributes of cooperative learning outlined by the Johnson and Johnson are inherent within each curriculum.
- The curriculum approach nets improvements in students' self-esteem as well as academic achievement.

Minuses of the Curriculum Approach

The minus most frequently discussed regarding the curriculum approach center on social skill instruction. In the model, social skills are developed indirectly. No effort is made to instruct students directly on how to work cooperatively. Although the approach works very well with skilled class-room managers and with well-behaved students, many teachers report that it breaks down when competition (as in TGT or CIRC) between groups becomes too intense, the teacher lacks strong management skills, or the students have little experience with or have little value for cooperative learning.

A second minus derives from the curriculum thrust. The detailed, step-by-step procedure for implementing cooperative learning within a set curriculum may discourage transfer of the approach to other curricular areas. For instance, if the teacher is using TAI for math, he or she may not recognize any way to use cooperative elements in reading or social studies.

A third minus is the very small number of developed cooperative curricula available for the classroom. Although some major educational publishers suggest some cooperative activities within their science and language arts texts, the scope of well-developed cooperative curricula is limited.

Model 3: The Structural Approach

Since 1967, Kagan has focused his research on the structural approach to cooperative learning (see Kagan 1992). Kagan's approach is based on the creation, analysis, and application of *content-free* structures that cause students to interact in positive ways in the classroom. Content-free structures are usable with any content and enable the teacher to make multiple applications of a single structure in a variety of subjects.

Kagan's structures fall into three groups: in turn, jigsaw, and match-ups (see Figure 1.5). These structures allow students to interact with content and each other in a variety of ways.

Pluses of the Structural Approach

The pluses of the structural approach begin with its simplicity. Each structure is easy to use. It takes less than one staff-development hour to master a single structure and to develop a variety of appropriate activities. The new structures blend easily with lecture format and provide practical ways to develop quick, informal student interactions and well-structured discussions.

Students also easily adapt to the new methods. Because of the number of structure options, a teacher can introduce more variety into the daily regimen and thus boost motivation.

As teachers build more extensive repertoires of cooperative structures, they can find numerous ways to create multidimensional lessons. For example, the direct instruction lesson shown in Figure 1.6 includes a number of opportunities for cooperative interactions. (The interactions are shown in italics in the figure.)

Kagan's Structures

A. **In Turn.** The teacher structures a task in which individuals take turns in a prescribed order. Included among these are round robin, response in turn, round table, four corners, and three-step interview.

B. **Jigsaw.** The teacher structures the task so that each student in the group is given a part of the information to study and then share with other group members. When members teach their material to one another, the whole is greater than the parts. Level I jigsaw, level II jigsaw, co-op–co-op, and think-pair-share all follow this format.

C. **Match-Ups.** The teacher structures student-to-student tasks, which formally and informally create cooperative situations. Included here are match mine, numbered heads together, co-op cards, and partners.

Figure 1.5

Sample Lesson on Interview Techniques

ANTICIPATORY SET: The teacher calls a student to the front of class and models an interview with the student. "*Who* are you? *What* is your age? *Where* were you born? *When* did you start school here? *Why* do you think I am asking you these questions?" (The answer to the why question is: to model an interview that uses the basic five questions—who, what, when, where, and why.)

OBJECTIVE: The teacher shows the lesson objective on the overhead: "To develop interview questions in preparation for a news article."

INPUT: The teacher shows the newspaper model, explains the key questions, and demonstrates how the parts of the graphic are used. She uses the questions asked in the anticipatory set to demonstrate.

CHECKING FOR UNDERSTANDING: The teacher tells the students to *turn to a neighbor.* Next, the teacher asks *one student in each pair to explain to the partner* how to use the newspaper model to generate the questions. After three minutes, the teacher tells the groups to stop. Several listeners from the pairs describe what they heard. Other students give corrective feedback as needed.

GUIDED PRACTICE: The teacher distributes one copy of the model to each *pair.* The roles of recorder and checker are assigned. The *pairs review the roles and cooperative guidelines* as the teacher monitors and assists the pairs as needed. After this round, several pairs describe the questions they asked and explain why they made each selection. Again, corrective feedback is encouraged. A second round of models is given out for additional practice.

INDEPENDENT PRACTICE: For homework, students are given a blank sheet of interview instructions and are asked to *interview a household member* of their choice.

CLOSURE: On the next day, *each pair joins a second pair to review and critique* each other's interview questions. Then, students engage in an all-class discussion about interview questions: Which questions are most important? Why? What benefits the writer?

Figure 1.6

Another plus of the structural model is that structures readily lend themselves to problem solving and the application of thinking tasks. For example, partners can work at any level of thinking as illustrated in Figure 1.7. (Also, see chapter 4 for more information on the three-story intellect.)

Minuses of the Structural Approach

The simplicity of the structural approach is a double-edged sword. Because the structures look "fun and cute," a teacher may save the structures for Friday afternoon fillers. Consequently, students get the message that these are play activities, and they miss the potential richness of the cooperative structure.

A second minus is that the structural approach assumes a great deal about student transfer of the cooperative ethic, cooperative skills, and cooperative behaviors. The structural approach works best as a hook and does not include direct social skill instruction or formal group processing. Therefore, the cooperative skills are transferred more by osmosis than by formal instruction. As with the curriculum approach, the lack of direct instruction in cooperative learning limits transfer of the cooperative skills beyond the specific task—only the super learners are likely to make the transfer to other tasks. Teachers need enthusiasm, assertiveness, and ability to hook students into cooperative tasks.

Levels of Thinking and Partner Interaction

Thinking Level I: Gathering Information
1. Assign a list of vocabulary words to each pair in a team. Ask partners to coach and quiz each other on the meanings of assigned words. If any pair is unsure of a definition, tell the pair to "travel" to another pair for advice.
2. When all pairs are ready, conduct a final check for mastery in each team. Follow this with a quiz in which teams compete against each other.

Thinking Level II: Processing Information
1. Tell each pair to use the vocabulary words to create a story about the current season of the year. If any pair gets stuck, let it "travel" to another pair for help.
2. Tell each pair to share its story with the team. Encourage the team to explain why each story was done well.

Thinking Level III: Applying Information
1. Ask each pair to hypothesize about the changes that might occur to their chosen season of the year if global warming increases in the next decade.
2. Tell pairs to share their hypotheses in a team. Assign one person in each team to list the hypotheses on a sheet of newsprint. Encourage the teams to discuss and rank their hypotheses based on which effect would be most disastrous.

Figure 1.7

A third minus of the structural approach occurs when the teacher restricts the use of cooperative structures to low-level and routine classroom tasks (e.g., spelling words, worksheets, computation drill and practice, etc.). Students quickly perceive such limited use as a gambit to manipulate quick interest.

Model 4: The Group Investigation Approach

Group investigation, as described by Sharan and Sharan (1976), includes five stages (see Figure 1.8). In stage 1, students work together to plan how they will find answers to key questions about a topic of mutual interest. The teacher frames the broad topic. Students investigate this "big" question (e.g., What do you think will happen if the United States produces twice as much nuclear waste per year each year for the next decade? How would our American society be different today if we had lost World War II? What can we learn from a study of plant life?) If students need stimulation, the teacher provides a potpourri of print or video materials, a guest lecturer, or a field trip. Questions are reviewed in teams, and then classified and synthesized into subtopics for small-group investigation.

Sharan and Sharan's Group Investigation Model

Stage 1: Posing the big question and forming groups by interest

Stage 2: Identifying the inquiry problem and planning how to research

Stage 3: Dividing up the work and gathering information

Stage 4: Preparing the report

Stage 5: Presenting and evaluating the report

Figure 1.8

In stage 2, students brainstorm what they want to know about the topic. Teams formulate the problem statement and help each other discuss and plan the search process.

In stage 3, teams break the work into individual or pair investigation tasks and each student or pair selects a subtopic to investigate. Each then gathers the assigned information, analyzes it, and draws tentative conclusions.

In stage 4, teams translate their results into a report for the class. The teacher schedules the reports.

In stage 5, teams make formal presentations and the teacher guides discussions on their results. Finally, students evaluate their work.

The teacher plays the major facilitating role through each stage of this inquiry process.

A classroom teacher who uses both the conceptual and structural approaches calls the group investigation approach the "ultimate jigsaw." "For my classes," she wrote, "group investigation is the most powerful and empowering of the cooperative methods."

Pluses of the Group Investigation Model

If the teacher wants the optimum structure for encouraging inquiry, student-to-student interaction, cooperative social skill development, creative problem solving, and communication skills, the group investigation approach provides it. If teacher want the maximum opportunity to use their facilitation skills with students, group investigation provides it. If teachers want students to delve deeply into a concept in the curriculum, then they will find no better motivator.

Minuses of the Group Investigation Model

On the other hand, if the teacher is concerned about curriculum coverage, or there is a supervisor who expects students to sit quietly in rows or wants to know what each student is doing every moment, then group investigation will not work. If students cannot handle the open-ended tasks or are not well prepared for positive interaction, question asking, problem solving, and consensus seeking, then group investigation will fall flat. If parents expect uniform assignments, daily quizzes, and most important, grades, grades, grades, teachers should not even consider using group investigation.

See Figure 1.9 for a summary of the 4 models.

Model 5: The Blueprints for Achievement Synthesis

A study of these various approaches shows that no *one* approach is sufficient or superior. Obviously, cooperative learning in some form is a necessary tool for use in every effective classroom. In this context, the practical teacher is best served by adopting a design that borrows the best ideas from each approach.

As we listened and worked with teachers in their classrooms, it became more and more obvious that a synthesized model that ties together cooperative learning and critical and creative thinking was needed for transfer. We see cooperative learning as an essential ingredient for developing students who are more able to think critically and creatively. We sometimes sketch a picture of cooperative learning as a jet engine with critical and creative thinking skills as the fuel. When put together, they produce a powerful thrust for soaring to new frontiers of discovery and adventure.

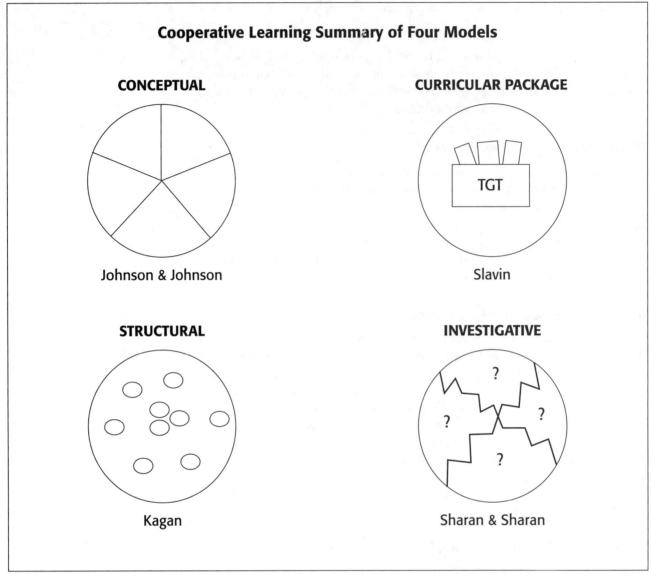

Figure 1.9

The blueprints for achievement model of cooperative learning synthesizes the most effective elements of the earlier models with the more recent research on explicit thinking skills, metacognition, cognitive organizers, research-based best practices, and learning for transfer. The synthesis uses the acronym BUILD: build in higher-order thinking for transfer, unite teams in face-to-face interaction, invite individual learning, look over and discuss the interaction, and develop social skills in cooperation for life (see Figure 1.10).

The Essential Concepts Plus One

Johnson and Johnson's conceptual model outlines the five essential ingredients that distinguish cooperative learning from other forms of group work and that support success in cooperative learning in the classroom.

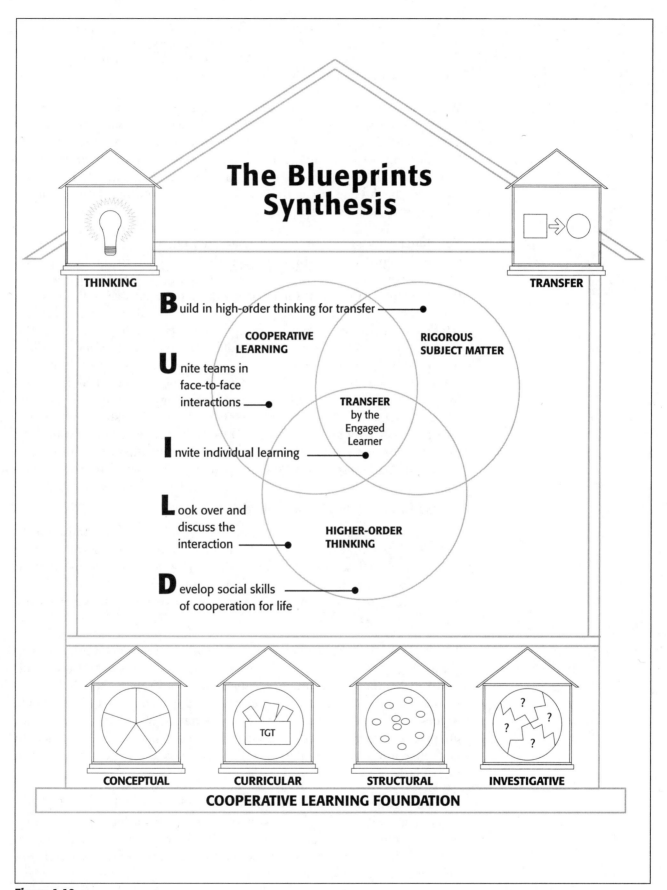

The Blueprints Synthesis

THINKING

TRANSFER

Build in high-order thinking for transfer

COOPERATIVE LEARNING

RIGOROUS SUBJECT MATTER

Unite teams in face-to-face interactions

TRANSFER by the Engaged Learner

Invite individual learning

Look over and discuss the interaction

HIGHER-ORDER THINKING

Develop social skills of cooperation for life

CONCEPTUAL **CURRICULAR** **STRUCTURAL** **INVESTIGATIVE**

TGT

? ? ? ?

COOPERATIVE LEARNING FOUNDATION

Figure 1.10

When combined with cognitive processing (lessons focused on higher-order thinking tasks) the element of thinking for transfer is also added. When each and every lesson is structured from this transfer perspective, even more dynamic changes occur in the classroom.

What Kagan's curricular model calls *cooperative structures,* trainers in other fields (Blanchard, Peters, and University Associates in business training and development, Canfield in self-esteem, Raths in values clarification, and Goodman in creative problem solving) have called *strategies.* Whichever name is used, the common element is that this staff development approach encourages the quickest transfer and use without falling into the workbook mentality.

The blueprints synthesis model uses an inductive approach. Teacher trainees begin with basic strategies that are easy to apply and use. Trainees work together to plan how to weave these basic strategies into the classroom. After the trainees have experienced strategies, both as students and as teachers, they explore the conceptual framework for the strategies. Learning about the concepts prevents trainees from using the strategies as isolated games. After they do an intensive classroom application of the strategies, trainees focus on more sophisticated strategies. These strategies require students to master higher-level social skills and to concentrate on problem solving and reasoning in a variety of contents (e.g., mathematics, language arts, science). In the final stage of learning, trainees receive mentor coaching and work on curriculum renewal. Both extend the use of cooperative learning and cognitive instruction to teamwork and problem solving as key components for effective transfer.

Pluses of the Blueprints Synthesis Model

The blueprints model demands a long-term and intense commitment to staff development. Moreover, it expects that what happens in the training program, as well as what happens in the classroom, will be used. With this synthesis, teachers begin switching from a focus on recall and quick answer tests to a focus on transferring knowledge and skills across the curriculum and into life.

Teachers who use this model need to have a high tolerance for ambiguity. If they expect that every problem has one right answer, the first precondition for developing the intelligent behaviors and social skills is lacking. In the blueprints model, greater emphasis is placed on helping students process and apply information than on having them memorize great quantities of detailed information. Teachers most often are asked to challenge and extend thinking and less often to inoculate students with information.

Teachers using this model also need strong planning skills and a creative bend. They will not have a page-by-page recipe or a lock-step teacher's guide. Teachers must feel comfortable with their own ability to design lessons that incorporate not only cooperative learning, but also intelligent behavior and reasoning skills.

The blueprints model pushes a school on essential curricular change. Thinking and cooperating require more time for in-depth exploration of concepts, in-depth practice of skills, and an emphasis on inquiry rather than answers. When coverage curriculum is the norm and isolated facts the king, little time is left for quality thinking or intense cooperation. If the school district is not ready to challenge the restrictive time limits and coverage of materials and to redesign curricula with transfer in mind, teachers can expect students to have a more difficult time with transfer.

The blueprints model does not, however, necessitate a total curricula changeover. But it does facilitate change by encouraging teachers to set new priorities in their curricula. For example, teachers might ask, What are the most important concepts to establish firmly versus what are the facts to cover more quickly?

This model also encourages teachers to see thinking skills as tools for unifying and integrating their curriculum. For instance, they can teach prediction in depth with language arts lessons and use science, mathematics, and social studies materials for students to practice thinking skills in cooperative groups.

In effect, the combination of cooperative learning and cognitive development is not just equal to a mathematical addition. Cooperation plus thinking is not the same as $3 + 3 = 6$. The combination of cooperative learning and cognitive development is more like a squaring of components in the classroom ($3^2 = 9$). Add still another factor—a transfer-based staff-development program with structured coaching and support—and a powerful, cubing change that produces effective, multidimensional results is engaged ($3^3 = 27$).

Minuses of the Blueprints Synthesis Model

The blueprints model takes time. In an already crowded curriculum, with more and more coverage being required, where is the time for group processing, metacognition, or social skills? To do these functions well, content coverage must give way.

This model requires intense and supportive staff development for most implementors. This means the district needs to fund not only intensive training days but also coaching teams, administrative inservice training, and opportunities to restructure curriculum.

Student learning derived from the blueprints model is difficult to test with standardized instruments. This is especially true when trying to measure students' transfer of concepts, their ability to reason, *and* their acquisition of knowledge. To succeed, assessments other than pencil-and-paper scantron tests are needed.

The blueprints transfer model asks students to strive for intelligent behavior, not test results. This is well outside the norms imposed by the interest in quick tests of isolated facts and skills.

Specs

Based on the extensive research presented, there are four compelling reasons to use cooperative learning in the classroom (Figure 1.11). First, research shows that cooperative learning aligns with the *standards*. Second, using cooperative learning strategies improves *teacher quality*; teachers who use cooperative learning employ a *robust repertoire* of strategies that meet the needs of diverse learners. Third, cooperative learning promotes students' acquisition of *real-world skills* that are necessary for lifelong learning. Fourth, a number of recent publications explain that cooperative learning is one of the *best practices* for increasing student achievement and is the most conducive strategy for integrating with other power strategies of instruction.

Four Compelling Reasons for Using Cooperative Learning

- Cooperative learning research and standards

- Teacher quality and repertoire

- Real-world skills for lifelong learning

- Best practices research

Figure 1.11

STANDARDS AND COOPERATIVE LEARNING

To understand the power of cooperative learning as a teaching/learning strategy in the contemporary classroom, one need only refer to the comprehensive body of research explained earlier in the Draft section. For example, Johnson and Johnson (1999b) note more than 600 studies that illustrate the positive effects of cooperative learning in students' cognitive and affective abilities. Essentially, cooperative learning increases student achievement and enhances self-esteem more effectively than most instruction of an individualistic nature.

Cooperative learning also shows up in the standards of learning. Cooperative learning is implied and explicitly stated in most state standards documents. In the examples shown in Figure 1.12, it is evident that the principles of cooperative learning permeate various content, process, and performance standards.

Cooperative Learning as Reflected in the Language of Standards

- Listen attentively and recognize when it is appropriate to speak.

- Read and discuss published letters.

- Express opinions.

- Understand that in any group there are different points of view.

- Evaluate one's own and other's work.

- Generate ideas for possible solutions through group activity.

- Participate in small-group projects and in structured tasks.

- In a group setting, test solutions against design specifications.

- Treat all individuals equally and respect diversity and special needs.

- Work cooperatively in a group.

- Understand the importance of accepting individual differences.

- Apply communication techniques.

- Identify tasks that require a coordinated effort and work with others to complete the task.

- Examine problems and proposed solutions from multiple perspectives.

- Understand the relationships of the individual groups.

- Apply (mathematics) operations and concepts in the workplace.

(Standards adapted from _New York State Learning Standards_ [New York State Academy for Teaching and Learning 2001], and _Show-Me Standards_ [Missouri Department of Elementary and Secondary Education 1996].)

Figure 1.12

COOPERATIVE LEARNING AS AN ESSENTIAL TOOL FOR A QUALITY TEACHING REPERTOIRE

"What if . . . poor and minority students are performing below other students not because something is wrong with them or their families, but because most schools don't bother to teach them what they need to know?" This question was posed by Haycock (1998b, p.1) in a seminal piece entitled, _Good Teaching Matters: How Well-Qualified Teachers Can Close the Achievement Gap._ To close the achievement gap between poor- and high-performing classrooms, quality teachers can use cooperative learning in both. Parents have known since time began that teacher quality matters, and it matters a lot. Every child is entitled to a quality teacher.

Quality teachers have high expectations for all learners. When low-performing students are challenged with rigor, higher-order thinking, problem solving, real-world scenarios, and real-world learning, they meet expectations (Haycock 1998b). Their achievement increases, and yes, their test scores go up. "When students 'construct knowledge' through 'disciplined inquiry', . . . this cognitively integrated knowledge is more likely to be owned and internalized by students . . . The evidence indicates that assignments calling for more authentic intellectual work actually improve student scores on conventional tests" (Newmann, Bryk, and Nagaoka 2001, pp. 29–30). Given this research, reasons to use cooperative learning are clear. It is an essential tool, if not *the* essential tool, for inclusion in every teacher's instructional repertoire. Without the skilled application of cooperative learning, it is hard to imagine how a teacher can help students hurdle the achievement barriers.

What makes for skillful application? Skillful applications come from teachers who

- know the structures and strategies of cooperative learning;
- understand when and how to use those structures and strategies within the curriculum;
- refine and adapt strategies to the unique demands of her students;
- integrate cooperative learning with other research-based instructional tools into high-content and high-challenge lessons on a daily basis; and
- use the powerful tool not just as an activity, but also as a powerful means to transform a classroom into an achievement-centered community of learners.

No one should doubt the value of cooperative learning with students who come to the classroom ready and eager to learn. Yet, many doubt that it can work well with low performers who have learned to resist any attempts to school them.

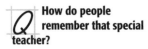 **How do people remember that special teacher?**

People remember teachers who made a difference with these sentiments:

- They cared.
- They listened.
- They knew who I was.
- They knew their subject.
- They made learning exciting.
- They helped me.
- They encouraged me.
- They loved teaching.

However, educators can't pretend not to know what good teachers do. Just ask people about teachers who have made the difference in their lives and the laundry list of predictable qualities emerges: They cared. They listened. They knew who I was. They knew a lot about their subject matter. They made learning exciting. They were passionate about their subjects. They kept in touch. They helped me. They encouraged me. They knew a lot about kids. They loved teaching.

Although most have heard the anonymous refrain—They don't care what teachers know until they know they care—it seems that parents and students do care that teachers know a lot about what they teach. In fact, this deep understanding of the subject matter helps create the quality in the quality label. Students pick up on the passion evidenced by true experts, and they get hooked into learning. "Simply put, students learn more from 'good' teachers than from 'bad' teachers under virtually any set of circumstances" (Wenglinsky 2000, p. 3).

But, what does this have to do with cooperative learning? It's a pretty straight-forward correlation, really. Teachers who fit the profile of quality also fit the profile of teachers who make a difference and these teachers embrace a robust repertoire of instructional strategies. They use all the tricks in their bag to design complex experiences that engage students in the teaching/learning process. Good teachers know when it is appropriate to use certain strategies.

For example, good teachers know just when, how, and how much cooperative learning to use in the various types of learning tasks. They know when to use partners, and when to use small groups. They know what member roles are needed and how to design complex, problem-centered learning that taps into the diverse talents of the group. Good teachers know how to infuse social skills into teamwork, and how to help students process and reflect on their own learning. Quality teachers have the highest expectations for all students and the highest expectations for their own effectiveness. They search out cooperative learning tools and other research-proven strategies that give the achievement advantage to all students.

REAL-WORLD APPLICATION: THE SCANS REPORT

The third compelling reason for using cooperative learning in today's diverse classroom is real-world application. A good example of real-world application is the SCANS report (Secretary's Commission on Achieving Necessary Skills 1991). Paralleling the Goals 2000 Education Bill, the United States Department of Labor issued the SCANS report that outlined the skills high school students need to succeed in the world of work. The report identified a three-part foundation—basic skills, thinking skills, and personal qualities—and five workplace competency areas—resources, interpersonal, information, systems, and technology. (See detailed list in Figure 1.13. For a blackline master, see C1.1 in Appendix C.)

The interpersonal section of the SCANS Report relates directly to cooperative learning. Cooperation is an integral skill for success in the world of work. The report states the skills specifically: participates as a member of a team, teaches others new skills, exercises leadership, negotiates, and works with diversity. These skills are practiced, rehearsed, and developed in cooperative learning tasks. SCANS and cooperative learning are clear companions in the educational agenda.

The SCANS Skills and Competencies

Foundation

1. *Basic skills:* Reads, writes, performs arithmetic and mathematical operations, listens, speaks.

2. *Thinking skills:* Thinks creatively, makes decisions, solves problems, visualizes, knows how to learn, and reasons.

3. *Personal qualities:* Displays responsibility, self-esteem, sociability, self-management, integrity, and honesty.

Workplace Competencies

1. *Resources:* Identifies, organizes, plans and allocates resources.
   - Time
   - Money
   - Materials and facilities
   - Human resources

2. *Interpersonal:* Works with others.
   - Participates as member of a team.
   - Teaches others new skills.
   - Exercises leadership.
   - Negotiates.
   - Works with diversity.

3. *Information:* Acquires and uses information.
   - Acquires and evaluates information.
   - Organizes and maintains information.
   - Interprets and communicates information.
   - Uses computers to process information.

4. *Systems:* Understands complex inter-relationships.
   - Understands systems.
   - Monitors and corrects performance.
   - Improves or designs systems.

5. *Technology:* Works with a variety of technologies.
   - Selects technology.
   - Applies technology.
   - Maintains and troubleshoots equipment.

(Adapted from Secretary 's Commission on Achieving Necessary Skills [SCANS] 1991.)

Figure 1.13

COOPERATIVE LEARNING AND RESEARCH-BASED BEST PRACTICES

There is strong support for the value of cooperative learning among sources that identify research-based best practices—Cawalti (1995); Joyce, Weil, and Calhoun (2000); and Marzano, Pickering, and Pollock (2001).

Cawalti

Cawalti in *Handbook of Research on Improving Student Achievement,* states, "With justification, cooperative learning has become widespread in American schools. Not only can it increase academic achievement, but . . . students learn teamwork, how to give and receive criticism and how to plan, monitor and evaluate their individual and joint activities with others" (1995, p. 17). In addition, the contributors to Cawalti's book provide specific information on using cooperative learning and other strategies in core disciplines such as mathematics, science, social studies, and language arts.

Joyce, Weil, and Calhoun

Joyce, Weil, and Calhoun, in their *Models of Teaching,* call cooperative "partners in learning," a part of their social models family. The authors state, "There is considerable evidence that partnerships in learning have a positive effect on learning by students of all ages and in most content areas" (2000, p. 29). The authors imply that the cooperative learning model complements other teaching models and it is often integrated within models such as attaining concepts, scientific inquiry, and inquiry models, memorization, and simulations.

Marzano, Pickering, and Pollock

It is, however, the third group of commentators that give the strongest support for the blueprints model. They explain, "Of all the classroom grouping strategies, cooperative learning may be the most flexible and powerful" (Marzano, Pickering, and Pollock 2001, p. 91). Not only do they favor cooperative learning, but they also provide nine categories of instructional strategies for its implementation: (1) identifying similarities and differences, (2) summarizing and notetaking, (3) reinforcing effort and providing recognition, (4) homework and practice, (5) nonlinguistic representations, (6) cooperative learning, (7) setting objectives and providing feedback, (8) generating and testing hypotheses, and (9) cues, questions, and advance organizers. The blueprints model uses these strategies extensively.

Figure 1.14 illustrates the impact of the nine strategies, as reported by Marzano, Pickering, and Pollock 2001. (For a blackline master, see Blackline C1.2 in Appendix C.) The figure illustrates the impact of each strategy in terms of "effect size." Two concepts are particularly important when examining the figure: effect size and stanines. *Effect size* simply means the effect the intervention strategy had on the experimental group as compared to the control group. In this figure, effect size registers the amount of gain or loss evidenced in the group that used the strategy. A *stanine* is calculated from a normal distribution of scores with the greatest number of scores falling in the middle range and fewer scores falling in the outlier ranges. A bell curve, with its stanines illustrated, often appears in the format shown in Figure 1.15. (For a blackline master, see Blackline C1.3 in Appendix C.)

Categories of Instructional Strategies that Affect Student Achievement

Category	Ave. Effect Size (ES)	Percentile Gain	No. of ESs	Standard Deviation (SD)
Identifying similarities and differences	1.61	45	31	.31
Summarizing and notetaking	1.00	34	179	.50
Reinforcing effort and providing recognition	.60	29	21	.35
Homework and practice	.77	28	134	.36
Nonlinguistic representations	.75	27	246	.40
Cooperative learning	.73	27	122	.40
Setting objectives and providing feedback	.61	23	408	.28
Generating and testing hypotheses	.61	23	63	.79
Questions, cues, and advance organizers	.59	22	1.251	.26

Figure 1.14

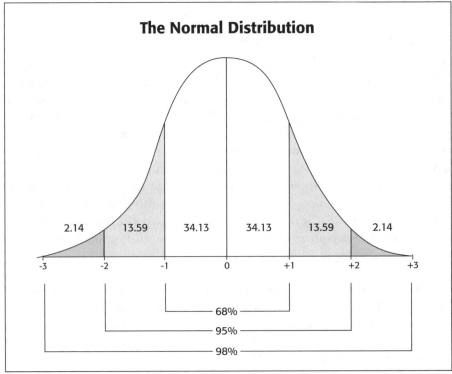

Figure 1.15

To compare the scores of the experimental group with the scores of the control group, a normal distribution curve for the experimental group is overlayed on a normal distribution curve of the control group. The difference, measured in stanines, is the effect size or the amount of impact evidenced by the group using the intervention.

For example, an effect size of 1.3 suggests improvement in scores jumped 4/3 stanines. Typically, results that show a change of 1/2 stanine or more indicate substantive gains. When examining Figure 1.14, note that the effect size of these nine families of strategies range from .59 to 1.61. All fall into the category of significant positive change.

Let's take a closer look at these nine strategies to discover the full dimension of each. (Please note: The strategies appear in the model lessons throughout the *Blueprints* text. Figure 1.16 shows the codes used to designate each strategy.)

Codes for Marzano, Pickering, and Pollock's Strategies

1SD: Identifying Similarities and Differences

2SN: Summarizing and Notetaking

3RR: Reinforcing Effort and Recognition

4HP: Homework and Practice

5NR: Nonlinguistic Representation

6CL: Cooperative Learning

7OF: Setting Objectives and Providing Feedback

8GH: Generating and Testing Hypotheses

9QCA: Questions, Cues, and Advance Organizers

Figure 1.16

Q How do the nine instructional strategies support the SCANS objectives?

A Most SCANS objectives are supported by more than one of the nine strategies (codes are shown in Figure 1.16):

Foundation: basic skills by 4HP; thinking skills by 1SD, 2SN, and 4HP; personal qualities by 3RR and 7OF

Workplace competencies: resources by 5NR and 9QCA; interpersonal by 3RR, 6CL, and 7OF; information by 2SN; systems by 6CL and 8GH; technology by 5NR and 9QCA.

Identifying Similarities and Differences (1SD)

The identifying similarities and differences strategy encompasses at least four facets or skill areas: comparing and contrasting, classifying, using metaphors, and developing analogies.

Comparing and contrasting involves comparing similarities and differences. For example, students might compare and contrast the attributes of two characters in a novel.

Classifying means to separate objects into categories by comparing the objects' similarities and differences. For example, triangles and rectangles fall into two different sets. Triangles have three sides, whereas rectangles have four sides. Therefore, rectangles do not fit in the set of triangles. They fall outside the set as non-examples.

Using metaphors implies similarities between two objects. For example, "the brain is a computer" implies similarities between a brain and a computer. Of course, every metaphor has its limitations. Although a brain and a computer share some similar attributes, some attributes are different. The metaphor simply emphasizes the similarities.

Developing analogies is another skill that requires knowledge of similarities and differences. For example, "a *tire* is to a *car* as a *page* is to a *book*" illustrates similarities in the "part to whole" comparison. But, the actual elements of tire and car differ drastically from those of page and book. Making the inferences that are necessary to complete analogies correctly is a highly sophisticated form of finding similarities and differences.

Summarizing and Notetaking (2SN)

The summarizing and notetaking strategy draws on learners' ability to see a whole from parts.

Summarizing requires the learner to have a tacit understanding of the idea to be summarized. The learner skillfully compacts knowledge to present a succinct digest that captures the essence of the whole. For example, students might be asked to summarize a news event into a few sentences or into a sound bite. Although a summary is simple recall of a larger piece, it does call for skillful inclusion and exclusion of facts.

Notetaking is a skill that distinguishes the importance of parts to create a personal whole. If you have ever borrowed class notes from a colleague, you have probably discovered the wide range of personal notetaking styles. Some are brief, others long winded! Some are all verbal, others are sprinkled with graphics. Some are organized and orderly, others are scattered and random. Students can be taught how to take notes in expedient and efficient ways. For example, teachers may introduce students to a mediated journal that is organized with labels or page headings for guided notetaking. The teacher assigns labels or headings to the journal pages to signal what is important for students to capture in their notes.

Reinforcing Effort and Recognition (3RR)

Reinforcing effort and recognition is a strategy that strengthens students' confidence in their identification of and progress toward worthwhile goals and activities.

Reinforcing effort with feedback that is immediate, specific, and concrete positively affects students' learning. Positive reinforcement should not be confused with continuous and unending praise that is simply part and parcel of some classroom rhetoric, but rather it should acknowledge genuine effort. For example, writing a comment on a sticky note and attaching it to a student's writing draft reinforces the student's effort.

Recognition means acknowledging each student's contribution to the class and appreciating each student's thinking. One way to acknowledge students is by using the human graph in which each student becomes part of a class graph (see Figure 1.17). The human graph allows each student to take a public stand, state an opinion, and support the opinion with a justifying statement. Thereby, each student is recognized as having an important idea to share.

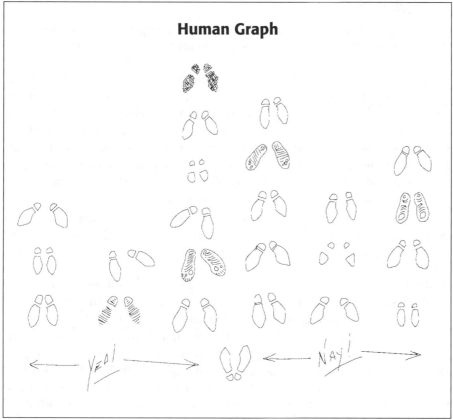

Figure 1.17

Homework and Practice (4HP)

Homework and practice encompass strategies that give students experience with content.

Homework benefits learning and achievement by calling for additional effort and processing away from the classroom, in a closer approximation of real life. Homework acts as a three-legged stool, bringing together the three human elements of education—student, teacher, and parents. Involving parents in structuring a time and place for homework sets the expectations for high achievement and results for all students.

Practice is the opportunity for learners to engage in the activity or skill, usually often or repeatedly. Much of school learning focuses on learning skills and memorizing facts and data. To retain this information requires practice, rehearsal, and repetition. Guided practice and independent practice are part of this picture. Practice that is guided, mediated by the teacher, and finally, independent (as in homework) provides the kind of rehearsal and repetition needed for students to learn, retain, and recall information. Coached practices and self-initiated independent exercises are needed to memorize multiplication facts, perform dance routines, run football plays, or make presentations at a competent and proficient level.

Nonlinguistic Representation (5NR)

Nonlinguistic representations build on the strength of visual presentations as more abstract and less fussy representations of details.

Graphic organizers are visual tools that help students see their thinking. Visual tools, such as mind maps, flow charts, and attribute webs, aid in analyzing and synthesizing new information and clarifying and focusing more familiar information. However, using visual representations as fill-in worksheets undermines the power of these tools. Instead, graphic organizers should be displayed on large newsprint as part of cooperative teamwork and used to foster lively conversation and critical analysis of the work. For example, asking students to do a concept map of their perception of a video on memory and learning provides a ripe opportunity for deep understanding and reflective insights. Encouraging students to create a picture of their thinking enhances the connections students make.

Multiple intelligences theory (Gardner 1983) supplies another forum for nonlinguistic representations of ideas . This theory recognizes eight ways of knowing: verbal/linguistic, visual/spatial, musical/rhythmic, logical/mathematical, bodily/kinesthetic, interpersonal, intrapersonal, and naturalist. Students are given multiple entry points into learning and are provided multiple exit points to demonstrate how well they have learned something. For example, students can be asked to create a model of the life cycle as a way to illustrate in nonlinguistic terms the same information that they might have written in an essay.

Cooperative Learning (6CL)

Cooperative learning is a foundational strategy that combines easily with other strategies. For example, think-pair-share partners might generate hypotheses together, a small group might create a poster depicting a visual metaphor for democratic values, or informal pairs may simply turn to their partners and summarize the salient points of an argument presented in the textbook. Whatever the mode, cooperative learning strategies create a forum for dialogue and reflection and promote communication skills, leadership, teamwork, and conflict resolution.

Setting Objectives and Providing Feedback (7OF)

Setting objectives and providing feedback is the set of strategies that guide and review student achievement.

Setting objectives is, without doubt, most frequently accomplished by adopting applicable standards. Creating robust, rigorous, and rich standards for student learning, with intermittent and measurable benchmarks, serves as a model for setting objectives for student achievement. Each content area has its basic set of concepts, skills, and procedures. For example, in life science one goal is that all students will know and be able to do investigations; therefore, the science objectives are clear. Teachers can use these objectives to guide students' investigation so that they may learn and apply concepts, skills, and procedures.

Providing feedback on how well an objective is met complements the strategy of setting objectives. Timely, specific, relevant feedback signals how well or how much the learner has accomplished. While feedback may be either formal or informal, the most powerful feedback comes from a specific, formal route—the scoring rubric. For example, as students create portfolios of their work, they can consult a predetermined rubric that shows that feedback (and judgments) will be given on appearance, content, and reflective thinking. Knowing the criteria and having fully described indicators for each criterion helps students anticipate relevant feedback on their final portfolio product.

Generating and Testing Hypotheses (8GH)

Generating and testing hypotheses actively engage student learners in their learning.

Generating hypotheses means that students generate ideas about what they think is going on. This process requires students to use higher-level thinking skills. They must engage with the information in dynamic ways, trying to make sense of whatever is occurring. Generating hypotheses is much more involved than memorizing inert knowledge. For example, as young students work with magnets, they begin to formulate ideas about why some objects "stick" and others "don't stick" to the magnets. To make the hypothesizing more explicit, the teacher might ask students to jot down their theories as they evolve.

Testing hypotheses is a natural follow-up to generating hypotheses. For example, after students have developed a theory about magnets and magnetic fields, they must test their theory with examples and non-examples. Through trial and error, they can refine their theory and write more credible hypotheses. Even in situations in which theories are untestable or unprovable (e.g., hypotheses about why the dinosaur disappeared), students can test their hypotheses through further research.

Questions, Cues, and Advance Organizers (9QCA)

Questions, cues, and advance organizers are strategies that help students develop deep understanding of both topic and process.

Questions have been a favorite strategy from the time of Bloom and his taxonomy (Bloom et al. 1956). Students are bombarded with questions at the six levels: from knowledge and comprehension to application, analysis, synthesis, and evaluation questions. They are asked to list, recall, use, dissect, create, and judge topics across content areas. When these questions are followed by skillful use of wait time (3–5 seconds) following a question, student responses are richer and more thoughtful (Rowe 1996). For example, when students are asked to rank their options for solving a tough math problem, they are being asked to *evaluate,* which is the highest level of Bloom's taxonomy. As teachers and students become skillful with questioning techniques, they become aware of the difference between divergent (fat) and convergent (skinny) questions. With this understanding, more in-depth thinking usually follows as they focus on the more robust kinds of questions. For example, the question becomes "How do you know who the hero is?" (divergent) instead of "Who is the hero of the story?" (convergent).

Cues provide memory pegs on which students can hang their thinking. Cues are the sparks that trigger the fuller flame. Cues might include acronyms that encapsulate a set of ideas or facts (e.g., HOMES—Huron, Ontario, Michigan, Erie, and Superior—for the names of the five Great Lakes). Cues might be musical in nature, signaling a particular routine. Cues can use visual icons to represent ideas, or they can be physical cues that trigger a mental model. Cues, in whatever form they take, provide the needed nudge to recall more and recall it faster—as a chunk of information.

Advance organizers provide a preview—an advanced look—at what is about to come. To know the power of advanced organizers is to understand the purpose and value of a syllabus, a table of contents, a chart, or a diagram. Advanced organizers prepare the mind for incoming information, stir up prior knowledge, and set up patterns for connecting new information.

Advance organizers also give students a way to organize their learning. For example, teachers may ask students to scan a chapter and create a web of ideas about what they discovered. This web then can serve as an organizer for further writing. In working with mediated journals, page labels provided by the teacher both guide students toward important material and provide an advance look at how the material is organized.

These nine strategies are woven throughout the *Blueprints* text. They are identified by their codes to cue the reader to the plentiful examples of these strategies in the book. When Marzano, Pickering, and Pollock say, "Cooperative learning is flexible," imagine how powerful it is when combined with the other eight strategies.

Setting Up the Scaffolding

Working the Crew

What is Big?
What is Small?
(Standards)

Although the word *standards* is bantered about throughout the educational community, students may have difficulty grasping what standards are. Even though adults have mastered real-world ideas about standards of measurement, standards for currency, or standards for the quality of a cut of meat, children may not understand what standards are or why standards are important. Because standards-based learning is the philosophical base of education today, it is never too early for students to begin thinking about standards.

This K–3 lesson includes a series of cooperative investigations and debriefings that introduce students to this sophisticated concept of a standard. Students work with the idea of a standard of measurement in very concrete ways. After students have a sense of what a standard is and why it is important, the teacher might discuss briefly the idea of standards of learning to bridge the abstract concept to the concrete manipulatives students have experienced.

Supplies for this lesson include items that students might use to measure two rugs, such as old gym shoes, yarn, boxes, newspapers, toys, kitchen utensils, tools, games, books, and items of clothing.

Divide the students into groups of three. Tell them each group needs to figure out a way to measure two rugs of different sizes. Instruct them to use any of the materials in the box to measure the rug. Then, after each team has agreed on the size of the rugs, they are to report their findings to the whole class using the chart on the board.

TEAM NAME	BIG RUG SIZE	SMALL RUG SIZE

After all groups have reported their findings, lead a discussion about what they did, how they did it, and what their conclusions are. Then, ask them to *compare* the various answers on the chart and *hypothesize* why they are so different. For example, you may ask a series of questions: Why does one group measure the big rug as 15 glasses long and 25 glasses wide, while another group records their findings as 9 papers by 14 papers? What is going on here? How will others know the real size of the rugs if they measure them with different things each time? Do we need to use the same thing each time? Do we need a standard of some sort? What is a standard?

Following the debriefing session, ask teams to think about their teamwork and to talk to each other. Ask them two of Mrs. Potter's Questions: What did you do well? What might you do differently if you work together again? (Mrs. Potter's Questions are shown in Chapter 2, Figure 2.6 and on Blackline C4.10 in Appendix C.) Then, sample some of the team responses. End by having students thank their partners.

Reflecting on the Design

Optional Reflection

Read "Rulers" from *Wally's Stories: Conversations in Kindergarten* (Paley 1981, pp. 13–16). See Appendix C for a copy of the story. The story tells about students' struggles with the very same activity of trying to measure two rugs.

# # #

BLUEPRINT
Middle School
Lesson

Codes 1SD
2SN
5NR
6CL
8GH

Setting Up the
Scaffolding

Working the
Crew

The Best Teacher I Ever Had (Teaching Quality)

The intent of this lesson is to develop the idea that quality teachers exhibit certain characteristics and that the same is true of quality students. Good teachers get results in terms of increased student achievement; good students get results in terms of deep understandings about their learning. So, what does *good* mean? Do educators know quality when they see it? Are there certain traits or characteristics that exemplify quality? Do teachers know how good, good is? What does a good teacher look and sound like? What does a good student look and sound like?

Ask students to work in pairs. Instruct them to think about a teacher who has made a difference in their lives and briefly tell their partners about that teacher. After both students in each pair have had an opportunity to tell a little bit about the teachers they chose, ask them to prepare to write about their teachers in a mediated journal entry. Explain that you will guide the writing by giving prompts. After a series of five or six prompts, students will have completed a brief paragraph about their best teacher.

Use the following prompts:
1. Name someone you believe is the best teacher you ever had.
2. Tell two traits about that teacher.
3. Describe (don't name) someone who is not a great teacher.
4. Tell how the two are different.
5. Write a concluding sentence.
6. Title your piece: The Best Teacher I Ever Had.

Ask partners to share their writings with each other and to look for the similarities and the differences between the two writings.

Now, ask the class to work in small groups, using web graphics and analyze these two ideas: a good teacher and a good student.
Discuss the traits of each and what the implications might be.

Ask the pairs to dialogue about what was easy and what was hard about the lesson. Have them speculate about the reasons why things were easy or hard. Sample some responses with the whole class.

# # #

Reflecting on
the Design

BLUEPRINT
High School
Lesson

Codes 1SD
2SN
5NR
6CL
7OF

Setting Up the
Scaffolding

Working the
Crew

On My Own (SCANS Report)

Begin the discussion with the idea that one of the inevitable outcomes of high school is that students will eventually be on their own. They may be on their own in college, military service, or a job, but eventually, they will join the ranks of those young adults who say, I'm on my own. The adult work world has certain expectations about what they should know and be able to do.

Tell the students that in 1991, the Department of Labor released a paper called *What Work Requires of Schools: A SCANS Report for America 2000.* (Secretary's Commission on Achieving Necessary Skills [SCANS] 1991). The national commission identified certain skills as necessary for high school graduates or persons entering the work force (see Figure 1.13 or Blackline C1.1 in Appendix C).

Students work in groups of four, with a recorder, materials' manager, reporter, and observer. Each group selects a career academy focus from these five academies:
- Health sciences
- Business, law, and transportation
- Communication, fine arts, and media technology
- Engineering, industrial technology, and science
- Education, social services, and tourism

Using one career academy as their point of reference, the teams are to review the SCANS report as presented in Figure 1.13 (or Blackline C.1). They are to determine how the report holds up today. Are the skills identified in the SCANS report necessary and valid for their selected career academy? Why or why not?

Each group is to present their findings in a multimedia presentation that illustrates either how five of the skills are used in the world of work or how they differ from the skills identified in the SCANS Report.

Have students write a journal entry using the lead:

> "When I'm on my own . . . ." Then, ask those who are willing to share their thoughts.

# # #

Reflecting on
the Design

Blueprints for Achievement

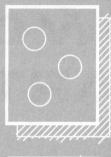

FORMING

PERFORMING

NORMING

CHAPTER 2

Phase I

FORMING

Level II
How Do I Get Started?

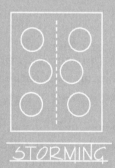

STORMING

CONFORMING

in the Cooperative Classroom

HOW DO I GET STARTED?

The best things and the best people rise out of their separateness; I'm against a homogenized society because I want the cream to rise.

—Robert Frost

Draft

Q What is a cooperative group?

A
- 2–5 students
- Teacher-selected
- Mixed by ability, motivation, gender, race
- Shared academic goal
- Targeted social skills
- Self-assessing

Q When do I start using cooperative groups?

A Start using cooperative groups right away. Cooperative learning takes time to develop. The sooner you start, no matter how small a start, the better. It is best to start with informal structures (e.g., think-pair-share, prediction pairs) before proceeding to more formal structures (e.g., jigsaw, graphic organizers).

How do I get started? is the most frequently asked question by classroom teachers new to cooperative learning. They are in the forming phase. They know well that the first lessons in the first week of school set the tone for the year. The best starts for cooperative learning are made *prior* to any formal introduction of cooperative learning. By beginning with planning and preparing for the *what, why,* and *how* of cooperative learning, teachers can introduce a cooperative climate in the classroom.

Teachers who have used homogeneous groups (e.g., lab groups in chemistry), may wonder, What is different about the *Blueprints* approach to cooperative groups? Teachers who have played the role of information giver ask, Why use cooperative groups? These are good questions.

The answer to the first question—What is different about the *Blueprints* approach to cooperative groups?—is twofold. First, *Blueprints* introduces a very unique approach to cooperation; it asks the teacher to form a cooperative classroom that creates a context for higher achievement by all students. Second, *Blueprints* introduces tools for creating *mixed ability* or *heterogeneous* groups in which students can learn for understanding and transfer in *all* subject areas.

The answer to the second question—Why use cooperative groups?—is more complicated. First, the research shows that the *Blueprints* approach increases students' academic performance and improves their social skills. By providing learning tools, *Blueprints* especially helps low performers become higher achievers and develop the social skills to interact with each other and their teachers in more positive ways (see chapter 3 for social skills development). Second, the *Blueprints* approach benefits teachers. As they teach students how to use the cognitive tools, they see the fruits of their labors in higher test scores and increased student academic performance. As they teach students the social skills of cooperative learning, they see student behavior improve and students' time on task increase.

What is this thing called *cooperative learning*? How does it differ from traditional grouping procedures in the classroom? How does it change the teacher's role?

Cooperative learning is an instructional model for teaching students how to learn together. It uses heterogeneous groups as a tool for creating a more cooperative classroom in which students' achievement, self-esteem, responsibility, high-level thinking, and favorable attitudes toward school increase dramatically.

Cooperative groups include two to five students of *different* ability, skill, motivation, gender, or racial origin who work to achieve a *single* learning goal (see Figure 2.1). In the cooperative classroom, teachers use a variety of structures and strategies to build on-task attention, trust, and shared success.

Three Levels of Instruction

3 Transfer

2 Deep Understanding

1 Cooperative Climate

What Is a Single Academic Goal?

A group of students applies collaborative social skills to achieve a single academic goal. All group members share the goal and work together as a single unit to achieve it. Individual goals give way to and focus on the group goal at all levels of academic work.

At the first level, the factual level, the group works as a unit to ensure each member "gets all the facts." For instance, if the common goal is to recall the definitions of ten key vocabulary words, the members help each other learn the words.

At the second level, the processing level, the group works to include all members in the process of meeting the goal. For example, if the goal is to challenge the group to compare the attributes of two authors, then each member contributes to the comparison.

At the third level, the transfer level, the group works to meet a complex goal. (e.g., to solve a complex problem). Again, it is the group, not each individual working alone, that is responsible for the group's success.

Think of a cooperative group as a group of lifeguards at a beach. One day, when the waves are high, the lifeguards spot a swimmer in distress beyond the breakers. Each guard knows he or she cannot swim through the breakers alone. Together, two—a male and female—jump into their boat. They work as a team with one goal—to get over the breakers and save the swimmer. One goal, different abilities.

Figure 2.1

Specs

Cooperative learning structures may be informal or formal. The basic difference between the two is that formal structures require the use of specific tools—roles, guidelines, success criteria, and group assessment strategies—that define how participants interact to achieve the common goal; informal structures only require the students to interact with each other to achieve a single goal.

INFORMAL STRUCTURES

The easiest way to start creating a cooperative classroom is to try a few *informal* cooperative learning strategies. Informal structures enable students to sample, experience, and enjoy cooperative learning. At the same time, informal structures help teachers see how the new approach works with their students and to gauge their own comfort level in managing the increased activity in the classroom. Teachers may include informal approaches in their standard lessons with little modification. These informal strategies quickly and easily initiate cognitive rehearsal and unite teams in the classroom.

Cognitive rehearsal, a key concept for understanding cooperative learning, rests on the principle that the one who talks is the one who learns. In traditional classrooms where the teacher talks to students ninety percent of the time, it is the teacher who benefits from cognitive rehearsal. The teacher talks and learns while the students passively record information in their heads, notebooks, or computers, which rewards students with better memories. On the other hand, when students answer questions or discuss the material with the teacher, they benefit intellectually. They also benefit when they interact with each other in small groups.

Informal cooperative learning *starts* students on the way to serious cognitive rehearsal. The key is to have student pairs spend at least two minutes at the beginning of a cooperative lesson preparing for new content, explaining a thought, or assessing what they have learned.

The informal strategies for promoting cognitive rehearsal do not require roles, guidelines, and other methods used in formal group tasks. Each of the eight informal strategies—shown in Figure 2.2 and explained in detail in the following paragraphs—takes little more than two to five minutes of face-to-face interaction. The teacher just decides when to use a tool, prepares instructions, and goes to it!

Think-Pair-Share

The *think-pair-share* rehearsal strategy can be used to

- help students summarize key points after a lecture,
- begin a new topic or unit by having students discuss prior knowledge,
- stimulate student thinking about an important piece of information,
- check students' understanding of a topic,

Q **What is cognitive rehearsal?**

A Cognitive rehearsal means that students verbally share, explain, or assess their ideas or concepts with each other. Cooperative learning and cognitive organizers are instructional models used to facilitate cognitive rehearsal.

Informal Cooperative Structures

Think-Pair-Share

Explain Why

Business Cards

KWL

Prediction Pairs

We Bags

I Learned Mail-Gram

Pair Review

Figure 2.2

- bring closure to a lesson,
- deepen students' short-term memories, or
- promote student transfer of a concept.

With each of these uses of the think-pair-share strategy, give similar instructions:

> *Before the lecture.* To start, say something like this: "Today, I am going to describe (topic). After I define each term, I'm going to ask you to (a, b, c, d, or e) with a partner." Fill in the second blank with one of the following: (a) summarize the key points, (b) describe what you already know about the topic, (c) pick one idea of importance to you and explain it, (d) tell how the information is important to you, or (e) explain something new you learned about the topic. Sample student ideas after 10–20 seconds.
>
> *After the lecture* (or at appropriate intervals during a longer lecture). After an appropriate amount of time, ask students to *turn to the person* on their (right or left) side, and take turns doing one of the activities (a, b, c, d, or e; see above). Allow time (2–3 minutes) for each person to share.

Explain Why

Explain why encourages students to rehearse their reasons for selecting answers. Before a lesson, ask students three to five multiple choice questions. After students answer each question, invite several students to explain *why* they selected their answers. Write students' answers on the board and explain to students that they should discover the correct answers as they study the lesson.

Business Cards

Business cards is a motivational strategy for rehearsal that involves the entire class. First, give each student a 3" x 5" index card and explain the purpose of a business card (e.g., to greet other people, to tell about yourself, or to explain an idea).

Then, model how to complete the business card. Display the card on an overhead or whiteboard and give the following instructions:

1. Write your first name in the middle of the card using capital letters (e.g., TOM).
2. Write the name of your school beneath your name (e.g., ML King School).
3. In the upper right corner of the card, write a *success* you had this week at school, home, or play (e.g., made a friend, got a 95 on a quiz).
4. In the upper left corner, write your learning *goal* for this week (e.g., improve vocabulary quiz score, finish a paper).
5. In the lower right corner, write a *benefit* for doing your homework (e.g., higher grades).
6. In the lower left corner, write the title of your *favorite* book (e.g., *Curious George, The Grapes of Wrath*).
7. Demonstrate your best cooperative skill (e.g., give a pat on the back, smile, or give an "Atta boy").

See Figure 2.3 for a sample of a business card and Blackline 2.1 in Appendix C.

Finally, after all students have completed their cards, instruct everyone to find a partner. After the pairs settle, each student should choose one of the corner topics (success, benefit, goal, or favorite) and explain to their partner *why* they selected the topic. After one or two minutes, ask students to switch partners and select a different corner to share. Students continue switching until all four corner topics have been discussed.

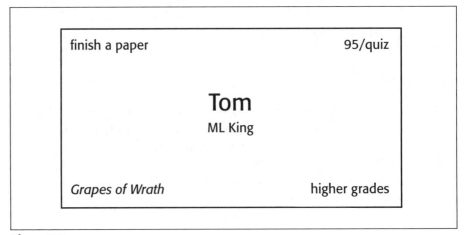

Figure 2.3

KWL

KWL stands for *what we Know, what we Want to know, and what we Learned*. Introduced by Ogle in 1986, this cognitive rehearsal strategy helps with pre-lesson diagnosis.

Ask students to find a partner. Announce the unit or lesson title (e.g., safety, photosynthesis, *Moby Dick,* whole numbers).

Give each pair a worksheet with three column headings at the top: What We Know, What We Want to Know; and What We Learned (see Blackline C2.2 in Appendix C). Invite pairs to list all they *know* about the topic in the first column and all they *want* to know about the topic in the second column. Match the pairs into foursomes so they can share their lists.

After finishing the unit, allow time for student pairs to write what they *learned* in the third column. Encourage students to discuss and their answers.

Prediction Pairs

Prediction pairs may be used when students can share an activity (e.g., reading a book). Begin by having students select a partner. Give each prediction pair a book or short story to read together. Ask partners to choose who will act as recorder and who will act as reader. Ask recorders in each pair to create a chart with two columns: What Will Happen Next and Reasons Based on Content.

Explain that after the reader reads each page aloud, the pair should predict what will happen next in the story. The recorder should write the predictions on the chart in the What Will Happen Next column. Predictions might be incidents both partners agree to. Then, the recorder should list the pair's reasons for the predictions in the Reasons Based on Content column. The pairs should include supporting evidence from the pages they have read.

After students complete an appropriate number of pages, invite pairs to share their prediction charts with another pair.

We Bags

To use the informal strategy *we bags*, ask students to select a partner and give each pair a paper bag. Invite the pairs to decorate the bags with their names, favorite books or foods, or names of places they have visited. Then, ask the groups to fill their bags with objects that have special meaning to them. When pairs are finished decorating and filling their bags, tell them to join another pair. Each person should introduce his or her partner to the foursome by discussing each item in the bag.

I Learned Mail-Gram

The *I learned mail-gram* strategy supports rehearsal after a lesson. Invite each student to complete and sign a mail-gram (a card) that has this stem: I learned . . . . (See Blackline C2.3 in Appendix C.) Next, match students into pairs to share their mail-grams. Rotate sharing pairs several times.

Pair Review

Pair review works well as a closure task for short lessons. Ask students to form pairs. Then, divide the lesson's information into two equal parts and ask one student to review the first half and the other student to review the second. Be explicit as to what each member should look for in the text (e.g., three key ideas, definitions of five vocabulary words).

After students have independently reviewed their half of the material, ask them to share their findings with their partners. Be sure to specify how many ideas each partner should share.

After pairs finish sharing with each other, ask them to rank the most important words, ideas, or concepts they found, and list the reasons for their rankings. This activity encourages deeper processing and strengthens students' short- and long-term recall of items or concepts. When students use graphic organizers, such as a ladder or steps, to record their ideas, their recall is further enhanced. Use pair reviews for checking homework, reviewing pre-tests, recalling prior knowledge, or renewing old acquaintances.

Hints for Implementing Informal Structures

To prevent students from taking advantage of the looser structure of these strategies, be sure to walk students through their first cooperative experience. When the teacher devotes time to explaining the reasons for each step, students begin to understand the underlying value as well as the steps of the process. The basic KWL is an easy starter. Start by announcing what students are going to do (work with the partner), why they are going to do it (to help each other), and what the common goal is (recall what they know about a topic). Next, tell students how to do the task (move your chairs quietly, put your heads together, and quietly talk with each other). Set a tight time limit for the work. When they finish their charts, ask pairs to share their ideas with on other pair or the whole class. When the task is done, be sure to compliment the students on how well they did the task and the quality of their answers.

FORMAL STRUCTURES

After students are comfortable working in pairs, it is time to upgrade the level of cooperative work and use formal task groups. Task groups increase the amount of student-to-student cognitive rehearsal in a lesson.

Task Groups

Initial task groups should include three students, preferably of different ability or motivation. Task groups are more *formal* than the informal pair activities described in the previous section. That is, task groups are structured explicitly to include:

- roles,

- cooperative guidelines,

- criteria for success in meeting a group goal, and

- a group assessment strategy.

Task groups support various models of instruction and can be used with any content lesson in the curriculum. In the direct instruction model, a teacher designs formal cooperative task groups with an anticipatory set, input, guided practice, or closure (see Appendix B for an example). In an inquiry lesson, a teacher creates cooperative lessons for gathering information, processing concepts, or making applications (see Appendix B for an example). Tasks as simple as learning vocabulary and practicing computation or as complex as contrasting two authors' styles or testing a physics hypothesis benefit from formal cooperative structures.

Introducing the Jigsaw

To start students in the more formal cooperative task groups, introduce them to the procedures in a simple, fun way. After they demonstrate a working knowledge of the procedures, move into content. One exceptionally useful structure to start with is the jigsaw. Two forms of jigsaws are introduced—the simple portmanteau jigsaw and the more complex concept jigsaw.

The Jigsaw Portmanteau

An easy way to introduce the jigsaw strategy is to use a jigsaw to learn vocabulary. To make it fun, students can create new words made up of two words put together. These are called portmanteau words, because they blend different concepts in a word that has a meaning of its own. (For some examples of portmanteau words, see Figure 2.4; for a diagram of a basic jigsaw procedure, see Blackline C2.4 in Appendix C.)

Try the lesson shown in Figure 2.4. This simple lesson demonstrates a round-robin jigsaw procedure with roles, guidelines, and group processing. Keep the list of new portmanteau words short so students can easily see and feel a jigsaw and learn the jigsaw procedures. In the processing that concludes the task, highlight the benefits of roles, guidelines, and jigsaw pieces for learning the words. After students demonstrate that they know how to jigsaw, use the same model to learn formal vocabulary words.

  What are task groups?

Task groups are formal group structures with
- roles,
- cooperative guidelines,
- criteria for success,
- a group goal,
- a group processing strategy,
- the ability to gather information, process concepts, or make applications.

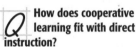 **How does cooperative learning fit with direct instruction?**

Cooperative learning works very well for a direct instruction lesson. See Appendix B for an example.

How does cooperative learning fit with the inquiry model?

 Cooperative learning fits well with the inquiry model. See the sample in Appendix B.

A Sample Starter: The Jigsaw Portmanteau

1. Select nine portmanteau words. Try these words created by students who learned the jigsaw portmanteau in their classes:

   Customerania (or customephrenia): the tendency of every salesperson in a store to ask May I help you? when you are just looking.

   Leaftover: the tiny piece of greenery stuck between someone's front teeth after eating spinach salad or soufflé.

   Socdroop: the tendency of socks that have lost their elastic to work their way down below the ankle.

   Chateauincinerade: The very, very well done steak that was accidentally left in the microwave for three hours.

   Linebind: When you go to the bank and are delighted that the line is short only to discover the person in front of you is depositing $500 in pennies.

   McLag: Having to wait longer for your order at a fast-food hamburger joint than at a restaurant.

   Aussification: What happens to most Americans who spend a long time in Australia.

   Acceleryeller: The person who thinks that when the stoplight changes to yellow it means to step on the gas.

   Diffizzication: What happens to any opened carbonated drink after sitting around for three days.

2. Divide the class into trios. Assign each group member three words. Give these instructions:

   Step 1: Learn the definitions of the three words. Draw a picture of each word. (You will use the sketch to teach the other members).

   Step 2: Conduct the first round of teaching and checking—each member teaches one word to the other members. Check the everyone understands the definition for each word. (Have each member review the definition.) Coach as needed.

   Step 3: Conduct a second round of teaching and checking.

   Step 4: Conduct a third round of teaching and checking.

   Step 5: Do a double check; make sure all groups members know all the words.

   Step 6: Take a quiz.

   Step 7: As a group, list the learning strategies you used to learn the vocabulary (e.g., check after each round, make and explain a sketch, give encouragement, etc.).

3. All students must know all the words within the fifteen minutes allowed for the exercise. To help, have one member quiz the other group members after each round of three and after the total nine. Then, after all the rounds, quiz the students.

Figure 2.4

The Content Jigsaw

A more formal type of jigsaw is the content jigsaw. This jigsaw can be used to gather a large amount of information in a short amount of time. By dividing the gathering task among the group members, the teacher sets the stage for an in-depth discussion of the core content. Let's look at the steps in the jigsaw procedure (see Figure 2.5).

Steps for the Jigsaw

1. Assign the information-gathering task.

2. Allot time for students to work alone and gather their fair share of the information.

3. Structure the groups.

4. Monitor the groups at work.

5. Assign time for the group assessment.

6. Assess individual knowledge with a quiz or written essay.

Figure 2.5

Step 1: Assign the information-gathering task. For example, if the trio's activity is to read a textbook chapter, the teacher may jigsaw the chapter in various ways:

- Divide the textbook chapter into three equal parts and ask each student to read one part.

- Assign three readings from different sources and ask each student to read one source and report to the group.

- Pose three questions about the textbook chapter, one question for each of the stories in the three-story intellect model (see chapter 4 and Blackline C2.5 in Appendix C for a blackline master of the three-story intellect). Then, student A reads to answer the first-story question (for facts), student B reads to answer the second-story question (for understanding), and student C reads to answer the third-story question (for transfer).

Step 2: Allot time for students to work alone and gather their fair share of the information. For less motivated students, allot time in class for coaching and checking. For more motivated students, make this a homework assignment.

Step 3. Structure the groups. Take time to establish the structure. Highlight the single goal and review the guidelines for cooperation. Assign roles (recorder, timekeeper, and checker) and review role responsibilities if necessary (see Appendix B for more information on roles).

Questions from the Three-Story Intellect

First-Story Verbs
Count, describe, name, recall, tell

Second-Story Verbs
Compare, distinguish, explain why, analyze, solve

Third-Story Verbs
estimate, evaluate, predict, imagine, judge

Emphasize the targeted social skill (e.g., active listening; see chapter 3 for a discussion of social skills). Set up the assessment criteria and rubric. The assessment should focus on how well the group worked together and the quality of the product. Keep individuals accountable but include a group presentation of the finished task.

Step 4: Monitor the groups at work. Coach and check for understanding as needed and help students keep their attention on the single goal.

Step 5: Assign time for the group assessment. Be sure to include an assessment of the *group* process using a tool such as Mrs. Potter's questions (Figure 2.6) or the PMI (Figure 2.7) as well as an assessment of each individual's contributions to the product.

Mrs. Potter's Questions

What were you supposed to do?

What did you do well?

What would you do differently next time?

Do you need any help?

Figure 2.6

PMI

What I liked (Pluses)

What I didn't like (Minuses)

Questions or thoughts (Intriguing Questions)

Figure 2.7

Step 6. Assess individual knowledge with a quiz or written essay. Even if tracking and ability grouping are the norm in a middle or high school classroom, teachers may structure content jigsaws or other formal cooperative tasks to meet the academic standard.

Consider an example taken from third-year (junior) English. The school tracks students into advanced placement (AP), average, and remedial groupings, and, students within each track exhibit a wide range of reading and writing abilities. The standard requires all students to analyze a significant American novel. To apply this standard equally and fairly to all students, teachers assign the same book, Hawthorne's *Scarlet Letter,* to students in all tracks. For departmental tests, each student must know the names and the importance of six major characters, twelve symbols, and nine events in the story. In addition, each student is expected to explain, using textual evidence, why a specific character made a certain moral decision. Finally, each student must write an essay about one or more characters. (The essay is graded by the teacher.) No collaboration is allowed during the assessment.

Although the assessment is individualistic, teachers use formal cooperative learning to maintain this standard in the AP and remedial classes.

In the AP class, students form cooperative task groups. Each group selects one contemporary film to compare with the novel. Students are given a worksheet with questions about character, theme, cultural references, symbolism, and setting. Each group jigsaws the questions; group members choose a part of the jigsaw to use as their focus when reading the novel. After students have read the novel, each group member takes one-half of a class period to lead the small group in a discussion of the novel from his or her focus. After all members have shared, the group synthesizes its understandings and prepares group members to write individual essays comparing the novel with the selected film. In addition, the group prepares and makes a presentation to the entire class. When all groups have presented, the teacher guides a closing discussion of the novel, emphasizing department-mandated facts and the moral decisions of the major characters. Then, finally, students individually take the test and write an essay.

In the remedial class, the teacher and the students spend ten days doing a chapter-by-chapter analysis of the text. Each class period begins with a review of the prior night's reading assignment, including characters, symbols, and important events. Then the teacher guides a think-pair-share discussion of the importance of the elements identified that day. At the end of chapter study, the teacher assigns students to formal task groups, and each student in every task group is asked to become an expert on two characters, four symbols, and three events (based on the standard). Each group must also create a mind map that combines all these features—characters, symbols, and events. For each element, the responsible student finds the text to support the group's position on the element. Groups spend three days drawing their mind maps and preparing for an all-class presentation. Presentations are graded by a rubric that highlights the accuracy of the quoted sources. After the presentations, the groups prepare members for a final examination on these elements. The examination tests factual knowledge and requires each student to write an essay explaining why a character made the decisions he did. Each test receives an individual grade.

After the Introduction

After students have completed a formal cooperative task, it is very important that they look back and debrief about what and how they learned. For the simple vocabulary jigsaw (the portmanteau), this may entail taking a few minutes to assess individual knowledge. For other, more complex cooperative tasks such as the content jigsaw, debriefing is an essential cognitive rehearsal. Debriefing reinforces the idea that cooperation improves individual achievement and solidifies students' recall and understanding of the core information. The simple jigsaw lesson, the portmanteau, demonstrates very powerfully to students that working together gives them better academic results than working alone. When students participate in *heterogeneous* groups (groups in which members differ in ability or motivation), they discover that each individual, whether they are higher or lower performers, score better by working as a team. Students also discover that assessment of content mastery is best done individually, but assessment of the group process is best done by the group.

During the time students are working in groups, what does the teacher do? Not only do students' roles change, but also the teacher's role shifts dramatically in a cooperative classroom (see Figure 2.8).

The Teacher's Role

From the traditional classroom:

- dispensing information from the front of the classroom

- performing for and entertaining passive students

- rewarding and punishing

- preparing for standardized tests

- grading workbooks and tests at the teacher's desk

- emphasizing teacher-student and student-material interactions

To the cooperative, achieving classroom:

- planning dynamic lessons for transfer of learning

- teaching students how to learn

- developing student responsibility through coaching and monitoring

- promoting active learning

- facilitating student self-evaluation

- encouraging and cheerleading mastery of skills and concepts

- extending participation

- intervening and correcting in the groups

- motivating high-level thinking

- building group skills

- balancing teacher-to-student, student-to-material and student-to-student interactions

Figure 2.8

How Cooperative Groups Differ from Traditional Groups

Traditional Learning Groups

- One goal and/or task learned at a time.

- Groups break up when product or task is finished.

- Social skills are assumed; they are not explicitly taught.

- One leader gets main role.

- Group is evaluated without looking at individual efforts.

- Teacher grades product.

- Homogeneous groups are created.

- Students are only responsible for themselves.

- Each student relies on him- or herself.

- No cooperative structure is included.

Cooperative Learning Groups

- Higher-order thinking is woven into every lesson.

- Teacher focuses on group interaction.

- Social skills are explicitly taught.

- Roles are shared and mixed.

- Individual contribution to group goal is evaluated.

- Group looks back and processes its interactions and group work.

- Groups are heterogeneous; students with different characteristics are mixed and matched.

- Members share responsibility for group.

- Students rely on each other.

- Cooperative structure is evident.

Figure 2.9

The changed teacher role hints at the differences between traditional groups and cooperative groups in a thinking classroom (see Figure 2.9).

As Slavin (1977a), Johnson and Johnson (1974), and other researchers of cooperative learning have shown, cooperative groups increase students' mastery of the basic skills. Reading and mathematics scores go up, grades improve, and students report that they prefer working together. But there is more, as Joyce reported in his meta-analysis of the effects of cooperative learning: "Cooperative learning procedures facilitate learning across all curriculum areas and ages, improving self-esteem, social skill and solidarity and academic learning goals ranging from the acquisition of information and skill through the modes of inquiry of academic disciplines" (Joyce, Weil, and Calhoun 2000, p. 15).

What Joyce points out is the most significant insight yet into the potential power of cooperative learning. As much as "pure" cooperative learning accomplishes when used as a stand-alone strategy, it provides a greater opportunity when combined with strategies that challenge students to think more skillfully, solve problems, or generate new concepts. In essence, the combinations that Joyce noted provide windows of opportunity that have exponential effects on student learning.

BUILD

Marcus and McDonald's (1990) acronym, BUILD, highlights the variables that produce the powerful results identified in the research on cooperative learning (see Figure 2.10). A lesson designed with all these BUILD variables is a robust and forceful cooperative learning event that has a high likelihood of getting excellent results. But, the likelihood that a lesson will have the powerful effects mentioned in the research decreases as the number of BUILD variables in the lesson decreases.

For each BUILD variable, the teacher can select from dozens of strategies to design each cooperative thinking lesson. Note in the portmanteau jigsaw (or in the sample lessons at the end of this chapter) how the lesson uses each of the variables. *Blueprints* addresses many strategies that teachers may use with the BUILD structure: student and teacher questions, graphic organizers, jigsaws and group investigations, problem solving, problem-based learning modules, and team projects. BUILD guides teachers in creating a strong, formal cooperative structure and serves as a framework for criteria to assess the quality of the cooperative task.

The BUILD Structure as a Rubric

Teachers create a BUILD structure by using the five steps of cooperative lesson planning (see Blackline C2.6 in Appendix C).

Build in higher-order thinking. To create cooperative groups in which student learning, achievement, and self-esteem are increased significantly, the teacher must build *higher-level thinking* into the tasks. Creating high-level thinking challenges automatically boosts cooperation because the group members recognize that they need help from the group to meet the challenge. Conversely, if the task is too easy, such as a simple fill-in-the-blank worksheet, students realize that they can do the

---

The BUILD Acronym

B = Build in higher-order thinking to challenge students.

U = Unite the teams so students form bonds of trust.

I = Invite individual accountability.

L = Look back and debrief what and how students learned.

D = Develop students' social skills.

(Adapted from Marcus and McDonald 1990.)

Figure 2.10

task more quickly, easily, and better by working alone without collaborators. High challenge fosters high collaboration. In turn, higher-level metacognitive discussion promotes the desired transfer.

Unite the team to form bonds of trust. When teachers tailor high-level cognitive tasks for the group, members form a united team—a team with a "sink or swim together" posture. When students know that they all make it together but none makes it alone, their motivation to cooperate is sparked naturally. Interdependence by team members to accomplish individual as well as group goals is an absolute key to the high-performance classroom.

Invite individual accountability. Another critical element to cooperative groups is helping each student know that he or she is accountable personally for achieving the group goal and learning the material. Often, students new to cooperative models are unskilled at learning and being accountable for the total picture at the same time. High-performing classrooms, on the other hand, gradually adopt deliberate, visible, and, sophisticated steps to invite individual accountability. These graduated moves range from quick, individual quizzes to more elaborate, independent, and appropriate applications of what a student has learned.

Look back and debrief what and how students learned. Taking time to *look over* what the group has done—planning, monitoring, and evaluating academic and cooperative tasks—is another critical element in the high-performing classroom. This metacognitive model promotes further application and transfer from the lesson and also fosters cognitive rehearsal among the group members. Without group processing time or group processing formats, little, if any, transfer takes place. Yet, when students evaluate their group behaviors and task results, they exhibit noticeable tendencies toward meaningful transfer.

Develop students' social skills. A final element for the high-functioning cooperative learning teams is the teacher's explicit attention to developing students' *social skills*. These skills are needed for communicating, building trust, promoting leadership, and resolving conflicts. Students develop into valuable, contributing, and empathetic members of groups when they have acquired specific social skills: active listening behaviors (e.g., paraphrasing, affirming, and clarifying), leadership skills (e.g., encouraging others), and conflict resolution skills (e.g., disagreeing with ideas but not people, listening to others' points of view, and seeking consensus).

Q **What kind of classroom interactions do we use?**

A To BUILD thinking in the cooperative classroom, three types of interactions to consider:

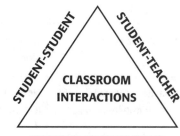

STUDENT-TEACHER = How teachers question and respond to students

STUDENT-STUDENT = How students talk and work with each other

STUDENT-INFORMATION = How students deal with the material

Applying the BUILD Rubric to a Lesson

As noted, a second important value of the BUILD model is its use as a rubric for evaluating a lesson's alignment with the cooperative framework. Figure 2.11 shows a rubric that teachers can use to plan and assess the potential effectiveness of their cooperative lessons (see Blackline C2.7 in Appendix C).

Without teachers deliberately integrating the five BUILD attributes, groups function simply as study groups, which have much lower impact on achievement. However, when teachers emphasize BUILD, formal cooperative groups develop the cohesion that facilitates higher achievement levels.

BUILD Rubric

To what degree does this lesson:	1	2	3	4
Build in higher-order thinking.	All facts and recall	Implied thinking	Application of specific skill	High challenge thinking and reflecting
Unite the team.	Task can be done alone	Uses roles and guidelines	Has common goal structures	Supports common goal
Invite individual responsibility.	No reason to work together	Uses one strategy	Uses two strategies	Uses three or more strategies
Look back and review.	Not called for	Content review	Content and cooperation review	All three functions— content, cooperation, cognition—reviewed
Develop social skills.	Not done	Forced by structure	Encouraged by structure, taught and reviewed	Expectation integrated

Figure 2.11

SUMMARY

When introducing cooperative learning, begin with informal strategies. Teach students a strategy such as think-pair-share, and use it each day. Add other informal strategies gradually. Introduce simple, formal strategies to give variety to cooperative instruction when students have developed a climate of cooperation. Return to the informal strategies and concentrate on building cooperation if students regress in their ability to work together.

Throughout *Blueprints,* specific strategies are provided for developing lessons and units that meet the BUILD criteria to a high degree. The BUILD Planning Chart (see Blackline C2.6 in Appendix C) provides a bird's eye view of the "best" of the BUILD strategies integrated into a planning matrix. See Appendix B for a model lesson.

BLUEPRINT
Elementary
Lesson

Codes......6CL
8GH
9QCA

Setting Up the
Scaffolding

Working the
Crew

T-E-A-M
(Together Each
Achieves More)

Students are used to working on individual tasks in school. Cooperative learning disrupts the game they have learned to play. This lesson helps students learn that working together increases individual achievement and is important to high performance—Together Each Achieves More (T–E–A–M). In cooperative learning, students must prove that they have learned with meaning rather than merely memorizing content. Three questions are associated with this high-content, high-challenge, and high-support lesson: What does each child understand? How has each student improved his or her thinking skills? What has each learned about working with others as a team member?

Use the *think-pair-share* and *explain why* strategies for this lesson. First, show the word T–E–A–M on an overhead. Invite students to *think* about times when they participated in a team and to answer this question: What did it take for team members to win the challenge together? Tell students to form *pairs.* Ask pairs to join their lists and agree on three answers to the question. Invite pairs to *share* answers with the whole class. List unduplicated answers on the board. Ask students to *explain why* the pair selected a specific answer. When the list is complete (about 3–5 minutes), invite students to select some examples from the list that match with T–E–A–M. Make a list.

Reflecting on
the Design

Conclude by asking students how this activity helped their concept of team-work. Call on individuals who have not yet spoken, if possible. Remember to wait for answers and give as many as students as possible the opportunity to respond.

# # #

BLUEPRINT

Middle School
Lesson

Codes 1SD
2SN
5NR
6CL
9QCA

Setting Up the
Scaffolding

Cooperative?
Competitive?
Or Individualistic?

On the materials table, place a pile of old magazines, one pair of scissors for every three students, a pad of newsprint with crayons or markers, and several rolls of masking tape. Tell the students that they are going to study three ways people work together. On the board, write the words *cooperative, competitive,* and *individualistic.* Put a T-chart under each (see Blackline C2.8 in Appendix C).

COOPERATIVE		COMPETITIVE		INDIVIDUALISTIC	
Looks Like	Sounds Like	Looks Like	Sounds Like	Looks Like	Sounds Like

Define each word (see below). Write the definition under the word and add examples.

> **Cooperative:** when two or more people work together toward a single goal (e.g., football players, airplane crew)
>
> **Competitive:** when one or more persons work against each other toward a single goal (e.g., two football teams try to win the game, race car drivers try to win a race)
>
> **Individualistic:** when one person works alone to reach a goal (e.g., a mountain climber, a house painter) according to a set criterion (e.g., 80 percent, etc.)

Ask members of the class to add other examples.

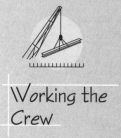

Divide the class into teams by asking them to count off by threes. Tell them that each three-person team is going to work toward a single goal. Before the students do the task, however, prepare the teams with materials and instructions.

Give each trio one hanger, 24" of string, one 8" X 11" tagboard, one pot of paste, one pair of scissors, and one magazine. Assign the roles of cutter (cuts out selected pictures), paster (pastes on squares) and arranger (ties pictures to hanger). The cooperative goal is to make a mobile using pictures (from the magazine) glued to tagboard squares (see illustration below). The middle piece of each mobile has one of the following team words: *cooperation, competition,* or *individualism.* Assign each group one of the themes and tell the groups that their pictures have to fit their assigned themes.

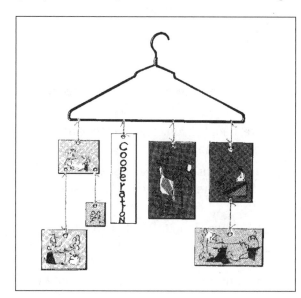

Allow 10 minutes for teams to construct their mobiles. Give teams another 3 minutes to ensure that each member can explain the picture selections made for their theme. When a member can explain the selections, then he or she signs the mobile. After all members have signed their finished mobiles, hang the mobiles throughout the room.

To explore how the students feel about the concepts of cooperation, competition, and individualism, ask them to give examples of positive and negative feelings about each of the three ways to interact.

For social skill processing, ask students to describe a cooperating behavior they used today.

For cognitive processing, simply have students describe their products (the mobiles).

For metacognitive reflection, tell groups to talk about *how* they thought through the task. What did they do first? second? third? Reinforce the value of cooperation by telling them that they will do many tasks during the year in which they will work cooperatively to think critically and creatively.

# # #

BLUEPRINT
High School
Lesson

Codes 1SD
2SN
6CL

Setting Up the Scaffolding

Torn Circles

On the board or on a transparency, write these words and describe the three types of interactions:

Cooperative: when two or more people work together toward a single goal (e.g., football players, airplane crew)

Competitive: when one or more persons work against each other toward a single goal (e.g., two football teams try to win the game, race car drivers try to win a race)

Individualistic: when one person works alone to reach a goal (e.g., a mountain climber, a house painter)

Elicit definitions of the words from students with sports examples of the three types of interactions:

Cooperation: seesaw, leap frog

Competition: Olympics, tug of war

Individualistic: swimming, tightrope walking

Divide the class into teams of three and assign the roles:

Material's manager: Gets the stuff.

Reporter: Gives report.

Observer: Talks about feelings.

Working the Crew

Explain to the students that the Torn Circles activity is a quick, but graphically concrete, example of the three types of social interactions. Ask them to focus on how they feel as they sample the three distinct interactions.

Competitive Task

Instruct students to *each,* by themselves, take a sheet of scratch paper (gathered by the material's manager) and tear a circle (see illustration below). The goal is to tear the roundest circle in the group. Reiterate: The winning circle will be judged by others for *roundness.*

After the individuals complete the task, instruct them to select the best circle in their groups of threes.

After the winner from each group is selected, have each side of the room select the three roundest circles.

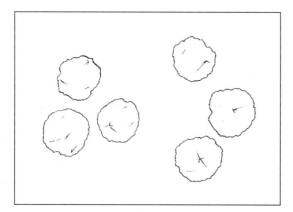

Ask the six finalists, one at a time, to place their circles on the overhead projector and, using a pseudo "applause meter," judge the best circle in the room. (First-place, second-place and third-place winners may be chosen.)

After the competition is over, ask students to describe how they are feeling to their groups of three. Ask reporters to sample the feelings experienced by their groups. Gather a list of words that describe students' feelings on the competitive tasks (e.g., anxious, stupid, angry, nervous).

Individualistic Task

Instruct students that again, they are to individually tear shapes. However, this time the torn shapes must *meet these criteria:*
- two straight sides
- two curves
- one hole

Any and all torn shapes that meet the criteria earn a 100 percent grade for the participants. Torn circles for the individualistic task might look like this:

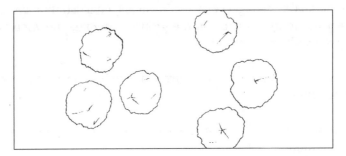

Again, talk with students about how they felt during this interaction. Gather words that describe their feelings when trying to meet individual criteria (e.g., successful, non-threatened, satisfied, a winner).

Cooperative Task

Instruct students that in this last interaction they are to each contribute a piece for a final collage comprised of three pieces. The final collage design should symbolize cooperation. Again, ask each student trio to design a collage that symbolizes cooperation using the group's three torn pieces (see example below).

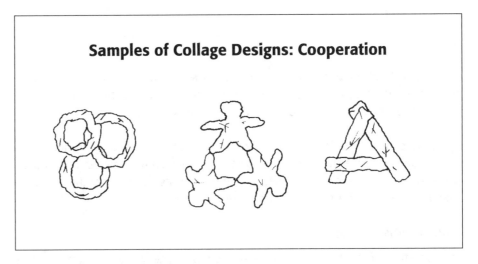

Samples of Collage Designs: Cooperation

Again, ask student what feelings they experienced as they cooperatively completed this task. Gather words that describe their feelings (e.g., supported, teamwork, pride, trust).

Throughout the three interactions, students focused on their feelings. Take time to compare and contrast the three lists of words describing the different feelings students had during the activities.

Reflecting on
the Design

To process socially, ask students to describe a social situation in which someone acted inappropriately.

To process cognitively, check that students understand the three types of interactions. Ask students to role play in groups of six these three words: *competitive, individualistic, cooperative.*

Finally, lead students to metacognitively transfer the concepts beyond this situation by directing each student to make an entry in his or her log. (The log is a student notebook of ideas, thoughts, notes, and so forth that may be referred to and added to throughout the year).) Have students complete one of the following lead-ins in their logs:

Cooperation is like _____ because both _____.

Competition differs from cooperation because _____.

The hardest part about cooperating is _____.

# # #

Blueprints for Achievement

FORMING

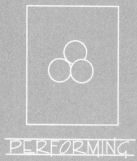
PERFORMING

NORMING

CHAPTER 3

Phase II
NORMING

Level 1

How Do I Develop
Students' Social Skills?

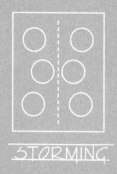
STORMING

CONFORMING

in the Cooperative
Classroom

Phase II
NORMING
Level 1

HOW DO I DEVELOP STUDENTS' SOCIAL SKILLS?

Lots of times you have to pretend to join a parade in which you are really not interested in order to get where you're going.

—Christopher Morley

Draft

In the *Blueprints* approach, the goal is to build a cooperative *classroom*. To do this, the teacher starts by creating behavior *norms* that guide the development of students' social skills—skills that help students interact so they might achieve the shared goals of the cooperative classroom. As the school year progresses and teachers guide the students through the many phases of group development, teachers see the students change from individuals who are centered on their own performance to individuals who enhance each others' performances by working together.

When students learn a new social skill, it is important that they
- understand the need for and value of the skill,
- know the chief behavior indicators of the skill,
- know when to use the skill,
- practice the skill,
- reflect on how they might improve their use of the skill, and
- persist in refining a skill until it is automatic.

Social skills are primarily developed in cooperative groups. These skills are the foundation for the management of cooperative classroom behavior and are needed for all interactions, large group and small. Because cooperative social skills are essential tools in a constructive and successful classroom management program, teachers need to take time to teach the basic, interactive social skills. Teaching and learning cooperative social skills is not an extra. The most effective teachers encourage students to use those skills both inside and outside of the classroom. Teaching these skills *reinforces* other classroom management techniques such as consequence charts, fair and equal application of discipline codes, and classroom rules that establish high expectations for positive behavior. There are five components in this process: deciding how to teach social skills, teaching social skills, choosing social skills, saving time to teach social skills, and planning what to do when students misbehave.

DECIDE HOW TO TEACH SOCIAL SKILLS

How does a teacher decide whether to teach a cooperative social skill formally or informally? The answer depends on the students' existing level of cooperative skills in a particular classroom. One class may have students who have strong interpersonal skills they developed at home or in previous classes; another class may have students who have little experience in these crucial skills. The experienced class needs little training on basic forming and norming skills and can advance to more sophisticated performing skills; the inexperienced class needs more training in basic skills.

In addition to considering the students' level of sophistication with cooperation, teachers need to remember that students learn skills in several ways. Some learn social skills from *informal* instruction woven into classroom expectations, roles, and guidelines. Others learn better through *formal* (or direct) instruction in the skills.

During *informal instruction* in social skills, the teacher reinforces previously learned cooperative skills. For example, the teacher might assign familiar group roles, such as encourager or recorder, or reinforce cooperative behaviors that students already know, such as "one person talks at a time." The easiest way to informally teach social skills is to reinforce cooperative behaviors, such as sharing, listening, and helping, when students display these in day-to-day activity. Every activity, every lesson can be strengthened by including informal cooperative skill development.

Formal instruction in cooperative skills is needed when students' behavior indicates that they lack skills. Formal instruction is especially helpful with younger students and with students who rebel against the cooperative learning climate of high expectations for on-task behavior. These students profit the most from direct instruction, guided practice, and constructive feedback in the development of the cooperative social skills.

TEACH SOCIAL SKILLS

The basic procedure for teaching a social skill includes using a hook lesson, teaching specific behaviors, providing practice, extending practice, observing progress, and reflecting on activity. Let's examine each step more closely using a lesson in listening as an illustration.

Hook strategies lay the groundwork. Encourage all students to develop the social skill (e.g., helping each other). Younger students, students who

Specs

Q **What social skill areas need to be addressed?**

A Communication (C), Trust (T), Leadership (L), and Conflict Resolution (CR) need to be addressed. (See Appendix B for an explanation of each of these.)

Teaching Social Skills Process

• Use a hook it strategy.
• Teach associated behaviors.
• Provide practice.
• Extend practice to reinforce skill.
• Observe students practicing the skill.
• Guide student reflection.

Q **How often should I work on social skills?**

A That depends on your students' needs. After instruction (one class period), practices of five-ten minutes each week for three or four weeks should ingrain the skill and set it as a norm. From that point, a five- to ten-minute reflection per day (elementary) or per week (middle/secondary) should suffice to imbed the skills and lead to high performance.

lack cooperative skills, or students whose peers reinforce negative social skills need more time to recognize, reinforce, and practice the essential cooperative skills. Start with a role play in which two selected students demonstrate to the class how *not* to help each other on a task. Follow this with a second role play in which two students show *how* to help each other on the same task.

Teach students the specific behaviors associated with the positive social skill. After the hook strategy, ask students to generate a list of behaviors for the social skill. Use a T-chart or web to record both the acceptable behaviors (e.g, helping each other) and non-acceptable behaviors (e.g, not helping each other). Add behaviors that students miss. Post the charts on the bulletin board or provide a copy for each student's notebook.

Next, lead students in guided skill *practice,* massed in short bursts. For instance, active listening pairs can practice with each other in three- to five-minute segments. Student A helps as student B follows instructions for completing a task. After the practice, A self-evaluates his or her helping practice. Then the partners reverse roles before the two list the ways they helped each other. Students need to continue practicing until the social skill becomes automatic. This takes time. During the hook, students entered the first stage of change: awareness. They perceived that they needed the skill and they increased their commitment to improve the skill. After they received positive feedback, they refine the skill until it becomes automatic.

Extended practices give students opportunities to reinforce the targeted skill. When discussing the criteria for lesson success, be sure to tell students what skill behaviors are expected of them. For example, you might say, I want to see at least five listening behaviors from each group or On your group evaluation, I expect you to report five examples of active listening.

Observe as students practice the desired social skill. Watch for both good and bad examples of the targeted social skill (or designate a student to look for examples). Some teachers use a checklist (see Figure 3.1) to record samples of the specified social skills while the groups work on task. After the groups process their work, recognize the positive examples you observed, and encourage all students to continue practicing the skills.

Student *reflection* is the final and most important step in the process, because it helps students develop intrinsic motivation. Guide reflection with stems, cues, a human graph, or Mrs. Potter's Questions (see chapter 2).

CHOOSE SOCIAL SKILLS

In addition to deciding *how* to teach cooperative skills (informally or formally), teachers need to select *what* skills to teach. Skills vary by phase (see Figure 3.2 and Blackline C3.1 in Appendix C). Let's start by looking at the forming skills, go on to norming skills, and finally, consider more advanced skills.

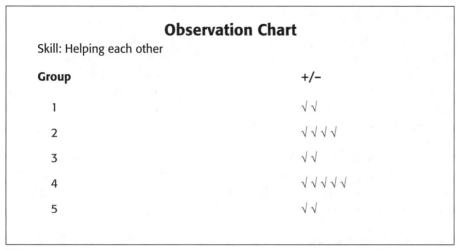

Observation Chart

Skill: Helping each other

Group	+/−
1	√ √
2	√ √ √ √
3	√ √
4	√ √ √ √
5	√ √

Figure 3.1

Phases of Introduction of Social Skills	
Phase	**Social Skills** **Communication (C), Trust (T), Leadership (L), Conflict Resolution (CR)**
Forming to organize groups and establish behavior guidelines	Use a 6" voice. (C) Heads together. (C) Listen to your neighbor. (C) Do your job. (L) Stay with the group. (C) Help each other. (L)
Norming to complete assigned tasks and build effective relationships	Include all members. (L) Let all participate. (L) Encourage others. (L) Respect each other's opinions. (T) Listen with focus. (T) Stay on task. (L)
Conforming to promote critical thinking and maximize the learning of all	Clarify. (C) Probe for differences. (CR) Paraphrase ideas. (C) Generate alternatives. (CR) Give examples. (C) Seek consensus. (CR)
Storming to function effectively and enable the work of the team	Sense tone. (C) See all points of view. (CR) Disagree with idea not person. (CR) Try to agree. (CR) Keep an open mind. (T) Contribute own ideas. (L)
Performing to foster higher-level thinking skills, creativity, and depth intuition	Elaborate on ideas. (C) Extend ideas. (C) Integrate ideas. (L) Synthesize. (L) Justify ideas. (CR) Reach consensus. (CR)

Figure 3.2

Q **How many skills do I teach?**

A It is not necessary to teach a large number of social skills nor *to cover* the entire list at each level. Procedural skills may be grouped for instruction with forming groups. After that, one skill well developed over a semester is more valuable than several "touched on."

Focus on Forming Skills

In the early *forming* stage, individuals learn how to contribute to and benefit from teamwork. This stage includes learning how to move into and out of a group, to speak in a group, to listen in a group, to help the group, and to keep the group on task. A slightly expanded form of these basic skills help teachers assess their classes' levels of forming skills (see Figure 3.3 and Blackline C3.2 in Appendix C).

Teachers may teach lessons that focus on forming skills that help students work on task in a group. Following are two sample lessons. The first addresses learning to control the volume of talking and the second focuses on moving into a group.

The teacher may use the first lesson when a class is too noisy. This direct instruction lesson reinforces the expectations for the appropriate noise level. First, use a hand signal to get the class' attention (see Appendix B). When all are quiet, explain the expectation (e.g., Speak in voices you can hear no more than six inches away.) or sit in a noisy group and demonstrate a six-inch voice. Guide the groups, then give them time to practice. When the class strays from the expected level of talking, use this as a teachable moment. Signal for quiet, look around, and use facial expressions to enforce the quiet hand signal. When all students stop talking, remind the class of the rule, and then move ahead. By insisting firmly and stubbornly that students respond to the hand signal and that their behavior meets the established voice level, the teacher establishes that there are times to work on-task in groups and times to give silent attention to the teacher. Remind students to use appropriate voice levels during group work. By using hand signals and reinforcing behavior, you not only command students' attention without raising your voice above a whisper, but you also train students to use appropriate voice levels when working with others.

The second lesson, teaches students how to move into groups. If the classroom has a permanent cooperative seating arrangement, students will need to move desks infrequently. If, however, desks need to be moved in and out of rows to create cooperative group seating, then the teacher must teach, practice, reinforce, and reflect on these appropriate procedures with students. One effective procedure follows:

1. Ask one row of students at a time to pick up their books and set them against the wall and then sit down.

2. Assign each student in the class to a group. Use cards with colored dots or group names, or choose another group assignment method. Assign roles appropriate for the lesson and the students: for example, calculator, reader, encourager, and so on. Display the desired group pattern on the overhead or board.

Assessing Your Class: The Forming Skills			
Skill	**Needed**	**Have**	**Comments**
Move into a group.			
Move out of a group.			
One person talks at a time.			
Stay with group.			
Control volume of talk (3″, 6″, 12″).			
Practice all roles.			
Keep hands and feet to self.			

Figure 3.3

3. Ask students to move their seats so they are sitting with their new group. Invite the students to form their groups quietly. If the class is too noisy, stop the activity (preferably with a hand signal) until all students are quiet. Reinforce the expectation for a quiet move and begin again.

4. Give positive reinforcement for a quiet move, and ask students to gather their books or to get their work materials from the wall.

5. After the task is done, instruct students to store their group materials, to rearrange their desks (put diagram on overhead or blackboard if necessary), and to sit down.

Q **What do I do if students slip into forming misbehaviors?**

A Go back and revisit the forming skills to remind students of the desired behavior.

Focus on Norming Skills

After establishing the forming behaviors, it is time to proceed to the norming phase of skills.

Every teacher wants and deserves student-to-student interaction behavior norms to be positive and encouraging. Unfortunately, the norms learned from television humor, sports figures, and the playground may be negative and discouraging. To change the norms from negative behaviors—put-downs, disrespectful slurs, and inattention—to positive behaviors, teachers need to identify specific social skills that lead to a more positive climate. The form in Figure 3.4 may be used to assess a class's level of norming skills. (See also Blackline C3.3 in Appendix C.)

Assessing Your Class: The Norming Skills			
Skill	**Needed**	**Have**	**Comments**
Sincere compliments			
Respectful statements and actions			
Attentive listening			
Encouragement			
Taking turns to speak			
Applauding success			
Pride in role			

Figure 3.4

One of the most effective social skill lessons you can teach your students focuses on a practical norming skill—encouraging. If students are to work cooperatively, they must learn to replace their negative behaviors (e.g., comic put-downs) with behaviors that encourage their peers. Peer encouragement is a highly useful skill for the cooperative classroom.

Solid formal instruction of a social skill requires the same careful preparation found in any procedural lesson. First, use a hook. For instance, to target the students' attention on the social skill, use a role playing activity, a structured group experience, or a story that illustrates the social skill lesson (see the sample middle school lesson [IALAC] at the end of this chapter). Other hooks include people searches, agree/disagree statements, or think-pair-share (see chapter 2). When creating a hook to teach encouragement, consider a using a film such as *Cipher in the Snow*. This film is a powerful illustration of the impact of discouragement on a child's life.

Next, use a T-chart as an aid to teaching what encouragement is and means in a group. Ask these questions: What does encouragement sound like? What does it look like? (See Figure 3.5 for an example T-chart and Blackline C3.4 in Appendix C.) After students develop the positive behavior chart, ask them to make a negative chart: What does discouragement look and sound like? T-charts may be developed for every cooperative social skill. T-charts help students understand the specific behaviors that make up a skill. Instead of dealing with abstract words, such as *encouragement* or *attentive listening*, the students work with specific behaviors and look at both sides of the coin.

Encouragement	
Sounds Like	**Looks Like**
"Keep at it."	Thumbs up
"Atta girl, Atta boy."	Pat on the back
"Way to go!"	Smile
"Here's another way to look at it."	Head nodding
"Great idea."	Beckoning hand
"Keep trying."	
"You're getting close."	

Figure 3.5

After creating a T-chart, prepare a display that will provide a daily reminder of the behaviors. For example, decorate a large bulletin board with words and pictures celebrating *encouragement,* put a model T-chart on the wall, or give students a T-chart handout that details the positive behaviors. At this point, emphasize the positive. Relegate negative behaviors to oblivion.

As needed, practice and continue practicing the behaviors with a role play, simulation, or embedded group task. Conclude the activity with a reflection using a stem: I like encouragement because . . . or Encouragement is most helpful when . . . .

Q **What social skills help define a cooperative climate in the classroom?**

A
- Encouragement
- Communication
- Trust
- Leadership
- Conflict resolution

Also, when putting together cooperative groups, take time to give students feedback on their progress in creating effective groups. This helps students to stay focused on setting the norm for positive interactions. One effective method for feedback is to put a chart on the bulletin board for all to see. Figure 3.4 outlines the essential cooperative skills of encouraging, listening, and staying on task. This list is a good start for a chart. As the groups advance—acquiring new skills or moving through the phases—add elements to the chart. Remind students that as they have studied various content topics, they also have learned how to improve their cooperative teamwork. Point out which elements past groups have implemented effectively.

Students also need to reflect on their own progress. Use the think-pair-share strategy to help students reflect. First, ask each student to think about his or her own progress in using the targeted cooperative skills. Next, ask students to share their individual reflections with their cooperative groups using a round robin. The round robin ensures that each person gets a chance to talk and to listen. When groups finish sharing, ask for volunteers to share with the entire class.

Focus on Advanced Social Skills

The forming and norming social skills are only the start. If students turn these skills into habits in a flash, as many do, they are ready to tackle the more advanced social skills in content lessons. At times, the teacher may pull aside those who need more practice while those who are using good social skills work on a special challenge assignment in the content.

The more advanced the class becomes in its collaborations, the more opportunities the teacher has to infuse social skills into lesson designs. As students become more accomplished with the social skills, they will create more products, spend more time on-task, and improve their achievement.

The most successful teachers of cooperative learning are natural modelers of the cooperative social skills. Successful teachers model positive social skills in all interactions with students, not just in demo lessons. They speak softly, often with 6-inch voices; they establish eye contact and focus their listening on what is said; and they probe for differences in ideas, not differences with the person. They avoid shouting at students, arguing, or dominating discussions. Most importantly, students experience this high level of social skills in action and more easily imitate what the teacher is doing. Thus, these teachers put in place the axiom: Do as I do *and* as I say.

Advanced social skills, just as the norming and forming skills, do not develop without deliberate, specific, and repeated attention. Each skill should be introduced explicitly. Integration of a skill and reflection on its use are the two keys most likely to open the door for self-monitoring groups. Review Figure 3.2 to discover which skills to teach at each phase of the group process.

For example, it is usually necessary to teach students how to disagree with ideas, not people, when groups reach the storming phase. Similarly, when groups show signs of exquisite performing and become high-functioning teams, it is appropriate to target the more sophisticated skills of reaching consensus and dealing skillfully with controversy. The direct instruction model works equally well at each phase.

The order of skills in Figure 3.2 is only a suggested sequence; the teacher needs to evaluate students' range of social skills and decide when to introduce them to a particular class. Although the skills are listed in an order that appears somewhat developmental, students may develop differently and teachers may need to adapt the sequence and spend more or less time teaching certain skills. Each teacher must decide on the final design for introducing social skills.

As social skill instruction develops during the year, it is important to explicitly include skills from each of the categories. Thus, the teacher may consult Figure 3.2 when trying to choose which social skills to teach, how many skills to include, and when to teach which skills. The caveat to all teachers is: *Do not try merely to cover all social skills.* Each skill needs to be modeled, practiced, and used throughout the students' time in the classroom. It is better for a class to master one social skill each semester than to merely cover twenty skills. Less is more.

SAVE TIME TO TEACH SOCIAL SKILLS

Teachers under inordinate pressure to cover curriculum may find it difficult to see where social skills fit. Let us say only this: when a teacher takes time to introduce the forming skills needed for basic classroom management or to teach the more complex skills at the norming or performing phases, the payoff is always greater mastery of content. Sometimes a teacher must forego teaching unimportant facts to find time to teach social skills. Most likely, students' improved social skills will *enable* them to concentrate their efforts and spend more time on-task and on-focus. The results of these efforts and increased student responsibility for learning are obvious; students not only increase their achievement at the moment, but also they improve their ability to collaborate with others for a lifetime.

PLAN WHAT TO DO WHEN STUDENTS MISBEHAVE

It would be a big surprise if cooperative learning changed students' predisposition to misbehave in school. Cooperative learning is not a magic wand that banishes misbehavior. Nor is it a cure-all. What, then, does a teacher do when students violate the norms of the cooperative culture?

First, the teacher must have faith in the culture of cooperation he has built in the classroom. If the teacher has taken time to build cooperative norms and teach basic social skills, he will find it far easier to correct and

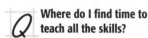

Q Where do I find time to teach all the skills?

A It is more important to develop one skill in a semester. This encourages students to internalize the skill. Picking one of the skills per semester is more beneficial than covering many.

control misbehavior throughout the school year. For example, using the class-generated T-chart of negative behaviors associated with a social skill, the teacher can review the T-chart of negative behaviors with a misbehaving student to identify the misbehavior and, then, focus on the corresponding positive behavior. This use of the class-generated list is a powerful reminder of what the class has identified, in specific detail, as unacceptable and acceptable behavior.

Second, the teacher must rely on commonsense classroom management skills. If students display simple, off-task behavior (e.g., side talking, misplaced hands, bumping, giggling, etc.), the teacher can follow proximity guidelines—they move closer to the mild offender, stand beside the offender, or establish eye contact using the dreaded "look." If students break their group task norms (e.g., overtalking, taking over the group) and do not respond to the proximity hint, the teacher may need to talk privately to the student, identify the misbehavior, voice displeasure with the misbehavior, and insist strongly that the student use the expected behavior. If a student repeats a misbehavior, teachers might want to warn that the student will be removed from the group or may just send the student to a work alone spot. (The spot should be as far removed from the working groups as possible, but within quick reach of the teacher.)

For students whose misbehavior is not cured by these basic strategies, teachers must escalate their reactions and use proper alternatives that are practiced at their particular school. When individual student misbehavior is more openly destructive or defies the teacher, teachers must immediately move to discipline methods that have worked best and have administrative support. These may include removal from the classroom, phone calls to parents, or after school or Saturday morning sessions. (The tactics for handling misbehaviors are listed in Figure 3.6.)

If misbehavior involves more than one student and is a significant ongoing challenge to the cooperative culture, address the problem in a classroom meeting with all students. The method in Figure 3.7, developed by Glasser (1986) and advanced by Burke (2000), adapts the problem-solving model to the correction of a classroom discipline problem.

Whether dealing with a discipline issue with one student, one group, or the entire class, it is important to be firm, fair, and consistent. Be sure to insist that each and every student abide by the norms set in the classroom and use the social skills that shape *this* classroom's cooperative culture.

Q What do I do when many students are misbehaving after I have taught the social skills?

A Work more with the whole class. Refocus and reteach the social skills to all the students.

What to Do About Individual Misbehaviors

1. Use teacher proximity.

2. Talk privately to student.

3. Remove student from group.

4. Assign student to work alone.

5. Seek administrative support.

6. Call parent.

7. Assign detention.

Figure 3.6

Notes: Be sure your students are prepared to work in a circle. More importantly, be sure you are comfortable with your ability to maintain focus and positive responses. The circle is best used "whole class" with an issue involving multiple members (e.g., tardiness). It works best in a group when it is a group issue. Do not use the circle to focus on one student's misbehavior.

The Classroom Circle

Step 1. Assemble the class in a full circle. Be sure to have eye contact with each and every student.

Step 2. Identify the reason for the circle (the misbehavior), feelings about it, why it must be corrected, and the purpose of the circle (consensus on expected behavior and solutions). Be firm and fair. Encourage responses that are not blaming others but are moving to a classroom agreement. (See Figure 3.5 or list you created with Blackline C3.4 for a list of encouraging behaviors.)

Step 3. Label the problem in behavioral terms. Discuss the expected behavior. Consider using a T-chart to list problem behaviors and review expected behaviors.

Step 4. Identify ideas for getting students to use the expected behavior.

Step 5. Use an agreement method to choose the best approach.

Step 6. Identify consequences for the next breakdown.

Step 7. Assess the circle's effectiveness.

Figure 3.7

SUMMARY

Cooperative learning promotes higher student achievement because it teaches students by word and by example how to work well with others. Students who know how to develop the social skills necessary for learning and who understand the notion that "many hands together are better than one hand alone," receive increased support and assistance to meet challenges of the curriculum, overcome obstacles to learning, and benefit from multiple viewpoints.

When teachers guide groups through the phases of development, students benefit beyond student achievement. The less stressful, more positive classroom culture that emerges from purposeful teaching of the essential social skills encourages students to help each other without bullying, violent interactions, or annoying distractions. When students work more cooperatively, teachers gain more time to teach the curriculum and to expand students' capabilities to successfully collaborate with family members and work colleagues throughout life.

BLUEPRINT
Elementary
Lesson

Codes 2SN
5NR
6CL
7OF

Setting Up the
Scaffolding

Tell/Retell

To teach students about attentive listening, prepare a bulletin board with an attentive listening theme. Show pictures of

- a class attending to the teacher,
- group members attending to each other,
- a class attending to a visitor, and
- a class attending to a student speaker.

Make a T-chart on attentive listening and display it on the bulletin board. (You may use Blackline C3.5 in Appendix C to create the T-chart.)

Attentive Listening	
SOUNDS LIKE	**LOOKS LIKE**
1. "uh huh"	1. eyes alert and focused on talker
2. "I see."	2. mirroring emotions
3. clarifying questions	3. leaning forward or toward speaker
4. silence	4. head nods at right time
5. paraphrasing	5. taking notes
6. (add others)	6. (add others)
7.	7.
8.	8.

Gather students around and explain the bulletin board and T-chart. Ask volunteers to share how it feels to have someone's full attention. Solicit several answers. Demonstrate with the principal, another teacher, or a volunteer what attentive listening looks and sounds like.

Divide students into pairs. Instruct one student in each pair to share a fun adventure. Instruct the other to attend closely so that he or she can repeat the story. Walk among the pairs and give a thumbs-up to each child you see listening.

Use this monitoring time to be aware of misbehaving students, especially during this time when interpersonal skills and social behavior are the focus. Be aware of the student who seeks attention, feels inadequate, makes a power play, is looking for revenge, or shows signs of emotional disturbances. When a misbehaving student exhibits a deficit in a social skill, review the strategies presented in Figure 3.6 and take time to address the social skill with clear, directed, and effective action. Grab that teachable moment when immediate corrective action is needed.

To encourage students to process affectively, ask them to briefly share their thoughts on the activity. Then, ask several listeners to tell the class what they heard in their partner interactions. Praise them for good listening (if appropriate). Ask the speakers to tell how it felt to have someone listen so carefully.

To process the social skill of active listening, ask students to tell about someone they think is a good listener.

To process cognitively, continue to practice on succeeding days. Begin each practice with a review of the T-chart on attentive listening. End each practice with praise to the attentive listeners.

After several short practices, have a class discussion on why listening attentively is a good idea, and when attentive listening is important in class and at home. This metacognitive talk helps students transfer the social skill beyond the lesson.

# # #

Working the Crew

Reflecting on the Design

BLUEPRINT
Middle School
Lesson

Codes 3RR
6CL
9QCA

Setting Up the
Scaffolding

IALAC

Use Simon's (1973) IALAC (I Am Lovable And Capable) strategy or tell the students a unique version of the IALAC story using the following sample. Show students the IALAC sign (see Blackline C3.2 in Appendix C for a blackline master of the sign).

(Name) , age _____ , woke up one school morning looking at _____ his/her pajama top. _____ saw a giant sign that said, IALAC. _____ knew at once this meant "I Am Lovable And Capable." _____ dressed and ran quickly to the kitchen. _____ was very excited. Before _____ could speak, _____ sister said, "You pea-brain, _(rip off a corner of the sign)_ what did you do with my new jacket?" "Nothing," _____ said. "Man," whined _____ sister, "_____ is a jerk." _(rip)_ "_____," said _____ unhappy mother. "You oughta know better. Why can't you use your brain _(rip)_ once in a while. Your big brother would never do nothing so stupid." _(rip)_ "But Mom," _____ said, "I . . . ." "Don't sass me back," said _____ mother. "You are such a smart mouth." _(rip)_ _____ saw _____ sister smirking. "Smart mouth, smart mouth." _(rip, double rip)_

By the time _____ left for the school bus, one-half of IALAC was ripped. On the school bus, George Burns said _____ was an idiot _(rip)_, cry baby, and jerk _(rip, rip)_. _____ sister laughed each time _(triple rip)_.

In the first class period, Mrs. Smartzolla asked _____ to put a homework problem on the board. _____ forgot a (name item) in the formula. "_____," Mrs. Smartzolla moaned, "how slow can you be? I've told you a thousand times." _(rip)_

In language arts, Mr. Thomas barked at _____ for getting the lowest score on the vocabulary quiz *(rip)*. He read how _____ had misspelled _____ to the whole class and said sarcastically, "I guess no one could ever accuse you of a gorgative brain." *(rip)* Everyone laughed *(rip for each laugh)*.

By the end of the day, _____ went home with a very small IALAC sign. _____ was very upset.

The next day, _____ woke to find IALAC on _____ pajamas, but very small. _____ hoped that today would be better. _____ wanted to keep _____ IALAC so much.

(Continue this story with additional IALAC demolition.)

Working the Crew

After the story, place students into groups of five, and give each group one piece of 3" x 5" newsprint and a marker. Appoint a recorder in each group. Ask groups to talk about the different ways their IALACs can get ripped. After five minutes, ask several recorders to share samples.

Instruct the groups to make a second list: What things can they do or say to add to people's IALACs? After five minutes, ask for samples.

Ask each group to pick the three best IALAC builders from its list. Gather ideas from the groups to make an unduplicated class list to hang in the classroom.

Reflecting on the Design

To process affectively, have students finish the following statement:
    It feels good when . . .

To process socially, ask students to take time today to use positive statements with a family member.

To process cognitively, post the encouragement T-chart (Figure 3.5 or list you created on Blackline C3.4 in Appendix C) and discuss how the class can use it to build each other's IALACs. On succeeding days, use these ideas for practice.

To process metacognitively, ask students to discuss what they did well in their groups, and what they would do differently next time to help their groups.

# # #

BLUEPRINT
High School
Lesson

Codes 5NR
6CL
9QCA

Setting Up the
Scaffolding

The Non-Listening Challenge

Divide the class into pairs. Ask students to think of a recent time when someone important paid close attention to them. As they recount the ways they knew that they were being listened to, make a T-chart for attentive listening. (You may use Blackline C3.5 in Appendix C to create the T-chart.)

Attentive Listening	
SOUNDS LIKE	**LOOKS LIKE**
1. "uh huh"	1. eyes alert and focused on talker
2. "I see."	2. mirroring emotions
3. clarifying questions	3. leaning forward or toward speaker
4. silence	4. head nods at right time
5. paraphrasing	5. taking notes
6. (add others)	6. (add others)
7.	7.
8.	8.

Identify the older and younger students in each pair. Designate the older student in a pair as partner A and the younger as partner B. Give the As the first set of instructions: Think of a time in the past year when someone did *not* listen to you. What happened? How did it feel? Ask As to prepare their stories while you give the Bs their instructions.

Give Bs these instructions: Review the T-chart on attentive listening. Now that you have reviewed how to behave when you listen with attention, you are to do your 100 percent, absolute, total best *not* to listen to your partner's story! You are to model non-listening behaviors.

Set these guidelines for the non-listening activity:
- All students must stay in the room.
- Speakers are to try their best to tell their stories.
- Students should not hurt each other.
- Students must stop when the teacher gives the signal (e.g., lights off, hands up).

After two minutes, stop the activity. Have each pair shake hands and ask the Bs to apologize to the As.

As students do this activity, move around the room and note their behavior. Be aware of genuine misbehavior in students, especially during this time when interpersonal skills and social behavior are the focus. Be aware of the student who seeks attention, feels inadequate, makes a power play, is looking for revenge, or shows signs of emotional disturbances. When a misbehaving student exhibits a deficit in a social skill, and take time to address the social skill with clear, direct, and effective action.

Even better, use this non-listening activity to capitalize on the opportunity to correct students who deliberately demonstrate poor listening skills. Use the opportunity to address the question, What do I do with the kid who takes over?, a common misbehavior in group interaction. Find a student who takes over the partner interview (there usually is one in the class), causing the dialogue to become very one-sided. Moving this student into a leadership role may be a good strategy for this situation. For example, tell the class to "freeze frame"in the midst of this partner interaction. Explain to students that, to reinforce the roles of each partner, one pair will model or role play an interaction. Select the pair with the partner who has taken over and have them model the desired actions. Surprisingly, the misbehavior disappears instantly, and the desired behavior is modeled in true leadership style. Note that the student selected to participate in the role play has actually modeled the very behavior he or she was lacking, a reinforcing activity if there ever was one.

Because the non-listening activity is intentionally set up to focus on misbehavior, several students might try this power play. Designating a leadership role for one offender in front of the class decreases other students' interest in engaging in a power play. So, be sure to highlight why the strategy (giving a leadership role) works.

Although this may be simple classroom management, addressing this incident within the context of social skill instruction adds power to the situation by using positive reinforcement. Teachers also can review the incident with the class or use the groups' reflection time to lead a discussion about how power plays can take over the group.

Reflecting on the Design

For affective processing, discuss the positive effects of attentive listening on the speaker and listener.

To process the social skill of listening, have students describe a television character who is a good listener.

To process cognitively, put a double T-chart for non-listening on the board. What did non-listening look like, sound like, and feel like?

For metacognitve processing, discuss with the class instances when they may have experienced the same negative feelings caused by non-listening.

# # #

Blueprints for Achievement

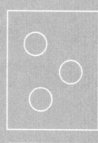

FORMING

PERFORMING

NORMING

CHAPTER 4

Phase II

NORMING

Level II

How Do I Create High-Challenge Tasks?

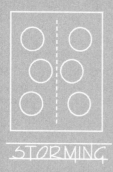

STORMING

CONFORMING

in the Cooperative Classroom

Phase II
NORMING
Level II

HOW DO I CREATE HIGH-CHALLENGE TASKS?

What spirit do we want our intelligence to have? Do we want children to be gifted and alienated? — literate and prejudiced? — brilliant and cynical? — intelligent and materialistic? — in need of help and ashamed? ... Unless we educate for wholeness in person and wholeness of our earth planet, we are not really intelligent .... The health and wholeness of our planet is not separable from health and wholeness of us as individuals.

—M.C. Richards

Draft

The brain is on our minds! During the decade of the 1990s, new brain imaging technologies ushered in a flurry of research on the brain and learning. The beginning of the millennium continues to see eruptions of new information about the brain, mind, memory and learning, and theories of intelligence. Discoveries about how the brain functions are being revealed at an unprecedented rate.

Keeping abreast of this plethora of data can be somewhat overwhelming. Even if educators were to achieve some level of understanding about the brain, learning, memory, and intelligence, it may be far too early to make conclusive statements about how brain research influences the teaching/learning process (Bruer 1999). Yet, it is not too early to use the emerging evidence to inform pedagogical practices (Brandt 1999).

To begin the journey into this new frontier—the human brain—educators need a foundation of understanding about brain functioning and its effect on learning. Then, educators may incorporate this knowledge into their decisions about schooling and recognize how these findings influence the *Blueprints* model.

Following is an exploration of brain/mind research from four perspectives: brain physiology, the principles of the brain and learning, the mind and memory, and theories of intelligence.

BRAIN PHYSIOLOGY

There are three basic physiological elements to the brain: lobes, functions, and brain cells.

The physiology of the brain, at the most basic level, consists of four lobes: occipital (vision), temporal (hearing), parietal lobe (touch and integration of the senses), and frontal lobe (thinking and problem solving). Figure 4.1 shows their relationship (see also Blackline C4.1 in Appendix C).

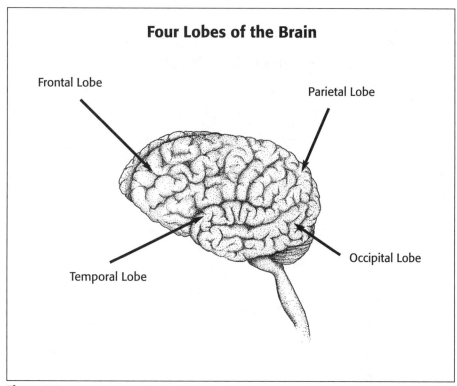

Figure 4.1

Q **Where can I learn more about the brain?**

A For a more comprehensive look at the brain, see the seminal piece, Sylwester's *A Celebration of Neurons: An Educator's Guide to the Human Brain* (1995).

Functions, the second area of brain physiology, comprise three major types that are integral to the actions and reactions of human beings and to the teaching/learning process:

- *Reflexive* Functions. Regulated by the brain stem, these include automated functions such as breathing, heartbeat, coughing, sneezing, digestion, and blinking.

- *Emotional* Functions. Previously thought to be encompassed in the limbic system (called the emotional brain), emotions are now believed to be processed throughout the brain (LeDoux 1996).

- *Cognitive* Functions. These functions are processed in the neocortex.

The third elemental part of brain physiology is the interaction of brain cells, or neurons, as they communicate with each other in the learning process. See Figure 4.2 for an illustration of neurons, their parts, and their connections to each other (see also Blackline C4.2 in Appendix C). Basically, neurons' *axons send* messages as electrical impulses from sensory input and their *dendrites receive* these messages in the form of neurotransmitters. Neurotransmitters, or chemical messengers, are received through the synapses or gaps in the dendrites, making multiple connections to other dendrites and, thus, creating neural networks. The neural networks are the crux of the brain's internal communication process and are needed for the learner to construct knowledge and to learn. Learning, a function of experience, occurs as dendritic connections are created and strengthened through use.

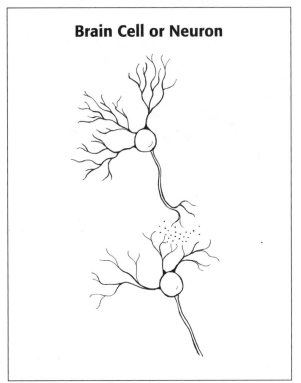

Brain Cell or Neuron

Figure 4.2

BRAIN PRINCIPLES THAT GOVERN LEARNING

The bridge between brain physiology and how one learns is captured in twelve principles formulated by Renate and Geoffrey Caine (1994; see Figure 4.3 or Blackline C4.3 in Appendix C). These principles incorporate insights from the research and serve as a theoretical foundation for making decisions about brain-based learning. Teachers need to look at the principles for general awareness and to understand the research implications for the cooperative classroom. Each principle and how it might guide the work of teachers using the *Blueprints* approach is discussed in detail in the following section.

Twelve Principles of Brain-Based Learning

Principle 1:   The brain is a parallel processor.

Principle 2:   Learning engages the entire physiology.

Principle 3:   The search for meaning is innate.

Principle 4:   The search for meaning occurs through patterning.

Principle 5:   Emotions are critical to patterning.

Principle 6:   The brain processes parts and wholes simultaneously.

Principle 7:   Learning involves both focused attention and peripheral perception.

Principle 8:   Learning always involves conscious and unconscious processes.

Principle 9:   We have at least two different types of memory: spatial (implicit) and rote (explicit).

Principle 10: We understand and remember best when facts or skills are embedded in natural, spatial memory.

Principle 11: Learning is enhanced by challenge and inhibited by threat.

Principle 12: Each brain is unique.

(Adapted from Caine and Caine 1994)

Figure 4.3

Principle 1: The brain is a parallel processor.

The brain can do many things at once: think, feel, imagine, and interact with other modes of information.

Implications. Good teaching orchestrates learning by using a robust repertoire of strategies that taps into many modalities. Teachers blend strategies such as cooperative learning with thinking strategies and other solid instructional tools. In this approach, effective instructors use a blend of strategies, rather than isolated pieces.

Principle 2: Learning engages the entire physiology.

The brain is a bodily organ that functions by biological rules. Although learning is as natural as breathing, it can be enhanced or inhibited by environmental and personal circumstances.

Implications. Because everything affects the brain's ability to learn, stress management, nutrition, exercise, and relaxation are all facets of managing healthy learning environments. Cooperative learning groups create a safe haven for taking learning risks and offer moments of activity and relaxation.

Principle 1 connects to

chapter 4: multiple intelligences and modalities

chapter 7: cognition and metacognition

Principle 2 connects to

chapter 3: forming teams, building trust

Principle 3 connects to

chapter 5: graphic organizers

chapter 7: thinking skills

chapter 9: application and transfer

Principle 3: The search for meaning is innate.

The brain strives to make sense of experiences. This search for meaning is natural to the human brain and is part of a human's survival instinct.

Implications. Learners make sense of the world when their learning environment is familiar and stable and, at the same time, is rich enough to satisfy curiosity and nurture inventiveness. Discussions in cooperative groups provide ample opportunities to search for meaning, especially when teachers shape the opportunities with a single, shared goal and the most appropriate tools for the group.

Principle 4 connects to:

chapter 2: cooperative learning and making meaning through dialogue

chapter 5: visual tools and graphic organizers

Principle 4: The search for meaning occurs through patterning.

Acting as both artist and scientist, the brain attempts to make meaning through organizing and categorizing information into discernible patterns. When it receives input, the brain tries to match the input to a known pattern or it creates a new pattern from the input.

Implications. Teachers help students discover or form patterns by presenting information in families or groupings. When information is presented in ways that allow the brain to extract patterns, learners often may find themes, integrate concepts, and use real-world analogies as they learn. Cooperative structures prove fertile ground for pattern making as group members generate and share diverse ideas and find the similarities that tie the ideas together.

Principle 5 connects to

chapter 2: using cooperative groups

chapter 3: developing social skills

chapter 8: resolving conflict

Principle 5: Emotions are critical to patterning.

Cognition and emotion cannot be separated. Learning is directly influenced by the learner's emotions—prejudices, biases, assumptions, and sense of efficacy.

Implications. Teachers attend explicitly to the feelings that accompany learning situations because they know that cognitive functioning is influenced by the students' emotional state. The small size of cooperative groups fosters safe and caring settings for students to explore the affective realms of learning.

Principle 6 connects to

chapter 2: cooperative learning

chapter 4: three-story intellect model

chapter 6: BUILD structure

chapter 9: transfer

Principle 6: The brain processes parts and wholes simultaneously.

The brain is divided into two parts (left and right hemispheres) that work separately and interactively at the same time. Therefore, the brain can process information in parts and as a whole simultaneously.

Implications. Teachers use the whole-to-part and part-to-whole principles to structure deductive or inductive lessons. Deductive learning begins with the whole and moves to the specifics. Inductive learning starts with specifics and moves to the whole. Both types of lessons are enhanced when students interact with one another in cooperative learning groups.

Principle 7: Learning involves both focused attention and peripheral perception.

As the brain focuses on one piece of information, it continues to scan and accommodate incidental information. The brain absorbs information from both the focal point of learning and the context surrounding the focal point.

Implications. Teachers organize learning within an enriched environment—one that offers ample peripheral richness for all learners. Within this environment, cooperative learning groups provide yet another tier of richness as students become aware of the nuances of teamwork.

Principle 7 connects to:

chapter 2: creating a cooperative learning culture

chapter 4: using a cooperative learning culture

chapter 7: thinking in high-challenge tasks

chapter 10: assessing achievement

Principle 8: Learning always involves conscious and unconscious processes.

Learners are not consciously aware of all that they learn. Much lurks beneath the conscious awareness of a learning experience. Because unconscious processing goes on all the time, people sometimes have an insight into a situation. This insight is unconscious processing paying its dividend.

Implications. Explicit attention to reflective processing helps students access their unconscious processing and enhances their learning situation. Cooperative learning provides the perfect setting for holding reflective dialogues.

Principle 8 connects to:

chapter 7: metacognitive reflection

chapter 9: explicit transfer strategies

chapter 10: multimodal assessment

Principle 9: We have at least two different types of memory: spatial (implicit) and rote (explicit).

Spatial or implicit memory is automatic. It needs no practice and rehearsal, because the experience itself provides automatic memory cues. Facts, skills, and conceptual learning however, often require explicit attention, rehearsal, and practice to produce long-term memory.

Implications. Robust student learning needs both rote and experiential learning experiences. Students in cooperative groups practice and rehearse together to promote rote learning. The creative energy of a cooperative group enhances experiential kinds of learning, such as problem solving and projects.

Principle 9 connects to:

chapter 4: experiential learning and memory systems

Principle 10: We understand and remember best when facts or skills are embedded in natural, spatial memory.

Embedding specific facts and data in meaningful contexts gives them meaning for learners. When information is integrated into an existing and recognizable schema, the brain is better able to connect new learning with what it already knows.

Implications. Lecture and direct instruction input must be accompanied by meaningful experiences. When teachers follow up direct instruction

Principle 10 connects to

chapter 6: BUILD; cooperative lesson development

with real-world applications, they enhance the learners' memory of the skill. Cooperative learning is the most appropriate strategy to use for experiential applications following a whole-group direct instruction lesson.

Principle 11: Learning is enhanced by challenge and inhibited by threat.

Again, the affective and the cognitive are intertwined. The brain is engaged by challenge and kicks in to resolve puzzlement. In turn, the brain reacts viscerally to threatening situations, which may cloud cognitive functions, at least momentarily.

Implications. Caine and Caine (1994) use the term *relaxed alertness* to describe the optimal learning state. Teachers strive to create an environment in which students are relaxed, but focused; at ease, but ready to zero in on learning. Cooperative learning groups are often just the right setting to achieve this sense of relaxed alertness.

Principle 12: Each brain is unique.

Although all human brains include similar systems, each person's brain is unique. Even the brains of identical twins are essentially different. Learning changes the structure and the chemistry of the brain, so each learner's unique experiences create a unique brain.

Implications. Multimodal teaching taps into individual differences and creates diversity for learners. Teachers engage various learning styles by structuring different types of group interactions in cooperative learning environments.

With some knowledge and understanding of the principles of the brain and learning, teachers are equipped to decide what strategies might be brain-friendly. Although no attempt has been made to correlate the strategies with brain research, these principles do provide a framework for best practices.

MIND, MEMORY, AND LEARNING

The *mind* is often thought to be the brain's work. That is, the term *brain* refers to the biological organ whereas the term *mind* refers to the brain's cognitive functions. Memory and learning are products of the mind, and it is these products that take educators to the heart of the situation. Sprenger (1999, p. 46) states that, "The only evidence we have of learning is memory." Therefore, educators shift their interest from the organic brain to the cognitive mind and ask pragmatic questions about how to promote memory and student learning. The following paragraphs explore the memory/learning process—how humans store and retrieve information in their memory systems and the types of memory systems—and discuss how cooperative learning enhances memory.

Sidebar (left margin):

Principle 11 connects to:

chapter 2: creating safe emotional climates in cooperative groups

chapter 4: engaging minds with the three-story intellect model

chapter 10: reducing assessment stress

Principle 12 connects to

chapter 4: multiple intelligences

chapter 5: graphic organizers

From Sensory Input to Memory Systems— How Humans Form Memories

Sights, sounds, touches, smells, and tastes are, literally, what memories are made of. These sensory inputs, or *sensory memory,* start the memory process (Sousa 2001). The brain may either reject or accept these sensory inputs for further processing. One key input on whether the brain accepts an input is *attention.* If an input does not grab one's attention, it never, consciously, gets into the memory system.

For example, consider the case of a woman listening to a song on the radio. If the sensory input (the song) grabs her attention, it becomes part of an *immediate memory* (a short, effervescent memory). But, when she uses the input (the song) in some other way—perhaps humming along with the song—she activates her *working memory* (a different type of short-term memory).

If the working memory makes meaning of the incoming input, the input is processed further, and the song is lodged in *long-term memory.* For example, the woman might recall a time when that particular song was especially significant to her; thus, she connects the input to previously created meaning and the song and incident enter her long-term memory. It is long-term memory that stores ideas for future reference. Long-term memory intertwines learning and memory.

Types of Memory Systems

In learning situations, students need to access information—facts, data, and concepts—from their memories and use it appropriately. This is no easy task, because memories are distributed throughout the brain; the good news is that they are connected to many networks of neurons. Although this implies that a memory can be accessed through multiple entry points or channels, the catch is that a memory must be reconstructed each time it is needed. For example, when a boy tries to recall his grandfather's face, he could use a number of sensory inputs—a sound, a smell, or a combination—to trigger his memory system and let his mind reassemble the picture of his grandfather's face.

In addition to categorizing memories by durability—immediate, working, and long-term—some researchers categorize memory by method of acquisition. Sprenger (1999) identifies five types of memory: semantic, episodic, procedural, automatic, and emotional. *Semantic memory* comes from rote learning (e.g., studying vocabulary, spelling, historical facts) that requires practice and rehearsal to create long-term memory. *Episodic memory* is contextual, locational, or spatial memory (e.g., an incident, a happening) and is easily accessed by relating it to a location. *Procedural memory* is muscle memory (e.g., typing, cycling) that has been rehearsed and practiced—producing a strong, lasting memory. *Automatic memory* is sometimes called a conditioned response (e.g., reacting to hot or cold water, stopping at a traffic light)—and becomes a reflex. *Emotional memory* (e.g., death, love) is the most powerful kind of memory and overrides every other kind of memory system.

Each of these memory systems is located throughout parts of the brain (frontal lobes, cerebellum, amygdala, hippocampus). Given this dispersal of storage, teachers try to involve as many of these systems as possible to foster students' learning—so that the learning makes sense, has meaning, and is relevant.

Memory and Cooperative Learning

Cooperative learning structures increase students' opportunities to pay attention to memory and learning. Often, students seem to attend to, process, and use information easier and better when they produce or perform as a cooperative team. Cooperative interactions—student discussions and dialogues within the small group—promote deep processing of information for meaning and relevance and help learners make sense of content. Teachers need to consider these critical points as they use *Blueprints*.

Refer to the portmanteau strategy in chapter 2, for a practical tool related to memory and cooperative learning.

THEORIES OF INTELLIGENCE

The final area of brain/mind research that pertains to cooperative learning concerns the expanding view of human intelligence. There are three theories, in particular, that seem to influence the concept of the cooperative classroom: the theory of multiple intelligences conceived by Gardner (1983; 1999); the theory of emotional intelligence presented by Goleman (1995), and the theory of moral intelligence proposed by Coles (1997).

The Theory of Multiple Intelligences

Gardner (1983; 1999) identified eight intelligences at work in the human mind and illustrated each intelligence by naming a prodigy who shows the intelligence in abundance (see Figure 4.4 or Blackline C4.4 in Appendix C).

Gardner postulates that each human has a jagged profile of the eight intelligences and suggests that schools need to provide equal opportunity for each of the students' intelligences to prosper.

Educators can find bountiful opportunities to incorporate multiple intelligences in cooperative classrooms. Teachers promote diversity in intelligences when forming groups and when delineating tasks so that different students lead at different times. Student performances naturally bring various intelligences into play and present golden opportunities for students to strengthen their weaker intelligences through interactions with others who might be stronger in those same areas. Purposeful and focused dialogue involving all group members is an integral part of cooperative learning. The multiple intelligences framework provides a perfect scheme for thinking about the personal intelligences.

Multiple Intelligences		
Intelligence	**Activities**	**Prodigies**
verbal/linguistic	reading, writing, speaking, and listening	T. S. Elliot
logical/mathematical	inductive and deductive thinking, mathematical reasoning	Michael Polanyi
visual/spatial	visual/spatial arts, architecture, sciences	Van Gogh
musical/rhythmic	musical appreciation, skill, and performance	Mozart
bodily/kinesthetic	hand/eye coordination; physical abilities of athletes, dancers, surgeons	George Balanchine
interpersonal	social, empathic, charismatic	Gandhi
intrapersonal	introspective, reflective, philosophical	Socrates
naturalist	classification of species, flora and fauna	Linnaeus

Figure 4.4

The Theory of Emotional Intelligence

Multiple intelligences also tie well to the theory of emotional intelligence (Goleman 1995). Goleman identified five domains of emotional intelligence:

- awareness of feelings,
- control and self-regulation over emotions,
- sense of empathy for others,
- relationships with others, and
- social skill repertoire.

(See Blackline C4.5 in Appendix C for a list of those domains.)

Cooperative learning develops these very skills and concepts.

The Theory of Moral Intelligence

The theory of moral intelligence (Coles 1997) correlates with the emotional world of learners. Thinking about what is right and wrong, and why, is an integral part of problem solving and decision making that is such a big part of cooperative teamwork.

Cooperative learning brings out all of the intelligences. Teachers who use these frames of intelligence—multiple intelligences, emotional intelligence, and moral intelligence—strengthen students' awareness of their strengths and of their capabilities to improve their weaknesses.

Specs

Brain physiology, principles of the brain and learning, memory systems, and intelligence theories bridge the biology of the brain to the cognitive functioning of the mind. This body of research is the basis for focusing on higher-order thinking in the cooperative classroom. *Blueprints* synthesizes this research into the three-story intellect model that encourages high-challenge learning and higher-order thinking. Teachers can use the three-story intellect to create high-challenge, cooperative tasks that move students beyond gathering facts to the higher achievement levels of processing and applying new knowledge in purposeful ways.

When students have learned the basic skills of forming groups and the norms for expected social behaviors in the classroom, teachers may begin to introduce "mind-full" tasks. These tasks promote *purposeful* "brain work" or higher-order thinking in cooperative groups. Skilled cooperative learning groups work with a dual focus: one eye on the academic goal and the other on the integration of social and thinking skills.

CRITERION FOR SUCCESS: THE THREE-STORY INTELLECT

When the basics of cooperative learning are in place, teachers face the important decision of how to set criteria for success for high-challenge academic work. Teachers ask, To what degree does the cooperative task engage and challenge all students in complex thinking and problem-solving processes to better understand and transfer the curriculum content of the lessons? Answers range from not at all to intensely.

Teachers use the three-story intellect model to set criteria for high-content, high-challenge lessons. This practical framework can be used to implement the mind/brain research principles and to structure thinking tasks within the curricular content. The three-story intellect model was inspired by Oliver Wendell Holmes, Jr.:

> There are one-story [intellects], two-story [intellects], and three-story [intellects] with skylights. All fact collectors, who have no aim beyond their facts, are one-story [minds]. Two-story [minds] *compare, reason, generalize,* using the labors of the fact collectors as well as their own. Three-story [minds] *idealize, imagine, predict*—their best illumination comes from above, through the skylight.

Holmes' remark serves as a reminder as well as a guideline for creating lessons that promote three levels of thinking and encourage transfer. Figure 4.5 illustrates the three-story intellect model.

Three-Story Intellect

Figure 4.5

Figure 4.6 shows a scale to gauge the level of challenge for cooperative lessons using the three-story intellect model.

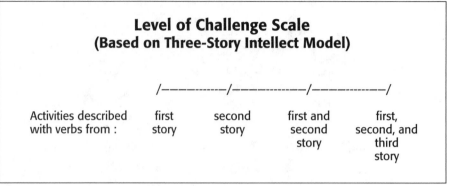

Figure 4.6

The First Story: Gathering Information

In the gathering stage, students find facts or recall information. This first level of cognitive functioning engages learners in typical school tasks: count, name, select, and describe.

To do tasks at this first level, students need to understand that information comes from many sources. Teachers who have acted as the sole source of information in the classroom (teacher as sage on the stage) will need to break with tradition by introducing alternate sources of information—textbooks, library books, videotapes, guest experts, newspapers, magazines, Internet sites and so on.

The first level of processing features skinny questions and answers. That is, teachers ask skinny questions—those that elicit yes or no, or single word answers from students. For example, a teacher might ask, Can you name the states in the United States? And students might answer, Yes. Or, the teacher might ask, Name two explorers. And the students might answer Bolivar, Columbus. Figure 4.7 illustrates skinny questions and answers that this level of processing produces. (See also Blackline C4.6 in Appendix C. Fat questions are discussed in the next section on second-story processing.)

Teachers can integrate first-story verbs into students' vocabularies by helping them learn the words as part of an assigned task. For example, cooperative learning groups may be asked to gather a compendium of information on various geographic regions of the United States (see Figure 4.8 for an abbreviated example). The teacher provides a checklist of requirements to guide students toward the academic goal. A list of skinny questions and a map depicting the information might be the group's final products. This is the first level, or first-story intellect, of cognitive skills—*gathering information.*

Asking "Thought-Full" Questions

FAT QUESTIONS

Fat questions require a lot of discussion and explanation with interesting examples. Fat questions take time to think through and answer in depth.

Examples:

Compare the billy goat's behavior to the troll.
Predict how Macbeth will die.
Estimate the number of sheep in an acre.

SKINNY QUESTIONS

Skinny questions require simple yes/no/maybe so answers, a one-word answer, or a nod or shake of the head. They take no space or time.

Examples:

Can you list the Presidents?
Name 3 people who . . . .
Count from 1–10.
Recall the definition for *cooperative.*
Remember this date.

Figure 4.7

Geographic Region: Midwest

SKINNY QUESTIONS

- What is the average income of people living in the Midwest?

- What is the rainfall for each region?

Figure 4.8

From a transfer perspective, these first-story verbs may be the most important vocabulary students learn in their school years. Why? Because they are the vocabulary used in most standardized test questions. Students who know these words are much more likely to understand the standardized questions and respond correctly. Figure 4.9 illustrates the occurrence of first-story words in standardized tests.

Three Sample Standardized Test Questions

1. Match the process of *thawing out* with its definition.
   a. gain heat
   b. gain cold
   c. lose heat
   d. lose cold

2. Select the element below that is not a type of fossil.
   a. Sandstone
   b. Casts
   c. Molds
   d. Petrified wood

3. Clouds and fog are made up of droplets of water that are formed on particles during a process named:
   a. Condensation
   b. Evaporation
   c. Precipitation
   d. Accumulation

Figure 4.9

Sequential Organization Sample (Do Not Jigsaw)

When you are driving to Detroit from Chicago, follow these steps:

1. Take I-90/I-94 South to the Skyway (I-90).
2. Take the Skyway (I-90) East to Indiana.
3. In Indiana take I-294 East to the I-94 junction (near Lake Station).
4. Take I-94 East to Detroit.

Divisible Structure

How does the culture of the United States differ from the Mexican and Canadian cultures, the other American countries that border on the United States?

In the United States, the citizens prize . . .

In Mexico, the citizens prize . . .

In Canada, the citizens prize . . .

When structuring cooperative group tasks at the first-story intellect level (gathering), teachers may ask each student to search through the entire body of information provided or they might jigsaw the task (see chapter 2 for an explanation of the jigsaw strategy). When using the jigsaw approach to task assignment, tasks need a divisible structure with individual parts that assemble into a whole picture. In a divisible structure, information cannot be locked into a sequence (e.g., a sequenced set of instructions). A sequential task, such as a set of instructions, cannot be jigsawed because information gathering by the second and third group members depends on what the first member does. Without access to the first member's information, the other group members cannot do their own task well. In a divisible structure, each individual in the group is assigned a measurable amount of material to gather and to report to the group. No one piece has to precede another in order to "get the whole picture." Because each member's information task is independent, each can gather the assigned information, report to the group, and then work with the group to achieve the common goal.

Consider two examples, one with a sequential form and one with a divisible structure.

- *Sequential.* A teacher might assign groups to follow six steps to solve a problem. If the teacher assigns two steps to each of three members of a group, students assigned the final steps will have a difficult time because the final steps depend on understanding the first two. It is *not* helpful to jigsaw sequential information.

- *Divisible.* A teacher might ask groups to describe the culture of three different countries. The material is organized in the same way for each country. The information one student gathers does not depend on information another student collects. Each can gather his or her part and then report to the group. When all reports are in, the teacher may ask additional questions to move students to the next levels of thinking (e.g., the teacher might ask, How are these countries alike or different? or Predict what would happen if a family had to immigrate from country A to country B.). It is helpful to jigsaw divisible material.

At level 1, it is better to ask students to gather information rather than to regurgitate it, memorize parts, or work on a group worksheet. Mindless recall tasks that have no structured interdependence provide little reason for students to work together. If one student has weak memory skills or makes a mistake, other group members have little chance to offer help. This leads to boredom, low energy, and conflict, especially if one person shirks his or her job on the team. Such an affective result directly opposes the desired goal of thought-provoking cooperative tasks. On the other hand, students who learn how to *gather* information gain a lifelong skill—knowing how to work together.

The Second Story: Processing Information

The second-story intellect involves students in *information processing*. Typically, mind-stirring second-story tasks include *comparing and contrasting, classifying, explaining, solving,* and *analyzing.* During second-story tasks, students interact with and internalize information. This level also moves students from interdependence at level 1 to a more intensified group collaboration. Although some students move to this level intuitively, most need time to formally review and learn the skills.

In the second-story processing stage, students manipulate new information and try to make connections to prior knowledge, previous experience, and/or developing concepts. Through this *process,* students gain an understanding of the content and are able to make sense of things. When learners manipulate knowledge and concepts, they anchor new ideas to personally relevant past experiences. Second-story processing helps individuals connect new and prior knowledge and assimilate concepts and ideas in personally relevant ways.

Q **How could I use a divisible structure for a cooperative lesson?**

A A jigsaw is an excellent task assignment strategy for gathering information that has a divisible structure. Follow these steps:

1. Assign students to groups of three.
2. Structure group roles and ask each group to choose a region to investigate.
3. Divide the needed information into three questions:
   a. What are the dates, places, and people described?
   b. What is the weather?
   c. What is special about the people?
4. Assign one question to each of the three students in each group.
5. Tell students to gather information about their questions and write answers to them.
6. Walk among the students and check for accuracy.
7. After 15 minutes, have each group member report to the small group and share answers to the questions. Encourage note taking.
8. Check for understanding by calling on random groups to share with the class.
9. Review the process.

After students master one-story questions—list, name, and describe—they are ready to tackle deeper questions about the study topic. Teachers can lead students to generate higher-level questions that pull in a lot of information by helping students distinguish between *fat* and *skinny* questions. Figure 4.7 illustrates the difference between fat, information-enriching questions and skinny, information-impoverishing questions. (See also Blackline C4.6 in Appendix C.)

Note: You may use blackline C4.7 in Appendix C to list questions and evaluate if they are fat or skinny.

When formulating fat questions (or divergent statements), students and teachers can refer to the second story to find appropriate verbs (Figure 4.5). The specific verbs shown at this level are key to the precise thinking processes that help students most with their academic tasks. The success or failure of teamwork depends on students working together to answer fat questions. Fat questions push students to look in different ways and different places just to find the information.

In the first-story example (Figure 4.8), students gathered information about various regions of the United States and created a map. The second-story task for this activity involves deeper processing of information. In essence, students make sense of the information for themselves by tying new facts and ideas to prior knowledge and experience. For example, after groups display and discuss the maps of the different regions, a teacher might ask students to find a partner and *compare* and *contrast* their regions, using fat questions that the pair generate—a second-story activity. The teacher might ask students to create a Venn diagram to help them analyze and make sense of the data (see Figure 4.10). The final product could be a short homework essay in which each student compares the region explored by his or her group to a similar region from a television show. In Figure 4.11, students have added fat questions to the earlier project in Figure 4.8.

In the example, students are required to *do something* with the gathered facts—in their group work in the classroom and individual work at home. Second-story processing calls for a different type of thinking than called for by the first-story fact gathering. Students must break the information into parts (analyze), find similarities (compare), and discover differences (contrast).

The Third Story: Applying Information

Beyond first- and second-story cooperative tasks reside those at the highest level of cognitive performance, the third-story intellect tasks. Third-story tasks ask students to apply the information they have gathered and processed. In third-story thinking, students *estimate*, *predict*, *imagine*, *apply*, and *judge*—they begin to use new ideas in meaningful ways.

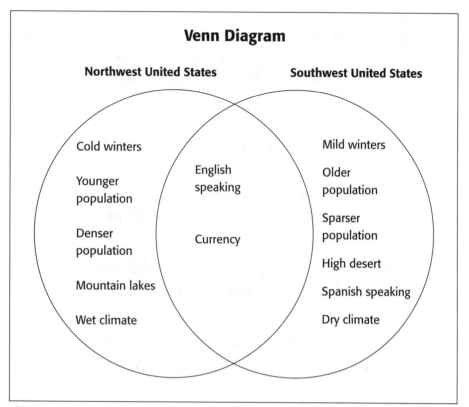

Venn Diagram

Northwest United States   Southwest United States

Cold winters   Mild winters

Younger   English   Older
population   speaking   population

Denser   Sparser
population   Currency   population

Mountain lakes   High desert

                                Spanish speaking

Wet climate   Dry climate

Figure 4.10

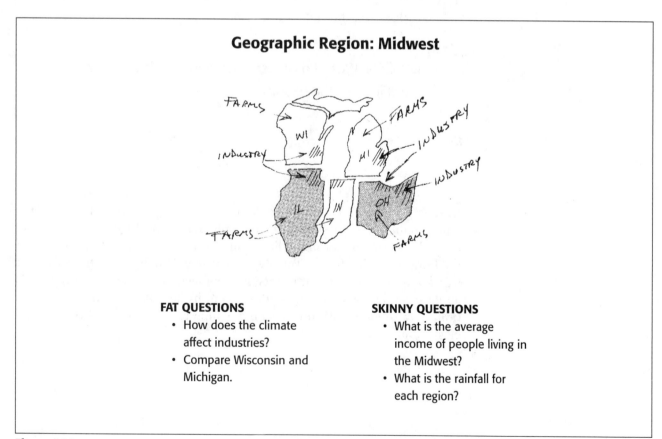

Geographic Region: Midwest

FAT QUESTIONS
- How does the climate affect industries?
- Compare Wisconsin and Michigan.

SKINNY QUESTIONS
- What is the average income of people living in the Midwest?
- What is the rainfall for each region?

Figure 4.11

Let's continue the example of gathering and comparing data on regions of the United States. The third-story academic task now requires sophisticated use of the information as students select a "what if" question for the group to tackle (see Figure 4.12 for examples).

What If . . . ?

Select one issue and prepare a brief five-paragraph essay stating your ideas. Give examples from your information.

1. Environment: What if the *greenhouse effect* continues? How will this affect the various factors in the regions?

2. Demographics: What if *senior citizens' migration* to the South continues? How will that affect the region?

3. Economics: What if the *recycling tax* goes into effect? How will that affect the region?

4. Politics: What if a *conservative governor* is elected? How will it affect the region?

Figure 4.12

Inherent in the "what if" speculations is an expectation that students know about current issues and can apply that knowledge to the lesson at hand. Expectations for immediate and relevant student use actually build the bridges needed for the transfer of learning. When students apply their new knowledge to relevant events, lessons seem meaningful. Without this application, lessons and curriculum seem irrelevant and bits of information seem isolated with little or no meaning to students' lives beyond the classroom.

HIGH CHALLENGE

When students engage in three-story intellectual tasks, cooperative learning groups take on an aura of a corporate think tank. Group members can sense a synergy within group tasks. The high-challenge approach creates a need for and an appreciation of the team as a whole. When teachers set aside time at the end of each task to review the thinking process used—naming, analyzing, comparing, predicting—students quickly perceive that teachers have high expectations for their mental engagement.

Although cooperative groups may be used for remedial work, if teachers use cooperative learning groups only for the drill-and-practice work of remediation, they undermine the value of the groups for complex and challenging tasks.

Teachers need *time* to lead students into three-story tasks. Students cannot be rushed into performing higher-level cognitive tasks or assimilating all three levels of the three-story intellect model. The sample lesson in Figure 4.13 demonstrates the *gradual* process that elevates student tasks to second- and third-story thinking. It is the slow but steady nature of student development that is sometimes missed when teachers first use cooperative lessons.

The sample lesson in Figure 4.13 shows how a teacher might build a three-story lesson. At the *first level, gathering information,* the teacher used a fat thought provoker—brainstorming. If the teacher also used *wait time* and *equal distribution of responses* (chapters 6 and 7 discuss these two techniques), he would motivate greater numbers of students to think of responses. Next, at the *second level,* the teacher divided students into pairs so they could engage in cooperative learning. Finally, at the *third level,* the teacher challenged the pairs to work together on reflection questions. The simple scaffold allows teachers to move the lesson slowly but surely in the best direction. They advance students' cooperative and thinking skills, improve students' understanding of content and provide lessons that are fast-paced, varied, interesting, and challenging. All of this adds up to increased student motivation that pays dividends in future lessons.

Sample Lesson: Mind Map

CODES: 5NR, 6CL, 9QCA

Tell the students that they will work together on a task and are going to be doing several things at once. First, they will practice working together. Second, they will think about how places in their neighborhood (town) are connected. Third, they will learn how to make a mind map that shows different ways that their world is connected.

1. Ask students to think about the neighborhood (in the city oR suburbs) or town (in a rural area) where they live and to brainstorm a list in words or pictures of the "places" in the town. Record answers on the board without comment. Following are two lists with suggested places, one for a neighborhood and one for a town:

Neighborhood	Town
school	grocery store
church	feed store
synagogue	train station
mosque	church
grocery store	gas station
police station	fast food restaurant
gas station	barn
my house	grain silo
drug store	drug store
clothing store	houses
fast food restaurant	school
bank	bank
library	

2. When the students reach their limit on brainstorming places, divide the class into pairs and ask them to draw a mind map for either a neighborhood or a town. (Following is an example of a mind map.) (For a blackline master, see Blackline C4.8 in Appendix C):

SAMPLE MIND MAP

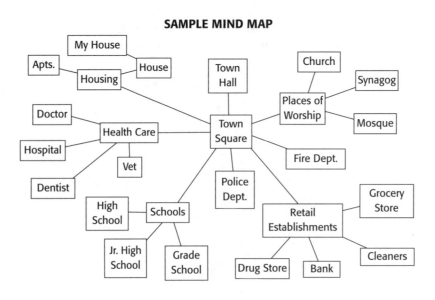

Figure 4.13

3. When groups are almost done drawing their mind maps, encourage them to finish in the next two or three minutes. Ask pairs to present their maps to the class. Ask each pair one or two questions from the three-story intellect model. Let partners consult on answers, but each should take a turn giving an answer. Following are examples of appropriate questions to ask.

Sample I	Sample II
Name your places. (One-story question)	Count the places you named. (One-story question.)
Explain why you connected _____ with _____. (Two-story question)	Sort the places on your map into _____ and _____. (Two-story question)
Estimate how long it would take you to walk from _____ to _____. (Three-story question)	Imagine what places might disappear and what new places might appear in the next ten years. (Three-story question)

4. When presentations are complete, ask students to vote on the following questions to assess their cooperation (thumbs up = good job; thumbs down = need to work on this; sideways = not sure):
   • In our pair, we each did our assigned job.
   • In our pair, we took turns answering the questions.
   • In our pair, we listened to each other.

Figure 4.13 (continued)

SUMMARY

Throughout *Blueprints,* the lessons at the end of each chapter integrate *gathering, processing,* and *applying* tasks. This compact hierarchy of thinking tasks can be a part of every lesson, no matter how brief or extensive the lesson is. The lessons at the end of this chapter address these three distinct levels in subject matter lessons. By including complexity and higher-level thinking tasks in students' lessons, teachers automatically build interdependence among members and create a sense of "teamness" in the groups. In addition, these lessons integrate the principles of brain-based learning, ensuring each lesson will be a mindful experience for students.

BLUEPRINT

Elementary

Lesson

Codes 2SN
6CL
7OF
9QCA

Setting Up the Scaffolding

Working the Crew

Bed-to-Bed

Through the school years, and even beyond, the typical, overused, and abused storytelling model uses the "bed-to-bed" format. For example, a young student may be telling about a personal experience:

> I got up (out of *bed*). I had breakfast. I went outside. I played with my dog. I had dinner. I watched TV and I went to *bed.*

An older student might use the bed-to-bed format for a book report:

> George Washington was born in Virginia in 1732. He became famous for leading the US patriots to victory in the American Revolution. He was elected the first president of the United States. He died in 1799.

Both examples are simplified, but they suggest the bed-to-bed narrative that seems to dominate students' writing styles. As a quick focus activity, have students turn to a *partner* and tell a personal bed-to-bed story about a trip they recently took. Stress the bed-to-bed model that is to be followed:

> We got up and got started at _____. We went to _____. We passed by _____. We arrived in _____ and went to bed.

When they have finished their bed-to-bed stories, tell students that they are going to practice telling a story using the three-story intellect model. To begin, they are to interview someone to *gather information.* Then, they are to *process the information* by charting, webbing, prioritizing, or using whatever technique helps them focus the material. Finally, they are to tell a story about the person's life in a biography by *applying the gathered and processed information.* They must explore fresh approaches to storytelling because their biographies must not fall into the bed-to-bed format.

To help students focus on interviewing techniques, especially questioning strategies, assign students the following task.

Task 1: To *gather information,* ask students to select a television interview show in which the host or hostess asks the guests questions. Brainstorm possibilities:

> Barbara Walters
> Paula Zahn
> Katie Couric/Matt Lauer/Ann Curry
> Oprah Winfrey
> David Letterman
> Tim Russett
> Chris Mathews
> Jay Leno
> Rosie O'Donnell
> Bill Mahr

Ask students to watch the selected show with pencil and paper in hand. Have them record the actual questions asked by the interviewer. The next day, revisit the definitions of fat and skinny questions with the students (see Figure 4.7 or Blackline C4.6 in Appendix C).

FAT QUESTIONS
Fat questions require a lot of discussion and explanation with interesting examples. Fat questions take time to think through and answer in depth.

SKINNY QUESTIONS
Skinny questions require simple yes/no/maybe so answers, a one-word answer, or a nod or shake of the head. They take no space or time.

Now, have students transfer their questions to a chart similar to the one below. Have them rate each question. (You may use Blackline C4.7 in Appendix C.)

Fat	Skinny	Questions
	X	How old were you when . . . ?
X		Would you rather . . . ?
X		Who has influenced you and how?
	X	Have you always . . . ?
X		What if you were to . . . ?
	X	Has anyone ever suggested that . . . ?

To *process information* with the fat and skinny questions as a guide, revisit the three-story intellect model (Figure 4.5). Using both the three-story intellect model and the fat and skinny questions' rating sheet, have students write interview questions.

In groups of three, with a recorder, observer, and reporter on each team, ask students to formulate a set of fat and a few skinny questions for an interview with a senior citizen (see example below). The completed sheet of questions serves as the interview guide for the three group members when they actually interview their subjects.

> **Sample Interview Sheet**
> 1. Tell me about a vivid childhood memory.
> 2. Compare yourself to a contemporary figure.

To *apply the information,* ask student to use their completed interview sheets and interview senior citizens at a local hospital or nursing home. (Relatives can become the interview subjects if a class excursion is not possible.) Suggest ways that students can capture the interview (e.g., taping the session or taking notes during the interview).

Following the interviews, discuss with students different methods they might use to write their biographies. Remind them not to use the bed-to-bed narrative format. Elicit ideas, including:

- Insert quotes.

- Show a dialogue.

- Write a song.

- Include poetry.

- Use flashbacks.

- Present episodes.

- Present a view from the eyes of a youngster (or another person).

When students have finished their biographies, suggest they present part of the biography to their interviewees as a way of thanking them for their cooperation and involvement.

Reflecting on the Design

For affective processing, ask students to complete a log entry using the following lead-in:

> The thing I liked most about this project is . . .

For social skill processing, ask students to describe how they show appreciation to a favorite relative.

For cognitive processing, have students generate uses for fat and skinny questions besides interviews.

For metacognitive processing, ask students to name and describe someone they think is a three-story intellect. Ask them to explain why they think that person is a "thinker." Suggest the following lead-in:

> _____ is a three-story intellect. She or he _____.
> That is why I nominate her or him as a three-story intellect!

# # #

BLUEPRINT
Middle School
Lesson

Codes 5NR
6CL
7OF
9QCA

Setting Up the
Scaffolding

Robert Frost's Poetry

Use trios to review the characteristics of Robert Frost's poetry. Have each trio use a web (a blank web is available in Appendix C, Blackline C4.9) to brainstorm all the characteristics they can recall about Frost's work.

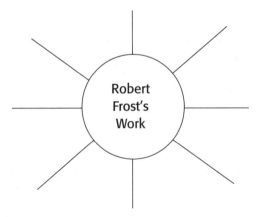

Next, have students select the three characteristics that make Frost's work most unique.

Conduct an all-class discussion about Frost's writing characteristics. Tell students that they will be using Frost's poem, "Stopping by Woods on a Snowy Evening," to study his poetry. Give each group a copy of the poem, individual notes, a worksheet and newsprint.

Explain that students are to work in the same groups of three to analyze Frost's poem "Stopping By Woods on a Snowy Evening." Their task is to see how closely the poem matches the criteria selected from the webs.

Before beginning, rotate the three roles—checker, reader, and recorder—and review the responsibilities for each. In each group, have the checker review cooperative guidelines.

Explain the criteria for success:

- Each group must present at least three arguments to defend the group's three selected characteristics.
- Each group member must be able to explain the group's choices.

Working the Crew

To process affectively, ask students to share how they felt during the activity.

To process the social skill of trust building, tell teams to create a poster-sized ad for their groups with the heading: How's Your Team Building Today?

To process cognitively, have each person write a three-paragraph essay explaining how this poem reflects the major characteristics of Frost's other poetry.

To process metacognitively, ask each group to review Mrs. Potter's Questions:

Reflecting on the Design

Mrs. Potter's Questions

1. What were you supposed to do?
2. What did you do well?
3. What would you do differently next time?
4. Do you need any help?

(For a blackline master of Mrs. Potter's Questions, see Blackline C4.10 in Appendix C.)

# # #

BLUEPRINT
High School
Lesson

Codes 1SD
5NR
6CL
9QCA

Setting Up the Scaffolding

Working the Crew

Create a Creature

Distribute a die to each group and tell students that the die will help them in the lesson. Show the three-story intellect model (Figure 4.5) and explain that students will gather, process, and apply information about classifying in a lesson called Create a Creature.

Assign students to groups of three and define these roles:

Researcher: Finds the information in the text.
Recorder: Charts the information.
Illustrator: Draws, diagrams, and labels the creature with the designated attributes.

To help students *gather information,* distribute a copy of a blank Create a Creature matrix to each group (see Blackline C4.11 in Appendix C for a blank matrix chart). Tell students to use the text and choose possible variables to complete the matrix. A completed matrix might look like the sample on the next page.

When students have completed the grids, ask each group to roll the die. For each roll, have the recorder circle the corresponding square in each column of the grid. For example, on the first roll for the first column, if the roll is 4, recorders would circle the fourth item in first column (bilateral); for the second column, if the roll is 2, they circle the second item (2 body segments). Groups continue tossing the die until all six columns have a circled item. A completed chart with circled choices appears on the next page.

To encourage students to *process the information,* ask them to *predict* what they might do next. Invariably, students figure out that the next step is to synthesize the various elements and create a creature using the circled items.

Lesson courtesy of Bob Kapheim, biology teacher, York High School, Elmhurst, IL.

Create a Creature—Classification Lab

	A Body Symmetry	B Segmentation	C Form of Locomotion	D Sensory Organs	E Support Structures	F Body Covering
1						
2	bi-lateral	none	none	eyes, ears & nostrils	bony skeleton	skin & hair
3	radial	2 body segments	2 or 4 walking legs	paired antennae	cartilaginous skeleton	scales
4	bi-laterial	3 body segments	legs & wings	compound eye & antennae	exoskeleton	skin & hair
5	bi-lateral	multiple segments	6 or 8 legs	tentacles	soft bodied	feathers
6	radial	2 body segments	fins	eyes, ears & nostrils	shell hinged	scales
7	bi-lateral	none	multiple walking legs	compound eye & antennae	shell carried	skin & hair

Create a Creature—Classification Lab

	A Body Symmetry	B Segmentation	C Form of Locomotion	D Sensory Organs	E Support Structures	F Body Covering
1						
2	bi-lateral	none	none	(eyes, ears & nostrils)	bony skeleton	skin & hair
3	radial	(2 body segments)	2 or 4 walking legs	paired antennae	cartilaginous skeleton	scales
4	(bi-laterial)	3 body segments	legs & wings	compound eye & antennae	(exoskeleton)	skin & hair
5	bi-lateral	multiple segments	6 or 8 legs	tentacles	soft bodied	feathers
6	radial	2 body segments	(fins)	eyes, ears & nostrils	shell hinged	scales
7	bi-lateral	none	multiple walking legs	compound eye & antennae	shell carried	(skin & hair)

Ask students to:
1. Illustrate the new creature.
2. Label the diagram with all the designated attributes.
3. Name the creature appropriately.
4. Have all group members sign the sheet.
5. Display the creatures on the bulletin board.

To help students *apply the information,* ask groups to select a creature other than their own. Tell groups to use the labeled attributes on the diagram and refer to the text for classification procedures so that they might classify the creature according to formal scientific methodology. When groups finish classifying the creatures in the appropriate manner, have the groups return the creature diagrams to the originators.

For affective processing, ask students to use the PMI structure to talk about the pluses and minuses they felt about the lesson:

Pluses (+) What I liked	
Minuses (-) What I didn't like	
Intriguing (?) Questions or thoughts	

For processing social skills, ask students to complete this stem:

Taking turns is both good and bad because . . . .

For processing at the cognitive level, have students share their classifications.

For processing at the metacognitive level, ask students to complete a log entry on the lab technique using this lead-in:

What if . . . ?

# # #

Reflecting on the Design

Blueprints for Achievement

FORMING

PERFORMING

NORMING

CHAPTER 5

Phase III

CONFORMING

Level 1

How Do I Expand Thinking
in the Classroom?

STORMING

CONFORMING

in the Cooperative
Classroom

Phase III
CONFORMING
Level I

HOW DO I EXPAND THINKING IN THE CLASSROOM?

The art of teaching is the art of assisting discovery.
—Mark Van Doran

Draft

As students improve their abilities to engage in small-group, student-to-student interactions, they begin to exhibit conforming behaviors—both cooperatively and cognitively. In the conforming stage, few students resist assigned roles and most allow others to share in the tasks. Students have mastered basic social skills; they listen, encourage, interact, share, agree, and stay on task. More students respond to fat questions, they offer more ideas when brainstorming and predicting, and they become more confident in using thinking tools. The teacher spends more time observing and giving feedback to students and less time intervening and managing classroom misbehavior.

In the conforming stage, teacher and students are ready to raise their achievement expectations to higher level. Just as students responded to higher expectations for cooperative interaction in earlier stages, they respond to higher expectations to think more precisely and thoroughly in this stage. What can a teacher do to promote more intense thinking by students? Beyond asking the right questions and structuring thoughtful dialogue, teachers can introduce students to graphic organizers.

RESEARCH ON GRAPHIC ORGANIZERS

The concept of graphic organizers is rooted in Ausubel's (1978) theory of "meaningful reception learning." Ausubel believes that the brain stores information in a hierarchy. For instance, the brain clusters highly generalized concepts together, followed by less inclusive concepts, and, finally, specific facts and details. Ausubel advocates that students use an advance organizer—a structured overview organizer—to display information hierarchically and graphically (see Figure 5.1). The structured overview always shows pertinent vocabulary in a hierarchical arrangement. Structured overviews are dynamic; as learners assimilate new information and experiences, they reorganize their information cognitively and change the graphic display to reflect the shifts. An advance organizer, such as the structured overview, may be prepared by the teacher and given to students before they read the text.

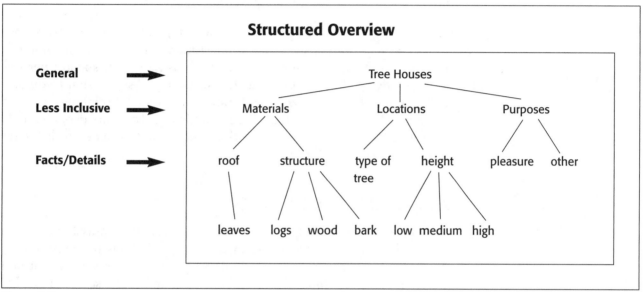

Figure 5.1

COGNITIVE MAPPING

According to Ambruster and Anderson (1980), Dansereau et al. (1979), Davidson (1982), and Vaughn (1982), cognitive maps (or organizers) improve students' retention of information. Lyman and McTighe (1988), suggest that the ability to organize information and ideas is fundamental to thinking. Cognitive maps help students of all ages and abilities develop the necessary organizational skills in all content areas.

Cognitive organizers provide a holistic picture of a concept by showing relationships and interrelationships. Lyman and McTighe (1988) explain that cognitive maps help students

- represent abstract or implicit information in more concrete forms,
- depict the relationships among facts and concepts,
- generate elaborate ideas, and
- relate new information to prior knowledge.

Ogle (1986) uses the KWL graphic organizer to help students connect to prior knowledge and past experiences and to reflect on their learning. In this acronym, the K stands for What I *Know*; the W for What I *Want* to

Know; and the L for What I *Learned.* Although originally developed to help students with reading, the KWL can be used in many instructional situations.

Bellanca (1990a, 1992) presents twenty-four different graphic organizers including those that help learners analyze (fishbone, Venn), evaluate (PMI, T-chart), and synthesize (thought tree, matrix) information. These graphic representations allow both students and teachers to see students' thinking. When students use these graphic organizers in cooperative groups, they share their thinking verbally and visually.

Hyerle (1996) presents yet another set of graphics and explains that thinking maps are constructivist tools students use to make meaning of information. Hyerle categorizes visual tools as those that support personal knowledge (mind mapping), isolate content tasks (decision tree), and promote the thinking process and transfer across all disciplines (systems thinking). Hyerle stresses that these graphic organizers are dynamic tools for interactive thinking and reflecting and are not designed to be static tools, such as a fill-in form.

MAPS AND MINDS TOGETHER

Cognitive organizers help students organize, retain, and assimilate concepts and ideas from kindergarten to college. Perhaps the most widely used graphic organizer is the attribute web, which targets a concept and structures attribute analysis. (Attribute webs are discussed later in this chapter.) Other types of maps include the flow charts, PMI, T-chart, right angle thinking, fishbone, hour glass, 5W, Venn diagram, and ranking ladder.

Cognitive organizers can serve as frameworks for class or group discussions and written work. According to Lyman and McTighe (1988), students learn better when cognitive maps are used in conjunction with think-pair-share cooperative strategies and metacognitive cues. Perhaps most important, students interact personally with the information when they use cognitive organizers. These maps make students' thinking visible, for both students and teachers. Cognitive organizers facilitate just the sort of thinking—clear, stable, and organized—that Ausubel (1978) suggests makes learning easier for students.

Specs

When teachers target graphic organizers to lesson content and thinking processes, they introduce students to powerful tools to improve their reading comprehension as well as their organizational and thinking skills. (Figure 5.5, later in this chapter, matches thinking skills with graphic organizers). Students not only advance their visual/spatial intelligence but also benefit from structures that improve their social interactions. Using graphic organizers, students learn to fit concepts with their prior knowledge and to transfer ideas to new situations. Teachers can more easily observe interactions, see who is contributing, coach as needed, and in the end, assess the results of the teams' work.

DEVELOPING STUDENTS' UNDERSTANDING WITH GRAPHIC ORGANIZERS

As Figure 5.5 (later in this chapter) illustrates, each graphic organizer promotes a specific thinking process. Graphic organizers are not merely worksheets. They extend students' thinking beyond low-level copying by promoting group cooperation, higher-level thinking, and high-level team achievement.

The search for how to raise student achievement parallels the National Aeronautics and Aerospace Administration's (NASA) 1960s man-on-the-moon project. For many years, NASA scientists tried to find a way to take humans to the moon and back safely. There were trials. There were failures. And, there were few successes. Finally, the scientists realized that there was no single solution; only a synthesis of many ways would work. Using a synthesis of ideas, they achieved that "one great leap" for humankind on July 20, 1969.

Raising student achievement is a parallel challenge. Instead of one right way, at least nine instructional approaches strongly support achievement gains (Marzano, Pickering, and Pollock 2001). Furthermore, education researchers demonstrated that combinations of cognitive methods, especially those grounded in cooperative culture, are more effective than one method applied by itself (Joyce, Weil, and Calhoun 2000). Educators recognize that instruction anchored in content and process standards helps improve performance for all students, regardless of race, nationality, socioeconomic background, or other out-of-date and biased differentiators. Thus, teachers must strive to couple cooperative tasks with complex cognitive tasks. They must BUILD higher-order thinking processes into high-challenge lessons by targeting specific micro-skills (Figure 5.2) or by stringing thinking skills together into a macro-process (Figure 5.3) approach to complex thinking. The more carefully this is done, the more likely it is that students will respond and engage in a high-challenge lesson.

Micro-Skills

Critical Thinking Skills

1. attributing
2. comparing and contrasting
3. classifying
4. sequencing
5. prioritizing
6. drawing conclusions
7. determining cause and effect
8. analyzing for bias
9. analyzing for assumptions
10. solving for analogies
11. evaluating
12. decision making

Creative Thinking Skills

1. brainstorming
2. visualizing
3. personifying
4. inventing
5. associating relationships
6. inferring
7. generalizing
8. predicting
9. hypothesizing
10. making analogies
11. dealing with ambiguity and paradox
12. problem solving

Figure 5.2

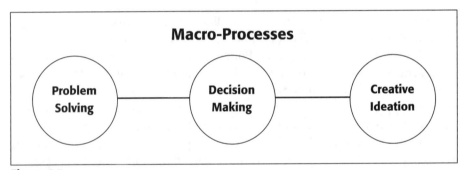

Macro-Processes

Problem Solving — Decision Making — Creative Ideation

Figure 5.3

STUDENT-TO-INFORMATION MODELS

Figure 5.4 shows fourteen graphic organizers (See also Blackline C5.1 in Appendix C.). Figures 5.6–5.19 show a sample of each of these organizers. (See also Blacklines C5.2–C.15.)

Teachers may introduce higher-order cognitive tasks to cooperative groups by using these organizers. Each organizer can be used to target a specific micro-skill for thinking (see Figure 5.5). Teachers may use the quick reference chart in Figure 5.5 to mix and match the organizers and skills to fit specific instructional targets of a lesson and create high-content, high-challenge tasks.

Graphic Organizers

Venn Diagram
Figure 5.6

Attribute Web
Figure 5.7

Mind Map
Figure 5.8

PMI
Figure 5.9

P+	
M–	
I?	

T-Chart
Figure 5.10

Looks Like | Sounds Like

Ranking Ladder
Figure 5.11

1 _____
2 _____
3 _____
4 _____

Right Angle Thinking
Figure 5.12

A _____

B _____

Flow Chart
Figure 5.13

Fishbone
Figure 5.14

KWL
Figure 5.15

What We **Know**	What We **Want** to Find Out	What We **Learn**

Hour Glass
Figure 5.16

Know/Recall

Topic

What If?

5W Model
Figure 5.17

Thought Tree
Figure 5.18

Matrix
Figure 5.19

Figure 5.4

Matching Thinking Processes with Organizers

Thinking Micro-Skills	Cognitive Organizers
comparing and contrasting	Venn diagram
attributing	attribute web
brainstorming	mind map
evaluating	PMI
visualizing	T-chart
prioritizing	ranking ladder
associating relationships	right angle thinking
sequencing	flow chart
analyzing	fishbone
predicting and evaluating	KWL
hypothesizing	hour glass
classifying	5W model
associating relationships	thought tree
classifying	matrix

Figure 5.5

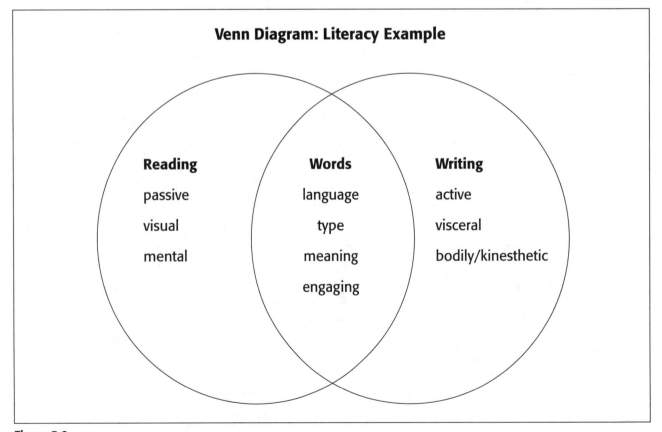

Venn Diagram: Literacy Example

Reading
passive
visual
mental

Words
language
type
meaning
engaging

Writing
active
visceral
bodily/kinesthetic

Figure 5.6

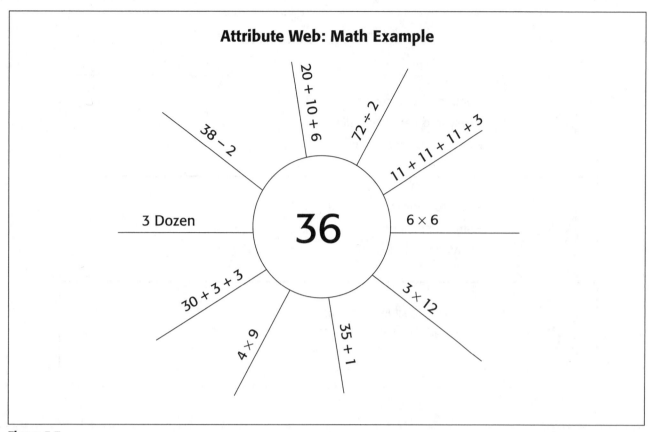

Figure 5.7

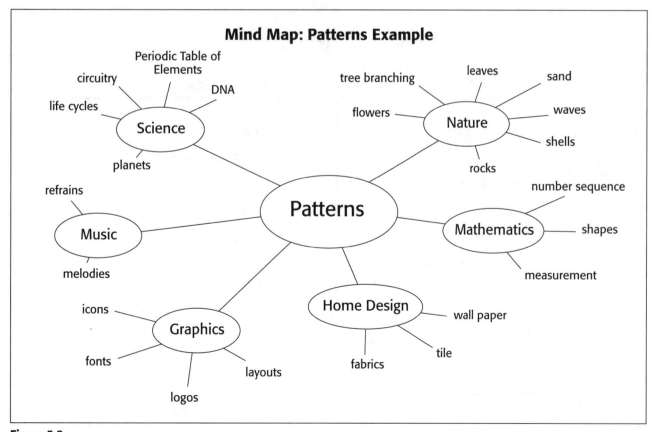

Figure 5.8

PMI: Research Example

P+	+ abundance of sources + easy to do electronically + interesting information
M−	− easy to digress − time consuming − sometimes frustrating
I ?	? levels of detail are amazing ? new paths revealed

Figure 5.9

T-Chart: Good Reader Example

Looks Like	Sounds Like
turning pages	quiet
focused	silent reading
head down	pages rustling
still	laughter
frequent	sighing
variety of materials	

Figure 5.10

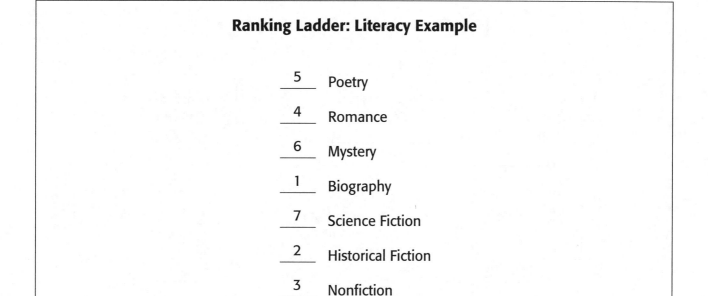

Ranking Ladder: Literacy Example

5	Poetry
4	Romance
6	Mystery
1	Biography
7	Science Fiction
2	Historical Fiction
3	Nonfiction

Figure 5.11

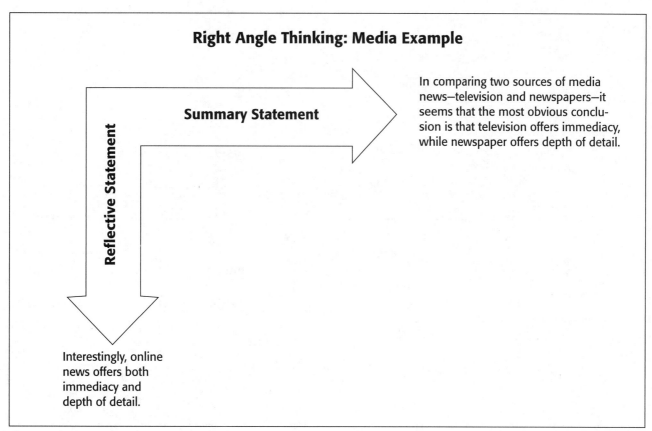

Right Angle Thinking: Media Example

Summary Statement

In comparing two sources of media news—television and newspapers—it seems that the most obvious conclusion is that television offers immediacy, while newspaper offers depth of detail.

Reflective Statement

Interestingly, online news offers both immediacy and depth of detail.

Figure 5.12

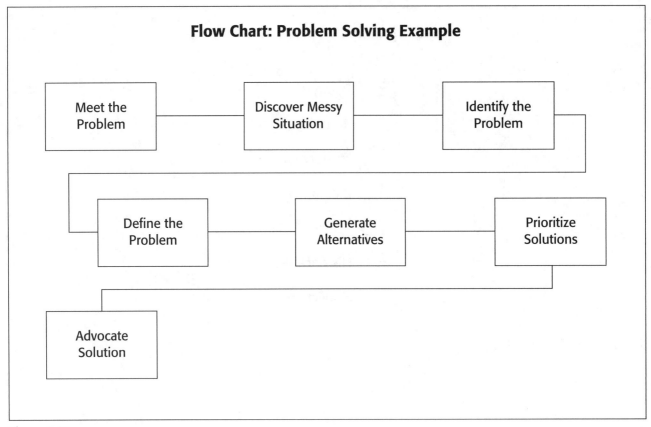

Figure 5.13

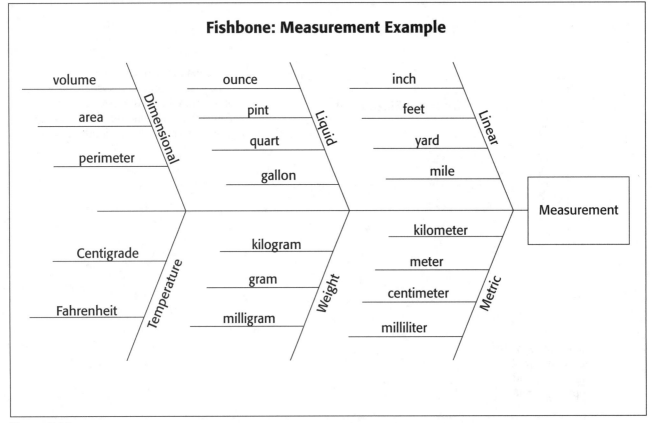

Figure 5.14

KWL: Brain Example

What We *Know*	What We *Want* to Find Out	What We *Learned*
• Some physiology of brain—cerebrum, limbic system, cerebellum • How brain cells "talk" to each other • The brain needs exercise, movement, water, and relaxation. • How short-term and long-term memory work	• How do nutrition and the brain work together? • How to facilitate long-term memory • About some diseases that affect the brain, such as Alzheimer's and Parkinson's • How MRI and fMRI work	• The brain is social. • The brain changes its structure and chemistry as a person learns. • Memory is learning. • Critical periods are not that critical—they are sensitive periods.

Figure 5.15

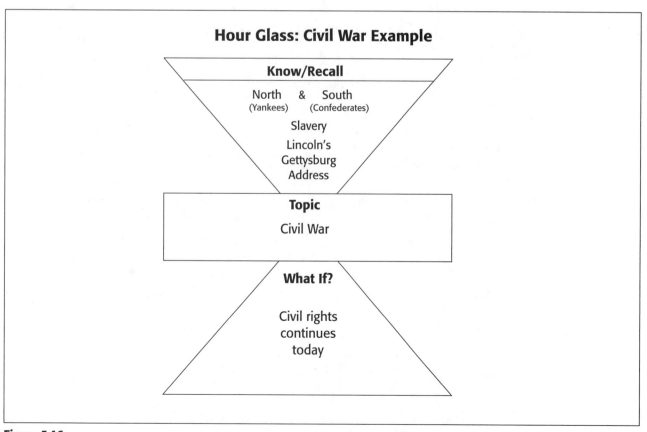

Figure 5.16

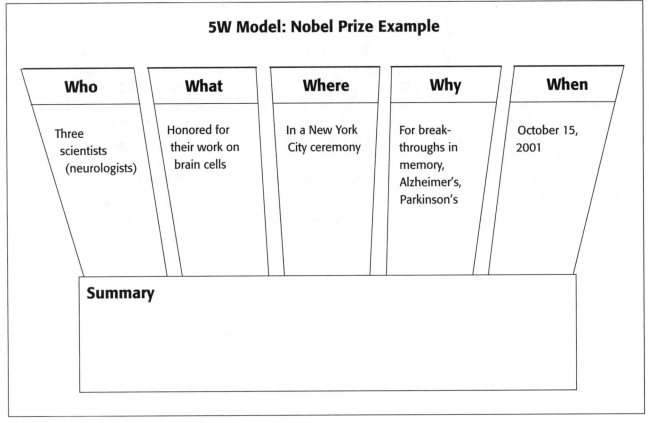

Figure 5.17

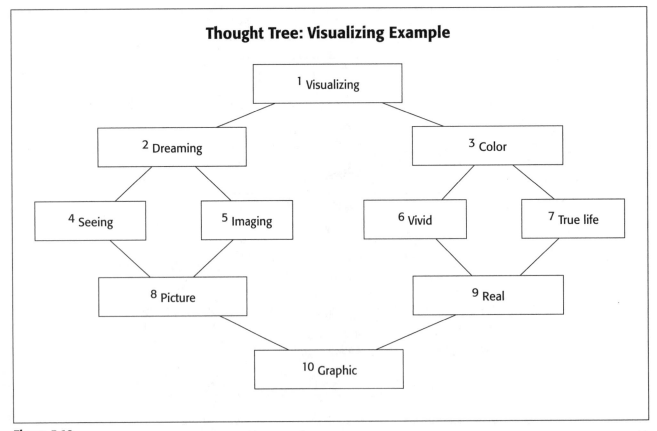

Figure 5.18

Matrix: Create a Creature—Classification Lab Example

	A BODY SYMMETRY	**B** SEGMENTATION	**C** FORM OF LOCOMOTION	**D** SENSORY ORGANS	**E** SUPPORT STRUCTURES	**F** BODY COVERING
1	bilateral	none	none	eyes, ears & nostrils	bony skeleton	skin & hair
2	radial	2 body segments	2 or 4 walking legs	paired antennae	cartilaginous skeleton	scales
3	bilaterial	3 body segments	legs & wings	compound eye & antennae	exoskeleton	skin & hair
4	bilaterial	multiple segments	6 or 8 legs	tentacles	soft bodied	feathers
5	radial	2 body segments	fins	eyes, ears & nostrils	shell hinged	scales
6	bilaterial	none	multiple walking legs	compound eye & antennae	shell carried	skin & hair

Figure 5.19

To help students learn to use the organizers, teachers first demonstrate an organizer to the whole class, then students practice using it in cooperative groups, and finally, teachers test individuals about its proper use. Students increase their achievement, productivity, and performance when they use graphic organizers to structure cooperation, cognition, and content connection.

CHOOSING AND USING A GRAPHIC ORGANIZER

Teachers can use Figure 5.20 to choose an appropriate graphic organizer for a lesson. (See also Blackline C5.16 in appendix C.) The sample lesson plan in Figure 5.21 uses the 5W model for a primary BUILD lesson that takes students through four stages: prior knowledge, generating knowledge, transfer, and assessment. (See chapter 6 for an explanation of these four stages.)

Graphic Organizer Lesson Outline

1. **Purpose of the Organizer:** What thinking does it instigate (e.g., analysis, comparison, cause and effect, etc.)?

2. **Appropriate Use:** In what stages of a lesson will this organizer work best?

3. **Timing:** How much time will it take to use this organizer?

4. **Materials:** What materials will the students need to use this organizer?

5. **Content:** How well does this organizer fit with the content objectives of the lesson?

6. **Instructions:** What do the students need to know to use this organizer correctly?

7. **Cooperative Structure:** What group structure will I use?

8. **Mediation and Assessment:** How will I focus students on what they learned and how they learned?

Figure 5.20

Teachers should keep in mind that the first lessons with an organizer may require extra time. Introduce the organizer using a fun, familiar, and easy topic. Assess students' understanding of how and why to use the organizer before moving on to using the organizer with course content.

When students are comfortable with an organizer, the teacher may integrate the organizer into any one of the four lesson stages—prior knowledge, new understanding, transfer, and assessment. (The four stages are discussed in chapter 6). Although some organizers seem to be linked to particular stages, such as the KWL to stage 1 (prior knowledge) or the PMI to stage 4 (assessment), others, such as the attribute web, may be used in any stage of the lesson. Teachers frequently use several different organizers in a single lesson. In the lessons at the end of this chapter, note how the lessons integrate a variety of organizers.

Ultimately, students will develop such skill with an organizer that they can make their own selections for use in their daily school work. Students involved in high-challenge tasks not only must do the task, but they must also decide how to best attack the task. Student self-determination is an overriding goal of the high-performance, high-challenge, cooperative classroom.

Sample Graphic Organizer Lesson Outline

Topic: Using the 5W Model

Organizer: The 5W Model (See Blackline C5.13 in Appendix C.)

Purpose: To gather and summarize information

Appropriate Use: Throughout lesson

Timing: 20–40 minutes

Materials: Copy of blank organizer, marking pens, information sources such as magazine or newspaper articles

Content: Topic of lesson

Instructions: (Develop via four stages—prior knowledge, new understanding, transfer, and assessment.)

Arrange students in groups of three. Assign cooperative group roles: reader, recorder, and encourager (who makes sure each student has an opportunity to speak).

Provide each group with an article and a blank copy of the 5W model. Instruct students to read the article and list facts under the appropriate headings.

Post the completed lists with their corresponding articles at different locations around the room. Rotate groups from station to station so that students can discuss several of the articles and lists. Review 2–3 examples with the class. Ask volunteers to explain why the 5 questions are important.

Explain to students that they will be writing their own newspaper articles. Brainstorm a list of current school and community events that could be used as topics. Select one topic to use as an example. Model listing facts for each of the 5 headings on the 5W model and writing a paragraph using those facts.

Invite each student to choose a topic, complete a copy of the 5W model, and write his or her own article. Provide corrective feedback on the completed articles and review 2–3 examples with the class, pointing out the strengths of each.

Cooperative Structure: Trios

Mediation and Assessment: Review completed organizers with monitoring and coaching; check for understanding of elements.

Figure 5.21

SUMMARY

Graphic organizers are powerful tools that expand student thinking by engaging many thinking skills and implementing many of the important principles of brain-based learning. These tools provoke inquiry in cooperative groups and generate thoughtful dialogue. When teachers use the cognitive organizers to promote understanding of text material, organize complex ideas, or mediate transfer, students benefit as they gather, process, and apply information using the principles of the three-story intellect.

BLUEPRINT
Elementary
Lesson

Codes 1SD
5NR
6CL
9QCA

Setting Up the
Scaffolding

Me-We (PMI)

Ask each student bring a stuffed animal from home.

Assign students to groups of two. In pairs, ask each to share his or her item and explain why the item is significant. Ask students to tell why they selected that particular item instead of another. What makes the stuffed animal special? Ask pairs to talk about how their animals are alike and how they are different. Discuss the differences as a class. On the board or chart paper, lead student pairs as they do a PMI evaluation on the pluses and minuses of being different. Take time to note ideas that are neither a plus nor a minus, but are just interesting thoughts about being different. An example PMI follows.

P (+)	More interesting.
M (−)	Like different things.
I (?)	Not just like me.

After the groups complete the PMI, discuss the word *different* with students. Mention that because people are different, sometimes they see things in different ways. For example, different things are important to each of us. Mention that these differences show up when people work in groups. People think of the "me" and not the "we." In order to get along with each other, sometimes people have to combine their ideas into a "me-we." Tell students they will soon discover what "me-we" looks like.

In the same pairs, have students create a "me-we" creature by making a drawing that combines their two animals. When they finish drawing, ask the pairs to name their "me-we" creature. For example, a lion combined with a teddy bear might be named libear.

Working the Crew

To process affectively, have students talk about a time that it felt good to be different.

To process the social skills of teamwork, have students list things they can do in pairs (e.g., seesaw, play tennis, play catch, etc.).

Reflecting on the Design

For cognitive processing, have students turn to their partners to tell one thing that is different about themselves.

For metacognitive processing, ask students to complete one of the following statements in a verbal wraparound:

I am special because . . .

(My partner) is special because . . .

Together we . . .

# # #

BLUEPRINT
Middle School
Lesson

Codes 1SD
5NR
6CL
9QCA

Setting Up the
Scaffolding

African and Asian Elephants

Form groups of three and assign the following roles:
> *Recorder:* Writes on chart.
> *Reporter:* Reports results.
> *Leader:* Talks about group.

Explain to students that the lesson has a double focus:
1. learning how to compare and contrast, and
2. using a Venn diagram as a graphic organizer to make thinking visible.

Show a Venn diagram model that illustrates the organizer's usefulness in listing similarities and differences. Explain how to use the Venn diagram to list similarities and differences in the different circles.

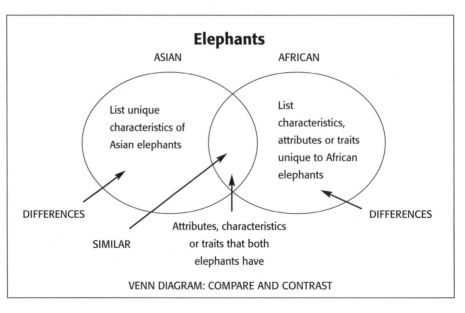

Elephants

ASIAN · AFRICAN

List unique characteristics of Asian elephants

List characteristics, attributes or traits unique to African elephants

DIFFERENCES

DIFFERENCES

SIMILAR

Attributes, characteristics or traits that both elephants have

VENN DIAGRAM: COMPARE AND CONTRAST

African and Asian Elephants

Elephants are the largest of all land animals, and they are among the strangest looking animals in the world, with their long trunks, big ears, and pointed tusks. There are two basic kinds of elephants—African elephants and Asian (or Indian) elephants. It is rather easy to tell one kind from another.

Asian elephants have smaller ears than African elephants. They have a high forehead with two rather large "bumps" on it. The back of the Asian elephant bends up in the middle, and usually only the males have tusks.

African elephants have very large ears. Their foreheads don't have big bumps on them. The back of an African elephant bends down in the middle, and both the males and females have tusks.

African elephants are larger than Asian elephants, and the males of both kinds are larger than the females. The average Asian male is about 9 feet tall (2.74 meters) at the shoulder and weighs about 10,000 pounds (4,535 kilograms). African males average about 10 feet tall (3 meters) and weigh about 12,000 pounds (5,443 kilograms).

However, some elephants grow much larger than this. The largest African male on record was more than 12 1/2 feet tall (3.66 meters) and weighed about 22,000 (9,979 kilograms). The single elephant weighed as much as 150 average-sized people.

Male elephants are called bulls, and females are called cows. Young elephants are called calves. When an elephant calf is born, it is already a big animal. It is about three feet tall (1 meter) and weighs about 200 pounds (90 kilograms). Baby elephants are covered with hair, but as they grow they lose most of it.

Elephants can live a very long time. Asian elephants may live as long as 80 years, and African elephants may live for 60 years.

Give each group a piece of blank poster paper, a marking pen, and a copy of the article "African and Asian Elephants" (see Blackline C5.17 in Appendix C).

Instruct students to read the piece. Ask the recorders to jot down the attributes of each type of elephant in the appropriate section of the Venn diagram.

After students have analyzed the characteristics of the elephants, ask the groups to draw some conclusions about the likenesses and differences of the elephants. Sample the ideas as a class.

For affective processing, ask students to perform a PMI evaluation of the Venn diagram, telling what they like and what they do not like. An example follows.

P M I

P (+)	Separates the characteristics
M (-)	Hard to write the shared characteristics in the small middle section
I (?)	How many circles could be used?

To process the social skills, have students compare good teamwork and poor teamwork.

To process at the cognitive level, have students use the completed Venn diagrams to formulate fat (divergent) and skinny (convergent) questions about other mammals. An example follows.

Fat
Write 3 FAT questions about elephants that will get FAT answers.
   1. Why do elephants live in warm places?
   2. What other animals are like elephants?
   3. Could an elephant be a pet?

Skinny
Write 3 SKINNY questions about elephants that will get SKINNY answers.
   1. Are elephants mammals?
   2. How many kinds of elephants are there?
   3. What kinds of foods do elephants eat?

Finally, to help students reflect metacognitively on other uses of the Venn diagram, have students:

1. Create a large Venn diagram using yarn laid out on the floor. Designate one circle for students wearing jeans, and the other for those wearing gym shoes. Ask students to move to the right place on the Venn. (Students with both jeans and gym shoes stand in the middle.)

2. Ask students to pair with a friend and to design a use for Venn diagrams in mathematics, science, literature, or social studies. The examples on the next page illustrate possibilities from science and social studies.

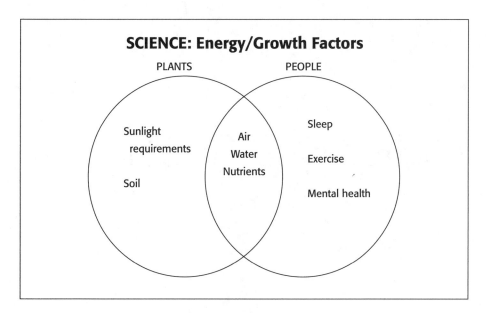

SCIENCE: Energy/Growth Factors

PLANTS   PEOPLE

Sunlight requirements

Soil

Air
Water
Nutrients

Sleep

Exercise

Mental health

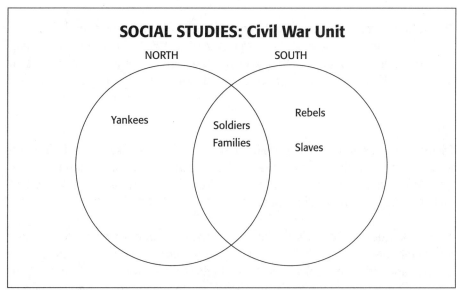

SOCIAL STUDIES: Civil War Unit

NORTH   SOUTH

Yankees

Soldiers
Families

Rebels

Slaves

# # #

BLUEPRINT
High School
Lesson

Codes 1SD
5NR
6CL
9QCA

Setting Up the
Scaffolding

Working the
Crew

Right Angle Thinking

This lesson introduces students to the thinking skill of associating ideas with the right angle thinking cognitive organizer (Figure 5.12). Discuss *association* with the class. Explain that they will describe what connecting one idea to another is like using the thought tree association technique (Figure 5.18).

Divide students into pairs. Explain that partners will take turns being "on focus"—that is, each partner takes on the role of speaker and listener in rotation. Ask students to draw a thought tree (see Figure 5.18 and Blackline C5.14 in Appendix C for a blackline master).

Now, ask students to individually complete the thought tree by associating ideas. Tell them to begin with the word *association,* think of two words related to it, and write one word in each box in the second line. Have students continue following the hierarchy of the boxes on the diagram, using a stream of consciousness. Students should move through the thought tree exercise as rapidly as possible. The more quickly the associations are made, the more candid the connections.

When students have completed the diagrams, ask each student to complete the following lead-in using word #1 and word #10 from the tree:

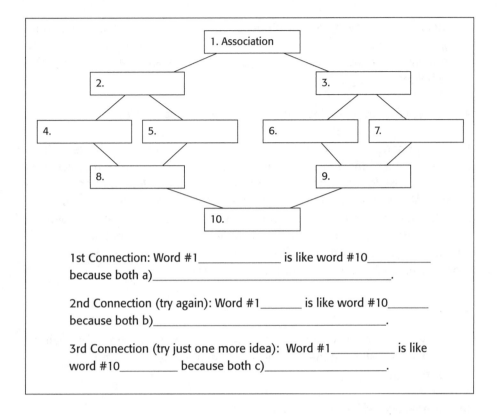

1st Connection: Word #1_____ is like word #10_____ because both a)_____.

2nd Connection (try again): Word #1_____ is like word #10_____ because both b)_____.

3rd Connection (try just one more idea): Word #1_____ is like word #10_____ because both c)_____.

Next, introduce students to the right angle thinking cognitive organizer (see Figure 5.12 and Blackline C5.8 in Appendix C for a blackline master).

Explain to students that they are to discuss a biographical character that they are familiar with. Explain that each partner takes turns taking on the role of speaker. As speaker, the partner uses the idea of association to discuss the biographical character he or she has been studying. The listener should jot down a summary of interesting information on the right-angle chart (in the arm for idea #1) and reflect and elaborate on the ideas in the space to the right.

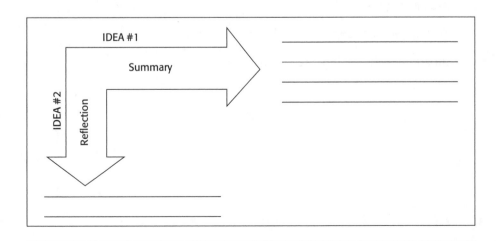

Listeners should also reflect on other ideas or thoughts from their personal experiences that they think connect to the original idea. Listeners should note these ideas along the vertical arrow (idea #2) and elaborate on them in the space below that angle.

Ask students to reverse roles and try the same exercise again.

To help students understand the importance of capturing associated ideas, elicit examples of incidents of serendipitous discoveries—ideas that occur as someone looks for something else—or of reflective thoughts that accompany an original idea. Suggest that the right angle thinking organizer is a visual tool that illustrates how students can deliberately capture the extraneous ideas or peripheral thoughts that naturally occur while focusing on something quite different. The learner constantly makes connections. Sometimes—many times—those reflective thoughts are worth capturing, too.

Reflecting on the Design

To engage students in affective processing, have partners share the feelings they had as they allowed their minds to follow the association and capture the "extra" thought.

To process social skills, have students recall:

A time I got a good idea from a friend . . .

A time I got a bad idea from a friend . . .

Process the cognitive content by asking partners to compare the biographical characters they discussed in the right angle exercise.

Finally, to lead students toward metacognitive transfer, have them reflect on one of the following questions in a log entry:

Associating ideas is . . .

Thinking at right angles might have helped me when . . .

Biographies spark thinking because . . .

# # #

Blueprints for Achievement

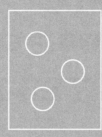

FORMING

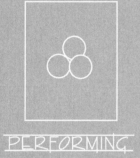

PERFORMING

NORMING

CHAPTER 6

Phase III

CONFORMING

Level II

How Do I Build Power
Lessons in the
Cooperative Classroom?

STORMING

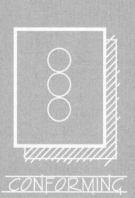

CONFORMING

in the Cooperative
Classroom

HOW DO I BUILD POWER LESSONS IN THE COOPERATIVE CLASSROOM?

Part of the teacher's art is to watch the balanced growth of their pupils.

—M. C. Richards

Draft

Creating powerful lessons is the crux of fostering high student achievement in cooperative learning groups. Teachers give students opportunities for high achievement when they use the fundamental principles of power lessons as underpinnings for the lesson-creating strategy, BUILD. When teachers embrace the foundational principles of the power lesson, which are embodied in the BUILD strategy, they create classroom lessons in the conforming stage with confidence, facility, and wisdom.

Blueprints sets a mind-challenging model of high expectations for student achievement: high content + high support + high challenge = high achievement. Knowing content is a necessary function of learning (high content). But, by itself, students' knowing content will not develop higher achievement. A second critical requirement is that teachers integrate cooperating, thinking, and deep understanding of content into a single lesson (high support). Then, students are challenged to understand meaning and to transfer the information (high challenge). When teachers integrate high content, high support, and high challenge, students meet high expectations (high achievement), thus completing the equation. In short, teachers combine content, challenge, and support to create power lessons for students' high achievement.

THE ANATOMY OF POWER LESSONS

Power lessons result from careful and creative instructional design. Instructional design is a process built on proven principles and practices of instruction. It integrates cooperative learning, higher-order thinking, and content mastery into a seamless and strategic flow. Effective teachers infuse the design principles in different ways in different lessons because each lesson uniquely embodies both the principles of design and the assembly of individual students and their individual learning needs and intelligences.

A Question of Flow

In power lessons, *flow* is the hallmark of a powerful lesson. Flow is "the state in which people are so involved in an activity that nothing else seems to matter," (Csikszentmihalyi 1990, p. 4). Flow occurs "when a person's body or mind is stretched to its limits in a voluntary effort to accomplish something difficult and worthwhile" (p. 3). Flow springs from sound, principled lesson designs. Strong lessons lead students to better mental engagement and intense cognitive rehearsal with the rich content of the curriculum. Students with engaged, active minds generate information (Feuerstein 1980), increasing their motivation to learn. Increased motivation leads to better performance on a variety of assessment measures, including standardized tests. However, when teachers employ the principles as ironclad, inflexible rules and ignore their personal knowledge and experience of individual learners, they create less effective lessons, and students achieve less. Teachers are most effective when they recognize that their knowledge and experience of their individual students is critical to applying the principles well.

Students have difficulty in reaching flow when teachers take a piecemeal approach to instruction. When teachers isolate thinking and/or cooperative learning activities, they may ignore the need for flexibility and personal decision making. Friday afternoon mind puzzles, an occasional graphic organizer, or a fun-filled people search may give a temporary energy boost to the class, but not as well as strategic, consistent, principle-based, and regular blending of thinking and learning processes into the content of the curriculum does. Teachers foster students' flow by choosing high-impact rather than low-impact activities. High-impact activities integrate thinking and cooperative activities with the content of the lesson. On the other hand, low-impact activities tend to be isolated additions tacked on a lesson to boost students' energy. Following are examples of low-impact versus high-impact activities.

It is Friday afternoon and the class is lethargic.

Low-Impact Activity. To raise the energy level, the teacher thinks about asking students to create a human graph on "Your Next Vacation" but only if all students have finished the assigned workbook pages on time.

High-Impact Activity. Anticipating the class's lethargy, the teacher planned to do a human graph to conclude her unit on world cultures. She asks each student to compare his or her own family activities to the activities of a family from a culture they studied during the past two weeks. She asks: Do you have many similarities, some similarities, or few similarities?

Before creating the graph, she tells students to turn to a partner and discuss their ideas. Then, she asks students to form the human graph. After they form the graph, she asks each student to identify at least one comparison and write it in a journal. Finally, she randomly selects students to contribute ideas to a composite list for the class.

It is the first week of the new block schedule.

Low-Impact Activity. The teacher discovers that her required lesson plan does not fill the allotted time. She instructs the students to read the assigned novel for the final fifteen minutes of the period. Rather than change her lesson plans, she makes silent reading the closing activity every day.

High-Impact Activity. The teacher has discovered that her required lesson plan does not fill the assigned time. To use the found time, when the students complete the lab experiment, she writes three journal entry stems on the board for each team to discuss and answer:

> What was the most important idea that you learned in this experiment?
>
> What is a question you still have about _____?
>
> How did working together benefit you and your partners?

After allowing the groups ten minutes to make journal entries and to discuss responses, she calls on a group member to share answers with the class. On each day during this lesson, she concludes with this same summative activity calling on different reporting groups each day.

It is time for the new science lesson. The principal has stressed inegrated lesson plans.

Low-Impact Activity. The teacher instructs students to take out dictionaries, look up the vocabulary words, and write their definitions in their notebooks. At the end of the period, she tells them to save these definitions for the unit test review.

High-Impact Activity. The teacher starts the lesson by telling students that vocabulary words are the keys that open the door to the content of the lesson. She also explains that they will be tested on vocabulary at the end of the lesson. The teacher posts the definitions for the words and assigns students in groups of three. She tells the groups to use the portmanteau jigsaw (see chapter 2) to help each other master the definitions. During the lesson each day, a different group explains how the words fit in the lesson. At the end of the lesson, the teacher tests students with a vocabulary quiz.

The new unit is Hamlet.

Low-Impact Activity. The teacher instructs the students to follow along as he calls upon one student after another to read the scenes. At various points, he explains a footnote.

High-Impact Activity. The teacher divides the class into groups of six. Each group assigns character roles for the first scene and practices reading the scene. When students have finished practicing, the teacher asks each group to list predictions about what is going to happen in this play. As a class, students create an unduplicated set of predictions for the play before moving to the next group assignment. Throughout the unit, the teacher points out the importance of making predictions and encourages students to repeat the prediction strategy.

The teacher begins a lesson for making graphs.

Low-Impact Activity. The teacher reads the instructions for making a graph. She distributes worksheets before telling the students to complete every other example. After 20 minutes, she calls on the first student in the first row to put his first graph on the board. The class is to review the student's graph, deciding if it is right or wrong. After the teacher approves the answer, each student corrects his or her own worksheet.

High-Impact Activity. The teacher introduces the unit on graphs with a human bar graph that illustrates the types of graphs in the unit. For graph content, she uses the number of minutes the students spend each day on study, work, play, and meals. To create the graph, for example, for the number of minutes students study each day, she does the following:

- She tells students to line up side by side in a straight line, which serves as the baseline.
- She designates one end of the baseline as the starting point— 0 minutes of study—and the other as the ending point—120 minutes of study.
- She instructs students who agree with either extreme to move to the corresponding end of the line. She encourages students who hold an in-between position to move as close to the appropriate end as they think indicates their position with regard to minutes of study.
- She tells students at each location to form a bar by moving into a line that is at a right angle to the baseline.
- She asks several students at different points on the graph to explain their positions.

When the human graph activity is completed, the teacher begins a KWL activity on graphs. She discovers that the students understand all that she had planned to teach in the graph unit and moves to the next unit.

The class is learning about end punctuation.

Low-Impact Activity. The teacher wants to use cooperative learning, so she puts students into pairs. She explains that each pair is a team and that teams will compete against each other. She gives each team a worksheet and tells them that the team that finds the most grammatical mistakes on the worksheet wins a prize.

High-Impact Activity. The teacher starts by asking the class to complete a KWL on end punctuation. As students work on the KWL, she notices that they are confused about periods, question marks, and exclamation points. She elects to start with the period and assigns pairs to complete a worksheet on periods. She reviews their worksheets and then asks random volunteers to make a general rule about the use of the period. When the class agrees on the rule for using periods as end punctuation, she asks new volunteers to punctuate sample sentences she has written on the board. She checks that the class understands before she gives pairs new practice sheets. When the pairs are done with the worksheets, she forms students into groups of four. The foursomes check each other's work and test the period rule by inventing and punctuating new sentences.

Standardized tests begin in four weeks.

Low-Impact Activity. The principal distributes old tests to each class for each subject. He requires teachers to stop daily instruction and to have their students do practice tests for each area each day.

High-Impact Activity. For preparation, the teacher uses a prior knowledge web to identify what test-taking strategies her students already know. She adds two strategies to the web that students do not know or mention. Each day, she gives students a sample test. She assigns students in pairs and asks them to go through the test, answer the questions, and note which strategies they used. While the pairs are doing this, the teacher checks answers and identifies the best strategies being used by a pair. After thirty minutes, the class summarizes and lists the best strategies from the pairs. At the end of the week, students summarize best strategies for test taking across the curriculum. At the start of the next week, the pairs review the best strategies they want to remember.

As the high impact examples show, cooperative or cognitive activities can become repeated and purposeful *strategies* that increase student achievement. To increase student achievement, teachers need to couple strategic thinking activities—such as advance organizers, higher-order questions, graphic organizers, and reflective journals—with cooperative structures—such as pairs and trios—to energize curricular content. These combinations provide powerful means for students to attain higher achievement goals.

Principles of Instructional Design

Flexibility

Cognitive Rehearsal

Variety

Functional Integration

Economy

Figure 6.1

Principles of a Power Lesson

Five design principles underlie the creation of instructional flow: flexibility, cognitive rehearsal, variety, functional integration, and economy (see Figure 6.1).

Principle 1: Flexibility. As the high-impact lessons in the previous section demonstrated, teachers needed to use flexibility in integrating strategies to create flow. Strategies differ depending on whether content is sequential or not.

Learning may or may not be a sequential, step-by-step process. Some subjects—such as mathematics—must be taught sequentially and do not allow for much flexibility. However, teachers must not be so rigid in following the steps that they miss teaching students the underlying concepts necessary for understanding the steps.

Take, for instance, the concept of *fractions.* Students need to know the correct procedures for using fractions. When taught just the procedures, however, students do not learn everything they need to know to correctly respond to every fraction problem on a standardized test or, more important, to apply fractions to real-life purposes. Memorizing a formula or a set of procedures is a good first step for student achievement, but tests do not ask students to list a memorized set of procedures. Instead, students must apply the formula and the procedures to solve problems. When students grasp the concept and understand how to analyze the word problem, they have the elements to solve the problem. Memorizing formulas and procedures is a means to an end, not an end in itself. Students with basic knowledge, conceptual understanding, and topically related thinking skills are more likely to answer test questions correctly than students with limited, memorized, sterile procedures practiced repeatedly on identical tests with identical problems.

Most other subjects follow a non-sequential pattern and allow for more flexibility in teaching. For instance, students may be asked to analyze a character in a novel. There is no sequence or set procedure to follow in this analysis. Teachers can choose from many strategies to help students in their analyses. As students read the novel, they infer characteristics from character clues: What does the hero or heroine say or do that gives clues to character? What other clues does the author provide? How does the student match those clues with prior experience to make successful inferences? When teachers provide students with tools such as graphic organizers, they help students gather and organize information. As students read, they fill in the various elements of the organizer, gather clues, and draw correct inferences.

The flow of a lesson must allow for flexibility, taking in to account the various ways that students learn, the nature of the material, and the type of student thinking called for by the lesson. There are neither magical formulae nor preset lesson designs. Instead, teachers decide how to organize the information for the most effective lesson.

Principle 2: Cognitive Rehearsal. Feuerstein (1980), Vygotsky (1962), Piaget (1972), and other theorists explain that learning occurs best when the mind is actively engaged in the task. Unfortunately, students are too often active, but too seldom engaged.

Curricular time constraints create a daunting choice for teachers daily: to spend or not to spend time transforming students into this active role. This choice seems more daunting when teachers perceive their students as too unruly, too slow, or too needy to move instruction beyond the pour-and-store model. When teachers have had little or no exposure to the many research-based teaching tools that support students' active engagement in learning, the task of implementing active learning may seem overwhelming.

In the *Blueprints* approach, teachers must change their commitment. This change starts with learning about selected best practice tools that have proven successful in all manner of classrooms, including those where students were noted for their unruly behavior and their low motivation and interest in learning.

Teachers engage students when they lead students away from passively receiving information to actively generating information. Among the most effective of these tools for promoting student success is the one called *cognitive rehearsal.*

What is cognitive rehearsal? *Cognitive rehearsal* happens when the student thinks about and replays his or her responses to an intellectual challenge—a question, a puzzle, or other forms of inquiry. Effective readers, for example, make regular use of cognitive rehearsal. As they read a passage, they rehearse the information in their minds, making sure they understand what they read. Teachers can stimulate students' thinking by requiring students to rehearse information by writing, drawing, or other means of reflection. (For more information on cognitive rehearsal, see chapter 2.)

Educational research has shown that several tools effectively promote cognitive rehearsal. Kerman (1979) discusses several teaching tools based on research into teachers' expectations in the classroom (Figure 6.2).

In addition to the tools in Figure 6.2, teachers may rely on both the informal and the formal cooperative strategies shown in Figure 6.3. (See chapter 2 for a full explanation of formal and informal strategies.)

Teaching Tools to Support Cognitive Rehearsal

- Wait time: Ask a question and then wait 3–5 seconds before selecting a student to respond (Rowe 1996).

- Equal distribution of responses: Purposefully select different students to answer questions.

- Clarifying questions: Ask questions that require students to explain answers, describe rationale, and give examples.

- Higher-order questions: Ask questions that require students to use more complex thinking skills than called for by fact-seeking questions.

(Adapted from Kerman 1979.)

Figure 6.2

Cooperative Strategies

Informal Cooperative Strategies
- TTYPA (Turn to Your Partner, and . . .)
- think-pair-share
- think-write-share
- what if pairs
- round robin

Formal Cooperative Tasks
- jigsaw
- expert jigsaw
- cooperative group (2–5)
- project teams
- problem-based learning teams

Figure 6.3

Principle 3: Variety. Variety is the spice of learning. According to Hunter (1971), teachers introduce motivational variety by selecting cooperative structures and thinking tools and molding these structures and tools into strategies.

For example, consider a teacher beginning a new unit. During the first lesson, she may ask students to identify all the words associated with the unit concept (e.g., character, plot, etc. in literature). She asks each student to write a personal list in a journal. Then, she leads the class to complete a KWL, listing responses on the board, or jigsaws a definition search for words to add to the KWL.

During the second lesson, she asks students: What three important words from yesterday help you recall what you know about *character*? She pulls three random names from a hat and ask the chosen students to present their lists. Next, she uses these words to introduce the character in the novel the class is to study. After this introduction, she uses the prediction strategy with the entire class. Then, she asks students to predict what will happen in the novel. (She may choose to place students in cooperative groups to do the predictions.) After students finish predicting, the teacher assigns the first reading. Finally, she ends the class period by asking students to complete an individual journal entry starting with the stem: Today, an important prediction I made about this story was . . . . (Or, she could end with pairs sharing what they have learned, a summary that they made, or a round robin: Today, I learned . . . .)

Even as she teaches the lesson, the teacher has multiple opportunities to add variety beyond the tools and strategies she originally selected. She can mix grouping patterns (whole class, heterogeneous groups, homogeneous groups), strategies, tools, content, organization, and so forth. By making each day different, she keeps lessons from falling into a predictable pattern and keeps students interested and actively engaged. Variety is the spice of each lesson.

Principle 4: Functional Integration. The seamless integration of content, thinking, and cooperative learning is essential to higher student achievement. As teachers balance time with engagement, they can integrate cooperative learning (pairs, trios) with strategies that promote thinking (analysis, evaluating, predicting, summarizing) to explore content. Teachers can also mix and match techniques (questioning strategies, KWL, think-pair-share, launch questions, etc.) to control pace, variety, and interest in each stage of a lesson's development.

In the *Blueprints* model, teachers use four stages to develop and integrate cooperation, thinking, and content during a cooperative lesson (Figure 6.4 or Blackline C6.1 in Appendix C). In each stage, effective teachers consider the principles of flexible flow, cognitive rehearsal, and variety.

Stages of a Cooperative Lesson

Stage 1: Assess prior knowledge.

Stage 2: Gather and understand new information.

Stage 3: Transfer new concepts.

Stage 4: Assess learning.

Figure 6.4

For instance, in stage 1, the teacher might ask student pairs (cooperative structure) to make predictions (thinking skill) based on what they already know about George Washington Carver. In stage 2, the teacher might ask student trios (cooperative structure) to make a web (thinking tool) about Carver's characteristics gathered from a story they have read. After student groups have gathered this information, the teacher might ask selected groups to present their webs to the class and ask a volunteer to create an all class web of unduplicated characteristics on the board. The teacher might want to ask clarifying questions (stage 2) using appropriate wait time and equal distribution. Then, in stage 3, the teacher might ask each student to summarize Carver's most positive traits (thinking) and call for pair-share groups (cooperative structure) to discuss the question: How can we personally benefit from having similar characteristics? Finally, in stage 4, teachers ask student pairs to use a PMI (thinking) cognitive organizer and, perhaps, a lesson rubric to assess what they have done.

Principle 5: Economy. Economy—the principle of less is more—comes into play in many ways in the *Blueprints* approach. First, teachers spend less time talking, giving students more time for cognitive rehearsal. Teachers spend less time delivering content, using more time for giving instructions, coaching student pairs, eliciting responses from all, and mediating meaningful understanding of the content. Teachers spend less time dominating activity in the classroom (thus, students spend less time listening to them) and more time strategically planning how to help more students think more (thus, students spend more time doing their own thinking—finding prior knowledge, predicting, analyzing, asking questions, summarizing—and helping each other). Finally, teachers design unit instruction to cover less detailed information in order to have more time to build understanding of a targeted concept, to create transfer, and to assess students' deeper understanding of the content.

The bottom line of these five principles is simple: power lessons depend on teachers empowering students to be active, engaged generators of knowledge. To break through students' resistance and to help them build flow into their learning is a tough task. From the first stage of lesson design through the final one, teachers must signal their expectations that it is the students', not only the teacher's, job to be the workers and thinkers in the classroom.

Assessing Power Lessons for Lesson Power

Teachers may want to assess a lesson's power. A rubric can help teachers review, both before and after a lesson, the elements and strategies that worked in a lesson or an unit. Figure 6.5 identifies desired elements for an assessment based on the principles of power lessons and suggests a scale for evaluating a lesson's lesson power (see also Blackline C6.2 in Appendix C). (Several of the more specific entries in the rubric are developed to support the BUILD technique, which is discussed next.)

Rubric for Evaluating Power Lessons for Lesson Power

To What Degree Have I		By What Means
provided *flexibility?*	1 2 3 4 5	_____
engaged students with *cognitive rehearsal?*	1 2 3 4 5	_____
provided *variety?*	1 2 3 4 5	_____
integrated		
content?	1 2 3 4 5	_____
cooperation?	1 2 3 4 5	_____
cognition?	1 2 3 4 5	_____
and developed prior knowledge?	1 2 3 4 5	_____
and generated new understanding?	1 2 3 4 5	_____
and facilitated transfer?	1 2 3 4 5	_____
and assessed process?	1 2 3 4 5	_____
and assessed results?	1 2 3 4 5	_____
and aligned with standards?	1 2 3 4 5	_____
been *economical* (less is more)?	1 2 3 4 5	_____

Figure 6.5

Lessons built on the principles of power lessons give students the power to outstrip their own expectations for how much and how well they can learn. Teachers can use the power lesson principles and the BUILD framework, which is based on the principles of instructional flow, to design power lessons that lead students to high achievement. See Figure 6.6 and 6.7 for a review of the BUILD framework and chapter 2 for an earlier discussion of BUILD.

BUILD Framework

B – Build in higher-order thinking that requires critical and creative thinking (brainstorming, inventing, performing) to stretch the mind.

U – Unite the teams so students establish a group identity.

I – Invite individual accountability by assigning roles to group members.

L – Look back and debrief *what* and *how* students learned.

D – Develop students' social skills by setting guidelines for students to accept others' ideas.

Figure 6.6

BUILDING POWER LESSONS

Examples of power lessons abound throughout *Blueprints*. For example, the portmanteau vocabulary lesson (chapter 2) is an example of a power lesson at the information-gathering stage of the three-story intellect. At the second-story (processing) level, examples of power lessons are the grade and content-appropriate lessons at the end of each chapter. For instance, consider the lesson built around a study of Robert Frost's poetry in chapter 4. The teacher asked students to recall what they knew about Frost's poetry and record the gathered information (first-story activity), then compare (second-story processing) the assigned poem with the gathered information. After forming students into cooperative groups, the teacher asked them to explain why (second-story processing) they chose certain characteristics. Finally, students were asked to independently write an essay using what they had learned about the poetry (third-story processing). Examples of power lessons that take students to the third story are prevalent. For example, in the Me-We lesson in chapter 5, students use a PMI graphic organizer to assess (third-story processing) the animals in the story. In the African and Asian Elephants lesson (chapter 5), students use a PMI organizer to assess their use of a Venn diagram.

BUILD : Cooperative Lesson Planner

	B **B**uild in High-Order Thinking *Problem Solving, Decision Making, Creative Ideation*	**U** **U**nite Teams *Build Trust & Teamwork*	**I** **I**nsist on Individual Learning *Insure Individual Learning & Responsibility*	**L** **L**ook Over & Discuss *Plan, Monitor & Evaluate*	**D** **D**evelop Social Skills *Communication, Leadership, Conflict Resolution*	
1	Critical and creative thinking	Bonding and group identity	Assigned roles	Goal setting	Paraphrase	I hear I see...
2	3-to-1 technique	Shared materials	Quiz	PMI	Affirm	That's a good idea
3	Problem solving	Single product	Random responses	Human graph	Clarify	Tell me more!
4	Decision making	Jigsaw	Individual application	Teacher observation sheet	Test options	What else?
5	Fat & Skinny Questions	Lottery	Individual grades	Student observer feedback	Sense tone	That feels___
6	Application	Bonus points	Signature. I agree! I understand!	Success award	Encourage others	No put-downs!
7	Transfer within/across/into	Group grade	Round robin (Wraparound)	Log entry	Accept others' ideas	Set DOVE guidelines
8	Graphic organizers	Group reward	Homework	Individual transfer or application	T-chart	Looks like Sounds like
9	Metacognitive exercises	Consensus	Bonus points	Team ad	Disagree with ideas not people	Other point of view
10	Making metaphors	Extended projects	Expert jigsaw	Mrs. Potter's questions	Reach consensus	5 to fist

Figure 6.7

Teachers begin lesson design by considering the three basic elements: cooperation, thinking, and content. They do this by asking several questions:

- Which of the cooperative and cognitive strategies in my repertoire are appropriate for helping students learn this material?
- What do students already know about the subject area?
- What is the cooperative climate of the classroom?
- What are the students' capabilities to use cooperative strategies?
- What are the students' capabilities and readiness to use a designated cognitive strategy?

With answers to these questions, teachers can select the cooperative and cognitive strategies to teach the lesson. They may begin BUILDing cooperative lessons using the BUILD Cooperative Lesson Planner (Figure 6.7, also see Blackline C6.3 in Appendix C).

Teachers begin their BUILD process by asking five more questions that help them set the parameters of their planning:

1. What is it that I want my students to know and/or do at the completion of the lesson?
2. What are the cooperative strategies that will best help them know and do what is intended?
3. What is the information that they will need to know and do what is intended?
4. What are the cognitive strategies that will best help them know and do what is intended?
5. How will I know they have accomplished what I intended?

Let's go through the BUILD process using an example from US history. A standard has been set for students: They are to demonstrate the ability to write a grammatically correct, three-paragraph essay communicating understanding of how two American leaders took effective action in ending a social conflict.

Note that this standard addresses two types of achievement: content and process. The content focuses on students' knowledge of social conflict and effective leaders in American history. The process requires students to demonstrate, understand, compare (second-story processing) and assess effectiveness (third-story processing). Finally, the standard integrates content from the students' English class by insisting on grammatical correctness in the three-paragraph essay model.

Based on their understanding of the standard, content, and process, teachers respond to the first question: What is it that I want my students to know and do? They want their students to know about major social conflicts in the American story, the resolution of each, and the leadership role that brought the conflict to a satisfactory end. They want students to apply an assessment rubric to the social conflicts and to the involved leaders (third-story processing). Finally, they want students to have a strong grasp of the facts (first-level processing) so that they can demonstrate their understanding by *explaining why* they selected specific leaders (third-story processing).

Teachers might develop a simple assessment rubric for the leadership content of this lesson, for example:

1. Knows key facts about the selected leader.

   Scale: Knows all 90% 80% 70%

2. Knows key facts about the selected social conflict.

   Scale: Knows all 90% 80% 70%

3. Demonstrates understanding of criteria for effective leadership.

   Scale: Number of reasons: 4 3 2

4. Demonstrates ability to assess leadership with a criteria.

   Scale: Number of examples: 4 3 2

Teachers recognize that students' understanding of content is only a start to meeting the goal. Students are also asked for a "demonstration of ability to write a grammatically correct three-paragraph essay." Students need to know grammar and what is an acceptable "three-paragraph" essay. Teachers need to plan how to introduce or review these components.

When students know the three-paragraph format and grammar from prior lessons, teachers' planning is simplified. The design for the lesson centers on the rubric that students will use to bridge from past, related lessons to this historical content lesson. Teachers add two items to the content rubric that address prior knowledge of grammar and essay structure:

5. Uses correct spelling, sentence structure, and grammar.

   Scale: Number of errors: 0 2 4 6

6. Uses correct structure and logic for a three-paragraph essay.

   Scale: all logically correct, all formally correct, some formal breakdown, lacks structure

The rubric is presented to the students at the start of the lesson to clarify the lesson's intent and to provide signposts to success.

When teachers know what they expect students to understand and do and are aware that these high expectations will require complex thinking and challenging tasks, they are ready to outline their instructional strategies.

It is at this point that the BUILD Lesson Planning Chart (Figure 6.7) helps teachers think through the key stages of a well-designed lesson. The chart is an instruction repertoire in a matrix. Teachers may use the chart not only to recall the variety of strategies available but also to easily view a variety of ways to apply each one the four stages of lesson design: developing prior knowledge, generating new understanding, transferring understanding inside and outside the curriculum, and assessing the process and its results (Figure 6.4).

Stage 1: Prior Knowledge

Based on the standard that frames this example historical lesson, three pieces of content merit prior knowledge investigation: grammar, essay structure, and historical content.

In this first stage of developing students' prior knowledge, teachers help students recall prior knowledge they have on the content and processes of the lesson. Among the teacher's strategy choices are KWL graphic organizer, think-pair-share, attribute web, questions, or the fact matrix.

In this case, teachers might organize by using whole-class strategies to review prior knowledge. First, they might do a KWL on the history with pairs and a whole-class listing of their results. At the next session, they might do a matrix to review of the grammar they want to highlight. Finally, they could do T-chart on what an effective three-paragraph essay looks and sounds like. This step-by-step series of prior knowledge strategies would be appropriate for a class that needs to move through all material at a steady and detailed pace for a comprehensive and detailed review.

The KWL is the structure most often used in stage 1. By pairing students, teachers initiate the cooperative element and intensify students' engagement with what they already know. When first introduced to the KWL strategy, some teachers are concerned about eliciting sufficient and appropriate responses, especially if their students have been conditioned to expect teachers to be the doer and teller. This is a legitimate concern. Teachers may combat the problem by prompting and assisting with the first two questions (the K and the W), giving students a chance to be comfortable with their new interactive roles before they answer the third question (the L).

Completing the lesson and KWL shows students that they are building on their prior knowledge and constructing their own learning. Sometimes, teachers need to step in and mediate student feelings of competence and success. Teachers actively guide student thinking when they mediate, a practice derived from the work of Feuerstein (1980), a pioneer in metacognition. *Mediating* means that teachers use their questioning strategies, wait time, distribution of responses, fat questions, and so on to probe, enlighten, and clarify student understanding. Questions may focus on meaning of the concepts, on transfer, on student feelings of competence, on the social interaction, or on other factors.

The plus of eliciting prior knowledge with a KWL, matrix, or T-chart is its thoroughness; the minus is the amount of time it might take. The prior knowledge check should take no more than 10% of the time allotted for the lesson. For the class that moves quickly, teachers can jigsaw this element. For example, teachers might assign one-third of the pairs to develop a "what we know" web for the essay structure, another third of the pairs to work with the KWL on the content, and the final third to create a grammar matrix. Each group would then make a presentation to the others or use an advanced jigsaw process to share their findings.

What is most important is that teachers' decisions are made in context: teachers consider class comfort and skill with cooperative learning, the content of the lesson, and the total amount of time for the lesson as they choose their strategies.

Stage 2: Generating Knowledge

In the second stage, teachers show students that there are multiple sources of information from which they can gather, process, and apply knowledge. Although teachers may not be the fountain of all knowledge dispensed in the classroom, they are the students' source for learning about effective tools for gathering information, such as graphic organizers.

For the standard-based history lesson, teachers may choose from several graphic organizers to help students gather information on the conflict and leadership content.

The simplest tool is an attribute web that groups of three or five students complete to gather information about different leaders. The matrix and the fishbone lend themselves to developing deeper student understanding, and the Venn diagram allows each group to review and compare two leaders.

When teachers select the fishbone, for example, they ask students to do first-story and second-story thinking in a single task. After teachers assign each group a historical leader and a conflict to analyze, students complete the fishbone:

1. Groups assign a member to be recorder, materials manager, searcher 1, searcher 2, and timekeeper. They review the responsibilities of each role.

2. Teacher and groups walk through the procedure for completing the organizer:

   • In the head of the fishbone, write the leader's name and the conflict he or she had to resolve.

   • On each major bone, write one cause of the conflict.

   • On the next set of bones, write examples from the group's research.

- Repeat the steps for the solutions used.
- Decide whether the solutions showed the leader to be effective and be prepared to explain why.

To help teachers evaluate the group's effectiveness, they might ask students to use the ranking ladder or a PMI organizer. If they use a PMI, teachers ask students to chart What were the pluses of this leader's decisions? What were the minuses? What questions do you have about the leadership in this conflict? It is appropriate to allot 60% of the lesson's total time to stage 2 of the lesson.

Stage 3: Transfer

The third stage, often overlooked, is essential in every lesson. In this stage, teachers mediate students' understanding of the lesson's key concepts. Student understanding grows best if teachers' questions mediate the meaning and the transfer possibilities of the lesson. A class-wide presentation of completed organizers heightens students' sense of accountability and motivation. Teachers can call on one or two groups to present their information and ideas to the class for each organizer in the lesson, or they can wait until the groups have finished and then call on each to respond to fat questions about the meanings of their investigations. To use fat questions, teachers give each group a fat launch question, such as these examples for this lesson:

Group 1: Tell us why you think your most effective leader succeeded.

Group 2: Tell us why you think the leader was effective.

Group 3: What weaknesses do you think hurt the leader's effectiveness?

Group 4: What questions do you want to ask your most effective leader about his or her decisions?

Group 5: What would you predict your most effective leader would do in resolving (some current conflict)?

With these starter or launch questions, teachers mediate the students' learning experience that began with the development of prior knowledge and has moved through processing with a graphic organizer. After a group presents its response to the class, teachers may ask follow-up and clarifying questions to ensure that all group members have a chance to respond. Then, teachers may involve the audience (the class) by asking them questions:

- How does this appraisal compare with _____?
- What interests you most about this leader's _____?
- Why do you think _____?

As well as mediating the students' understanding of the lesson's meaning, teachers need to mediate students' transfer of knowledge, skills, and achievement across the curriculum and beyond the school walls. Teachers might ask transfer mediating questions:

- What else are you studying (have you studied) where an understanding of a leader's effectiveness is important? Why do you think so?

- How can you use these criteria for today's world leaders? Why do you think so?

It is appropriate to use 25% of the lesson's total time to mediate meaning and transfer.

Stage 4: Assessment

In the final stage, teachers assess students' achievement in three elements: content, cooperation, and thinking. Every lesson does not need to assess all three elements, but, it is important that students learn to be accountable with at least one element in each lesson.

Assessing Content. Teachers can use any number of assessment approaches: an individual quiz, journal entry with a lead-in (e.g., I learned that a leader's role in resolving conflict included . . .), short essay (e.g., Explain why your leader was effective), or graphic organizer (e.g, Rank the characteristics of effectiveness on the ranking ladder and explain your top choice, or Make a T-chart showing what leadership effectiveness looks and sounds like). Students expect, and deserve, assessment tasks that align with lesson criteria and, more important, that test their individual learning. Learning may come from group collaboration, but assessment targets individual results. Teachers can return to the KWL to review the lesson with the class before assessing content individually. In fact, this activity can complete the KWL started by pairs in stage 1. By reestablishing the same pairs, students experience continuity with the initial activity when they generate their list of what they *learned* in the lesson. Teachers might conclude the review with a class list on the board and a mediated discussion of the meaning of the key concepts.

Assessing Cooperation. To assess cooperative behavior in the groups, teachers may ask students to reflect on how well they worked together during parts of the lesson. Informal task group strategies—such as the think-pair-share, business cards, we-bags, and I learned mailgrams—work well in assessing cooperation. Other strategies—such as log entries, social skill review, and role review—are also helpful when structured with Mrs. Potter's questions.

Assessing Thinking. Assessing thinking assessment starts with assessing the criterion of *fluency*: How many times did students make statements aligned to a specific thinking skill? For example, typical questions include: How long is the brainstorm list? How many predictions were accurate?

Teachers can assess individual thinking when they ask students to complete such statements as: I have improved my thinking in this lesson by . . . and To improve my thinking, I will . . . . Teachers may ask students to complete a PMI chart, a right angle thinking organizer, a ranking ladder, or entries in a journal to assess students' achievements. Teachers may give students an index card and ask them to write their names, the lesson title, and date on one side and, on the other side, list their answers to these stems: Three ways I used my thinking skills well in this lesson . . . and Three ways I will work to improve my thinking . . . .

Teachers may also use rubrics aligned to the specific thinking skill orproblem solving process used in the lesson` as a checklist for observations or ask students to self-assess their thinking skills. Teachers must also choose between structuring this opportunity to invite individual accountability (the I in BUILD), to enhance higher-order thinking (the B), or build on teamwork (U).

SUMMARY

Significant gains in student achievement are difficult to come by. However, the task is not impossible. First, teachers carefully plan for the integration of content, cooperation, and thinking into a coherent, power-packed lesson. Second, teachers carefully attend to which strategies are used in each stage of the design. Finally, teachers carefully infuse the four stages (prior knowledge, generate knowledge, transfer, and assessment) throughout the BUILD lesson. When teachers incorporate these elements in their lessons, they make the right choices for each student in their classroom and can readily see each and every student climb the achievement ladder.

BLUEPRINT

Elementary

Lesson

Codes 1SD
         6CL
         7OF
         8GH

Setting Up the
Scaffolding

Mammal Mania

Using a BUILD cooperative lesson planner (Figure 6.7), scan and select key elements for the lesson Mammal Mania. The BUILD acronym (see below) helps teachers systematically note specific lesson details, and the BUILD planner helps them choose the appropriate tools for the critical elements of a higher-order thinking/cooperative lesson (see example on next page; see Blackline C6.3 in Appendix C for a blackline master).

BUILD Acronym for Mammal Lesson

B – Requiring critical and creative thinking (brainstorming, inventing, performing) stretches the mind.

U – Establishing a group identity unites each team.

I – Assigned roles keep members accountable for tasks and learning.

L – Mrs. Potter's questions structure quality review.

D – Setting guidelines for students to accept others' ideas (DOVE Guidelines) enforces social skills. (**D**-Defer judgment; anything goes; **O**-Opt for original; different ideas; **V**-Vast number is needed; and **E**-Expand by piggybacking on other's ideas)

Mammal: Cooperative Lesson Planner

B	**U**	**I**	**L**	**D**	
Build in High-Order Thinking	**U**nite Teams	**I**nsist on Individual Learning	**L**ook Over & Discuss	**D**evelop Social Skills	
Problem Solving, Decision Making, Creative Ideation	*Build Trust & Teamwork*	*Insure Individual Learning & Responbility*	*Plan, Monitor & Evaluate*	*Communication, Leadership, Conflict Resolution*	
1 Critical and creative thinking	Bonding and group identity	Assigned roles	Goal setting	Paraphrase	I hear I see...
2 3-to-1 technique	Shared materials	Quiz	PMI	Affirm	That's a good idea
3 Problem solving	Single product	Random responses	Human graph	Clarify	Tell me more!
4 Decision making	Jigsaw	Individual application	Teacher observation sheet	Test options	What else?
5 Fat & Skinny Questions	Lottery	Individual grades	Student observer feedback	Sense tone	That feels ____
6 Application	Bonus points	Signature. I agree! I understand!	Success award	Encourage others	No put-downs!
7 Transfer within/across/into	Group grade	Round robin (Wraparound)	Log entry	Accept others' ideas	Set DOVE guidelines
8 Graphic organizers	Group reward	Homework	Individual transfer or application	T-chart	Looks like Sounds like
9 Metacognitive exercises	Consensus	Bonus points	Team ad	Disagree with ideas not people	Other point of view
10 Making metaphors	Extended projects	Expert jigsaw	Mrs. Potter's questions	Reach consensus	5 to fist

Next, select appropriate thinking skill(s) for the lesson from the list of micro-skills for thinking (see Figure 5.2 in chapter 5). Following is an illustration of one set of choices for the mammal mania lesson:

Micro-Skills

CRITICAL THINKING SKILLS	CREATIVE THINKING SKILLS
1. attributing	1. brainstorming
2. comparing and contrasting	2. visualizing
3. classifying	3. personifying
4. sequencing	4. inventing
5. prioritizing	5. associating relationships
6. drawing conclusions	6. inferring
7. determining cause and effect	7. generalizing
8. analyzing for bias	8. predicting
9. analyzing for assumptions	9. hypothesizing
10. solving for analogies	10. making analogies
11. evaluating	11. dealing with ambiguity and paradox
12. decision making	12. problem solving

Working the
Crew

Using the chosen micro-skills and the BUILD guide for designing the lesson, incorporate the specific components into the plan. For example, in preparation for a spring field trip to the zoo, which is a culminating activity for the mammal unit in science, a teacher created the following lesson using the selected elements.

STAGE 1: PRIOR KNOWLEDGE

The class brainstorms an attribute web for mammals.

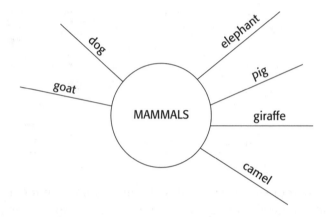

Then, students turn to a partner and recall the critical attributes of mammals, checking to ensure that all listed animals fit the definition.

STAGE 2: GENERATE KNOWLEDGE

The teacher arranges students into groups of three and assigns the roles of recorder/illustrator, animal trainer, and actor. Students review the responsibilities of the roles.

The teacher explains to the groups that their first task is to select an animal from the unit and to invent a team name that signifies their mammal selection. A group name creates a group identity. For example, a group name might be the Elephant Explorers.

Then, the teacher tells students that they are to use a strategy, called That's a Good Idea. The strategy builds on the social skill, accepting others' ideas, and a creative thinking skill, personifying an animal that can talk and behave like a person. Tell students the goal is to use their mammal to create a fictional character (an animal) that can behave in human ways. They must brainstorm at least six improvements to add to their mammal.

Here is how they proceed: The *first* person personifies the mammal by giving it a human trait (e.g., The elephant can ride a bike).

The *second* person tells why that trait is a good idea (e.g., That's a good idea because he can get around faster) and then gives another trait for the elephant (e.g., He can also talk).

The *third* person tells why the previous trait is a good idea (e.g., That's a good idea because he can communicate with others) and then adds another idea (e.g., He flies kites too).

Continue around the group until all members have praised another's idea *and* added a trait to the animal. (Let students know they may pass but they cannot say: The same thing he said.) The recorder writes the traits and praises on a group chart.

After the recorder has listed all the suggested improvements, the illustrator draws the animal in a way that shows the personified characteristics.

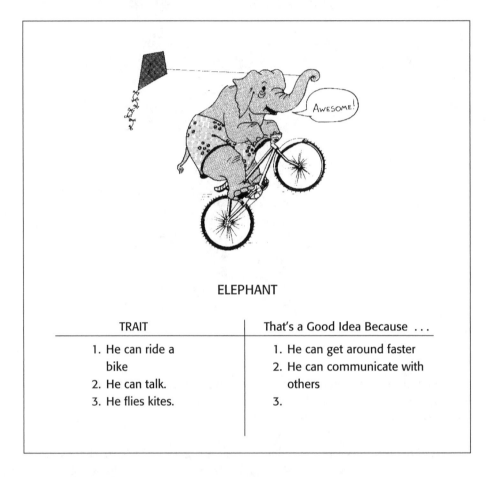

ELEPHANT

TRAIT	That's a Good Idea Because ...
1. He can ride a bike	1. He can get around faster
2. He can talk.	2. He can communicate with others
3. He flies kites.	3.

For the final task, the animal trainer and the animal actor perform a brief skit incorporating the various human characteristics. These performances can be done for another small group or for the whole class.

STAGE 3: TRANSFER

For affective processing, ask students to become the animal. Ask them to imagine the actions and feelings of the mammal. Then, in their groups of three, have them finish this statement:

I want to be more like (animal) because . . .

For social skill processing, have students discuss why it is important to add ideas to the group and to accept others' ideas.

Reflecting on
the Design

STAGE 4: ASSESSMENT

For cognitive processing, have students talk about the thinking skill *personifying* and answer these questions:

> What was difficult about trying to change the animal into a human-like character?

> Why is using That's A Good Idea (responses in turn) a good idea?

For metacognitive processing, have the groups talk through Mrs. Potter's questions:

> What were we supposed to do?

> What did we do well?

> What should we do differently?

> Do we need any help?

(For a blackline master of Mrs. Potter's questions, see blackline C4.10 in Appendix C.)

# # #

BLUEPRINT
Middle School
Lesson

Codes 1SD
6CL
7OF
9QCA

Setting Up the
Scaffolding

Metric Matters

Using a BUILD cooperative lesson planner (Figure 6.7), scan and select key elements for the lesson Metric Matters. The BUILD acronym (see below) helps teachers systematically note specific lesson details, and the BUILD planner helps them choose the appropriate tools for the critical elements of a higher-order thinking/cooperative lesson (see example on next page; see Blackline C6.3 in Appendix C for a blackline master).

BUILD Acronym for Metric Lesson

B – A graphic organizer creates a higher-order thinking lesson.

U – Bonus points in groups unite the teams.

I – A wraparound ensures the individual learning process.

L – Answering What? So what? Now what? forces students to look back on the lesson.

D – Encouragement is targeted for social skill building.

BUILD : Cooperative Lesson Planner

	B Build in High-Order Thinking	**U** Unite Teams	**I** Insist on Individual Learning	**L** Look Over & Discuss	**D** Develop Social Skills	
	Problem Solving, Decision Making, Creative Ideation	*Build Trust & Teamwork*	*Insure Individual Learning & Responsibility*	*Plan, Monitor & Evaluate*	*Communication, Leadership, Conflict Resolution*	
1	Critical and creative thinking	Bonding and group identity	Assigned roles	Goal setting	Paraphrase	I hear I see...
2	3-to-1 technique	Shared materials	Quiz	PMI	Affirm	That's a good idea
3	Problem solving	Single product	Random responses	Human graph	Clarify	Tell me more!
4	Decision making	Jigsaw	Individual application	Teacher observation sheet	Test options	What else?
5	Fat & Skinny Questions	Lottery	Individual grades	Student observer feedback	Sense tone	That feels ____
6	Application	Bonus points	Signature. I agree! I understand!	Success award	Encourage others	No put-downs!
7	Transfer within/across/into	Group grade	Round robin (Wraparound)	Log entry	Accept others' ideas	Set DOVE guidelines
8	Graphic organizers	Group reward	Homework	Individual transfer or application	T-chart	Looks like Sounds like
9	Metacognitive exercises	Consensus	Bonus points	Team ad	Disagree with ideas not people	Other point of view
10	Making metaphors	Extended projects	Expert jigsaw	Mrs. Potter's questions	Reach consensus	5 to fist

Next, select appropriate micro-skills for thinking from the list (see Figure 5.2 from chapter 5). Following is an illustration of one set of choices for the metric matters lesson:

Micro-Skills

CRITICAL THINKING SKILLS

1. attributing
2. comparing and contrasting
3. classifying
4. sequencing
5. prioritizing
6. drawing conclusions
7. determining cause and effect
8. analyzing for bias
9. analyzing for assumptions
10. solving for analogies
11. evaluating

12. decision making

CREATIVE THINKING SKILLS

1. brainstorming
2. visualizing
3. personifying
4. inventing
5. associating relationships
6. inferring
7. generalizing
8. predicting
9. hypothesizing
10. making analogies
11. dealing with ambiguity and paradox

12. problem solving

The following lesson is described—using the selected elements—as it might occur based on the Sharan and Sharan (1976) group investigation model.

Sharan and Sharan Group Investigation Model

Step 1:   Posing the big question and forming groups by interest

Step 2:   Identifying the inquiry problem and planning how to research

Step 3:   Dividing up the work and gathering information

Step 4:   Synthesizing, summarizing, and writing the report

Step 5:   Presenting by groups and evaluating

STAGE 1: PRIOR KNOWLEDGE

Tell students that they will use a cooperative strategy—encouraging others—as they use the metric system in two subject areas. The focus for thinking skills will be brainstorming, prioritizing, problem solving, and transferring.

Begin by asking the class to fill in a graphic organizer (such as a mind map) with various aspects of metric matters that groups know or may want to investigate. Allow students to brainstorm many ideas.

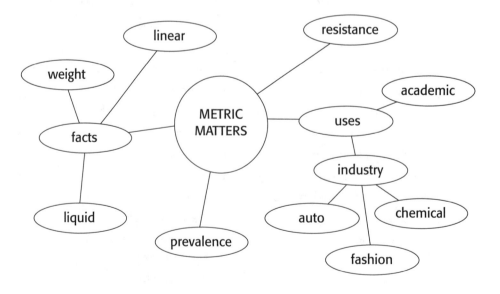

STAGE 2: GENERATING KNOWLEDGE

Then, apply the Sharan and Sharan group investigation model to shape the lesson.

Step 1: Pose the big question and form groups by topics of interest. Ask students to review the mind map on metrics that the class created and to arrange themselves in groups of three according to their specific topics of interest.

Step 2: Identify the inquiry problem and plan how to research. Instruct groups to discuss ways to gather information. Suggest library resources, primary resources such as interviews, and other media possibilities. Also, recommend the librarian as a quick resource.

Step 3: Divide the work and gather information. Tell students to use the jigsaw model to gather information. Groups are to divide the research into pieces, and each member is to take a piece of the puzzle to complete. Ask groups to set a date and time to reconvene with their completed parts. Ask a checker to see that all members contribute.

Step 4: Synthesize, summarize, and prepare the presentation. You may wish or need to instruct students in the refinements of the jigsaw model. That is, you may need to give group members definite ways to teach each other about their particular parts as each member contributes to the whole. Share these techniques with students as they prioritize, share, synthesize, and summarize information:

Ways To Teach Another

tell

model

demonstrate

draw

give examples

use visuals

make analogies

quiz

Emphasize that each member needs a thorough understanding of each separate piece; otherwise, their group and individual syntheses may be fragmented and superficial. High-performing groups create a synergy so that the final piece may be far richer than any work done by a single student.

Reflecting on
the Design

Step 5: Present and evaluate. First, tell student groups to use problem solving to create a final presentation that demonstrates how the metric matters they investigated can be applied across at least two content lessons. Groups can present to another group or to the whole class. Give bonus points to each group member who actually applies the idea in another class. (Require proof from the other teacher.)

STAGE 3: TRANSFER

For affective processing, ask students to discuss their feelings about the group investigation jigsaw. Do a quick wraparound with this stem: I felt . . . .

For social skill processing, have students talk about how they encouraged each other.

STAGE 4: ASSESSMENT

(*Note:* This is a continuation of Sharan and Sharan's fifth step, evaluate.)

For cognitive processing, have students discuss the pros and cons of the group investigation process that they just used.

For metacognitive processing, ask students to discuss the "So what?" aspects of group investigation. How can they parlay this model into other situations— "Now what"?

# # #

Codes 2SN
6CL
7OF
9QCA

Setting Up the
Scaffolding

In Defense of
Human Rights

Using a BUILD cooperative lesson planner (Figure 6.7), scan and select key elements for the lesson In Defense of Human Rights. The BUILD acronym (see below) helps teachers systematically note specific lesson details, and the BUILD planner helps them choose the appropriate tools for the critical elements of a higher-order thinking/cooperative lesson (see example on next page; see Blackline C6.3 in Appendix C for a blackline master).

BUILD Acronym for Human Rights

B – Application of the group investigation information builds in higher-order thinking.

U – The jigsaw unites the members as they rely on each other to complete the assignment.

I – Individual criteria ensures individual learning by forcing students to state their reasoning.

L – PMI allows time to look over and discuss all aspects of the lesson.

D – Reaching consensus gives students practice in using their social skills.

BUILD : Cooperative Lesson Planner

	Build in High-Order Thinking	**U**nite Teams	**I**nsist on Individual Learning	**L**ook Over & Discuss	**D**evelop Social Skills	
	Problem Solving, Decision Making, Creative Ideation	*Build Trust & Teamwork*	*Insure Individual Learning & Reponsibility*	*Plan, Monitor & Evaluate*	*Communication, Leadership, Conflict Resolution*	
1	Critical and creative thinking	Bonding and group identity	Assigned roles	Goal setting	Paraphrase	I hear I see...
2	3-to-1 technique	Shared materials	Quiz	PMI	Affirm	That's a good idea
3	Problem solving	Single product	Random responses	Human graph	Clarify	Tell me more!
4	Decision making	Jigsaw	Individual application	Teacher observation sheet	Test options	What else?
5	Fat & Skinny Questions	Lottery	Individual grades	Student observer feedback	Sense tone	That feels ____
6	Application	Bonus points	Signature. I agree! I understand!	Success award	Encourage others	No put-downs!
7	Transfer within/across/into	Group grade	Round robin (Wraparound)	Log entry	Accept others' ideas	Set DOVE guidelines
8	Graphic organizers	Group reward	Homework	Individual transfer or application	T-chart	Looks like Sounds like
9	Metacognitive exercises	Consensus	Bonus points	Team ad	Disagree with ideas not people	Other point of view
10	Making metaphors	Extended projects	Expert jigsaw	Mrs. Potter's questions	Reach consensus	5 to fist

Next, select appropriate strategies from the list of micro-skills for thinking (see Figure 5.2 from chapter 5). Following is an illustration of one set of choices for the In Defense of Human Rights lesson.

Micro-Skills

CRITICAL THINKING SKILLS	CREATIVE THINKING SKILLS
1. attributing	1. brainstorming
2. comparing and contrasting	2. visualizing
3. classifying	3. personifying
4. sequencing	4. inventing
5. prioritizing	5. associating relationships
6. drawing conclusions	6. inferring
7. determining cause and effect	7. generalizing
8. analyzing for bias	8. predicting
9. analyzing for assumptions	9. hypothesizing
10. solving for analogies	10. making analogies
11. evaluating	11. dealing with ambiguity and paradox
12. decision making	12. problem solving

You may want to use the Sharan and Sharan (1976) group investigation model for this lesson. The model is shown below.

Sharan and Sharan Group Investigation Model

Step 1: Posing the big question and forming groups by interest

Step 2: Identifying the inquiry problem and planning how to research

Step 3: Dividing up the work and gathering information

Step 4: Synthesizing, summarizing, and writing the report

Step 5: Presenting by groups and evaluating

Working the Crew

STAGE 1: PRIOR KNOWLEDGE

Tell students that they will use a cooperative group to investigate the topic In Defense of Human Rights. Each group will present a five-minute snippet to the class that delineates a particular right of human beings that has been abused throughout history. The scenarios are to project an empathetic viewpoint. Humor may be used. Good taste and appropriateness will be part of the grading criteria.

After the presentations, each student will apply the information presented by writing a paper on a human rights position other than the one researched by his or her group. In other words, students are to gather information from the other groups' presentations in order to formulate their individual positions on human rights issues.

Step 1: Pose the big question and form groups by topics of interest. As a class, brainstorm a number of human rights issues (e.g., the US Bill of Rights, right to bear children, choose own spouse, hostages, treatment of mentally ill, censorship, woman's rights, POWs, homeless, free speech, citizenship, assembly, discrimination, free elections). Write the list on the board. Ask students to form groups of 3–4 students according to topics of interest drawn from the board. Suggest that each team create a group name to designate its topic.

STAGE 2: GENERATE KNOWLEDGE

Step 2: Identify the inquiry problem and plan how to research. Using the jigsaw model, teams discuss and plan their research procedures. Be sure the groups include a variety of sources for gathering information and visualizing past abuses of human rights.

Step 3: Divide up the work and gather information. Ask group members to take individual responsibility for specific pieces of the whole project. Have group checkers collect completed assignments and data from the various members. Have groups set a date, time, and place to share their various segments.

Step 4: Synthesize, summarize, and prepare a report. Student teams reassemble with their respective pieces of information. In the jigsaw format, as each person shares his or her piece of information care is taken in how that sharing is done. This is really the teachable moment, when each member of the group teaches the other members of the group. Remind students that each member is responsible for learning all the pieces of information as they fit them together into a total picture, their presentations.

STAGE 3: TRANSFER

Step 5: Presentations by groups. After reaching consensus on a format for presenting, have student groups present their In Defense of Human Rights pieces to the class. Require students to use an observation sheet as a reference prompter when they evaluate the information and write their papers. Or consider videotaping the presentations.

STAGE 4: ASSESSMENT

(*Note:* This is a continuation of Sharan and Sharan's fifth step, evaluate.)

For affective processing, ask groups to discuss this question: How did your feelings influence your performance?

To process the social skills, ask students to describe an instance when their behavior infringed on someone else's rights.

Reflecting on
the Design

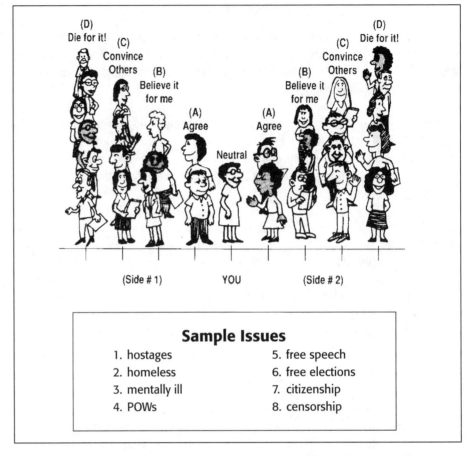

Sample Issues

1. hostages
2. homeless
3. mentally ill
4. POWs

5. free speech
6. free elections
7. citizenship
8. censorship

For cognitive processing, use the human graph to take readings on the issues discussed in this lesson (see sample human graph and issues above). Have students display their intensity of feelings using the ratings *agree, believe it, convince others, die for it.* Then ask students to evaluate their thinking by stating their individual criteria for their decisions on other topics (see a sample list of topics below).

For metacognitive processing, evaluate Sharan and Sharan's group investigation model with a PMI chart. (See Blackline C5.5 in Appendix C for a blackline master.)

GROUP INVESTIGATION	
PLUS (+)	
MINUS (–)	
INTERESTING (?)	

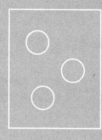

FORMING

PERFORMING

NORMING

CHAPTER 7

Phase IV

STORMING

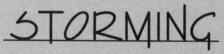

Level 1

How Do I Keep Them
Thinking in the
High-Achieving Classroom?

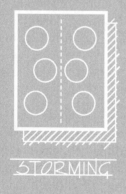

STORMING

CONFORMING

in the Cooperative Classroom

HOW DO I KEEP THEM THINKING IN THE HIGH-ACHIEVING CLASSROOM?

We have in our thinkery, a well-experienced power to think our-selves out of trials and difficulties.

–F. R Feland

Draft

In the *storming* phase, students work up a storm to achieve high expectations in the high-challenge classroom. They accept increasingly complex intellectual and collaborative challenges and recognize that increased rigor is required in their thinking.

During this phase, teachers introduce a hierarchy of complex thinking behaviors. This hierarchy (or taxonomy) of cognitive behavior begins with micro-skills, compounds into macro-processes, and culminates in metacognitive behavior.

COGNITIVE RESEARCH

Cognitive research on complexity in thinking falls into two categories: cognition and metacognition (or reflection). In the early 1980s, cognitive research focused on explicit instruction on thinking skills. This research fostered the thinking skills movement. At the same time, research about reading focused on teaching students to practice metacognition—thinking strategically about how one thinks. Metacognition emerged not only as a driving force in teaching reading, but also as a mirroring technique that helped learners reflect on all aspects of their own thinking and behavior. Subsequently, the metacognitive strand sparked additional theory and research on the transfer of learning.

Cognition

A number of experts in cognition suggest that thinking skills should be explicitly taught. Costa, in *Developing Minds* (1985a, 2002), pulls together these beliefs about explicit thinking skills:

1. Thinking most often is taught indirectly, but a direct approach is needed.

2. Learning how to think is not an automatic by-product of studying certain subjects.

3. Students will not learn to think better simply by being asked to think about a subject or topic.

4. Students do not learn how to engage in critical thinking by themselves.

5. Competent critical thinking is not an incidental outcome of instruction directed toward, or that appears to be directed toward, other ends.

6. Thinking skills instruction must be direct and systematic prior to, during, and following students' introduction to and use of the skills in the classroom.

Researchers debate whether explicit thinking skills should be taught separately or infused into the existing subject area curriculum. There are, of course, pros and cons for each side (Figure 7.1).

Explicit Thinking Skills

	PROS	CONS
Thinking infused in content	• Easy transfer • Enhances content	• Teachers may be unskilled in the teaching of thinking skills
Thinking taught separately	• Guarantees these will be a spot and slot for thinking • Targeted to tests and grade levels, therefore teachers will teach thinking	• Takes more time • No transfer

Figure 7.1

Blueprints takes a middle path between teaching the skills separately and infusing them in the content. *Blueprints* sticks to the middle path and places a strong focus on the transfer of learning for all children. The infused model eases the students' way for fruitful transfer, creative application, and relevant student use throughout the curriculum. By itself, the separated model seems to reinforce students' perceptions that curriculum consists of unconnected little boxes of content. In other words, mathematics is not art, art is not science, and thinking is not any of these—the curricula are fragmented. Feuerstein (1980) and others support a combination of both explicit thinking skill instruction and subsequent application to curricular content. By bridging skill instruction and content application, teachers foster strong transfer of student learning. This transfer, in turn, helps students develop deep understanding of the thinking processes for future, ongoing applications on their own.

Metacognition—Thinking About Thinking

According to Swartz and Perkins (1989), metacognition refers to knowledge about, awareness of, and control over one's own mind and thinking. Costa (1985a, 2002) calls this "thinking about thinking." Marzano and Arredondo (1986) also speak of awareness and control over one's own thinking.

Brown (1978) describes the metacognitive processes in relation to reading. Brown's description of good and poor readers illustrate what is meant by metacognition:

- The good reader reads and reads and reads and, suddenly, hears a little voice saying, I don't know what I just read. The reader has read and spoken the words on the page in her mind, but in a "word-calling" sense; she has only read the words but has not grasped their meaning. Suddenly, she becomes aware of this deficit and realizes she has lost contact with the context of the text. Her mind signals her to adapt a recovery strategy—reread the beginning of the paragraph, recall a thought, scan the text for key words, and so forth.
- The poor reader reads and reads and reads and never realizes that she is not understanding what she is reading. She does not notice her lack of comprehension because she has never gotten meaning from text. She says the words in her mind, but she is a not reading in the real sense of reading.

Learning to understand and articulate one's own mental processes is a necessary link to fruitful transfer. Costa (1984) suggests that metacognition has three parts: the ability to know what you know, know what you do not know, and wonder why you are doing what you are doing. When processing metacognitively, students are aware of their own thoughts, strategies, feeling, and actions and how they affect others (Costa and Kallick 2000). They become aware of their own thinking (what goes on inside their heads) prior to, during, and after a learning activity. In the classroom, metacognitive processing implies planning, monitoring, and evaluating learning activities (Figure 7.2).

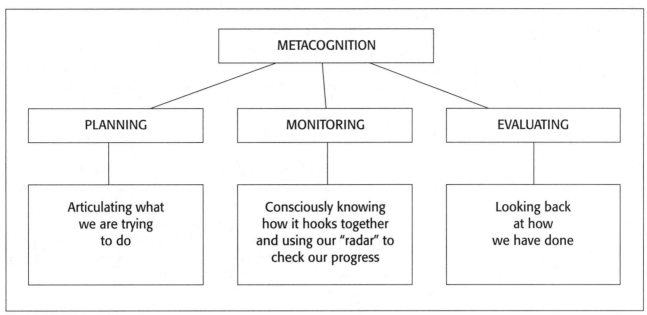

Figure 7.2

Swartz and Perkins (1989) gauged the sophistication of thinking by four increasingly metacognitive levels: tacit, aware, strategic, and reflective (Figure 7.3).

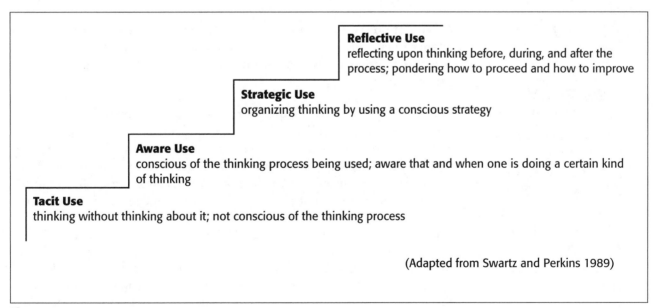

Figure 7.3

Whimbey's (1975, 1977) paired-partner think-aloud model demonstrates all four levels of metacognition. In this strategy, a problem solver thinks aloud as he or she works through a situation while the monitor cues the thinking aloud with specific questions or prompts. Thus, instead of *tacitly* solving the problem, unaware of the strategies used, students become *aware* of their thinking at a conscious level. In addition, over time, the problem solver and the monitor both map out *strategic* use of problem-solving patterns. *Reflective* use is inherent in the think-aloud technique.

Teachers can use metacognitive *prompts* to help students monitor and direct their own thinking. Metacognitive questions teach students about thinking and promote the kind of metaphorical thoughts, generalizations, and mindful abstractions that form powerful bridges for complex transfer (Perkins and Salomon 1988). Beyer (1987) elaborates on a cueing technique to prompt metacognition and suggests teachers use the following questions to foster metacognitive behavior in students:

- What am I doing?
- Why am I doing it?
- What other way can I do it?
- How does it work? Can I do it again or another way?
- How would I help someone else do it?

Some additional lead-ins are:

- How is _____ like _____?
- I wish I'd known this when _____.
- Next time, I am going to . . . .

The questions and lead-ins may be discussed within the group or reflected on individually in a log entry. These and similar questions encourage students to examine their own thinking and behavior in ways that foster generalization.

Mrs. Potter's questions (Figure 7.4) ask the standard metacognitive questions that promote reflective thinking and foster future applications. Teachers can use these questions repeatedly to help students process their thinking during cooperative learning tasks in the classroom. When the questions are posted on the board, students have a constant reminder to use metacognition and transfer. The questions can easily become part of the processing that follows a cooperative task. (A blackline master of Mrs. Potter's questions, Blackline C4.10, is available in Appendix C.)

Beyer (1988) suggests modeling direct instruction of a thinking skill and using thinking guides to promote planning, monitoring, and evaluating. Students can use Figure 7.5 to assess their own behavior. The tool is a strategy based on de Bono's (1973) PMI cognitive organizer. Students look at the affective with the PMI, the cognitive with their answers, and the metacognitive with questions for processing their thinking. This evaluation ties directly to the learning situation.

Mrs. Potter's Questions

1. What were you expected to do?

2. In this assignment, what did you do well?

3. If you had to do this task over, what would you do differently?

4. What help do you need from me?

Figure 7.4

Three Levels of Processing

Affective: How did it feel?

P (+) Pluses	
M (-) Minuses	
I (?) Interesting	

Cognitive: Assess your answers and/or strategies:

> What answer did you get?
> What else?
> Tell me more.
> Give an example.
> Please illustrate.

Metacognitive: Why bother? How can I use this?

> Can I duplicate?
> Can I replicate?
> Can I integrate?
> Can I map?
> Can I innovate?

Figure 7.5

The evidence is clear that explicit attention to the metacognitive—the stuff beyond the cognitive answers—promotes transfer and application of knowledge, skills, concepts, and attitudes in novel situations.

Csikszentmihalyi (1990) takes metacognition to a higher level and talks about a "state of flow" in which the learner experiences elements of enjoyment, such as a challenging activity that requires skill, the merging of action and awareness, clear goals and feedback, concentration on the task at hand, the paradox of control, the loss of self-consciousness, and the transformation of time. The "merging of action and awareness" is a metacognitive state in which the learner is aware of "the positive aspects of human experience—joy, creativity, the process of total involvement with life" (p. xi).

Teachers are now armed with research findings that report the efficacy of cognitive and metacognitive tools in today's classrooms:

- Teachers make the difference (Haycock 1998a).
- Schools make a difference (Edmonds and Frederickson 1979).
- Intelligence is modifiable (Feuerstein 1980).
- Learners can monitor and control their own performance (Brown 1978).
- Learners are active, strategic, planful, and constructive (Anderson, et al. 1985).

Specs

In the storming phase, students are ready to learn explicit thinking skills such as comparing, predicting, and classifying and to apply these skills to more holistic processes such as problem solving. As students become skilled in specific thinking strategies, they practice using the skills in various content and in real-world problems. Finally, students reflect on the micro-skills and macro-processes as they begin to transfer these ideas in purposeful ways (Figure 7.6).

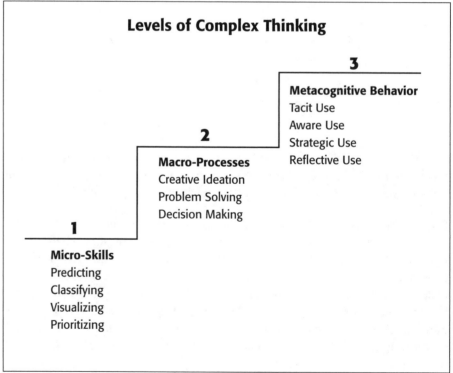

Figure 7.6

MICRO-SKILLS

Micro-skills encompass a spectrum of explicit thinking skills. Some micro-skills, labeled *critical thinking skills,* require mental processing that is *analytical and/or evaluative in nature.* Others, labeled as *creative thinking skills,* trigger mental processing that is *generative or productive* in nature. Both critical and creative thinking skills support problem solving and decision making. An extensive list of typical micro-skills, critical and creative, is shown in Figure 7.7. Most skills are embedded in school curricula. In the *Blueprints* classroom, teachers stop assuming all students will "get" these skills by osmosis; instead, they select those that will most benefit student achievement and teach each one explicitly. With explicit instruction in the micro-skills, students build a repertoire for *selective* use when groups attack the tasks assigned in their course work.

Micro-Skills

Critical Thinking Skills	**Creative Thinking Skills**
1. attributing	1. brainstorming
2. comparing and contrasting	2. visualizing
3. classifying	3. personifying
4. sequencing	4. inventing
5. prioritizing	5. associating relationships
6. drawing conclusions	6. inferring
7. determining cause and effect	7. generalizing
8. analyzing for bias	8. predicting
9. analyzing for assumptions	9. hypothesizing
10. solving for analogies	10. making analogies
11. evaluating	11. dealing with ambiguity and paradox
12. Decision making	12. problem solving

Figure 7.7

There is no magic way to teach a micro-skill. Whether the teacher elects a direct instruction lesson design, an inquiry design, or an embedded design, a micro-skill lesson follows the same stages as a sound content lesson: prior knowledge, generate knowledge, transfer, and assessment.

The Four Stages of a Cooperative Lesson
1. Prior Knowledge
2. Generate Knowledge
3. Transfer
4. Assessment

Stage 1: Prior Knowledge

Teachers first identify the thinking skill students need to learn in order to complete a content lesson. Then they check students' prior knowledge of the skill. Take, for instance, the micro-skill, comparing. A teacher might elicit synonyms for the word *comparing* by asking students to describe what they do when they compare two items. (The teacher might show a sample such as two pencils with slight differences to help students focus on comparing.) While students explain how they compare items, the teacher asks students to identify as many synonyms as possible from their comments. The teacher lists the words on the board, highlighting words such as *alike, likeness, same, similar,* and so forth. Next, the teacher might use a think-pair-share activity in which students identify ways in which the sample items fit these words. Also, the pairs pick out other items in the room that fit these words and explain to each other how the items fit. Finally, the teacher elicits multiple responses from the pairs and then summarizes their ideas to create a definition of the term *compare*.

Stage 2: Generate Knowledge

In this stage, teachers point out how frequently students compare items in their schoolwork. They give an example from recent classroom experiences such as two countries in geography, two cultures in world history, two elements in chemistry, or two settings in a story. Then, a teacher might select two students to stand before the class and instruct groups of three to list the "samenesses" that they can see between the two students. After listing what students can see, the teacher asks the trios to make a second list of positive "samenesses" that they also *know* about the two students but which are not observable (e.g., both have a brother, both like to help people, both live on Washington Street). The teacher concludes the session by discussing why both lists are important.

Stage 3: Transfer

To promote transfer of this thinking skill, teachers might ask students to think of other times they have compare objects or found "sameness." They can do this by using a simple jigsaw activity. First, the entire class brainstorms a master list. Then the class forms groups of three and each group selects one item from the master list, makes a chart showing both the observable and the non-observable similarities, and explains why it is important to note both kinds of similarities in the context of the study. Next, students use a simple rubric to measure each similarity. When the groups are finished with their comparisons, the teacher selects three students at random to report similarities to the class. After the reports, the teacher asks members of the non-reporting groups to explain why it was important to include observable and non-observerable similarities.

Stage 4: Assessment

Teachers wrap up the skill instruction with an assessment on *comparing*. For example, they might ask each trio to use a rubric to assess how well the group performed their task of comparing and to use Mrs. Potter's questions to evaluate how well the members worked together. They might ask a team member in each group to record the group's answers to the questions and then to prepare a written summary of the answers. The teacher collects these answers before asking for some groups to share that did not make public representations in Stage 3. Finally, a teacher might conclude with this round robin: About comparing, I have learned . . . . (This sample lesson takes about 40 minutes.)

Students benefit most from explicit skill instruction when teachers introduce the skill at the beginning of a unit in which the skill is central to unit tasks. For instance, a standard in the literature curriculum for the year might be: Students will know how to *compare* characters in a short story. Because comparing has been identified as an important concept in the standard, teachers should not assume that all students know how to compare. Rather, they should take the time—40 minutes in this case—to conduct an explicit lesson on comparing. This gives students a concentrated introduction to the concept before they launch into the major literature lesson. The explicit skill instruction prepares students to transfer what they know about comparing to the literature lesson.

MACRO-PROCESSES

Although micro-skills are distinguished here to clarify and emphasize each skill, it is unlikely that the mind uses micro-skills in separate and disparate procedures. When students are proficient using the micro-skills, they process combinations simultaneously as they navigate a particular situation or problem. For example, they may brainstorm and prioritize simultaneously.

When students combine micro-skills either in series or use micro-skills simultaneously, they enter the next hierarchical level of thinking, *macro-processes*. Macro-processes include critically analyzing a problem, brainstorming alternatives, setting criteria, evaluating choices, and deciding on solutions.

When they string together the micro-skills for thinking, teachers parlay discrete and separate mental procedures into the macro-processes needed for problem solving. For example, teachers might ask students to use a Venn diagram so that they use the micro-skills of creative and critical thinking to solve problems and make decisions.

METACOGNITIVE BEHAVIOR

At the highest level of the cognitive hierarchy—beyond the cognitive in its purest sense—is metacognitive behavior. After students have used micro-skills and macro-processes, they need to practice metacognition—thinking about how they approached and solved the problem. That is, when students engage in metacognitive behavior, they focus on thinking *about* their thinking, not about the problem itself. This "ah ha" process helps students talk about and make sense of their learning and behavior (Figure 7.8).

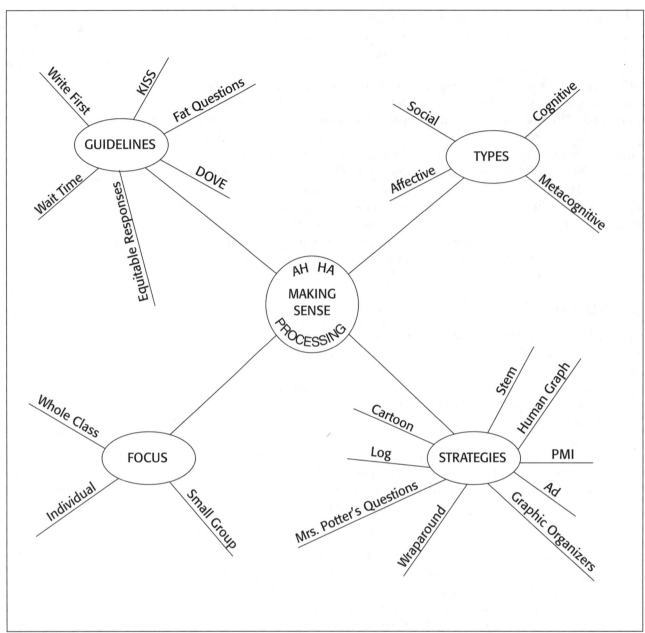

Figure 7.8

For example, when students recite a memorized piece, they are demonstrating cognitive processing. However, when they begin to explain *how* they memorized the piece, they are thinking metacognitively. This metacognitive level promotes transfer through awareness and discussion. Students can use the Are You Cooperating Today? poster (Figure 7.9) to distinguish various types of reflective processing about cooperation.

Students need to go beyond thinking metacognitively about cooperation and think metacognitively about thinking skills and processes (Figure 7.10). In a rich investigation project, students have excellent opportunities for metacognition. Teachers can organize rich investigation projects

Figure 7.9

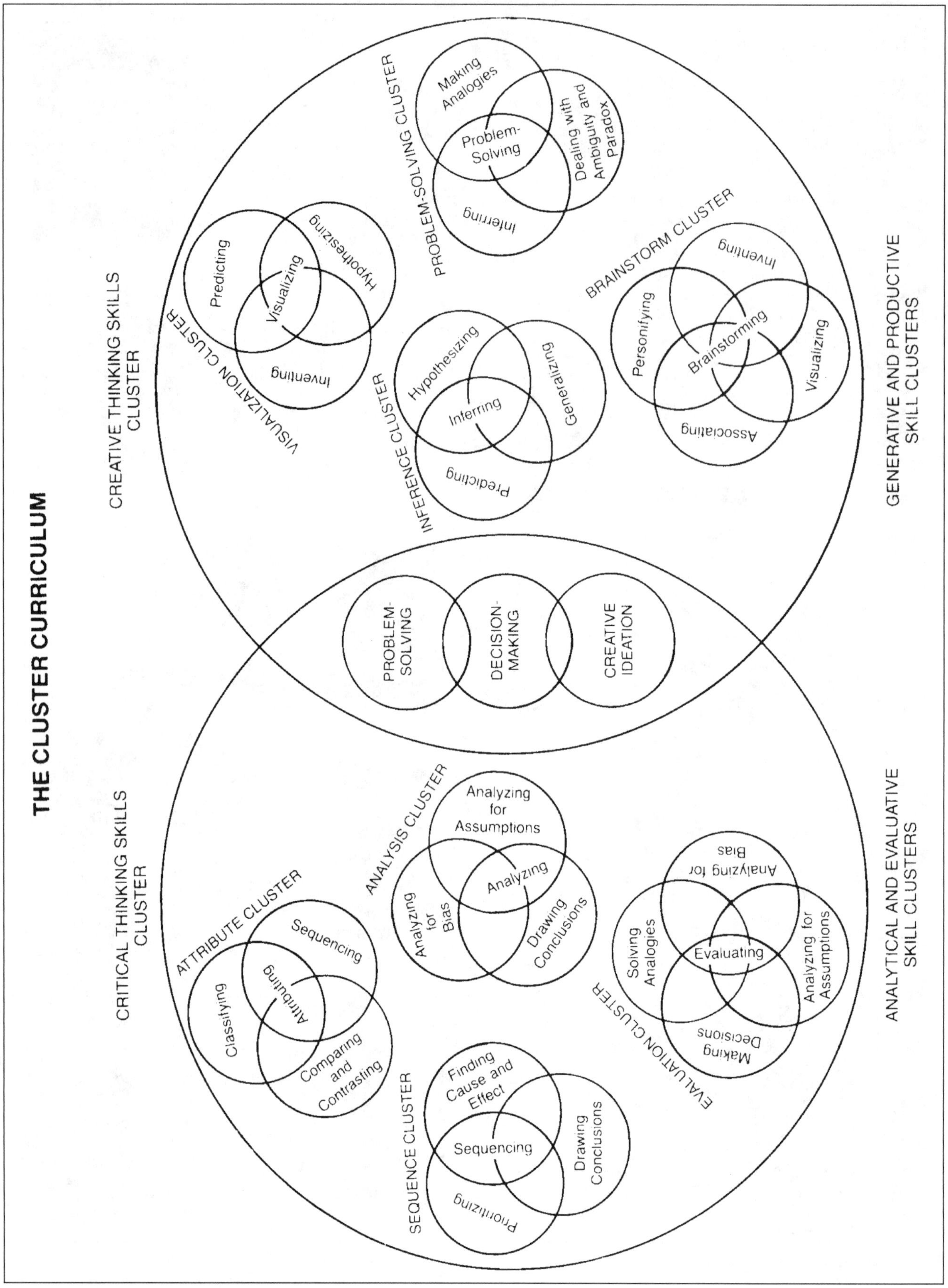
THE CLUSTER CURRICULUM
CRITICAL THINKING SKILLS CLUSTER
ATTRIBUTE CLUSTER
Classifying
Attributing
Sequencing
Comparing and Contrasting
SEQUENCE CLUSTER
Finding Cause and Effect
Sequencing
Prioritizing
Drawing Conclusions
ANALYSIS CLUSTER
Analyzing for Assumptions
Analyzing
Analyzing for Bias
Drawing Conclusions
EVALUATION CLUSTER
Solving Analogies
Analyzing for Bias
Evaluating
Analyzing for Assumptions
Making Decisions
ANALYTICAL AND EVALUATIVE SKILL CLUSTERS
PROBLEM-SOLVING
DECISION-MAKING
CREATIVE IDEATION
CREATIVE THINKING SKILLS CLUSTER
VISUALIZATION CLUSTER
Predicting
Visualizing
Hypothesizing
Inventing
INFERENCE CLUSTER
Hypothesizing
Inferring
Generalizing
Predicting
PROBLEM-SOLVING CLUSTER
Making Analogies
Problem-Solving
Dealing with Ambiguity and Paradox
Inferring
BRAINSTORM CLUSTER
Inventing
Personifying
Brainstorming
Visualizing
Associating
GENERATIVE AND PRODUCTIVE SKILL CLUSTERS

Figure 7.10

in a variety of ways, both simple and complex. For example, a project may be as simple as creating a collage of a historic period, a literacy theme, or scientific principle; writing a children's storybook, a short story, or an essay replicating a famous author's work; conducting a laboratory experiment; or going on a field trip. Or, a project might be as complex as the Design a Decade lesson at the end of this chapter.

Both students and teachers learn that doing by itself is low on the achievement influence scale. Collecting bears for a bear theme, building a model fort for a history unit, or painting a classroom collage to brighten the room are nice activities, but they are *not* rich investigations. A rich investigation requires these elements:

- cooperative teamwork,
- application of micro-skills and macro-processes,
- application of social skills,
- metacognitive reflection,
- alignment to standards and curriculum, and
- assessment of content.

In contrast to an activity project, when students participate in a rich investigation project that meets these criteria, they engage their intellects in a vigorous curricula over a protracted period of time. As students move toward the macro-processes of problem solving, their motivation for cooperation is elevated. The metacognitive stage explicitly brings forward students' mental procedures and guarantees future application and transfer across content and into life situations. All three levels of higher-order thinking—micro-skills, macro-process, metacognitive reflection—are needed if groups are to continue successfully in the cooperative classroom. Complex tasks embedded with rich project investigations command a "think tank" attitude by all participants.

PROMOTING STUDENT REFLECTION: METACOGNITIVE STRATEGIES

Teachers' greatest challenge in the *Blueprints* classroom is promoting student reflection or metacognition. The challenge is most difficult when students are comfortable in the passive role of information acquirer, where both teacher and student expectations for active thinking and student-student interaction are low. Yet, as teachers move to meet this challenge—the active mental engagement of all students—they quickly grasp the power of guided student reflection. They focus not on *what* students think but on *how to use* students' developing thinking skills to increase learning and encourage higher achievement.

Metacognition in the classroom is the capstone of teachers' careful work to create a cooperative culture where students know and respect each other's ideas and ways of knowing and thinking patterns. For students with strong interpersonal intelligence, reflection comes easy. For most, however, developing reflective habits and skills takes time. Why is it important for all students to develop what Gardner (1983) labeled the interpersonal intelligence? Because it is through these reflective practices that students solidify their understanding of curricular content, develop cross-content transfer, and transfer beyond the curriculum. When students recall not only details and procedures but also grasp the concepts that make transfer possible, they acquire the depth of understanding that is so important for increased success in standardized tests, teacher-made tests, essays, and other measures.

How do teachers prepare students for reflection? They develop quality cooperative cultures—the quality of student reflection is directly proportioned to the quality of the cooperative culture (Figure 7.11). In cooperative classrooms, teachers have established behavior norms that encourage all students to think independently and interdependently. The stronger the norms of mutual respect, listening, encouragement, and caring, the stronger the trust and willingness to share ideas and reactions.

The Reflective Classroom

Looks Like	Sounds Like
Waiting for the talker to finish	"That's a good idea."
Nodding agreement	"I'd like to clarify"
Taking notes on peer's ideas	"Let's see if I understand _____."
Heads together	"Good thinking . . ."
Making journal entries	"I agree . . ."
Taking turns	"Way to go _____."
Low voices	"Here's another idea . . . ."
High fives	"You can do it."
Thumbs up	"Thanks for sharing."
Using organizers	

Figure 7.11

What starter strategies encourage student reflection? Modeling by the teacher and the teaching social skills are two useful strategies.

Teacher Modeling

A teacher can model reflection in a number of ways. When he asks a question, he waits three to five seconds before calling on the first student. (This technique, called wait-time, was created by Rowe [1996].) When a student's answer is incomplete, he invites other students to add to the response and check for understanding. He also can be careful to seek an

---

Three Techniques for Achieving Equal Distribution of Reponses

Names From a Hat

Put all student names on slips of paper in a hat or box. Explain why you are using a hat. Pull a name after asking the question. Put the pulled name in another box not to be used until the first hat or box is empty. (This idea comes from Sally Berman via personal communication.)

Round Robin

Use a stem such as "I learned" or "I predict." Ask each student to respond in turn to the same question. Encourage active listening. Allow students to say, "I pass." Stay with one stem for all or introduce a new stem every five to seven students. (This idea comes from Joel Goodman via personal communication.)

Number Boards

Give each student a number and post names with numbers on a board. Ask a volunteer to call a number. The student with that number is asked a question. Change student numbers with each task. (This idea comes from Mary Hoffman via personal communication.)

Figure 7.12

equal distribution of responses by using such techniques as drawing names from a hat, using a number board, or asking students to respond in a round robin (Figure 7.12). As students respond, the teacher listens carefully to each answer and acknowledge the student's willingness to respond.

The same techniques work for group reports to the whole class. The teacher can also structure equal responses within small groups as a way to insist on individual participation. The small-group round robin promotes equal time in making reflective responses and in completing elements of a task.

Teaching Social Skills

Cooperative learning requires students to hone their social skills. As shown in chapter 3, when teachers teach social skills, they influence not only how students work in their small groups, but also how they work within the total classroom and with each other in individual interactions.

To effectively promote cooperative behaviors, teachers set high expectations for student classroom behavior and discreetly correct student behaviors that are contrary to the trust-enhancing climate. When necessary, they insist that any student who deviates from these high expectations bring his or her behavior into the norm or lose the benefits of community participation.

Where in a *Blueprints* lesson is metacognitive reflection most appropriate? Teachers can prompt effective metacognitive reflection throughout the lesson. When developing prior knowledge, they ask the students to reflect on past experience. When deepening understanding, they may use graphic organizers or the three-to-one technique (Figure 7.13) to help students cognitively reflect on the content.

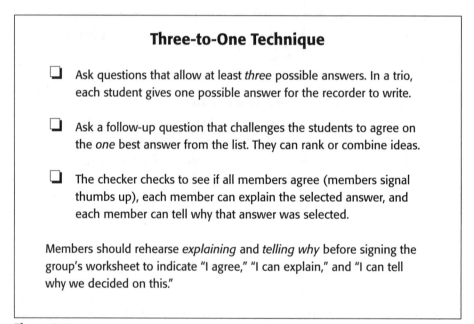

Three-to-One Technique

❏ Ask questions that allow at least *three* possible answers. In a trio, each student gives one possible answer for the recorder to write.

❏ Ask a follow-up question that challenges the students to agree on the *one* best answer from the list. They can rank or combine ideas.

❏ The checker checks to see if all members agree (members signal thumbs up), each member can explain the selected answer, and each member can tell why that answer was selected.

Members should rehearse *explaining* and *telling why* before signing the group's worksheet to indicate "I agree," "I can explain," and "I can tell why we decided on this."

Figure 7.13

Most often, teachers use reflective practices to assist students' assessment of knowledge, pair cooperation, or thinking in the lesson. Teachers may select from a number of assessment tools that help students reflect on their achievements. Students can complete the chosen technique in writing, orally, by drawing, with the whole class, or in a small group. Stems, Mrs. Potter's questions, and PMI are useful techniques (Figure 7.14).

Stems

About ____(topic)____ ,

    I learned . . .

    I am pleased that I . . .

    I discovered . . .

    I'm proud that I . . .

    I understand that . . .

    I know . . .

(From Joel Goodman via personal communication.)

Mrs. Potter's questions

1. What were you expected to do?

2. In this assignment, what did you do well?

3. If you had to do this task over, what would you differently?

4. What help do you need from me?

(From Bellanca and Fogarty 1986)

PMI

P(+) Pluses	
M(−) Minuses	
I(?) Interesting	

(From de Bono 1973)

Figure 7.14

THE CHALLENGE OF METACOGNITION

The successful use of metacognitive strategies depends on the culture of cooperation and cognition that the teacher has established. When teachers ask students to do cooperative tasks and large numbers of students stay silent, fool around, make negative comments about other students' responses, or let one student take over all the metacognitive work in the group, students are saying, We are not ready for this challenge. Successful metacognition depends on student readiness and willingness to do the most difficult type of sharing—thinking about thinking. Teachers can develop students' readiness by following these guidelines:

1. Start by asking students to write responses to stem statements. Keep these in student journals or on index cards that students sign. Do not ask for public reading.

2. Establish cooperative rules.

3. Start cooperative sharing of metacognitive reflection in pairs. Ask pairs to share pre-written responses to stems.

4. For individuals who are especially reticent, provide private prompts and encouragement and establish the right to pass.

5. Move to trio sharing of written stems. Allow the right to pass. For all-class sharing, have a volunteer from each group read a selection or summary of stem responses.

6. Encourage the class to honor the right to pass. If more than one or two pass in a round robin, drop back to group round robins.

Using private or public metacognitive strategies brings richness to student learning. Although it *seems* to take time from the content element of the curriculum, student metacognitive reflection on a regular basis is the hallmark of the highest quality of teaching and learning. Developing a cooperative-cognitive-metacognitive classroom takes patience, instructional skill development, and a strong commitment to higher achievement for all students.

BLUEPRINT
Elementary
Lesson

Codes 2SN
4HP
6CL
8GH
9QCA

Setting Up the Scaffolding

Meeting Magnets

In the *micro-skills* phase of the introductory lesson on magnets and their characteristics, use the letter below to gather objects and items for experimenting. Have students *predict* which items are likely to be attracted to the magnets

---

Dear Parents,

Please help us gather objects from around the house, garage and attic that will help us in our science experiments with magnets.

Send small items that we can keep in our lab (nuts, bolts, screws, nails, bottle caps, corks, clothespins, etc.).

Thank you,

Grade 1

Working the Crew

and why. Next, experiment with the assorted items to find out which *are* attracted to the magnets and which *are not.* Record the results on the tally sheet next to the appropriate item.

In the *macro-processing* phase, to *synthesize* and *analyze,* have students dis-

Draw items and circle YES if attracted to magnets or NO if not attracted to magnets.		
1 YES NO	2 YES NO	3 YES NO
4 YES NO	5 YES NO	6 YES NO
7 YES NO	8 YES NO	9 YES NO
10 YES NO	11 YES NO	12 YES NO

cuss with a partner some rules about magnets. Then have them compare the rules with other partners (using *metacognitive processing*). Rewrite, revise, and evaluate the results as a class.

To process for the affective, have students tell:

What was hardest to do . . .

What was easiest to do . . .

To process the *social skills,* ask students to talk about how they helped each other during the task.

To process the *cognitive,* encourage students to discuss the predictions they had prior to the experiment and if they were good ones or not.

For *metacognitive processing,* tell students to talk about something they learned in this lesson that they can use somewhere else.

#

Reflecting on
the Design

The Good, Good Story

In working with the *micro-skills*, use the Good, Good Story to focus on the skills of *brainstorming* and *analyzing* for precision of language. Read the story and discuss the overuse of the word *good.*

THE GOOD, GOOD STORY

The GOOD boy got a GOOD grade on his GOOD report. However, his GOOD friend did not feel very GOOD that day. So when the GOOD boy told his GOOD friend about his GOOD report, his GOOD friend did not reply in a GOOD manner.

Instead, his usually GOOD mood was not so GOOD and his reply was not as GOOD as expected. Luckily, the GOOD boy, who was always GOOD, just used his GOOD sense and took the not-so-GOOD remark in GOOD humor.

It was a GOOD thing too because just as the GOOD boy broke into a GOOD smile, the GOOD principal of the GOOD school appeared. He nodded hello as all GOOD principals do and went about his GOOD tasks.

Needless to say, the GOOD boy had a GOOD day and his GOOD friend had a GOOD lesson that day. Be GOOD to your GOOD friends and they will be GOOD to you. And in the end, that will be GOOD for all.

Working the
Crew

In cooperative groups of three, have students assign these roles: recorder, reporter, and observer. Responding in turn, students should use the micro-skill of brainstorming to list overused words. These should include words that appear frequently in their own writing. To prime the pump, suggest words such as *nice, said, a lot, like,* and *then.*

Overused Words	
LIST	RANKING
nice	
said	
a lot	
like	
then	
also	
everybody	
always	

After compiling the list of words, ask students in each group to use the micro-skill of *prioritizing* to rank them from the *most* overused to the *least* overused (in their opinion). (Note: This ranking is based on their use and overuse of the words and is a somewhat subjective ranking.) Next, have groups select one word to slot into a story similar to the Good, Good Story.

Notice that the micro-skills used in this first part of the lesson involve brainstorming—a creative, generative skill—and prioritizing—an analytical and evaluative critical thinking skill.

Now, to take the micro-skills into a problematic situation in which students are required to process the information as they interact with it, the *macro-processing* stage of cognitive instruction begins.

Remaining with their original task groups of three, have each group write a progressive story or tale in the style of the Good, Good Story. Instruct students to:

1. Select an overused word to use for slotting into their writing of the Good, Good Story.
2. Use an ABC order to structure sentences, having the recorder begin with *A*. The recorder uses the selected word at least three times in a sentence that begins with the letter *A*.
3. The recorder passes the paper to the next group member who must now start a sentence with the letter *B* and include the overused word at least three times.
4. At this point, the story might look like this:

> Selected Word – Nice
> Although a nice man in a nice brown suit was having a nice breakfast in a nice diner, a not-so-nice event occurred.
> Before the nice man could think of a nice way to help the victim who seemed so nice, a nice young man appeared with a nice fresh roll.
> Calling his nice name...

5. Continue the procedure until each group member has had a least two turns and the story is complete.

Note that students must piece a number of micro-skills together in this macro-process stage as they synthesize elements. Each student must brainstorm with fluency and demonstrate flexibility in shifting thoughts as the story line shifts with each member's added sentence. *Analysis* is required as each author evaluates which letter to use and whether or not the sentence makes sense.

To sample students' feelings about the task, use a PMI chart to talk about what they liked and didn't like, or comments or questions they have.

Precision of Language

P(+)	
M(−)	
I(?)	

To process the social skills, have students discuss a point where they got stuck in the task and how they got unstuck with someone's help.

Using a continuum to process the cognitive content, have students quickly brainstorm words to slot in for each extreme. Focus on the concept of precision of language.

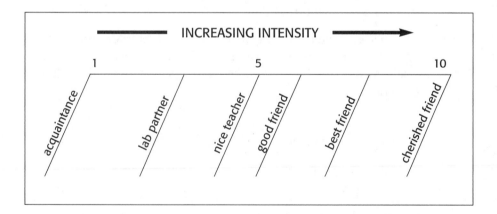

To process metacognitively, ask students to agree or disagree with this statement:

Not being precise with language can get you into trouble.

Next, have them do a log entry with this lead-in:

By stringing several thinking skills together, I . . . .

# # #

BLUEPRINT
High School
Lesson

Codes 1SD
2SN
6CL
8GH

Setting Up the
Scaffolding

Working the
Crew

Design a Decade

As a culminating unit in contemporary American history, tell the students they have to prepare a metaphorical presentation of a decade for review. Place students in groups of three with the following roles:

Scribe:	Keeps records
Historian:	Seeks resources
Orator:	Reports findings

Using the micro-skill of brainstorming, have each group of three complete the following chart by generating three words they associate with each decade. This is an initial focus activity to prime the pump, but students may use books and other resources.

List three words for each decade.			Rank
1900–09 _____ ,	_____ ,	_____ ,	____
1910s _____ ,	_____ ,	_____ ,	____
1920s _____ ,	_____ ,	_____ ,	____
1930s _____ ,	_____ ,	_____ ,	____
1940s _____ ,	_____ ,	_____ ,	____
1950s _____ ,	_____ ,	_____ ,	____
1960s _____ ,	_____ ,	_____ ,	____
1970s _____ ,	_____ ,	_____ ,	____
1980s _____ ,	_____ ,	_____ ,	____
1990s _____ ,	_____ ,	_____ ,	____
2000–09 _____ ,	_____ ,	_____ ,	____

Following the brainstorming and upon completing the chart, each group should *prioritize* the decades according to their favorites (ranking the list).

Using the group rankings, assign or ask students to select a decade for their design project. Next, have students quickly select an identifying name for their group that indicates their chosen decade.

Decade	Group Name
1900-1909	_____
1910s	_____
1920s	_____
1930s	_____
1940s	_____
1950s	_____
1960s	_____
1970s	_____
1980s	_____
1990s	_____
2000-2009	_____

Using the *macro-processing* skill of *problem solving,* students should use any and all resources necessary to research, gather, and review information about their decades. Instruct students to select ten to twelve snapshots or key elements from their decades.

Snapshots Capturing the 1970s

Now, after groups have decided on ten to twelve snapshots that depict the significant events or moments of their decades, ask the team members to bridge the snapshots by providing connectors between them.

In the 1970s, environmental issues such as litterbugs were a major focus. Nuclear power plants were also springing up amidst major controversies. A bridge or connector between these two might be the idea of conflict or opposing ideas.

Bridges provide a synthesizing process to the snapshot activity. Instead of having ten to twelve isolated snapshots floating around, bridges allow teams to find relationships between seemingly disparate ideas. In bridging the snapshots, students begin to see emerging patterns or overriding themes.

After bridging their snapshots, teams are able to sift out key attributes of their decades. These key attributes help members create extended metaphors for their decades (using the *metacognitive processing* stage) when they prepare to present their decades to the class.

After processing and analyzing the critical attributes of a decade through the bridging snapshots activity, ask each team to use the key components to create an extended metaphor representing its decade.

For example, the decade of the 1930s might be compared to a roller coaster ride that has gotten out of control. Like a rollercoaster, the stock market climbed precariously to the top and then suddenly rushed downward.

Once student teams have created their metaphors, instruct each team to:
1. Use its metaphor and develop comparisons for each snapshot.
2. Illustrate the metaphor on large paper with appropriately labeled parts.
3. Prepare to present the metaphor to the class.

For example, if the decade is compared to a parade, then the various elements depicting the significant events of the decade can be matched to the standard components of a parade (see example below or see Blackline C7.1 in Appendix C.). The metaphor model can be virtually anything that is a concrete, tangible concept that lends itself to easy comparison.

Reflecting on
the Design

For affective processing, have each student team create a song that reflects how the members feel about their decade.

To process the social skills, ask students to describe how they helped each other make bridges as they tried to finish the task.

For cognitive processing, have students take their ten to twelve snapshots and write an equation that includes all of the elements depicted in the snapshots.

For metacognitive processing, ask students to reflect on how they used the following skills and processes in completing their projects:

we used micro-skills of thinking to . . .

we used macro-processes of problem solving and decision making to . . .

we transferred ideas when we . . .

# # #

Blueprints for Achievement

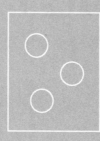

FORMING

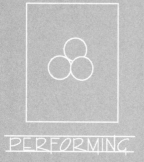

PERFORMING

NORMING

CHAPTER 8

Phase IV

STORMING

Level II
What Happens When
They Do Not Agree?

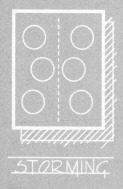

STORMING

CONFORMING

In the Cooperative Classroom

WHAT HAPPENS WHEN THEY DO NOT AGREE?

"First of all," he said, "if you can learn a simple trick, Scout, you'll get along a lot better with all kinds of folks. You never really understand a person until you consider things from his point of view..."
"Sir?"
"...until you climb into his skin and walk around in it."
—Harper Lee, To Kill a Mockingbird

Draft

The storming phase signals both *unrest* and *progress* in the small group process. While individual students vie for position and recognition in their small groups during this phase, teachers cannot overlook the rich opportunities for expanding and extending students' cooperative skills that this phase presents. Above all, they must ensure that student storming results in productive achievement and increased cooperation.

Teachers can facilitate the storming phase by exploring the types of disagreements the groups are experiencing. Teachers can provide complexity to the cooperative tasks so students sense that they are engaged in an authentic sink or swim situation. The more difficult or complex the task, the more intense the interaction becomes. And this intense involvement encourages more sophisticated cooperative behavior. Student teams begin to engage in problem-solving and decision-making processes required to achieve the desired outcomes.

However, just as the intensity of interaction increases, so too does the likelihood of unresolved conflicts. These conflicts are predictable and arise throughout the course of group growth. Teachers need to teach explicit agreement and disagreement strategies if the groups are to continue growing and succeeding. In addition to ensuring that the students review and reinforce the social skills learned earlier, teachers stretch students in two new ways:

1. They tell students about formal and informal tactics to use for helping people who disagree to come to an agreement.

2. They teach specific strategies. They define and model how arguing, persuading, giving in, avoiding, voting, compromising, mediating, delaying, arbitrating, reconceptualizing, negotiating, consensus seeking, ignoring, and humoring are useful conflict resolution strategies in small group work

Initially, the teacher may choose to intervene in conflicts in order to model appropriate conflict resolution skills. She may seize these teachable moments to intervene privately, or if the group agrees, she may use the intervention as a whole class demonstration. If the teacher chooses to conduct a whole class demonstration, she must take specific, careful steps to generalize the problem. The teacher can call on at least eight tactics for resolving conflict:

1. Check that both sides understand the other's point of view.

2. Ask each side to explain its points while the other side listens attentively and takes notes.

3. Encourage each side to ask clarifying questions and to paraphrase the ideas of the other side.

4. Give participants time to reflect silently.

5. Tell participants to identify agreements and write them on the board and label disagreements as facts, ideas, interpretations, goals, or beliefs.

6. Help participants focus on disagreements using an appropriately labeled strategy.

7. Review the process with everyone when a final agreement is reached.

8. Encourage both sides, together, to summarize the resolution.

After the teacher models the desired behavior, students begin to learn formally the strategies for reaching agreements and building their repertoire of social skills for conflict resolution. As they develop expertise in the different methods for dealing with controversy, students also begin to develop awareness and skill in knowing not only *how* but also *when* to use each particular tactic. By profiling this metacognitive aspect of using the strategies for agreeing and disagreeing, teachers foster lifelong transfer of students' vital interpersonal skills.

What Do You Do When You Disagree?

- ❏ **Argue**—stand firm
- ❏ **Persuade**—justify, reason, appeal to
- ❏ **Vote**—majority rules
- ❏ **Compromise**—combine, modify
- ❏ **Mediate**—neutral party facilitator
- ❏ **Arbitrate**—agree to abide by decision of arbitrator
- ❏ **Delay**—table it, sleep on it, wait
- ❏ **Reconceptualize**—rethink, find new angles
- ❏ **Negotiate**—give and take
- ❏ **Give in**—give up, cave in, play martyr
- ❏ **Seek Consensus**—talk, cajole, juggle, adjust, modify
- ❏ **Humor**—veer away from confrontation
- ❏ **Avoid**—ignore or postpone

Figure 8.1

INTRODUCING CONFLICT RESOLUTION TECHNIQUES

Teachers begin introducing conflict resolution tactics by asking students to examine their own past behavior. Distribute the checklist in Figure 8.1 and give students time to understand the various strategies. (For a blackline master, see Blackline C8.1 in Appendix C.) As a class, elicit definitions and examples of each.

Then, encourage students to assess their own use of the various techniques in a quick self-examination or think-pair-share interaction. Even a show of hands (How many have ever argued? compromised?) will activate prior knowledge of use of these strategies.

When students relate examples of their conflict resolution strategies, they are motivated to see the benefits of resolving conflicts. When teachers

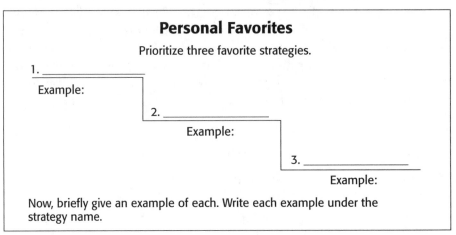

Personal Favorites

Prioritize three favorite strategies.

1. _____
   Example:

2. _____
   Example:

3. _____
   Example:

Now, briefly give an example of each. Write each example under the strategy name.

Figure 8.2

begin with student-initiated examples of the conflict resolution tactics, they can guide students to extend the tactics to larger academic or social contexts. A portmanteau vocabulary strategy, a web or concept map, or a journal entry can help students learn the technical terms of conflict resolution. The step chart is helpful in deepening student reflection on prior use of the skills. Ask students in a think-pair-share to prioritize their favorites in a chart like the one shown in Figure 8.2.

Tug O'War Thinking Creed

We pledge to . . .

Tug at ideas, not people.

Examine all sides of the issue.

Actively listen and clarify.

Modify our position when appropriate.

Seek the best decision, not the winning position.

Figure 8.3

Consider introducing and posting the Tug O' War Thinking Creed (Figure 8.3 or Blackline C8.2 in Appendix C.) as a reminder of expected behavior. Also, take time to demonstrate several communication techniques for resolving a conflict, such as listening carefully, searching for common ground, moving from easy to difficult, switching points of view, and lightening up.

Listen carefully to the other's position. Teachers encourage students to listen to one another by applying the PACTS skills:

Paraphrase:	Let me say what I think I heard from you . . . . Am I on target?
Affirm:	I appreciate that _____ is your (*goal, belief, opinion, etc.*). I can see you are firm about your (*goal, belief, opinion, etc.*).
Clarify:	I'm not clear on what you are saying. Could you clarify with an example?

Paraphrase

Affirm

Clarify

Test options

Summarize

> *Test Options:*   Let me state in different words what I think you are saying.
>
> *Summarize:*   Let me summarize the points you have made.

(A blackline master of PACTS, Blackline C8.3, is included in Appendix C.)

After making a PACTS statement, the speaker needs to allow the other person or group to respond and make corrections. This creates a dialogue between the supporters of opposing views. The purpose of the dialogue is to ensure that the opponents understand each other's point of view or position—they both have listened well and have grasped the other's position. Now, they can more readily find common ground.

Search for common ground. Many disagreements get lost in circular arguments that confuse and confound multiple issues. As opponents use their PACTS skills, each should list agreement points and label the conflict type (facts, goals, opinions, etc.). It also helps to do the same for disagreement points.

Move from easy to difficult. Agree on the easiest points—usually related to tools and facts—first. (See discussion of types of disagreement under stage 1: Prior Knowledge in the next section.) Resolving disagreements on beliefs is the most difficult task and requires more intense application of listening carefully, searching for common ground, and agreeing on easy points.

Switch points of view. When opposing groups reach a dead end, it helps improve understanding of the other's position when members switch positions and role play each other's viewpoint. This technique can play a major part in resolving the conflict.

Lighten up and laugh it up. Good humor can take the edge off of conflict, especially when emotions are heavy. The best approach is to avoid making fun about the other's position, but go ahead and make fun of your own.

TEACHING CONFLICT RESOLUTION SKILLS

Teachers might want to select particular skills that students need to add to their repertoire and teach a weekly or monthly lesson for those skills. The four-stage lesson design provides a consistent instructional framework for these lessons.

Stage 1: Prior Knowledge

Ask the students to share conflicts or disagreements they have had with friends, other students, or have seen on television. Make a list (_____versus _____) to illustrate.

Ask the students to label each example as one of the following:

   a. conflict of means or tool

   b. conflict of opinion, point of view, or interpretation

c. conflict of goal or intent

d. conflict of fact

e. conflict of belief

Discuss which types are easier to solve. Ask volunteer students to explain why.

Stage 2: Generate Knowledge

Assign students to groups of three. Ask each group to create a conflict that matches one of the conflict types. For example, two opposing track teams have a *goal* conflict; two lawyers can disagree on the *facts* in a case; members of two religious groups have different *beliefs*). Give each group a sheet of newsprint. Tell them they are to describe the conflict without naming the conflict type by writing it on the paper. When the groups are finished writing their descriptions, each group exchanges completed conflict descriptions by giving them to another group. Receiving groups use the descriptions to understand the problem, select an appropriate method for solving the problem, and then create a short role play using the solution. Each group presents their solution to the class using the round robin technique.

Stage 4: Assessment

(Do this step before Stage 3: Transfer.) Take three minutes for the class to rate and discuss the appropriateness of the solutions.

Stage 3: Promote Transfer

(Do this step after Stage 4: Assessment.) Ask each student to write in his or her journal about the techniques most usable in classroom group conflicts. Urge students to select a method outside their usual comfort zone. After the students finish writing, ask for volunteers to share.

After teachers have introduced the basics of conflict resolution to students, they can use the following lessons to introduce and practice the consensus-seeking technique. (Note that each lesson has similar content but is specifically tailored to the appropriate grade level.)

BLUEPRINT
Elementary
Lesson

Codes 1SN
5NR
6CL
7OF
9QCA

Setting Up the
Scaffolding

Top Three

Pass out one piece of a puzzle to each student. (See sample below. For a black-line master, see Blackline C8.4 in Appendix C.) Be sure to distribute complete sets of the puzzle pieces. (Each piece has a partner piece.) Instruct each student to find the partner with the piece that completes his or her puzzle.

SELL	VOTE	STALL	ARGUE
TALK INTO	MOST WINS	WAIT	FIGHT
GIVE IN	LEAD	GIVE AND TAKE	GIVE A LITTLE
QUIT	JUDGE	AGREE	BOTH GIVE SOME

After students have found their puzzle partner, tell them to discuss the words for agreeing and disagreeing that are on their puzzle pieces. Then talk to them about consensus. Introduce the word *consensus* and the rules for seeking consensus:

> Consensus=group opinion or agreement
> _____
> - Voting is outlawed.
> - No horse-trading allowed.
> - Don't give up.

Now show students the following consensus chart. Modeling with your hand, demonstrate how members signal the group (5-to-fist) as they call for a consensus reading.

Consensus Chart—5 to Fist			
5		(5 fingers)	All for it; top priority
4		(4 fingers)	Yes; high on my list
3		(3 fingers)	OK with me
2		(2 fingers)	Let's talk more
1		(1 fingers)	Will trust group
FIST		(fist)	No! An alternative is ____.

Model the consensus-seeking process with a selected group of three. Tell them to rank the following three vegetables, from their most favorite to their least favorite: spinach, peas, broccoli. Tell them to signal (5-to-fist) for each item when it is mentioned. Each student must give a signal for each item. Begin with spinach.

SPINACH

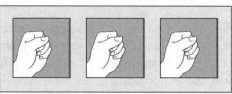

This first reading is easy. With three fists, consensus is reached, the alternative is anything but spinach. Spinach is last. Go on to peas.

PEAS

Talk about the fact that there must be one item that everyone agrees is their first choice. They must discuss the item until they can decide on the same reading. (Then, ask about broccoli.)

PEAS

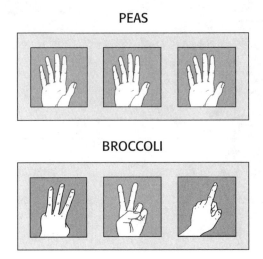

BROCCOLI

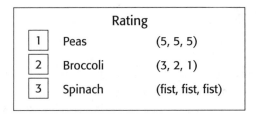

Finally, display the results of the voting.

	Rating	
1	Peas	(5, 5, 5)
2	Broccoli	(3, 2, 1)
3	Spinach	(fist, fist, fist)

After students have worked on the vegetable problem, they are now ready for a new problem—selecting the top three books for elementary students.

Tell the students that today they will make some important decisions as the experts for the elementary students in their school. Explain that their job is to select the best three books for students ages 5 to 11 throughout the country. Explain that they will make decisions about which three books they think every elementary student should read before leaving elementary school. These are the must-read books because they are the absolute best! Explain further that their decisions will be made into a list called The Top Three, which will be posted in each classroom in the building for other students and teachers to consider.

Have the students get into groups of three and assign these roles:
>   *Recorder:* writes down ideas
>   *Researcher:* picks up resources needed
>   *Reporter*: tells the results of the task and teamwork

Instruct groups to brainstorm a list of 15 books they think are possibilities for The Top Three list and write them on a newsprint sheet. They should include their favorite books and others they have heard of. Help with spelling as a facilitator.

Working the Crew

Possibilities for the Top Three List

1. _____   6. _____   11. _____

2. _____   7. _____   12. _____

3. _____   8. _____   13. _____

4. _____   9. _____   14. _____

5. _____   10. _____   15. _____

Discuss the DOVE guidelines for brainstorming and accepting others' ideas. (See below. A blackline master of the DOVE guidelines, Blackline C8.5, is included in Appendix C.)

DOVE

Defer judgment; anything goes
Opt for original, different ideas
Vast numbers are needed
Expand the list by piggybacking on ideas

After brainstorming 15 must-reads for The Top Three list, review the consensus chart (5-to-fist) with the students. Explain that through discussion and use of the 5-to-fist agreement model, they are to determine the top three books, naming book #1, book #2, and book #3. Allow time for discussion and the 5-to-fist activity. Facilitate as needed. Ask teams to list their selections on a chart and collect the team ratings at the end of the session.

Top Three Books

1._____

2._____

3._____

Team_____

Grade_____ Date_____

After reviewing the teams' rankings, compile the nominated book titles into a class list. Include all books listed by the teams.

Have each team review the class list and discuss the added book titles. The class goal is now to select by consensus the top three books from the class list.

To encourage open discussion on all nominations, reorganize the students into new teams of three. Using discussion and the 5-to-fist strategy, tell student teams to rank the top three.

Reorganize teams again with all new members. Again, rank the top three books by team.

Reorganize! Rank the top three books by team. The continued reorganization of new threesomes and the subsequent new rankings eliminates the ownership issue in which students stay loyal to their own nominations. However, if the continued regrouping and re-ranking becomes tedious or too time consuming, modify this step accordingly. Keep in mind that a group agreement needs to be reached in some manner. The specific design of that group agreement will vary.

After several group interactions, try a class ranking. Allow informal groups to *discuss, persuade,* and *justify* as they seek class consensus. This may take more time than was planned. If this happens, there is no reason why they can't stop and continue at another time or on another day. It is not uncommon for committees to take several sessions to arrive at an agreement. If this is the case, talk to students about what's happening. Reassure them that reaching agreement requires time to talk, clarify, and shift positions, and that to make good decisions it often takes quality time.

After a class decision has been reached, post the results.

> **Top Three Books
> by Agreement**
>
> 1._____
>
> 2._____
>
> 3._____
>
> _____'s Class
>
> Room_____

Reflecting on
the Design

For affective processing, have students web the feelings they have when they are in conflict or disagree with another person.

After webbing their feelings, students should complete this statement:

Conflict is like ___ because both _____.

For social skill processing, ask students to complete the stem:

Reaching agreement is good for our group work because . . .

For cognitive processing use the human graph (see Blackline C8.6 in Appendix C).

Ask students to move to the corresponding side of the human graph for each of the following opposing statements:

(Statement #1)	or	(Statement #2)
All students should read _____.	or	All students should not read _____.
Fiction is better than nonfiction.	or	Nonfiction is better than fiction.
A favorite author is _____.	or	A favorite author is not _____.
Books are better than television.	or	Television is better than books.

For metacognitive processing, have students complete these stems:

The hardest part about reaching agreement is . . .

The easiest part about reaching agreement is . . .

Another opportunity to use the 5-to-fist activity might be . . .

BLUEPRINT
Middle School
Lesson

Codes 1SN
5NR
6CL
7OF
9QCA

Setting Up the
Scaffolding

Top Five

Pass out one puzzle piece to each student. (See sample below. For a blackline master, see Blackline C8.4 in Appendix C.) Be sure to distribute complete sets of the puzzle pieces. (Each piece has a partner piece.) Instruct each student to find the partner with the piece that completes his or her puzzle.

AVOID	HUMOR	ARGUE	TAKE TIME OUT
IGNORE	JOKE	FIGHT	WAIT
BOTH GIVE SOME	SELL	GIVE UP	GIVE AND TAKE
COMPROMISE	CONVINCE	QUIT	AGREE

After students have found their puzzle partners, tell them to discuss the words for agreeing and disagreeing that are on their puzzle pieces. Then talk to them about consensus. Introduce the word *consensus* and the rules for seeking consensus:

Consensus-group opinion or agreement
• Voting is outlawed. • No horse-trading allowed. • Don't give up.

Now show students the following consensus chart. Modeling with your hand, demonstrate how members should signal the group (5-to-fist) when they call for a consensus reading.

Consenus Chart—5 to Fist			
5		(5 fingers)	All for it; top priority
4		(4 fingers)	Yes; high on my list
3		(3 fingers)	OK with me
2		(2 fingers)	Let's talk more
1		(1 fingers)	Will trust group
FIST		(fist)	No! An alternative is ____.

Model the agreement-seeking process with a selected group of three. Tell this group to rank the following sports with their favorite as number one:

- ☐ Baseball
- ☐ Basketball
- ☐ Football

They must signal with the 5-to-fist strategy for each one as it is mentioned and discussed.

BASEBALL

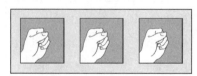

No one wants baseball as first. They suggest that since all agree—make it number 3 or last. Now go on to basketball.

BASKETBALL

Now, discuss the agreement cycle below to help students understand the dynamics of reaching agreement. Then, have students work on basketball again.

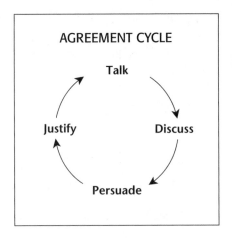

BASKETBALL

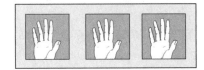

Continue with football.

FOOTBALL

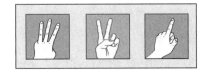

Ranking

1	Basketball	(5, 5, 5)
2	Basketball	(3, 2, 1)
3	Football	(fist, fist, fist)

Now, with the sports example in mind, give students the following task: By agreement of the class, select the top five, must-read books for all middle school students.

Tell the students that today they will make some important decisions as the experts for middle students in their school. Explain that their job is to select the top five books for students ages 10 to 13 throughout the country.

Working the
Crew

Elaborate on these instructions by explaining that they will make decisions about which five books they think every middle student should read before leaving middle school. These are the must-read books because they are the absolute best! Explain further that their decisions will be made into a list called The Top Five, which will be posted in each classroom in the building for others to consider.

Arrange students into groups of three, and assign these roles:
  Recorder: writes down ideas.
  Researcher: picks up resources.
  Reporter: tells results.

Instruct the groups to brainstorm a list of 25 books they think should be on The Top Five list and write their ideas on a large piece of paper. They should include their favorite books and other books they have heard of.

Must-Reads
Contenders for the Top Five

1. _____	9. _____	17. _____
2. _____	10. _____	18. _____
3. _____	11. _____	19. _____
4. _____	12. _____	20. _____
5. _____	13. _____	21. _____
6. _____	14. _____	22. _____
7. _____	15. _____	23. _____
8. _____	16. _____	24. _____
		25. _____

Figure 8.26

Discuss the DOVE guidelines for brainstorming and accepting others' ideas. (See below. A blackline master of the DOVE guidelines, Blackline C8.5, is included in Appendix C).

DOVE

Defer judgment; anything goes
Opt for original, different ideas
Vast numbers are needed
Expand the list by piggybacking on ideas

After brainstorming 25 book contenders for The Top Five list, review the 5-to-fist consensus model with the students. Explain that through discussions and use of the 5-to-fist consensus model, each team is to determine the top five books, naming book #1, book #2, book #3, book #4, and book #5. Collect the team rankings at the end of the session.

After reviewing the team rankings, compile the nominated book titles into a class list. Include all books listed by the teams. Have each team review the class list and discuss the additional book titles. The class goal now is to select by consensus the top five books from the class list.

To encourage open discussion on all nominations, reorganize the students into new teams of three. Using discussion and the 5-to-fist strategy, have student teams rank the top five.

Reorganize teams again with all new members to rank the top five books.

Reorganize! Rank the top five books by team. The continued reorganization of new threesomes and the subsequent new rankings eliminates the ownership issue in which students stay loyal to their own nominations. However, if the continued regrouping and re-ranking becomes tedious or too time consuming, modify this step accordingly. Keep in mind that a group consensus needs to be reached in some manner although the specific design of consensus will vary.

After several group interactions, try a class ranking. Allow informal groups to *discuss, persuade,* and *justify* as they seek class consensus. This may take more time than was planned. If so, there is no reason why they can't stop and continue at another time or on another day. It is not uncommon for committees to take several sessions to arrive at a consensus. Talk to students about what's happening. Reassure them that reaching consensus requires time to talk, clarify, and shift positions, and that to make good decisions it often takes quality time.

Once a class decision has been reached, post the results.

**By Agreement
Top Five Books**

1._____
2._____
3._____
4._____
5._____
Team_____
Grade_____ Date_____

Reflecting on the Design

For affective processing, have students web the feelings they have when they are in conflict or disagree with another person.

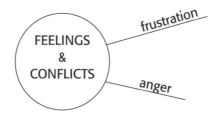

FEELINGS
&
CONFLICTS

frustration

anger

After webbing their feelings, students should complete this statement:

Conflict is like ___ because both _____.

For social processing, have students complete a PMI chart on consensus.

For cognitive processing, use a human graph (see Blackline C8.6 in Appendix C).

Ask students to move to the correct side of the human graph for each of the following opposing statements:

(Statement #1)		(Statement #2)
All students should read _____.	or	All students should not read _____.
Fiction is better than nonfiction.	or	Nonfiction is better than fiction.
A favorite author is _____.	or	A favorite author is not _____.
Books are better than television.	or	Television is better than books.

For metacognitive processing, have students complete the following stems:

The hardest part about reaching consensus is . . .

The easiest part about reaching consensus is . . .

Another opportunity to use the 5-to-fist activity might be . . .

BLUEPRINT
High School
Lesson

Codes 1SN
5NR
6CL
7OF
9QCA

Setting Up the
Scaffolding

Top Ten

Pass out one puzzle piece to each student. (See sample below. For a blackline master, see Blackline C8.8 in Appendix C). Be sure to distribute complete sets of the puzzle pieces. (Each piece has a partner piece.) Instruct each student to find the partner with the piece that completes his or her puzzle.

PERSUADE	MEDIATE	VOTE	RECONCEPTUALIZE
APPEAL TO	USE NEUTRAL FACILITATOR	MAJORITY RULES	RETHINK
HUMOR	ARGUE	NEGOTIATE	COMBINE
VEER FROM CONFRONTATION	STAND FIRM	GIVE AND TAKE	COMPROMISE

After students have found their puzzle partners, tell them to discuss the words for agreeing and disagreeing that appear on the puzzle pieces. Then talk to them about consensus. Introduce the word *consensus* and the rules for seeking consensus:

> Consensus-collective opinion or agreement
> _____
>
> - Voting is outlawed.
> - No horse-trading allowed.
> - Don't give up.

Now show students the following consensus chart. Modeling with your hand, demonstrate how members should signal the group (5-to-fist) when they call for a consensus reading.

Consensus Chart—5 to Fist			
5		(5 fingers)	All for it; top priority
4		(4 fingers)	Yes; high on my list
3		(3 fingers)	OK with me
2		(2 fingers)	Let's talk more
1		(1 fingers)	Will trust group
FIST		(fist)	No! An alternative is ____.

Model the consensus-seeking process with a selected group of four. Tell them to rank the following items according to personal preference:

- ☐ Tapes
- ☐ CDs
- ☐ Videos
- ☐ DVDs

They must discuss and signal their ratings with the 5-to-fist strategy for each item until they see a decision they all can agree upon.

TAPES

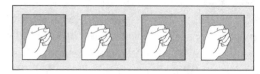

No one wants the tapes first. They suggest a simple alternative: Let's make this last on the ranking.

Now, move on to CDs, DVDs, and videos.

CDs

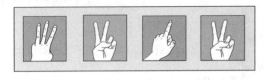

DVDs

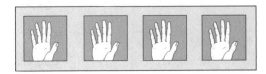

VIDEOs

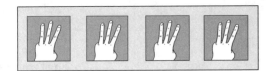

When students finish voting on all four musical forms, ask them to record their results:

Ranking

1	DVDs	(5, 5, 5, 5)
2	Videos	(3, 3, 3, 3)
3	CDs	(3, 2, 2, 1)
4	Tapes	(fist, fist, fist)

Now, with the music example in mind, give the students the following problem:

Select the top 10 books for secondary school students. Today you are going to make some important decisions as the experts for the secondary students in schools throughout the country. Your job is to select the top 10 books for secondary school students. You should choose ten books you think every secondary student should read before leaving high school. These are the must-read books because they are the absolute best! Your decisions will be made into a list called The Top 10, which will be posted throughout the school for others to consider.

Working the Crew

Assign students to groups of three, and assign these roles:

Recorder: writes down ideas

Researcher: picks up resources needed

Reporter: tells the results of the task and teamwork

Instruct groups to brainstorm a list of 25 books they think are possibilities for The Top 10 list and write them on a large piece of paper. They should include their favorite books and other books they have heard of.

MUST-READS
Contenders for the Top 10 Books

1. _____	9. _____	17. _____
2. _____	10. _____	18. _____
3. _____	11. _____	19. _____
4. _____	12. _____	20. _____
5. _____	13. _____	21. _____
6. _____	14. _____	22. _____
7. _____	15. _____	23. _____
8. _____	16. _____	24. _____
		25. _____

Discuss the DOVE guidelines for brainstorming and accepting others' ideas. (See below. A blackline master of the DOVE guidelines, Blackline C8.5, is included in Appendix C.)

DOVE

Defer judgment; anything goes
Opt for original, different ideas
Vast numbers are needed
Expand the list by piggybacking on ideas

After brainstorming 25 must-reads for The Top 10 list, review the 5-to-fist consensus model with the students. Explain that through discussions and use of this 5-to-fist consensus model, they are to determine the top 10 books, naming book #1, book #2, book #3, etc. Collect these team rankings at the end of the session.

Top 10 Books

1._____
2._____
3._____
4._____
5._____
6._____
7._____
8._____
9_____
10._____

Team_____

Grade_____ Date_____

After reviewing the team rankings, compile the nominated book titles into a class list. Include all books listed by the teams. Then review with the class the consensus cycle shown below to help students understand the dynamics of reaching agreement.

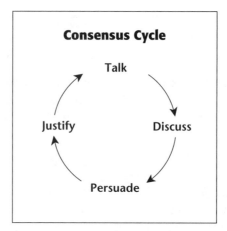

Consensus Cycle

Talk

Discuss

Persuade

Justify

Have each team review the class list and discuss the additional book titles. The class goal is now to select, again by consensus, the top 10 books.

To encourage open discussion on all nominations, reorganize the students into new teams of four. Using discussion and the 5-to-fist strategy, have student teams rank the top 10.

Reorganize teams again with all new members. Again, rank the top 10 books by team.

Reorganize! Rank the top 10 books by team. The continued reorganization of groups and the subsequent new rankings eliminates the ownership issue in which students stay loyal to their own nominations. However, if the continued regrouping and re-ranking becomes tedious or too time consuming, modify this step accordingly.

After several group interactions, try an all-class ranking. Allow informal groups to *discuss, persuade,* and *justify* as they seek class consensus. This may take more time than was planned. If so, there is no reason why they can't stop and continue at another time or on another day. It is not uncommon for committees to take several sessions to arrive at a consensus. If this is the case, talk to students about what's happening. Reassure them that reaching consensus requires time to talk, clarify, and shift positions, and that making good decisions often takes quality time.

Reflecting on the Design

For affective processing, have students web the feelings they have when they are in conflict or disagree with another person.

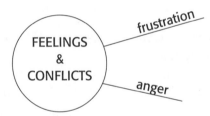

After webbing their feelings, students should complete this statement:

Conflict is like ___ because both _____.

For social skill processing, have students tell how they can facilitate reaching consensus.

(continued on next page)

For cognitive processing, introduce the human graph (see Blackline C8.6 in Appendix C).

Ask students to move to the corresponding side of the human graph for each of the following opposing statements:

(Statement #1)		(Statement #2)
All students should read _____.	or	All students should not read _____.
Fiction is better than nonfiction.	or	Nonfiction is better than fiction.
A favorite author is _____.	or	A favorite author is not _____.
Books are better than television.	or	Television is better than books.

For metacognitive processing, have students finish these stems:

The hardest part about reaching consensus is . . .

The easiest part about reaching consensus is . . .

Another opportunity to use the 5-to-fist activity might be . . .

Blueprints for Achievement

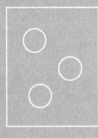

FORMING

PERFORMING

NORMING

CHAPTER 9

Phase V

PERFORMING

Level I

How Do I Promote Transfer
in the High-Achieving
Classroom?

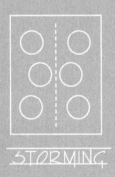

STORMING

CONFORMING

in the Cooperative Classroom

HOW DO I PROMOTE TRANSFER IN THE HIGH-ACHIEVING CLASSROOM?

Perhaps the most important single cause of a person's success or failure educationally has to do with the question of what he believes about himself.

—Arthur Combs

Draft

Isn't all learning for transfer? Educators frequently ask this question about the teaching/learning process, signaling that transfer is a constant source of controversy and confusion.

To transfer learning means to take what is learned in one situation and use it in another situation that is either quite like or quite different from the initial learning situation. The idea seems quite straightforward. An example might be the new driver who transfers learning from the driver's education course to driving any and all vehicles. Another example might be someone reading a book. The reader learns how to use survey as an overview methodology, and then applies the skill in an immediate reading assignment and also in future reading activities.

However, transfer of learning is more complex and multidimensional than simple duplication of skill use. Since the mid-1970s, experts seem to agree that transfer shows a natural dichotomy: simple and complex. Researchers suggest many terms to describe both sides of the dichotomy (Figure 9.1): simple and complex (Fogarty 1989), near and far (Wittrock 1967), horizontal and vertical (Joyce and Showers 1983), automatic and mindful (Perkins 1986), low road and high road (Salomon and Perkins 1988), similar and cued (Hunter 1971; Beyer 1987), spontaneous and guided and scaffolded (Sternberg 1984), and practiced and mediated (Feuerstein 1980).

Moye (1997) explores the critical factor of transfer and examines the conditions that foster transfer of learning for teachers in training. She notes that, in other life situations, people have come to expect transfer and,

Dichotomy in Transfer

LOW LEVEL	HIGH LEVEL
simple	complex
near	far
horizontal	vertical
automatic	mindful
low road	high road
similar	cued
spontaneous	guided and scaffolded
practiced	mediated

Figure 9.1

thus, transfer needs to permeate educational efforts in school reform and professional development.

The natural dichotomy in Figure 9.1 seems to be fairly easy to sense and understand. Yet, there is another dichotomy in thinking about transfer that seems to take precedence. This second, overriding division in transfer theory asks whether transfer is best served with *generalized* teaching or with *content-specific* teaching. There are three views worth looking at, presented metaphorically: Bo Peep, lost sheep, and good shepherd.

BO PEEP THEORY

"Leave them alone and they'll come home wagging their tails behind them." This short piece of doggerel summarizes the basic position that presently holds the educational community in its grip. According to Perkins (1990), it describes standard instructional practice: teach content, give students immediate and continuous practice, and transfer of learning is sure to follow.

For example, this theory presumes that when students are taught the periodic table of elements and practice recognizing and analyzing the atomic structure of the elements, they will somehow transfer this factual information into relevant applications. With sufficient and varied practice, some students may actually do this. Then again, some may not. This theoretical approach also presumes that students who learn the periodic table of elements somehow transfer concepts about patterns, symbolic notation, and how to chart information by simply working with the table in fact-oriented tasks. Although there is some possibility of transfer of content as a result of varied practice, there is a much slimmer possibility of transfer of patterning, notation, and how-to information. Bo Peep does not have any sheep coming home.

LOST SHEEP THEORY

In fact, again according to Perkins (1990), over time, transfer has become the *lost sheep* of the educational community. How has this lost sheep theory evolved to the point that it somehow overrides all other evidence?

Historically, educational dogma dictated that curricula adhere to the adage: Latin, geometry, (or the like) train the mind. However, in the early 1900s, Thorndike (1903) and others presented convincing evidence that suggested that training the faculties did not transfer in generalized ways. These researchers favored schooling in which the initial learning situation simulated as closely as possible the anticipated transfer situation. In fact, they advocated learning that encompassed identical elements for the two situations. Training would be specific, and transfer would occur.

Polya (1957) advocated a diametrically opposed view in mathematics. That is, Polya believed that a general, generic, and heuristic approach to problem solving was the key to the transfer of learning in diverse settings.

And so the controversy began with the basic and enduring formulations of arguments for transfer from specific, similar contexts and transfer from generalizable heuristics. Unfortunately, buried within the controversy is one overlooked but illuminating fact: neither side—context-bound, specific training nor generalizable principles and rules—shows overwhelming and convincing evidence of transfer.

Perkins' summation: "Transfer ain't that great, right now. We're not getting the transfer we want" (1990). In fact, transfer is so lacking and so rare that it has become what Perkins calls the lost sheep of education. A teacher's lost sheep explanation might sound like this: If transfer does not work, if I cannot seem to get the transfer I want, then I'll just do better in highly focused subject-oriented lessons. Thus, teachers will ignore transfer. If transfer is not there for their students, its lack is not a big issue. Teachers will just teach well what they can teach.

GOOD SHEPHERD THEORY

Fortunately, the winds of curricular change have recently rekindled the fading embers of transfer, which had been close to becoming forgotten ashes. A number of voices from the thinking skills movement have focused on the transfer issue again, igniting sparks of urgent concern. Although the controversy surrounding transfer-as-context-bound or transfer-as-generalizable remains a somewhat unresolved issue, agreements about transfer of learning do show evidence of promise for the educational community. For example, teaching Latin does not seem to transfer in terms of a more disciplined mind because, it is now agreed, Latin may not have been taught to cultivate transfer. And, although teaching general heuristics—does not seem to transfer into problem-solving steps in the writing process even when transfer has been explicitly considered, intricate and powerful implications have emerged from work in both areas.

In essence, current transfer research suggests that when teachers pay attention to transfer in contextual learning situations and when teachers accompany general strategies with self-monitoring techniques, students can transfer. However, in both context-bound and general heuristics approaches, transfer occurs when teachers shepherd it.

Thus, there is Perkins' (1990) *good shepherd theory*: When teachers provoke students to practice and reflect, transfer is fairly easy to achieve. Transfer *can* be mediated. The good shepherd theory gives new hope for students achieving transfer and new responsibility for teachers to teach for transfer. After all, isn't all learning for transfer?

HUGGING AND BRIDGING FOR TRANSFER

To begin to change Perkins' summation "Transfer ain't that great, right now" to "Transfer is greater than ever, right now," teachers need to examine two critical choices that foster the transfer phenomenon. Salomon and Perkins (1988) identify the first as a choice between automatic transfer (low road) and abstracted transfer (high road). They describe the second critical choice as choosing between two mediation strategies: hugging for low road and bridging for high road transfer. Hugging means teaching to enhance the resemblance between situations that foster low road or automatic transfer. Bridging means teaching to mediate the needed processes of abstraction and making connections that promote high road transfer (Salomon and Perkins 1988).

Beyer (1987) refers to mediation as cueing what to do, when to do it, and how to do it. Perkins (1986) further suggests that anticipatory tactics and retrieval tactics promote transfer. Using these categories—anticipatory tactics and retrieval tactics—suggests the division shown in Figure 9.2.

THE TRANSFER CURRICULUM

Transfer Tactics		
	ANTICIPATORY	RETRIEVAL
High road	• abstracting rules • anticipating applications	• reflect by generalizing the problem • focus retrieval in one particular context • make metaphors
Low road	• immediate practice • varied practice • matching lesson to target outcome	• spaced, varied practice over time

Figure 9.2

Fogarty's (1989) look at adult learners suggests a continuum of transfer behavior within the dichotomy of simple and complex transfer. The learner levels, originally developed for adult creative transfer, apply similarly to student transfer as shown in Figure 9.3. (See Blackline C9.1 in Appendix C for a blackline master.)

Fogarty's six categories of situational dispositions toward transfer describe learners' transfer behaviors ranging from simple (overlooks, duplicates, replicates) to complex (integrates, maps, and innovates). When teachers are aware of the learners' transfer levels and monitor transfer through appropriate cueing questions, they promote creative transfer, which is increasingly complex. For the learner who is simply *duplicating* the skill or strategy, which is a somewhat low level of transfer, the teacher might cue with a question: Can you think of an adjustment you can make so that this idea is useful in another context? This cue may be enough to spark movement toward *replicated* transfer in which the learner personally tailors the idea to suit his or her needs. The reflective questions based on transfer levels (Figure 9.4 or Blackline C9.2 in Appendix C) help teachers move students toward deeper levels of transfer. For example, if a student always draws figures in an identical way, the teacher might suggest that the student change the eyes or hair on the figure or even the size of the figure. By suggesting this, the teacher propels the student toward creative divergence and more complex transfer. The metacognitive reflection questions can be self- or peer-monitored with both adult and student learners. Note the shifts that are required as one wrestles with the transfer cueing questions in Figure 9.4.

Transfer Cueing Questions

Overlooking
Think of an instance when the skill or strategy
would be inappropriate.
I would not use _____ when _____.

Integrating
Think of an analogy for the skill or strategy.
_____ is like _____ because both _____.

Duplicating
Think of an opportunity passed when you could
have used the skill or strategy.
I wish I'd known about _____ when _____.

Mapping
Think of an opportunity to use the new idea.
Next _____, I could use _____ when _____.

Replicating
Think of an adjustment that will make your
application of _____ more relevant.
Next time I'm going to _____.

Innovating
Think of an application for a real-life setting.
I could use _____ when _____.

Figure 9.4

A Continuum

FROM TRAINING TO TRANSFER: LEARNER SITUATIONAL DISPOSITIONS

Birds		Transfer Disposition	Teacher (Training) Transfer	Student (Classroom) Transfer
Ollie the Head-in-the Sand Ostrich		Overlooks	Does nothing; unaware of relevance and misses appropriate applications; overlooks intentionally or unintentionally. (resists) *"Great session but this won't work with my kids or content"...or "I chose not to use...because..."*	Misses appropriate opportunity; overlooks; persists in former way. *"I get it right on the dittos, but I forget to use **punctuation** when I write an essay."* (Doesn't connect appropriateness.)
Dan the Drilling Woodpecker		Duplicates	Drills and practices exactly as presented; Drill! Drill! Then stops; uses as an activity rather than as a strategy, duplicates. (copies) *"Could I have a copy of that transparency?"*	Performs the drill exactly as practiced; duplicates. *"Yours is not to question why - just invert and multiply."* (When dividing fractions) (No understanding of what she/he is doing.)
Laura the Look-Alike Penquin		Replicates	Tailors to kids and content, but applies in similar content; all look alike, does not transfer into new situations; replicates. (differentiates) *"I use the web for every character analysis."*	Tailors, but applies in similar situation; all look alike; replicates. *"Paragraphing means I must have three 'indents' per page."* (Tailors into own story or essay, but paragraphs inappropriately.)
Jonathan Livingston Seagull		Integrates	Raised consciousness; acute awareness; deliberate refinement; integrates subtly; with existing repertoire. (combines) *"I haven't used any of your ideas, but I'm wording my questions carefully. I've always done this, but I'm doing more of it."*	Is aware; integrates; combines with other ideas and situations. *"I always try to guess (**predict**) what's gonna happen next on T.V. shows."* (Connects to prior knowledge and experience.)
Cathy the Carrier Pigeon		Maps	Consciously transfers ideas to various situations, contents; carries strategy as part of available repertoire; maps. (associates) *"I use the webbing strategy in everything."*	Carries strategy to other content and situations. Associates and maps. *Parent related story - "Tina suggested we **brainstorm** our vacation ideas and rank them to help us decide."* (Carries new skills in life situations.)
Samantha the Soaring Eagle		Innovates	Innovates; flies with an idea; takes it into action beyond the initial conception; creates enhances, invents; risks. (diverges) *"You have changed my teaching forever. I can never go back to what I used to do. I know too much. I'm too excited."*	Innovates; takes idea beyond initial conception; risks; diverges. *"After studying flow charts for computer class student constructs a Rube Goldberg type invention."* (Innovates; invents; diverges; goes beyond and creates novel.)

Figure 9.3

251

Joyce and Showers (1980) also looked at transfer of learning by adult learners in staff development programs. They suggest that, although horizontal transfer shifts directly into the classroom teaching situation, vertical transfer requires adaptation to fit the conditions. High transfer requires understanding of the purpose and rationale of the skill and the know-how to adapt it with executive control.

SHEPHERDING TRANSFER

Perkins, Fogarty, and Barell (1989) approach teaching for transfer as the key to more thoughtful instruction. By focusing curricula on the knowledge, skills, concepts, principles, attitudes, and dispositions (the "somethings") to be transferred and focusing on transferring these within content, across disciplines, and into life (the "somewheres"), teachers expertly tailor instruction by mediating the hugging and bridging strategies of transfer (the "somehows") (Figures 9.5 and 9.6). (For a blackline master of Figure 9.5, see Blackline C9.3 in Appendix C.)

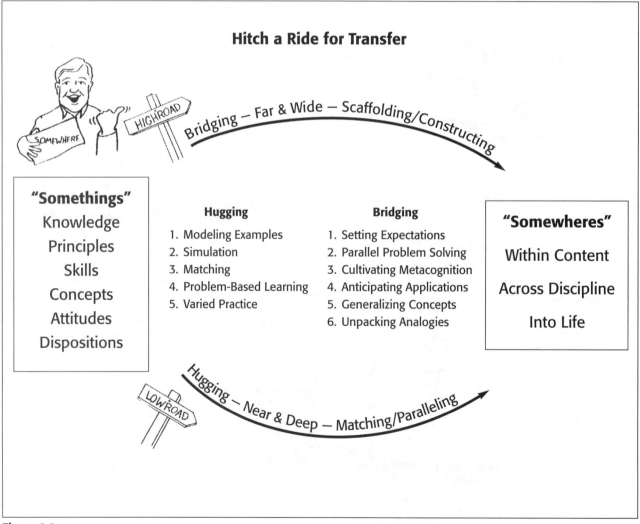

Figure 9.5

The Transfer Model

Something	Somehow	Somewhere
Concepts	HUGGING: bring instructional experience closer to target you want	WITHIN LESSON CONTENT:
Skills		Subtraction
Attitudes	Modeling	Addition
Knowledge	Simulating	Multiplication
Dispositions	Matching	Fractions
Principles	Problem-based Learning	
Habits of Mind	Practicing	ACROSS DISCIPLINE:
Content Standards		Math
Process Standards	BRIDGING: use mindful abstractions	Science
		Social Studies
Criteria:	Expectations	Language Arts
❏ _____	Problem Solving	Fine Arts
❏ _____	Metacognition	Technology
❏ _____	Applications	
	Generalizations	INTO LIFE:
	Analogies and Metaphors	Personal
		School
		Work
		Family

Figure 9.6

When teachers work with the model of "somethings" to transfer "somewhere," their instructional strategies of the "somehows" take on greater emphasis in the teaching/learning situation. In essence, they reshape curricula with the pieces that have what Fogarty (1989) calls *transfer power,* and teaching for transfer becomes an explicit part of the lesson.

In short, effective teachers sum up the "sheep" transfer theories as follows:

1. The *Bo Peep theory* only leads to the loss of one of the key aspects of the learning situation, the transfer of learning;

2. Ignoring transfer (the *lost sheep* theory) leads educators to miss the transfer, use, and application of learning in new settings—the essence of learning.

3. When teachers pay attention to transfer and guide it as a *good shepherd* herds sheep, then they take learning to new heights for learners of all ages and in all situations.

After all, isn't all learning for transfer?

When teachers teach students how to use the basic reflective tools that promote transfer, they are helping students with transfer of learning. These are integrated into the *Blueprints* teaching and learning model. Sometimes, a single, well-constructed transfer tool lesson familiarizes students with the vocabulary for metacognition (thinking about their thinking).

Three adaptable start-up lessons can be used to demonstrate three very useful transfer tools: stems, asking questions, and metacognitive reflection. These lessons show how teachers may incorporate both hugging elements (e.g., matching, modeling, simulating) and bridging elements (e.g., setting expectations, using analogies, generalizing) into their lessons.

TRANSFER TOOL: STEMS

Helping students focus on what they are learning and motivating them to write or share how they think about what they are learning, doing, or thinking are difficult challenges for teachers. One simple tool to help this challenge is the stem or lead-in statement. Like a stem that connects the leaf to a limb, the stem statement connects a student's thinking to the course content. The stem serves as the backbone for cooperative group or whole class ideas for writing or discussing content and for embedding transfer skills in the students' repertoire of learning techniques.

Begin by developing students' prior knowledge of the concept of *stem*. Review the word *stem* with the class. (In primary grades, show a leaf and stem). Ask students:

- What does the word stem mean to you?
- Give examples of stems in nature and all around you.
- What is the purpose of each different stem?

After students finish their discussion, display a graphic on the board or overhead showing the stem statement: (see Figure 9.7). Yesterday, I learned . . . . Solicit several responses (see Figure 9.7 for one example). Write the responses on multiple stems to show that each person's answer is a valid answer. Use either a list or show a leaf-like illustration with each student's statement attached.

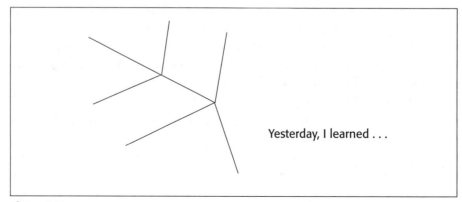

Yesterday, I learned . . .

Figure 9.7

When students are comfortable with the concept of a stem, explain to them that they are going to learn how to use the stem statement as a tool for discussing ideas in class and as a lead-in for their writing and discussion tasks.

Choose three stems from Figure 9.8 and write them on the board. (For a blackline master of Figure 9.8, see Blackline C9.4 in Appendix C.) Tell students that at the end of the day or class period they will write a response to one of these stems and then share the response with a partner.

Stem Statements

Today, I learned . . .

From this lesson, an idea I had was . . .

Today, I discovered is . . .

A problem I'm having is . . .

A connection I've made is . . .

I wonder . . .

What if . . .

Compared to . . .

Knowing _____, then _____.

If _____, then _____.

A surprise I had was . . .

Figure 9.8

When it's time to use the stem (e. g., at the end of the lesson, class period, or day), return to the three stems listed on the board and model each stem for the class. Link samples to the content studied.

Ask each student to select one of the stems and complete it. (Students may write their responses in their logs or journals, on a note card, or on other paper designated by the teacher.)

Tell students that this is the *think* time before going to pairing and sharing. Allow two to four minutes for the thinking task. Then, create pairs and ask them to exchange responses without judgment. After they have shared as pairs, ask volunteers to share their own statements.

Because this is an introductory lesson, it is important to assess student understanding of the strategy. Focus student reflection on the stem by putting these transfer stems on the board for all to see:

- A stem statement is . . .

- Another time or place in my school day that I could use a stem is . . .

- Stem statements are like leaf stems because . . .

Ask students to complete the stems. Follow the same think-pair-share sequence as the students used for the earlier stem completion activity but add a round robin for the final sharing so that all students participate. Explain that the first volunteer starts with a response to the first stem, and then each person to the volunteer's right responds in turn with a response. After about a third of the class has responded, switch to the second stem for responses. Do the same with the final stem until all students have given a response.

Before starting the round robin, establish the rules for responding. Acknowledge a student's right to pass and not to read or share a stem response. (If a student passes, simply acknowledge him or her with a "thank you" and go to the next student in turn.) At the same time, tell students that if they say, "My response is the same as so-and-so's," they are to read their response to the class anyway. In the beginning, be sure to emphasize the expectation that students may share without fear of negative feedback. As the class learns to share, you may ask students either to complete the statement or pass without offering the option of duplicating an earlier student's response.

Conclude the activity by thanking the class for the many ideas shared for transferring this strategy across the curriculum and for making the metaphor connection.

When students are familiar with the use of stems, multiple opportunities arise for their use. Teachers may even encourage more expansive responses. When brought into play at the end of each lesson, stem statements stimulate students' transfer. The students may use as little as two or three minutes for completing a stem statement in a journal or in the cooperative groups, or they may need more time to use the stems to start a discussion on how the learning from the lesson may be applied across the curriculum. To promote wider use of stems, a class brainstorm of thought-provoking verbs for the stems may help. To make this list, show students the three-story intellect model (see Figure 9.9 later in this chapter) and ask them to turn each verb into a possible stem for transfer.

Finally, remember that stems can appear at other times than the end of a lesson. For example, teachers may want to use a stem at a lesson's start for checking prior knowledge (e.g., What I know about_____ is . . .) or ask students to complete a stem as a bridge between lesson elements (e.g., A question I have about_____ is . . .).

TRANSFER TOOL: ASK THE RIGHT QUESTION

A basic marketing principle is: Ask the right question and you get answers you want. Ask the wrong question and you get answers you do not want. As the research on reading comprehension demonstrates, good readers ask the right questions as they read (Brown 1978). In the classroom, teachers can help all students learn to ask the right questions and use the answers to achieve deeper understanding of content and skills.

The first step to fostering student achievement in transfer is to introduce students to thinking verbs by displaying the three-story intellect model (see Figure 9.9 or Blackline C2.5 in Appendix C). Students who master the three-story intellect labels and definitions can use them as hooks on which to hang their thinking patterns in different content areas. These verbs help students recognize what they are being asked to think about and facilitate development of their thinking skills.

Start with the following focus activity to develop students' prior knowledge. On the overhead or board, display this Will Rogers saying: Even if you are on the right track, you will get run over if you just sit there. Show the following statements (use boldface for the thinking verbs/nouns) and ask students to respond to them:

In your own words, **explain** what the quote means.

What is **the connection** of this quote to your schoolwork?

Propose your own theory about life.

Do you **agree** or **disagree** with Rogers' quotation?

When students have finished writing their answers, ask several students to share their responses. Then, show students where each question fits on the three-story intellect model and explain why it is important for them to learn this vocabulary.

Use practice in the content of the next lesson to advance student understanding and use of questioning strategies. Select a story, text chapter, a few paragraphs, a video, a newspaper editorial, or magazine article related to the theme or topic of the lesson. Divide students into trios. Give each trio a copy of the material, a large sheet of newsprint, marking pens, and tape. Have each group select a recorder, task director, and timekeeper. Review their roles and the DOVE guidelines:

D - Defer judgment.

O - Opt for outlandish.

V - Vast numbers are needed.

E - Expand by piggybacking.

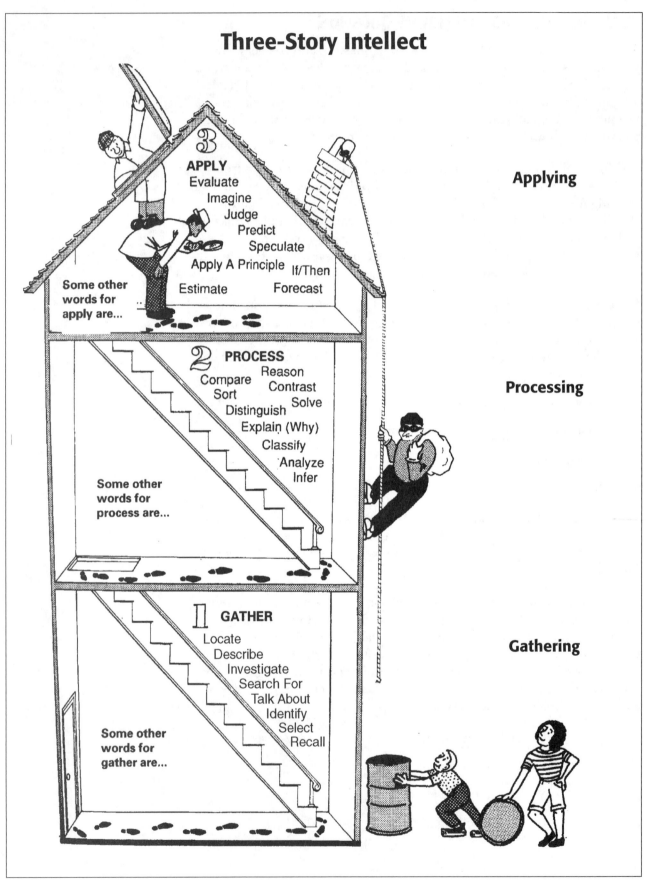

Three-Story Intellect

Applying

Processing

Gathering

Figure 9.9

258

Allow fifteen minutes for the task. Each group reads the material and composes three questions, one from each level of the three-story intellect model.

When the groups are finished making up their questions, join each trio with another trio. Ask trios to exchange material with each other. Next, they are to read the materials and check that the other trio's questions fit the three-story intellect model, and then answer the questions. After fifteen minutes, the two trios should discuss each other's responses and talk about how the responses apply to other school structures.

To assess what students have learned about asking questions and to promote additional use of this knowledge, ask students the following:

- Explain in your own words why it is important to ask the right question.
- Explain how you might use the different levels of questions if you were a teacher.
- What would happen if you had to answer second- and third-story questions in every class?
- Determine how skilled you are in asking questions and what you need to improve.

Adapt these requests to the students' grade level. Seek multiple responses and open discussion. To extend respondent's thinking, ask for clarification whenever possible.

TRANSFER TOOL: METACOGNITIVE REFLECTION

Critical thinkers are often described as people who can evaluate the quality of their learning, thinking, and problem solving. They have learned how to make logical judgments about important ideas that they study, read, see on television, or hear about from peers, politicians, or neighbors. The thinking skills required for this evaluation, however, are complex. Many students resist first attempts at critical thinking, but with encouragement, easy-to-use tools, and persistence, they can become evaluators and critical thinkers. Starting as non-responders, students grow in confidence to give amplified assessments that review what they have learned, how they have learned, the quality of their thinking, and the quality of their interactions with each other. When students achieve this confidence in the tools for assessment in the cooperative classroom, they readily transfer the tools and the confidence to other schoolwork, to their home lives, and to the world outside the classroom.

Begin this lesson on metacognitive reflection with a think-pair-share activity. Ask students to recall a recent instance of a television show and think about what they liked and disliked about the show. Then, in pairs, ask them to share their thinking. Solicit multiple answers from the pairs before asking students to generalize about the common connections in their examples. What do they perceive as similar among several or all of the ideas? Record the responses and introduce the vocabulary words *assessment* and *evaluation*. Help students understand that what they have just done fits the definitions of *assessment* and *evaluation* and ask the pairs to identify other examples of assessment.

Give each pair a copy of the Mrs. Potter's questions (see Blackline C4.10 in Appendix C):

- What were we expected to do?
- What did we do well?
- What would we do differently the next time we have this task?
- What help do we need?

Ask each pair to take turns responding and recording answers to the questions. If the speaker is too brief, the recorder can give hints but not the answer. They are to focus on the television show they just finished assessing. Model with one student how to answer the questions and have a volunteer recorder write the responses on the board.

Allow ten minutes for the paired interviews. Walk among the groups to encourage and coach. Let students do the talking and answering.

After the interviews, ask for volunteers to share. Pick one or two different recorders for the answers to each question. Check for understanding of the four questions.

Next, assign a cooperative group task as practice in another lesson. Structure the task with a thinking strategy that extends their thinking about the content of the lesson. Let the students know that at the end of that lesson they will use Mrs. Potter's assessment questions to evaluate their thinking. Assign the learning task in cooperative groups of three. Remind students to use roles, guidelines, and other tools to support their groups. Monitor and coach the groups during the task.

Review Mrs. Potter's questions. Give a worksheet to each group and ask the group to respond. Focus Mrs. Potter's questions on

- cooperative learning expectations in the task,
- thinking in the task, and
- both cooperative learning expectations and thinking.

Model some sample responses. Check for understanding of the task and allow five to seven minutes for the groups to work. If time allows, call upon random groups to report sample answers to the questions.

SUMMARY

These transfer tool lessons highlighted transfer elements. Note the use of both hugging and bridging strategies integrated into the lesson design. For a high-transfer lesson, it is important that the design include purposeful attention to the tools that promote transfer of content, thinking, and cooperation. When students know how to use the transfer tools, teachers can continue to incorporate the tools in future lessons so that students master them.

Learning these transfer tools works best when students practice them weekly. Teachers need to stress the appropriate "somehows" (e.g., modeling, simulating, problem solving, generalizations, etc.) that take these tools "somewhere" (e.g., Where *in this class* might you use Mrs. Potter's questions? When in *other classes* could you use Mrs. Potter's questions? *Outside of schoolwork,* what would be an appropriate time to use Mrs. Potter's questions? *How else* have you used Mrs. Potter's questions?).

The most effective mediation of transfer, however, includes mediation of content. The teacher, as guide on the side, *purposefully* asks the questions that engage students in thinking about how the central ideas and skills of a course apply in situations far removed from the immediate meaning of the concepts. This means teachers devote daily time—at least 20% of a class period—to help students transfer the meaning of what they have learned. When teachers couple this mediation within cooperative learning strategies, they ensure the highest degree of readiness for their students who, working alone on the test, need to find the best answers to the challenging test items.

How might this content mediation work? At the most basic level, the transfer-oriented teacher uses the informal cooperative strategies, such as think-pair-share or prediction pairs, to focus students on the transfer of content to a variety of "somewheres." Consider examples from a middle school music class. The unit focus is rhythm. Each week as the class practices for its winter concert, the teacher introduces a new piece with a different rhythm. Her students, representing a variety of ethnic groups, welcome her multi-ethnic selections, which were made also with the intent to extend their understanding of rhythm. At the end of the week, the teacher sets aside twenty minutes for student transfer work. She matches students in pairs, gives each pair a worksheet (Figure 9.10), and asks them to complete as many "think" questions as possible. After the pair agrees on its best answers, she selects different pairs to share one response.

---

1. Score this week's rhythm with numbers. _____

2. What other songs do you know with this rhythm?

   _____ None

   _____

   _____

3. Pick a household product, car, or service for a television advertisement. Tell how you would make this advertisement using this rhythm.

4. What are some other ways someone could use this rhythm?

Figure 9.10

Or the teacher might use the prediction pair for this lesson. After pairing students, she gives each pair a worksheet. After agreeing on the best answers, she selects random student pairs to share with the class. She guides the discussion that follows with PACTS guidelines (Figure 9.11). For this lesson, she might use Figure 9.12 for stimulating students' reflection.

PACTS

Paraphrase

Affirm

Clarify

Test options

Summarize

Figure 9.11

---

1. Identify with numbers the rhythm for this week. _____

2. Tell where else you have heard this rhythm.

   _____

3. Predict what would happen if . . . (Be specific.)

   _____

Figure 9.12

Such guidance goes beyond facilitation or questions that just make it easy for students to understand the concept. In the guidance role, teachers are mediators. They stand "in the middle" between student and course material and target questions that *challenge* students. Feuerstein (1980) points out the importance of this distinction between *facilitation* (i.e., make easy) and *mediation* (i.e., challenge). He notes that the teacher with high expectations does not lower standards by watering down curriculum or making the thought process easier. Instead, as a mediator, the teacher words and rewords the tough issues and helps students discover meaning and, as a result, builds their confidence in what obstacles they can overcome. When this occurs, students are all the more ready to make additional, appropriate transfers.

Thus, by making all teaching and learning reach for transfer, the argument that pits *generalized* teaching against *content-specific* teaching becomes a false dichotomy. Rather than being confronted with an either-or choice, teachers develop effective transfer by choosing both. For the practical teacher in the *Blueprints* classroom, this collaboration becomes the doorway leading to high achievement.

BLUEPRINT
Elementary
Lesson

Codes 1SD
                5NR
                6CL
                9QCA

Setting Up the Scaffolding

Working the Crew

Scavenger Hunt

One of the well-documented methods to raise student achievement is formal instruction in the use of analysis and classification in finding similarities and differences. Students are required throughout the curriculum to analyze and classify content. Seldom are they formally prepared to sharpen these skills. The better their preparation, however, the better they perform in the classroom and on standardized tests that use these skills.

From the earliest grades, students make patterns based on similarities and differences. In the first grade, they must know how to distinguish types of triangles, letter sounds, and types of machines; in high school, they distinguish and classify animals and plants in biology. And, outside the classroom, students are surrounded by examples of classification at work: the supermarket shelf, zip codes, credit card numbers, and the yellow pages, to mention a few.

To develop *prior knowledge,* ask three students to come to the front of the class. Pick three with very visible common characteristics such as hairstyle or shirt color. Ask the class to identify the characteristics that all three have in common. Watch out! They may find more than you intended, but that is okay!

After students finish this activity, introduce the vocabulary for this activity: *analysis, characteristic, classification, likeness,* and *difference.* (Use appropriate words for the grade level.) Use the portmanteau activity (chapter 2) to help students master these words using examples from their daily lives (e.g., Analysis is to divide a whole into many parts such as a whole pie that has apples, sugar, crust, etc.).

Most important, check for student understanding of the concept *classification,* a major thinking method for sorting objects and ideas into groups according to their likenesses. Post a mental menu that may facilitate student transfer and development of the skill of classification (see below or Blackline C9.5 in Appendix C).

Classifying

Cluster words that are alike.

Label the cluster.

Untangle subclusters.

Evaluate connections in the clusters.

Set the patterns.

Assemble groups of three by asking students to find two other classmates who share at least two similar characteristics. Explain that they are going on a scavenger hunt and that each student, working alone, has five minutes to gather no more than five items from the designated area (classroom, playground, etc.). Give examples of objects to collect, and send the students on their way.

When the hunters return to their trios at the end of five minutes, each group arranges its items on the floor or a desk. Each trio looks for ways to sort the items and comes up with at least three groups that have a single similarity in each (C). Next, the trios label their grouped items (L) and identify subgroups of items (U). Then, they identify the reasons for the connections (E). Finally, on a sheet of newsprint, each trio names its grouped items and identifies the key characteristic(s) of their grouped and sub-grouped items (S).

Reflecting on the Design

For cognitive processing, ask one or two trios to share their work. Ask teams to explain why they made each group and how they used CLUES.

Ask each trio to discuss and decide how the skill of classifying could help in one of these content areas: science, art, reading, mathematics, or social studies. Ask for volunteers to share their ideas with the class.

For metacognitive processing, conclude the lesson with a round robin response to this stem:

   Classification is an important thinking skill because . . .

Or ask students in their groups to discuss Mrs. Potter's questions with a focus on evaluating the thinking in the cooperative groups.

# # #

Codes 5NR
6CL
7OF
8GH
9QCA

Setting Up the
Scaffolding

Working the
Crew

That's a Good Idea!

Energy and enthusiasm help engage students in cooperative tasks. Sometimes students need a boost of energy to overcome lethargy, such as after lunch. Activities like this lesson can provide that boost. At the same time, this kind of activity meets the criteria for high challenge and high support for working on a high content lesson that promotes transfer.

Brainstorming is a thinking strategy for generating ideas. Sometimes, brainstorming is too random and individualistic. To counter these characteristics, begin this activity by putting students into groups of five. Assign roles of materials manager, recorder, process director, reporter, and encouragement manager. Give each group several marking pens and large pieces of newsprint.

Next, introduce the lesson. This problem-based lesson is taken from a social studies unit on westward expansion of the United States. Tell the class that the lesson has two parts. In part one, the class learns the "good idea" strategy, and in part two, the students practice to transfer the skills and structures they learned into the problem "How do we . . . ?" (If the topic modeled here does not fit your curriculum, select a different topic and adapt the strategies to it.)

PART 1: DEVELOPING MANY GOOD IDEAS
Assemble the groups, and review the DOVE guidelines:

D - Defer judgment.

O - Opt for outlandish.

V - Vast numbers are needed.

E - Expand by piggybacking.

Remind the class of the two purposes of the task: (a) to learn new ways of generating ideas that will solve a problem and (b) to use these new ways in a problem-solving lesson.

On the overhead or board, draw a T-chart and label the left-hand column Improvement and the right-hand column Because. Tell students to list an improvement to a vehicle of transportation under Improvement, and tell why that improvement is a good idea under Because.

Next, engage the entire class in brainstorming all the vehicles of transportation they know. Record these on the board for all to see. Prime the pump by listing car, airplane, and bus. No duplicates are allowed.

When the list is long enough for each group to have several choices, instruct each reporter in a group to select one means of transportation. Again, avoid duplicates but encourage wild and crazy ideas. (With middle graders, it helps to articulate some boundaries on ideas so that ideas are not offensive or risqué.)

Each group uses a round robin that starts with the recorder and moves clockwise around the group. The recorder suggests an improvement he or she would like to see in the vehicle to make a 2,000-mile trip comfortable and fun for the members of the group traveling together. The next person responds: That is a good idea, because . . . . After completing the stem, that person adds another improvement and the next person says: That is a good idea because . . . . As each group member takes a turn, the recorder fills in the chart. Plan to make at least two rounds or spend ten minutes maximum on this part of the activity.

Next, groups work together to draw a sketch of the vehicle. Post the completed sketches for all to see and then ask reporters to explain the new vehicle.

PART 2: SOLVING A PROBLEM

Instruct each group to read the text material on the westward expansion (or substitute some other source of information). Tell groups to rotate roles. Then, ask groups to construct a web that visualizes the barriers a family might face moving west to California from the east coast. The family would have the pleasure of traveling in the vehicle designed in part 1.

After groups have listed the barriers, ask them to select five to seven barriers that they can argue were the most difficult to overcome for a family in the westward movement. Rotate the group roles once again. Instruct each group to use the develop-many-good-ideas strategy from part 1 to list ways to overcome each barrier by making improvements on the vehicle. Again, conclude this step by a group drawing of the vehicle with its improvements.

Reflecting on the Design

Invite each group to display its vehicle to the class. With each member contributing in a presentation, the group explains the barriers selected, the vehicle improvements chosen, and the reasons for the improvements.

For cognitive processing, instruct each student to select one major barrier to a family's successful crossing to California and write a five-paragraph essay describing what the student thinks might be the best solution to overcoming that problem. Tell students that they are to use this outline:

1. The barrier: a problem to overcome
2. The best possible solution: a description
3. Reason 1 for the solution
4. Reason 2 for the solution
5. Summary

Students may either do this task during class time or as a homework.

For metacognitive processing, conclude by asking each group to use Mrs. Potter's questions to discuss this lesson. Responses may cover content, thinking, and/or collaboration but should highlight the problem solving done by the group. If time allows, invite the reporter from each group to report the group's ideas to the class.

# # #

BLUEPRINT
High School
Lesson

Codes 2SN
5NR
6CL
8GH

Setting Up the
Scaffolding

Working the
Crew

Do You Want to Bet?

The research on effective readers (Pearson, et al. 1984) tells teachers that one of most important skills is making predictions. They describe students who have grasped how to take data in a story or essay and can tell what will happen next with great accuracy. These students maintain a high level of interest in the material as they continue reading, because they want to see if their predictions come true. This skill carries over to working with information across the curriculum. The more skilled the student is in using data to make safe predictions, the more successful the student is in understanding the material. The stronger the student's ability to understand, the more likely the student will succeed in testing situations.

Begin the lesson by asking students what they already know about the word *prediction*. Invite pairs to complete a web showing their ideas. Ask three pairs to come to the front of the class and explain their webs.

After the third group finishes their demonstration, ask the pairs to create a question about what they think they need to know about making predictions as a reading tool. Randomly call on pairs to share their questions. List the questions on the board.

On the board or overhead, display the BET menu:

B = Base on facts.

E = Examine clues.

T = Test your prediction.

Set up cooperative groups of three with the roles of reader, recorder, and time-keeper.

Explain that the BET menu is a reminder of the steps a sound predictor takes when making a prediction. In the next task, they are going to make some predictions about a story and may want to refer to this menu.

Distribute one copy of "The Dinner Party" by Mona Gardner to each group. (See Blackline C9.6 in Appendix C). Instruct the reader to fold the copy on the BET lines and to read the first segment to the group. At the end of the first segment, ask the groups to BET what will happen in the next segment of the story and to support their prediction with clues from what they just read. The recorder writes these down as the members identify facts, discuss clues, or just guess.

The Dinner Party
By Mona Gardner

The country is India. A colonial official and his wife are giving a large dinner party. They are seated with their guests—army officers, government attachés and their wives, and a visiting American naturalist—in their spacious dining room, which has a bare marble floor, open rafters, and wide glass doors opening on to a veranda.

(BET what will happen next. Why do you think so? Find data to support your idea. Read to verify.)

A spirited discussion springs up between a young girl who insists that women have outgrown the jumping-on-a-chair-at-the-sight-of-a-mouse era and a colonel who says that they haven't.

"A woman's unfailing reaction in any crisis," the colonel says, "is to scream. And while a man may feel like it, he has that ounce more of nerve control than a woman has. And that last ounce is what counts."

(BET . . .)

The American does not join in the argument but watches the other guests. As he looks, he sees a strange expression come over the face of the hostess. She is staring straight ahead, her muscles contracting slightly. With a slight gesture she summons the native boy standing behind her chair and whispers to him. The boy's eyes widen and he quickly leaves the room.

Of the guests, none except the American notices this or sees the boy place a bowl of milk on the veranda just outside the open doors.

(BET . . .)

The American comes to a start. In India, milk in a bowl means only one thing—bait for a snake. He realizes there must be a cobra in the room. He looks up at the rafters, the likeliest place, but they are bare. Three corners of the room are empty and in the fourth the servants are waiting to serve the next course. There is only one place left—under the table.

His first impulse is to jump back and warn the others, but he knows the commotion would frighten the cobra into striking. He speaks quickly, the tone of his voice so arresting that it sobers everyone.

"I want to know just what control everyone at this table has. I will count to three hundred—that's five minutes—and not one of you is to move a muscle. Those who move will forfeit fifty rupees. Ready!"

(BET . . .)

The twenty people sit like stone images while he counts. He is saying ". . . two hundred and eighty . . ." when, out of the corner of his eye, he sees the cobra emerge and make for the bowl of milk. Screams ring out as he jumps to slam the veranda doors safely shut.

"You were right, Colonel," the host exclaims. "A man has just shown us an example of perfect control."

"Just a minute," the American says, turning to his hostess. "Mrs. Wynnes, how did you know that cobra was in the room?"

A faint smile lights up the woman's face as she replies, "Because it was crawling across my foot." ——

After five minutes, move the groups to the next segment and ask them to repeat the reading, predicting, and explaining. Monitor and encourage but do not join any groups. Continue to the end of the story.

Reflecting on the Design

For cognitive processing, call on random volunteers to respond to these four questions:

1. How accurate were your predictions (bets)? If you guessed the correct end, why were you able to do so? If not, where did you go wrong?

2. What did you learn about making predictions during this lesson?

3. How is this method of reading different from other methods you have used?

4. When might you use this approach in other schoolwork? In non-schoolwork?

Give many students the chance to respond by distributing responses equally.

# # #

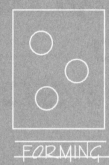

FORMING

PERFORMING

NORMING

CHAPTER 10

Phase V

PERFORMING

Level II
What About Grades,
Standards, and Test Scores?

STORMING

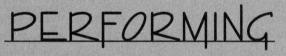

CONFORMING

WHAT ABOUT GRADES, STANDARDS, AND TEST SCORES?

There are days when spelling Tuesday simply doesn't count.
—Rabbit in <u>Vinnie the Pooh</u>, A. A. Milne

Draft

In this age of accountability, classroom teachers may feel an inordinate amount of pressure to test and measure. The current mania for standardized test results means that more time in the school year is allocated to tests and measurement. This pressure is most often translated into teacher confusion about instructional priorities: What do I do about tests and grades for cooperative learning and critical thinking? Behind this question is the teacher concern:

> I am expected to make sure all my students do well on the standardized tests for basic skills. The tests don't measure cooperative learning or thinking. If I spend time on thinking and cooperating, I will have to take instructional time from the basic skills. If I take time from the basic skills, my students may not do as well on the standardized tests. If they do poorly on tests, I will be blamed.

Such concern is both earnest and legitimate. On the one hand, teachers see the opportunities for learning inherent in the thinking and cooperative classroom. On the other hand, standardized tests heighten the pressure for accountability. Even more, teachers want to be accountable. Teachers want tests to match what the students are learning so they can know how well they are teaching. In spite of what some publicity-hunting politicians might assert, most teachers do want to do the best they can in helping their students learn.

Teachers who see the value of learning from a cognitive and cooperative perspective can measure student understanding, student cooperation, and student thinking in effective ways. Although these methods are not yet readily accepted as valid measuring devices by those who understand little about the science of educational measurement, many researchers describe them as more authentic and certainly more supportive of the total learning process. In this context, it is important to remember that cooperative learning and critical thinking are *means* to an *end*. It is more practical to think about assessment from two perspectives:

1. *Testing student knowledge:* the effective teacher uses classroom tests and district tests to determine the students' knowledge of the course content (e.g., mathematics, science) including concepts, skills, and procedures.

2. *Assessing authentically:* teachers look at what students can do with content. For example, students write an essay to demonstrate their ability to use a prescribed format, paint a picture to show brush technique, complete word problems to show ability to solve problems, and so forth. Teachers assess students' thinking skills (e.g., analyze data, compare characters) or cooperative learning (e.g., social skills), thus assessing not only what students *know* but what they can *do* with what they know.

AUTHENTIC ASSESSMENT

What does *authentic assessment* mean? According to the dictionary, *authentic* means reliable, trustworthy, supported by unquestioned evidence and *assessment* means appraisal, evaluation, and estimation of value (Merriam-Webster 1998). In an educational sense, authentic assessment means the evaluation of a student's learning through a *broad array* of unquestionable evidence. This evidence may include portfolios, logs, student artifacts, and test scores. It means weighing not only what students do, but also how they plan, make decisions, and evaluate themselves during a task. Authentic assessment gathers evidence from a variety of sources to paint a portrait of a student's growth as a thoughtful learner. Not limited to standardized tests, authentic assessment sees the student's whole performance and does not reduce the student's work to a single number, test score, or grade.

How does a teacher evaluate what a Scantron does not? Although authentic assessment is easy to advocate, implementing assessments such as using logs, student artifacts, and observation charts can be difficult in the actual classroom. Several time-tested ingredients, mostly predating the accountability mania, provide solid assessments of student performance, even of such seemingly esoteric processes as thinking and cooperating. These ingredients include establishing statewide standards and identifying core concepts.

STATEWIDE STANDARDS

National organizations such as the National Council for Teachers of Mathematics (NCTM) and the American Association of Science (AAS), have prepared national standards in specific content areas. Most states in the United States have used these to develop their own standards in all subject areas.

A standard establishes an ideal. For instance, the US National Board of Standards has established weight and distance standards, among others, that guide everyday living. *All* scales in the grocery store must comply with the weight standards; *every* new highway built must meet the standard for measuring distance.

A key to understanding standards used in education is the word *every*. When a state sets a standard that says "Every student will . . .," it sets a marking point for *all* students and sets a goal that *all* schools need to meet. This single standard for a state or nation is contrary to former educational practice in the United States. Traditionally, each local school board decided on the content of curriculum; therefore, the states had no way to measure statewide consistency in key areas of instruction. With a statewide standard, however, a state identifies what every child in every school needs to *know* (content) and be able to *do* (performance).

CORE CONCEPTS

For the first time in US education, all classroom teachers have a set of standards for each content area and are expected to help learners reach those standards. Nowhere is this more apparent than in mathematics and reading instruction. Students have a greater chance to score well on the state standardized tests when teachers review the applicable standards and give more attention and time to teaching the *core concepts* of an ever-expanding curriculum. For instance, standards-based curriculum in mathematics centers on eight to ten key concepts, such as numerical operations and fractions. By selecting the core concepts of a content area as the driving principle for setting instructional priorities, effective teachers focus student attention on the most important elements of the curriculum.

To teach these elements in depth, teachers organize a curriculum that separates a multitude of facts from a selection of organizing concepts. Choosing specific core processes enables teachers to create assessments directly connected to the curriculum content. For instance, in an oral quiz, a teacher can query knowledge-based information using verbs from the first story of the three-story intellect model or assess understanding of the core content by framing second-story processing or third-story application queries (Figure 10.1).

Three-Story Intellect

First-Story Queries (Gathering)

Name three characters in the story.

Tell what happened to Lincoln at the Ford Theatre.

List the steps in the science procedure.

Second-Story Queries (Processing)

Compare how the Democrats and the Republicans approached ____.

Explain why Anne came to Green Gables.

Explain the differences between living in a city and living on a farm.

Third-Story Queries (Applying)

Estimate how many 1-inch bolts are in this jar.

Predict the outcome of next month's election.

Evaluate the quality of your persistence.

Figure 10.1

Explain Why
• Give multiple reasons.
• Provide an example with a reason.
• Be sure reasoning is logical.

For journal entries, teachers can choose self-assessment lead-ins at the end of a task:

In this assignment, I stayed with the tough parts when/by . . .

I looked for alternatives in doing this task when . . .

I show persistence best when I . . .

I didn't quit when ____ because . . .

Teachers may also lead class discussions by asking coaching questions or giving feedback:

Who will share a time when you stuck with a tough task?

How did you overcome the urge to quit?

To assess students' ability to apply information, teachers might create a story that asks students to solve a problem. For instance, when students are studying light refraction, teachers might use a three-story intellect approach to pose *factual* questions about the physics of light, to ask students to *explain why* certain principles are important, and to encourage students to *use* the principles to solve a problem presented as a story. For example, a teacher might pose this problem and these questions:

Q **How much time do I give for discussing students' ideas and reflections?**

A In a 55-minute lesson the guideline is five minutes attention to prior knowledge, twenty-five minutes to content work, and twenty minutes for reflection and discussion. The remaining five minutes go to logistics.

> The lighthouse keeper was instructed to change the wattage of his light so that sailors could see its beams at three times the current distance of three miles.
>
> What must he understand about light?
>
> What steps will he have to take to accomplish this task?

When teachers provide scoring guides, called *rubrics,* they help students focus on critical elements of a lesson or unit by signaling the important fundamentals of the core content. There are two important steps in creating such a rubric: setting the criteria and selecting the media.

SET THE CRITERIA FOR EACH EVALUATION

Knowing what is going to be evaluated during a lesson helps both the students and the teacher. When measuring thinking, teachers may choose from two essential measurement approaches: measuring intelligent behaviors (Costa 1991) or measuring specific thinking skills or processes.

Measuring Intelligent Behaviors

Costa (1991) recommends measuring intelligent behaviors. Costa and Kallick (2000) recommend that teachers identify intelligent behaviors, dispositions of thinking, or habits of mind. Figure 10.2 shows the characteristics of intelligent behaviors that Costa believes teachers and parents can teach, observe, and assess.

Characteristics of Intelligent Behaviors

- Persistence
- Decreasing impulsivity
- Empathic listening
- Flexibility in thinking
- Metacognitive awareness
- Checking for accuracy
- Questioning
- Problem posing
- Drawing on past knowledge
- Application to new situations
- Precision of language and thought
- Using all the senses
- Ingenuity, originality, insightfulness, and creativity
- Inquisitiveness, curiosity
- Enjoyment of problem solving
  (Adapted from Costa 1991 and Costa and Kallick 2000)

Figure 10.2

Measuring Thinking Skills or Processes

The second approach to measuring student thinking identifies specific thinking skills and processes that the teacher wants the students to use with the subject matter. The three-story intellect model provides a framework for those skills (Figure 10.3).

Three-Story Intellect Model for Assessment

Gathering	Processing	Applying
count	compare	evaluate
describe	sort	imagine
match	distinguish	judge
name	explain why	predict
recite	classify	speculate
select	analyze	apply a principle
recall	infer	if/then
tell	reason	forecast
	contrast	estimate

Figure 10.3

When selecting criteria, teachers may pinpoint the quantity and quality of evidence that they need by considering fluency, flexibility, precision and perseverance, thoroughness and logic, and transfer.

Fluency

Fluent thinkers come up with a greater number of ideas, so when teachers ask students to gather information (e.g., name the characters, list the cities, describe the attributes), they need only count the number of responses students give. For instance, a simple gathering task may ask the students to list the colors seen in a picture; a more complex gathering task would ask students to identify the positive characteristics of a literary character. The grade for the individual or the group is quantitative and depends on the number of items listed.

Flexibility

Not only does the teacher look for fluency (quantity), but also for how different the responses are (quality). Flexible thinkers can identify a wide range of divergent responses to a question. For instance, when students are asked to gather information about botanical diseases found on pine trees that grow in a certain climate, a teacher might look for responses that identified both common and rare trees. Or, when students are asked to provide reasons for the disease, a teacher might look for a variety of arguments and viewpoints.

Precision and Perseverance

In mathematics and other convergent subjects, precision and perseverance are important traits. When assessing precision, teachers look for the exact and detailed application of a standard. For example, in science, did the students weigh each chemical to the exact decimal given? In mathematics, did students use each of the steps as given? When assessing perseverance, teachers observe how long students stay with a difficult task and how many different times they try to solve a problem. For instance, when students are working on a three-step word problem, how many tries do they make before giving up or asking for help?

Thoroughness and Logic

When looking for thoroughness, teachers first count the number of appropriate examples a student provides in making an argument or in defending a point. For instance, when students write an expository essay to describe an historic event, teachers look for complete and full coverage of the event. When students prepare an argumentative essay about a critical social issue, teachers count how many pro and con arguments are given. Teachers also evaluate the appropriateness of the examples by applying the rules of logic to each example. For instance, when students argue against increased local taxes to fund schools, teachers would reject a biased argument that attacked the governor for his beliefs about abortion.

Transfer

Teachers can assess students' abilities to transfer ideas. Narrow transfers that simply duplicate ideas receive lower grades than broad transfers that show more creativity and individuality. For instance, when students are asked to provide examples of times they could use a cut-and-paste procedure in a word processor, one student might repeat an example already given in the text while another might describe the use of the procedure in preparing research documents in another class. The latter student's idea shows a greater breadth and depth of transfer.

Setting the criteria for which content to know and which cooperative learning skills to use follow a similar track. For each lesson, teachers select the content that is most important to know and specifies which thinking processes are important to that content (e.g., recall, compare, predict). In addition, they designate which cooperative skills students need to demonstrate as they work through the lesson (e.g., trust, listening, leadership.)

SELECT THE MEDIA

The second step in planning for assessment is to select the media students will use to show evidence of learning. In addition to questions and demonstrations, there are a variety of media tools available. When teachers apply criteria to students' thoughtful work, they work from models that provide concrete examples of the *degrees* of quality expected. Models not only help teachers measure the quality of each student's work but also provide a concrete way to give students accurate feedback. Various media for gathering evidence of learning include quizzes and tests, logs, ad campaigns, product portfolios, and extended projects.

Quizzes and Tests

Quizzes and tests ask students to define the thinking skill, to identify strong uses of the skill, to give a demonstration of the skill in a concrete problem, or to write instructions for another use of the skill.

Logs

Logs provide students with opportunities to discuss what they have learned about a topic, ask questions they have about a burning issue, relate feelings about tasks they are doing, record ways to think through a problem, monitor their thoughts while developing a concept, explain how they used a specific thinking skill, evaluate their thinking dispositions, and sketch the ways they might think about a project. Figure 10.4 shows an example of a log.

Ad Campaigns

Ad campaigns require students to use two or three different media (e.g., posters, magazines, video) to sell a concept that they have learned (e.g., photosynthesis, whole numbers, tragedy).

Product Portfolios

Product portfolios encourage each student to keep a representative collection of completed assignments and products (e.g., a series of writing assignments) and to prepare an explanation of the changes noted through the year—including a review of the changes that have occurred during a semester. Students also complete an evaluation of the changes with a PMI chart.

Extended Projects

Extended projects require students to pull together a key concept for the year. For example, students might complete an extended science project on nuclear energy and its effects on the community. Through this project, students can demonstrate their problem-solving ability and its growth through the project.

Note that all the media described seem to be analogous to student projects. They are! The key is that teachers use the projects as a means or medium to help students think about how they approach learning tasks and to encourage students to communicate how they plan, monitor, and evaluate their thinking. When performance criteria are in hand, students perform better and teachers measure easier.

Log/Journal Example

Thinking Log Task: In your log, write about how you thought through the lab experiment today.

STUDENT: **Limited Response** *I had to figure out the different ways the frogs ate bugs.*	TEACHER COMMENT You have identified the first step in the problem-solving model. I would like you to tell me more by using the chart for problem solving on page 9. How would you use the other steps?
STUDENT: **Incomplete Response** *I followed the seven steps and checked off each one. After I checked it off, I made sure that I had an example for each one.*	TEACHER COMMENT I am pleased that you followed the seven-step model. That is a great start. I would like to have you give some of the examples here and tell how you decided on which example each time.
STUDENT: **Adequate Response** *The first thing I did was figure out the different kinds of food the frog ate. I brainstormed some other ideas. Then the facts told me that the real problem was to know the ways the frog ate insects. Once I had this idea, I began to look in two articles for the best reasons. I used the quote from the scientist to make my choice. He is the expert. After that, it was easy to pick out the others.*	TEACHER COMMENT I like the several different types of thinking you identified: problem identification, brainstorming, judging expert opinion. You have a start in explaining in more detail what you thought about. I would like you to say more about some of the ways you used the quote to help you choose.
STUDENT: **Complete Response** *When I read the first paragraph about the frog's eating habits, I thought of the ways my little brother eats in the highchair. He has all sorts of ways to attack food. So does the frog. The question is, which way is best? Obviously, the frog and my brother will have different best ways. To figure out the best way for the frog, I thought about Dr. Pink's argument. Since he has studied the frog for 24 years, I accept him as reliable. I thought about questioning his theory, but I didn't have time to research the answers. I do still have the questions in my head.*	TEACHER COMMENT I liked the personal touch in the comparison to your brother. It brings your thinking to life. I also like how you keep asking questions and looking for several answers to each question. Another plus is how you thought about the expert. I am interested and would like to hear the questions.

Figure 10.4

GRADING COOPERATION IN THE CLASSROOM

In any situation, grading is a two-edged sword. On the one hand, good grades motivate students who care about grades. On the other hand, grades can have little or no effect on students who have a record of Cs, Ds, or Fs.

New users of cooperative learning often ask about grading and testing. In the age of "hard" measurement (e.g., standardized tests and Scantrons), there is little leeway for "soft" evaluation (e.g., student essays and portfolios) on topics such as cooperation, thinking, and transfer. When one respects teachers' judgments about student performance, many valued answers to the questions about assessing student performance exist. But, when one is searching for teacher-proof evaluation methods, the number of successful opportunities is much fewer.

The assessment of cooperation, thinking, and transfer is possible. Moreover, well-done assessment can end in solid grades of student performance. The catch is in the teacher's willingness to go beyond standardized tests and to use a variety of tools *with* the Scantrons.

The most important reason for assessing student thinking and learning is almost always the most forgotten: constructive feedback helps students refine and develop their thinking patterns. At times, assessment results get jumbled in state mandates, real estate appraisal competition, school report cards, and other less important factors. When teachers give *immediate* written feedback, they give students a major motivator for achievement. Delayed and general feedback has little effect on students' desire to improve. One task returned with extensive and thought-producing comments is far more effective than five returned with little more than a brief A+, "good job," or C.

Grades

When assessing thinking and cooperating in the classroom, grades have two roles: to summarize and report to parents how a student is doing in the class or to motivate those students *for whom grades are important.*

A teacher's extended written or verbal feedback helps students much more than grades to improve thinking and cooperating. When teachers *must* provide grades, they need to grade both individual work for achievement and group work for cooperation. Teachers can assess any classroom task. Using clear criteria for performance, they simply attach a letter grade to each criterion. For instance, in the log sample in Figure 10.4, the limited response might receive a D, whereas the complete response would merit an A. For a thinking task in which fluency is the criterion, students with five responses might receive a C, seven responses a B, and ten responses an A.

Group Grades

Some teachers elect to enhance and reward cooperative work by using group grades with content. Watch out! This practice can be dangerous. Parents of high achieving students who know how to play the grading game especially dislike group grades for content. Also teachers new to cooperative learning sometimes find it difficult to use group grades fairly and effectively.

Yet, group grades that focus on the cooperative activity can be useful. This practice, correctly introduced, can promote the "we sink or swim together" atmosphere inherent in team building. Some ideas for using group grades include raising the group average, raising individual scores based on improvement, and giving a bonus for cooperative skills.

Raise the Group Average

To use this technique, teachers first ask student groups to work together for several grading rounds. In the beginning rounds, teachers determine the average grade of each group for each task. Then, they add bonus points for improvement of a group's average in subsequent rounds. For instance, in a series of weekly spelling quizzes, each student can have one point added to his or her individual score for each point the group average is raised. In a variation of this method, teachers identify individual student's base scores in each quiz area (e.g., vocabulary, spelling, grammar, mathematics, science, reading) and base bonus points for the group on the individual's improvement.

Raise Individual Scores Based on Improvement

In this variation, each individual receives as many bonus points as other members of the group have earned. For instance, in an examination, the criterion for a B grade is 85 percent. For every student in the group who scores higher than 85, each student earns two bonus points. A variation on this method is to award each member bonus points only when the students who typically score below 85 percent score higher on this test.

Give a Bonus for Cooperative Skills

Some teachers base bonus points only on the observed use of cooperative skills. The teacher or a student observer uses an observation checklist during class work to tabulate observed social skills. A preset number of observed cooperative behaviors merits bonus points (e.g., five behaviors = one point). Other teachers provide bonus points based on the quality of group processing. This bonus approach requires that a preset criterion be announced to the class.

Pitfalls of Group Grades

Before teachers use group grades, they need to review the pitfalls of group evaluation. First, when they use a group grade for a heterogeneous group of high and low achievers, the high achievers must have the social skills to resolve conflict and encourage equal participation. When teachers ask very able students to work with resistant or less able students, they risk both the success of the less able students and the frustration of the more able. They should use group grades only when all students can work together using cooperative skills.

A second pitfall concerns parents' reactions to the group grading results. Teachers need to check parental perception of what cooperative learning is, especially the parents of the class' high achievers. When these parents think that their children's grades depend on only how well students work together or only how well their children succeed when working with less able children, the teacher and the principal will face the storm of adverse opinion. The wise teacher ensures that the parents know what cooperative learning is and how it benefits their children.

A third pitfall is the difficulty caused by keeping students in the dark about the grading criteria. When group grades are used, teachers must announce the success criteria at the start of the task.

Individual Grades

Often, teachers find it more appropriate to grade individual completion of a task rather than rely solely on group grades. For instance, although a group may study a short story together, each member responds individually to the study questions, turns in his or her own essay, and earns his or her own grade. In another example, when students work in the cooperative groups to learn vocabulary, practice computation, or answer recall questions, the common work they do is checked in the group and reviewed by the teacher. Then, after the students study teacher feedback and correct their group work, each takes an individual test or quiz and receives an individual grade.

No Grades

When teachers elect *not* to use grades as a motivator for cooperative learning, they still can invite a high degree of individual learning in the cooperative classroom by using a variety of tools: assign a checker, assign a traveler, build trust, review or introduce social skills, work directly with students' self-concepts, and tighten aspects of group structure.

Include a checker. When the teacher assigns the checker to check short lists of basic information (e.g., vocabulary words, steps in a task, etc.) in small parts and again before students take a test, then she encourages the short, guided reviews (massed practice) that enhance short-term recall, lead to increased mastery, and model a way to memorize.

Assign a traveler. When a group gets stuck with a concept, the group can send one student to another group to find out other options. This person could be the low achiever who is given special recognition in this role.

Perform trust activities. When a group's cooperative skills lag, the teacher can return to the trust activities or the team identity tasks (e.g., reviewing group goals, creating team flags, making a team ad, etc.).

Review the social skills or introduce new ones. When the teacher introduces a high-energy, high-involvement activity as the hook for a review of needed social skills, she can review the group's skills without a heavy hand.

Work directly on students' self-concepts. When the teacher structures activities for goal setting (individual and group), building encouragement, strengthening team identity, and discovering personal likes, she helps students experience classroom success, which is paramount to building self-esteem.

Tighten other aspects of group structure. When the teacher defines specific expectations for a jigsaw or group round robin, she tightens group work and improve students' achievements. As Pat Taylor, a geometry teacher in Richmond, Virginia, tells her students, "You are each accountable for every concept you learn in your cooperative groups." To back this up, she uses a variety of techniques to ensure that their focus is not on "What grade did you get?" but on "What did you learn about this mathematics topic?"

Practices in individual learning communicate to each student his or her personal responsibility for learning the concepts and skills. In addition to the ideas for improving student achievement without grades that have been suggested, here are other transfer techniques that increase individual learning:

1. *Answer a random oral quiz.* Pick one person from the group to answer the question. Ask others to fill in any missing elements.

2. *Take a post-activity quiz.* Have all students take a quiz at the end of the lecture or activity. Instead of grading the quizzes, have students compare and discuss their work.

3. *Write a paper.* Have all students write an essay, letter, or memo to summarize the lesson.

4. *Sign on the line.* Have each student sign the idea he or she contributed or the problem he or she solved.

5. *Explain to a neighbor.* Select one half of the class to explain why an answer was correct or incorrect to the other half of the class. Or orchestrate a human graph.

6. *Get signatures from all.* Have everyone in the group sign this statement: I made my best contribution.

7. *Hold a tournament.* Teams that raise the quiz scores of all its members earn points.

8. *Use a group evaluator.* Give one student in the group a checklist with which to observe and give feedback on participating, sharing ideas, and other social skills.

9. *Complete homework practice.* After successful group practice, assign and collect individual homework practice.

10. *Make a test.* Have each group create a test on a topic. Rotate group tests.

11. *Evaluate a neighbor.* Ask groups to use a PMI chart or Mrs. Potter's questions to evaluate individual performances in the group.

12. *Give round robin answers.* Use a round robin (also called forced response and wraparound) with different lead-ins to check skills.

13. *Share group products.* Ask each group to present its product to the class. Tell all members that they must have a role in the presentation.

14. *Explain the answers.* After one student gives an answer, select another to explain why it is or is not correct.

15. *Coach a partner.* Instruct groups that finish a task first to coach groups still working.

16. *Do a jigsaw or expert jigsaw.* After instructing student groups to jigsaw material, have them do an expert jigsaw in which students form expert groups to research the same material (see Figure 10.5 or Blackline C10.1 in Appendix C). They review and confirm their information before returning to their base groups to teach group members the material.

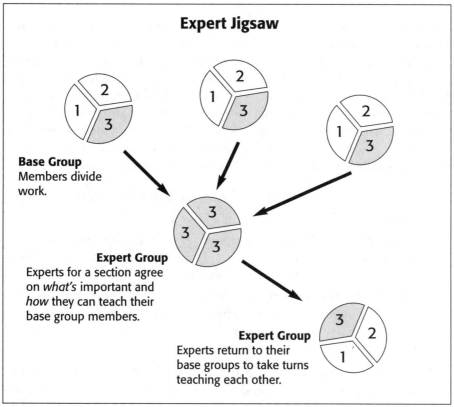

Figure 10.5

17. *Create individual applications.* Have each student brainstorm a way to apply or transfer a concept.

18. *Make log entries.* At the end of each lesson, tell students to complete the stem, I learned . . ., in their logs. Randomly check their entries.

19. *Use a teacher-observer.* Tell the class which participation skills will be observed. Wander through the class, make notes, and give feedback.

20. *Make a team ad.* Have students list the positive contributions of each team member on a team ad.

Student-Generated Team Grade

When teachers notice that their students are ready to go beyond the easy tools for inviting individual accountability, they may want to use the cooperative process itself to strengthen the team culture. To test the quality of students' cooperative interactions and the strength of the classroom's cooperative culture, teachers can challenge students to develop the grading criteria for appropriate team grades. The required standards are *fairness* (e.g., How will the grade be fair to each and every group member?) and *equality* (e.g., How will the grade represent an equal contribution?). The two criteria are linked and are not an either-or choice. To apply these standards, students need to give serious thought to both criteria to ensure that each is applied with rigor. This may be the ultimate test of cooperation.

When teachers elect to involve students in making team grades, they also include them in establishing criteria for the grading rubric. They might begin with an investigation of the two standards—fairness and equality—by asking: What do they mean? How will each work? What are the pitfalls? The investigation may be as simple as a facilitated, class discussion that starts with a think-pair-share or as complex as a group research project or a classroom circle (Glasser 1986). For whatever method selected, teachers must establish and facilitate the process and mediate the results, that is, the rubric used to evaluate the students' assigned work.

Teachers may involve students in creating a rubric with a classroom circle:

1. Arrange the classroom chairs in a large circle.

2. Introduce the task and its purpose (e.g., to involve you in creating the grading rubric for _____). Present the challenge and outline the discussion rules and procedures.

3. Present the two non-negotiable standards—fairness and equality. Stress the importance of these two criteria for the rubric. Facilitate a clarifying discussion if needed.

4. Pair students.

5. Tell pairs to select three to five criteria for one of the standards. (Half the groups are assigned *fairness* and half are assigned *equality*.)

6. After ten minutes, facilitate creating a list of possible and unduplicated criteria for each standard. Use additional questioning to guide the students as they pare the list to final criteria that seem most aligned and most appropriate. When necessary, uses 5-to-fist voting to move the groups to agreement before the end of the class period.

7. Draw one student's name from a hat and ask that student to make the master chart and distribute copies to each class member. (Figure 10.6 shows a format for the rubric. Also see Figure 10.7 for a sample rubric.)

Students not only receive cooperative and cognitive benefits when they create a team grading rubric but also deepen their understanding of content. The benefits to the teacher include enriching the classroom's cooperative culture and understanding how students perceive the priority of concepts, facts, procedures, and processes in the lesson's content.

Form of Rubric for a Team Grade

Criterion	Performance			
	Poor ——————Great			
Fairness				
Criterion 1	1	2	3	4
Criterion 2	1	2	3	4
Criterion 3	1	2	3	4
Criterion 4	1	2	3	4
Criterion 5	1	2	3	4
Equality				
Criterion 1	1	2	3	4
Criterion 2	1	2	3	4
Criterion 3	1	2	3	4
Criterion 4	1	2	3	4
Criterion 5	1	2	3	4

Figure 10.6

The rubric developed by a first-year teacher and his special needs students in a middle school music classroom is a perfect example of this process at its best. The teacher began rubric development with a discussion of the fair and equal standards. The project was a culminating activity for a six-week unit that drew on researching and report writing skills learned in language arts and bridged to his music class. The tasks in his music class were to study and learn to sing two Mozart songs for the spring concert and to study seven classical musicians from three cultures. The teacher's purposes for the unit were to introduce students to classical music and to develop students' understanding of music as a communication tool.

This novice teacher used collaborative rubric development not only to build students' cooperative behavior, but also to reinforce and integrate the two purposes. (See Figure 10.7 for the rubric.) The project, rated the best unit of the course by the students, ended with 3 As, 12 Bs, 13 Cs, and 1 D. In his assessment for his mentor teacher, the teacher noted that he was most pleased with how the rubric helped the students hone in on what was most important in the project and how it motivated the vast majority of the students to take very seriously the notion of individual responsibility in the group. Only one student elected to work alone.

Rubric for Project Pick-a-Piece

Task: Identify a musical piece from a classical composer of your choice. Complete a written research report and a presentation about the piece in any nonverbal mode.

Requirement: Each student may complete this project alone, in a pair, or in a group of three.

Standards: Fair and Equal. Teacher will use all agreed upon criteria below for each student's final presentation whether it is done alone, in a pair, or in a group.

1. Gathered research

   a. Research included assigned core idea(s), details, and sources.   1 2 3 4
   b. Research was complete.   1 2 3 4

2. Prepared report

   a. Research was presented in own voice (not copied).   1 2 3 4
   b. Report followed prescribed format, including footnotes.   1 2 3 4
   c. Report used correct grammar, sentence structure, and spelling.   1 2 3 4
   d. Report was interesting to read.   1 2 3 4

3. Presentation

   a. Original   1 2 3 4
   b. Communicated most important characteristics   1 2 3 4
   c. Captured and held attention   1 2 3 4
   d. Organized   1 2 3 4

4. Group Responsibility (pairs and trios only)

   a. Did fair share of tasks.   1 2 3 4
   b. Made an equal contribution to group effort.   1 2 3 4

Scale: 41–48 = A
            31–40 = B
            21–30 = C
            11–20 = D

Figure 10.7

SUMMARY

Blueprints follows the recommended best practices for assessing student learning of content, thinking, and cooperating. The *Blueprints'* three-story intellect framework adheres to current best practices that support student learning and invite individual accountability. *Blueprints* builds three-story lessons that integrate thinking, cooperating, and content and also builds three-story assessments that integrate all three elements. Standardized tests alone do not do the trick.

BLUEPRINT
Elementary
Lesson

Codes 5NR
6CL
7OF
8GH
9QCA

Setting Up the
Scaffolding

Sentence Boxes

Explain to the students that stories, directions, and other written forms are developed in an exact order to make sense. On the board, show a three-block sequence chart and number the blocks 1, 2, and 3 (see example below; see also Blackline C10.2 in Appendix C). Show the students the sequence of the numbers and the sequence of the boxes.

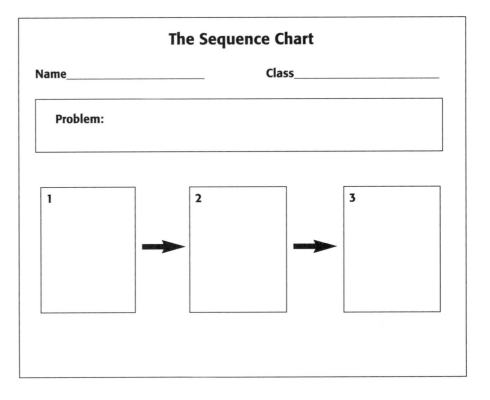

Arrange students in pairs. Give each pair these words: *I, school,* and *love.* Give each pair a blank three-word sequence chart. Have the pair agree on the correct order or sequence for the words and place them in order in the boxes.

On the board, record one pair's sequence. Ask for a show of hands from those that agree the sequence is correct. Check for disagreement and work until the sequence is correct and all agree.

Give each pair three additional word groups. Make at least one incomplete. Ask them to arrange all the words for a group to make a sentence in the boxes. For example:

> *Box, the, open* to create "Open the box."
>
> *Classroom, the, close, door* to create "Close the classroom door."
>
> *My, name, is, partner's* to create "My partner's name is _____."

Ask for volunteer pairs to put each response on the board. Gather agreement.

Working the
Crew

Explain that in this part of the lesson, students will put events in a story in order just as they have put words in a sentence in order. Let them know that each will be held individually accountable for two things: putting story items in order or sequence and helping the paired partner.

To help students make these expectations concrete, introduce these content and cooperation rubrics:

1. Sequence Rubric
   In your final story, you
   a. identified the key events   1 2 3 4 5+
   b. put the events in correct order   1 2 3 4 5+
   c. explained why you put each event in its place   1 2 3 4 5+

2. Cooperation Rubric
   In your pair, I saw you
   a. listening to your partner
      not at all   sometimes   most of the time   always
   b. helping your partner
      not at all   sometimes   most of the time   always
   c. agreeing with your partner
      not at all   sometimes   most of the time   always

Select a story to read to the class. After reading the story, ask for students to recall the events that happened. Write each event on the board as it is reported. Be sure to elicit a random group of responses, perhaps by drawing names from a hat. (This technique was developed and generously shared by master teacher, Sally Berman, at Palatine High School, Illinois.)

Provide each pair with a sequence chart with sufficient boxes to capture the number of events (see Blackline C10.2 in Appendix C). Number each of the recorded events on the board and instruct the pairs to agree on the sequence of numbers. Allow 15 minutes for this task.

Work with a random selection of volunteers to get the correct sequence. Ask students to explain why they placed events as they did.

When the class chart is correct, ask for a student volunteer to retell the story in his or her own words.

Consider repeating this task with one or more stories. When students are comfortable with making sequences, reinforce the skill by asking each pair to select a story to read and then make its own chart to present to the class. After pairs have demonstrated facility in sequencing a story with coaching, work for transfer by asking students to do one of the following:

1. Make a sequenced timeline of your own life history. Demonstrate with your own biography.
2. Make a sequence chart of instructions for doing a familiar mathematics or social studies task.
3. Make a sequence chart of instructions for doing a job at home for which you are responsible.
4. Make a sequence chart for a favorite event from your life or from a favorite TV show.

Assess individual capability to put items in a sequence by using the sequence rubric and assess cooperative work using the cooperation rubric. Use the sequence rubric to assess how each student places random words in one or more sentences and/or story events. Make an observation chart for the cooperative rubric and use it while the students are working in their pairs. You may give each student a copy of his or her completed chart or use the charts to enter a grade in the grade book.

To derive a grade, total the points scored on each task. For the word task, give one point for each distinction on a 1–4 scale. For the story sequence task, use the two rubrics, which have a total of 27 possible points in a perfect score. Translate these points to letter grades: 24–27 = A, 20–23 = B, 16–19 = C, and so on.

For affective processing, ask each pair to explain what they like and do not like about doing sequence charts. Show them a sample chart on the board. After the pairs are finished, make a class chart on the board and highlight key points.

# # #

Reflecting on the Design

BLUEPRINT
Middle School
Lesson

Codes 5NR
6CL
7OF
9QCA

Setting Up the
Scaffolding

The Reading Detective

Use a think-pair-share strategy to identify names of detectives your students know from television, comics, literature, real-life, and so forth. Use a round robin of student pairs to make a list on the board.

Ask the pairs to identify characteristics of a good detective. Use a random selection technique to construct a web of responses.

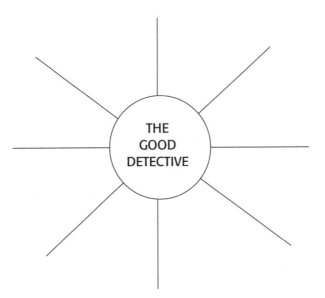

If students do not identify finds evidence from subtle clues, interprets clues, or makes inferences, add these to the web. Explain the terms as needed and add to the students' vocabulary list as a bridge to the notion that a good reader is a good detective able to find and interpret clues to character.

Explain that the goal of this lesson is for students to become better reading detectives. Outline the following activity and tell students that their work will be evaluated in three ways: (a) their identification of clues, (b) their inferences and good interpretations, and (c) their ability to work together and respect each other's opinions. Show students the following rubric that you will use to assess the completed work and the cooperative skills (add more items if you want):

a. Found an abundance of clues	1 3 5 7 9 12+ clues
b. Connected the clues to interpretations	1 2 3 4 5 6+ connections
c. Made correct inferences	1 2 3 4 5 6+ inferences
d. Showed respect for a different opinion	1 2 3 4 5 6+ instances

Working the Crew

Select a newspaper or magazine article on a current event or a short story from the literature curriculum.

Tell students to read the story or article as a homework assignment. Encourage them to look for clues about the most important character in the material and to build an attribute web similar to the one they did at the start of this lesson.

Ask for a student volunteer to use a facial expression to reveal his or her feelings about this assignment. Invite others to infer from the facial expression what the feeling is. Repeat this process with an invitation to make a gesture or use other body language and tone of voice to express this feeling as the volunteer walks around the classroom.

When students have completed these demonstrations, write INFER on the board and define the meaning of each letter (use the drama demonstrations to explain):

I Identify literal action (e.g., walking around the room, making a face)

N Note indicators of further meaning (e.g., smile, bounce in step, peppy "yes!")

F Find evidence of subtle clues (e.g., head nods, twinkle in eyes)

E Extend interpretation (e.g., kind of like the assignment)

R Restate interpretation based on subtle clues (e.g., loves the assignment)

Put students into groups of three and assign roles of recorder, encourager, and director. Review cooperative guidelines and highlight the social skill of respecting differences of opinion.

Ask each group to use INFER as the guide for making inferences about the character selected.

Matrix of Infer

	Clue	Clue	Clue	Clue	Clue	Interpretation
I						
N						
F						
E						
R						

Explore what *respect* looks and sounds like using a T-chart.

Respect T-Chart

Looks Like	Sounds Like

Now, select a group to present its INFER chart to the entire class. Invite students who disagree to do so in a respectful way. Repeat the chart presentation with one or two additional groups. Note that each group may have very different charts.

Provide feedback to the class by highlighting the solid inferences that each group made. Discuss difficulties encountered and possible solutions. If necessary, strengthen student skills in inference-making by repeating the above sequence on following days with one or more stories.

Assign a final story or article for home reading. Tell students that they will have to make their inference charts independently and that their work will be evaluated based on the rubrics.

Schedule time for students to work alone in order to complete the inference chart on the story or article assigned.

Use the rubric (or modify it) to assess the results and invite individual accountability. This rubric allows for a total of 24 points for the inferring process plus 6 points for the social skill (showing respect). After a student completes the inference chart, ask each to record up to six of the social skills on the class T-chart that he or she used in the group. Each demonstrated skill is worth a point. (You may add or subtract items based on your observations.) Use the following grading scale:

> 36–31 points = A
> 30–26 points = B
> 25–21 points = C
> 20–15 points = D

Students who fall below a grade they desire may take another story assignment and complete the individual chart. Average the two results together for the final grade.

Reflecting on the Design

The following reflection task helps students focus on transfer of the inferring skill to their other schoolwork. (Be sure to encourage students to apply their inference skills across the curriculum.)

1. Ask students to review the terms: *inference, subtle, interpretation,* and *clues* and to explain how these apply to a good detective and a good reading detective.

2. Ask students to explain *where* they would use the process and walk through *how* they would apply the skill. As each student takes a turn, encourage the others to listen with respect and observe the different ways each person can think about the same process.

3. Use wait time, random volunteers, and PACTS (Paraphrase, Affirm, Clarify, Test Options, Sense Tone) skills to extend the discussion.

4. Conclude with a summary statement.

5. As an alternative, use the trios to generate the *where* and to prepare a *how* chart for a class presentation.

# # #

BLUEPRINT
High School
Lesson

Codes 2SN
5NR
6CL
7OF
9QCA

Setting Up the
Scaffolding

End of Year Project

For the final six weeks of a course, introduce a project that helps students focus on the key concepts of the course. Introduce the project by explaining that its purpose is to help them develop a strong grasp of the key ideas of the course. This project will help them make sense of the various ideas and connect the pieces together.

Indicate the value of the project to the final course grade. Consider distributing grade points as follows: 20% for the project; 20% for the final exam; and 60% for the tests, quizzes, participation, homework, and essays throughout the semester or year.

Use a rubric for assessment:

1. The project illustrates the key ideas of the course:
   1 idea   2 ideas   3 ideas   4 ideas

2. The project links the ideas
   not at all   somewhat   well   lightly and clearly

3. The explanation of the importance of the ideas is strong
   not at all   somewhat   for the most part   exceedingly so

4. The project is an imaginative translation
   not at all   somewhat   for the most part   exceedingly so

5. The project shows a mastery of supporting details
   not at all   somewhat   for the most part   exceedingly well

6. The presentation of the project was strong
   not at all   somewhat   for the most part   exceedingly so

7. The presentation and the work showed signs of cooperative work
   not at all   somewhat   for the most part   exceedingly so

Grading Scale:
28–24 points = A
23–19 points = B
18–13 points = C
12–7 points = D

Working the
Crew

Begin with a brainstorm of the key ideas of the course.

After the list is complete and includes all the desired items, write each idea on a separate piece of paper and place them in a hat. Form groups of three and ask each group to select an idea from the hat. The group is to prepare a presentation for the class. All group members are to contribute to the preparation and presentation of its project.

Allow in-class time for each group to prepare their class presentation. The presentation should explain the idea, tell why the idea is important in the course, and provide details that illuminate the idea (including procedures and key vocabulary).

Groups also are to invent an artistic interpretation to communicate the idea. It may be a sculpture, a dance, a short story, a musical composition, a film, or whatever captures the group's understanding of the idea's essence. Groups are allowed twenty minutes each for their class presentations. All groups are encouraged to take notes on the presentations.

In addition, the group is to be prepared to respond as a panel to questions from the class about the presentation. The class will have the remainder of that group's presentation class time (one period) to dialogue about the project. They may ask such questions as:

What were you trying to do in this project (or some part of the project)? Why?

What was difficult? easy?

Who contributed what? Why?

What would you name the completed work?

What changes would you make now? Why?

How does this relate to the course?

What have you learned from doing this project about the course content? about your thinking process? about teamwork?

(Provide the class with the questions or ask the class to generate its own list of questions.)

You may choose one of the following options:

- Allow students to use the rubric to evaluate each project.

- Select a panel for each project.

- Ask each team to assess its own project.

- Allow individuals to assess themselves.

- Use some combination of the above.

Allow the groups ten to twelve class days to complete the project and prepare the presentation. Decide how much class time and how much out-of-class time you need to allow. At the minimum, schedule one day for each team's presentation.

Reflecting on the Design

For cognitive processing, invite students in a round robin to complete this stem:

> In this course, the most important thing (concept, understanding, learning) I gained was . . .

For metacognitive processing, invite each student to write a one-page reflection on what he or she learned about the course from this project. Return the students to the trios and allow them to share these reflections. Ask one student from each group to record a follow-up discussion that identifies similarities and differences. Select one group to share its results and then ask other groups to participate in a dialogue that illustrates similarities and differences among the groups.

# # #

Blueprints for Achievement

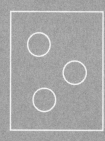

FORMING

PERFORMING

NORMING

GLOSSARY

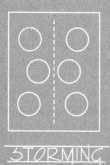

STORMING

CONFORMING

in the Cooperative Classroom

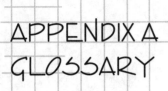

GLOSSARY

CONCEPTS

Agreement: When two or more individuals in a group assent to accepting divergent points of view in whole or part or can "live with" such views. All in the group do not necessarily buy in to the accepted terms.

Alignment: The way elements, strategies, and tactics of a lesson are connected to the lesson's goal and to the content standards. It also refers to the way a variety of lessons are related to a unit goal, the way units are related to a course goal, and the way assessment is related to the curriculum and instruction.

Assessment: The processes for weighing the worth of a student's assigned task, responsibility in a group, thinking, and/or products. Assessments are the tools of evaluation.

BUILD: The framework and acronym for creating cooperative-cognitive lessons: (1) **B**uild in higher-order thinking (2) **U**nify the teams (3) **I**nvite individual responsibility (4) **L**ook back and review (5) **D**evelop social skills. These are the necessary elements or critical attribute that define cooperative learning and set it apart from group work which may have none or a limited number of these attributes.

Cognition: The act of knowing and all of the rational processes that are sub-sets of knowing or finding meaning.

Cognitive rehearsal: Occurs whenever students verbally share, explain, or assess their ideas or concepts with each other or when they rehearse something mentally within their own minds.

Consensus: Resolving disagreement using formal strategies; all members of the group reach agreement about part or all of a position. Consensus building results from purposeful strategies that enable a group to resolve disagreements about facts, concepts, goals, or entire plans. One of the strategies is called 5-to-fist in which each member decides on a level of agreement (1 [low] to 5 [high]) with the idea or topic being discussed.

Cooperative learning: An instructional model for teaching students how to learn together. It uses heterogeneous groups as a tool for creating a classroom in which students' achievement, self-esteem, responsibility, high-level thinking, and favorable attitudes toward school increase dramatically. Its hallmark is the achievement of a shared goal.

Creative thinking micro-skills: Explicit thinking skills that enable a student to engage in finite, right-hemisphere thinking processes such as brainstorming, predicting, or synthesizing.

Critical thinking micro-skills: Explicit thinking skills that enable a student to engage in finite, left-hemisphere thinking processes such as categorizing, analyzing, or evaluating.

Deductive lesson: A lesson in which students are first presented with the big idea and then provided the details to explain or defend the idea. It is based on the deductive thinking model in which the individual begins with a hypothetical conclusion, looks for supporting evidence, and, when it is found, matches the conclusion to the hypothesis. The majority of textbooks and classroom lessons modify this design, presenting the conclusion first (seldom as an hypothesis) followed by the supporting details. For example, the teacher or the text might describe magnetic forces, and then students work with the magnets to see if they follow the rules discussed.

Direct instruction: A model of instruction in which all students in a classroom are taught at the same time in a prescribed step-by-step manner. There are several variations of the model. The most recognized is the Hunter (1971) model with its seven steps: anticipatory set, objective, modeling, checking for understanding, guided practice, independent practice, and evaluation. Direct instruction is often confused with the lecture approach because both are somewhat teacher-centered.

Emotional intelligence: A theory developed by Salovey and Mayer (1990) and popularized by Goleman (1995), a science writer. The theory describes the emotional intelligence as comprising understanding one's own feelings, exhibiting empathy for others, and regulating emotions to enhance living. Goleman suggests that this intelligence may be more important than cognitive intelligence.

Facilitation: Easing students' way through obstacles that appear to be blocking student learning. The teacher intervenes and shows students a simpler way to organize the task or simplifies the content for easier understanding. The teacher may, in effect, scaffold the learning for easier understanding.

Flexibility: The ability to think about a concept in many different ways.

Fluency: The ability to generate a large amount of ideas about a topic.

Formal instruction: Explicit instruction of a skill or concept using either a direct or indirect instructional model.

Heuristics: An aid to learning, discovery, or problem solving by experimental and trial-and-error methods.

High challenge: Teaching that requires students' to engage in rigorous and complex thinking processes.

High content: Using rich and rigorous curricular content that adheres to the content standards of the discipline.

High expectations: This term refers to the level of success that teachers expect of a student and how that expectation influences the student's actual achievement. High expectations are reflected in the rigor and challenge of the lesson for all children.

High road transfer: Salomon and Perkins (1988) coined this term to describe transfer that seems far removed or remote from the context of the learning situation. An example of high road transfer is when students become aware that the patterns evident in the periodic table set a model for searching for patterns in other phenomena or constructing similar matrices or grids.

High support: Using cooperative strategies to enrich a student's sense of belonging in a group.

Individual accountability: One of the required attributes that separates group work from cooperative learning (Johnson and Johnson 1974). The teacher holds each student accountable for his or her role in creating cooperative interactions and achieving the cooperative goal.

Individualized instruction: In this model of instruction each student works on a series of learning tasks at his or her own pace. The teacher provides the exercises one at a time; after the individual completes the task, the teacher corrects it, and the student moves to the next task.

Inductive lesson: A lesson in which students are asked to gather information before drawing conclusions. It is based on the inductive thinking process in which the individual gathers evidence, clues, or facts, and then, after finding the common elements, draws a conclusion about the information. In schools, this lesson design is most typically found in a science class. For example, students might play with magnets and then draw their conclusions about the qualities of magnets.

Informal instruction: Implicit instruction of a skill or concept that is embedded in a formal lesson with a larger scope.

Inquiry learning: A model of instruction in which students, usually working in groups, follow a series of open-ended questions to investigate a topic and reach conclusions.

Instructional flow: The controlled, smooth, and orderly pattern of instruction from the start of a lesson or unit until its end. A well-designed flow is marked by smooth and clear transitions among the parts and in relation to the lesson or unit goal.

Integration: Connecting or interwining the important elements such as cooperation, cognition, and content in a lesson.

Learning styles: Students posses different ways to process informattion—these are called learning styles. Certain strategies align to certain learning styles. As teachers diagnose student learning styles in their classroom, they are better able to plan lessons that will facilitate each child's best learning. Style theories focus on a variety of student differences ranging from color perception to ways of processing information.

Levels of transfer: Six levels of transfer related to learning: overlooking, duplicating, replicating, integrating, mapping, and innovating (Fogarty 1989).

Low performance: When a student's academic work results fall below the desired standards. Low performance is attributed to many factors such as motivation, interest, special needs, and social conditions. Low performance—unlike the designation, low ability—indicates that essential change and improvement is possible.

Low road transfer: Automatic, easy transfer of learning Salomon and Perkins (1988). An example of low road transfer is driving a car and then applying those same skills to driving a truck.

Mediated learning experience (MLE): Providing a learning experience that enables the teacher, using specific learning criteria, to challenge the student to master increasingly complex content (Feuerstein 1980). Each criterion specifies questioning strategies that the teacher can use to enable students to construct meaning in their individual, small group, or whole group work. MLE places primary attention on the teacher as a mediator or developer of the student's capacity to think and to apply the thinking strategies to ever more difficult content. MLE is most usually associated with Feuerstein's Instrumental Enrichment Program.

Mediation: A process used by a teacher to intervene between the students and the content, thinking, and/or the group process. In mediation, the teacher asks one set of targeted questions to challenge students to work systematically through their thinking or collaborating process. This is often followed by another set of questions that asks them to review that process, assess its use, and transfer it to new material. In this way, the teacher directs the students by challenging them to understand new, more difficult processes or content for overcoming the challenge and completing the difficult work without changing the process or making it easier to do.

Metacognition: Knowledge about, awareness of, and control over one's own mind and thinking. Metacognition is beyond the cognitive. For example, cognition is used to solve a mathematics problem; metacognition is used to discuss how the problem was best solved.

Mind-brain research: Research studies that focus on how the brain works and how those workings impact memory and learning.

Multiple intelligences: This theory, developed by Howard Gardner (1983, 1999), describes eight types of intelligences are that guide learning. In this theory, each individual learner has a jagged profile of intelligences and these intelligences are determined primarily by cultural influences and genetic predispositions. Some intelligences are stronger than others. By understanding each intelligence, a teacher, according to this theory, is able to offer students multiple entry points to learning in today's diverse classrooms.

Normal distribution: A continuous probability distribution of frequencies that is usually depicted by a bell-shaped curve. In the standard normal distribution, mean, median, and mode are equal. That means, in a normal distribution, the bulk of the instances cluster toward the center, with fewer occurring at either end of the scale.

Norms: Standards of behavior that are generally accepted (e.g., how one behaves in a group interaction). The norms are set both formally and informally by the group and are set over time.

Prior knowledge: Background knowledge or previous experience a student already possesses at the start of a lesson. The principle of prior knowledge calls for the teacher to introduce new knowledge by bridging back to prior knowledge. In some cases this may be prior knowledge of the actual topic; in others, the connection must be made with related knowledge.

Social skills: Skills that students use as they interact with others. There are general social skills for any interactive situation, such as communication skills. There are also social skills of specific value for interactions within a small group such as consensus seeking or deferring judgment.

Stages of design: The four stages that mark a well-designed lesson plan: accessing prior knowledge, gathering and understanding new information, transferring new concepts, and assessing learning.

Standards: The goals of the curriculum are represented by standards of learning within various content areas and across disciplines. Student learning standards are defined by criteria and indicators of quality. These standards "set the bar" for what is expected.

Criteria: Elements by which one ascertains the quality of a process or product. For example, one criterion for a persuasive speech might be the delivery of the speech.

Indicators: Criteria are often accompanied with indicators of quality. For example, the criterion for the delivery of a persuasive speech might include these indicators: *ineffective, somewhat effective, quite effective,* or *extremely effective.*

Strategy: An instructional or assessment method that is used at a specific place in a lesson design. Each strategy is selected to accomplish one or more specific purposes in a lesson.

Student achievement: The student's measured success rate in mastering the content of the curriculum. The success rate is usually measured and reported from standardized tests, but might also include overall grade point averages, as well as gains from one time to another.

Student-to-material interactions: This phrase describes how a student interacts with information, often from print or electronic learning materials.

Student-to-student interactions: This phrase describes verbal and non-verbal communication between students.

Student-to-teacher interactions: This phrase describes verbal and non-verbal communication between student(s) and the teacher.

Teacher Expectations and Student Achievement (TESA): This seminal work studied the strong relationship between how a teacher teaches and the level of student achievement. Conducted by Kermin (1979) and his associates with students and teachers in the Los Angeles School District, this study identified teacher behaviors related to high-expectation teaching that directly impacted the achievement gains of poor children who were expected to be low achievers. The study identified fifteen behaviors including wait time and teacher mobility around the classroom.

Three-story intellect: A model of thinking represented by the metaphor of a three-story building. This shortened and more focused adaptation of Bloom's taxonomy (Bloom et al. 1956) guides teachers in selection of the verbs associated with three levels of categories of thinking: gathering, processing and applying.

Gathering information: In the first level of the three-story intellect, students use thinking skills to find appropriate information from a variety of sources.

Processing information: In the second level of the three-story intellect, students use thinking skills to analyze and synthesize in order to better understand selected information.

Applying information: In the third story of the three-story intellect, students use information in other content areas or in different life situations.

Transfer: Bridging the old and the new and leading students to use academic content in situations that differ from those in which the content was learned.

Variety: Purposely using different, but appropriate, strategies and tactics within a lesson in order to motivate students.

Whole group lecture: This is a model of instruction in which the teacher talks to the students, usually as an entire class. During this talk, a teacher provides all the information that the students need to know about a topic. At given points, the teacher may test students on this information, which they acquire by studying the material alone or in groups outside of class time. This model is often wrongly described as direct instruction. Whole group instruction may also be an instructional strategy used at specific times in a lesson or unit along with other strategies.

METHODS

Advance organizers: These tools bridge students' prior knowledge or experience into a new lesson or unit and introduce new knowledge to students by presenting a preview. In essence, the student is privy of the information or the organization of the information in *advance* of learning.

Artifacts: Products of student work as assigned by the teacher. Products may result from completion of individual, group, or whole class activities.

Business card: An informal cooperative group task. Each individual responds to questions from the teacher to make a business card. At the teacher's signal, each person finds a person and exchanges cards. For as many times as needed, the teacher signals additional rounds. Cards may be used as a strategy to help students bond, to share information, to review for a test, or to assess a task.

Carousel: An informal strategy used to share information generated in formal cooperative groups that are studying different subtopics. Each subtopic group displays a poster showing the results of its assigned task in a space designated by the teacher. One member of the group stands with the poster. The other members stand by the next poster to the right. At the teacher's signal, the groups move to the right after discussing the content with the reporter who has stayed "at home." The process continues until all groups have circled back to their own poster.

Class circle: In this decision-making model established by Glasser (1986), the teacher guides students through steps of a decision-making model for resolving conflicts that affect the entire class.

Concept map: A graphic organizer that charts relationships among categories and subcategories of concepts and facts. It may be used to show multiple connections among items charted.

Cooperative groups: Groups of three to five students who work together to achieve a common goal according to the five BUILD criteria.

DOVE: DOVE is a acronym that means Defer judgment, Opt for original ideas, Vast numbers are needed, and Expand the list by piggybacking. This set of guidelines provided by the teacher standardizes cooperative group behaviors.

Equal distribution of responses: When a teacher selects a wide variety of students to answer questions. (This is a Teacher Expectations, Student Achievement [TESA] strategy). Teachers may elicit an equal distribution of responses through round robins, gatering names from a hat, using guided seating chart, and so forth.

Expert jigsaw: An advanced form of the jigsaw strategy. In this form, members of different groups who are studying the same piece of the jigsawed information get together to review and/or to plan. After this, the experts return to their base groups and present the information.

Explain why: In this informal group strategy, students work in pairs to answer a question and to agree on why the answer is appropriate.

Fat question: This type of question uses the second or third level of the three-story intellect and requires answers that are full of thought and allow a variety of possibilities for how and what is included in the response. This kind of question is divergent and open-ended.

Five-to-Fist: A tactic that allows students to signal a vote for up to five levels of agreement on a topic. The total score from all votes indicates the degree of agreement among group or class members.

Formal groups: Tactical groups that have specific components: a group, roles and responsibilities, guidelines, a rubric of expectations, and a thinking tactic.

Four corners: A formal cooperative group strategy in which students are assigned to or choose one of four subtopics located in each of the corners of the room. Groups discuss the topics for their corner and/or produce something.

Graphic organizers: Strategies that use visual representations of thinking to structure a specified thinking process. Organizers include Venn diagrams, webs, mind maps, right angle charts, etc.

Heterogeneous group: A group of students who are assembled with a purposeful consideration of the differences in their performance levels and/or demographic characteristics such as behavior, socioeconomic status, gender, motivation, ethnicity, etc. Heterogeneous grouping is encouraged by cooperative learning researchers.

Homogeneous group: A group of students with similar performance levels and/or other demographic factors such as behavior, gender, motivation, socioeconomic status, ethnicity, etc. Cooperative learning researchers discourage homogeneous groupings.

Hour glass: A graphic organizer that shows the connections between prior knowledge and new information.

Informal structures: Quick and easy cooperative grouping tactics in which students are informally matched in groups of two or three to discuss a topic. These tactics include think-pair-share, two heads together, prediction pairs, etc.

Jigsaw: Dividing information into equal parts and then reviewing the information in a formal group. Each group member studies an assigned section and teaches it to the other members of the group. The jigsaw is most appropriate when students need to study a large amount of information in a short time.

Journal: A reflection tool that enables students to maintain a daily or hourly log of thoughts or feelings in relation to their class work. Students may make independent entries or make entries at the instruction of the teacher. Teachers may invite students to group entries in the journal according to categories such as reflections on homework; reflections on group process; reflections on thinking; notes on reading tasks; graphic organizers to gather, process, or assess task information; etc. The teacher sets guidelines for confidentiality, for what is included and excluded in the journal, and so forth.

KWL: A graphic organizer used to brainstorm prior knowledge. The organizer is divided into three columns: what students *know* about the topic, what students *want* to know about the topic, and what the students have *learned* about the topic. Designed by Ogle (1986), this organizer is most commonly used to identify prior knowledge and to assess what new knowledge students have gained in a lesson.

Large group discussion: An interaction among all students in the class to guide their thinking about a topic with focused questions.

Launch question: A question that begins a discussion or inquiry on an important topic. This is the ultimate question that the discussion should answer.

Lecturette: A short (ten to twenty minutes) lecture of information or instructions by the teacher.

Modeling: When the teacher shows students how to use a skill by demonstrating it students may watch a video or observe a student who already knows how to use the skill. The teacher may model both the correct and the incorrect way to do the task. After the modeling, it is important that the teacher check for understanding. This is an essential strategy for helping all students learn new skills or tasks.

Mrs. Potter's questions: A questioning strategy that helps teachers assess student learning or enables students to self-assess thinking, cooperating, or content mastery. The questions are: What learning (thinking, cooperating) was expected? What did you do well? If you did the same thing again, what would you do differently? What help do you need to improve?

Name board: An equal distribution of responses tactic in which the teacher lists all students' names on a board. After asking a question and using wait time, the teacher chooses a name and calls on that person. The teacher may allow other students to call the names and may proceed in any order he or she selects. To avoid complacency among those called on early in the activity, the teacher may jump back to an earlier name occasionally.

Name cards: An equal distribution of responses tactic in which the teacher puts each student's name on an index card. After asking a question and giving wait time, the teacher uses the pack of cards to identify a respondent.

Name from a hat: An equal distribution of responses tactic in which the teacher places all students' names into a hat or bowl. After asking the question and allowing wait time, the teacher pulls a name from the hat for the first response and then proceeds to another question and/or elicits additional responses to the first question.

Newspaper model: A graphic organizer that uses five key categories of a factual story (who, what, when, where, why) to construct a summary.

PACTS: The acronym stands for **P**araphrasing, **A**ffirming, **C**larifying, **T**esting alternatives, and **S**ensing tone. These actions draw out or extend another's thinking about a topic. The teacher may create questions or may teach the questions to students for use in their student-to-student interactions.

People search: An informal cooperative strategy in which students search for others who can answer certain questions. The teacher gives students a chart that identifies a topic and ten to twelve items related to the topic. Students are invited to find a person to sign off on each item that the person can explain. At the same time, students get acquainted with each other and have opportunities to dialogue with a partner about certain topics. This provides cognitive rehearsal for both partners.

PMI: An assessment strategy devised by de Bono (1973) to review the pluses (P), the minuses (M), and the interesting questions (I) of a completed task or process. The teacher may guide the students with a PMI graphic organizer or ask the students to use it for solo or group self-assessment.

Portfolio: An assessment tool for gathering samples of student work (artifacts) and/or self-reflections and/or evaluations. Teachers may elect to use an all class portfolio, small group portfolios, or individual portfolios.

Portmanteau: A formal group strategy that jigsaws a list of creative words that students must learn in a short time. Students use the jigsaw with sketches of the words. Student teams ensure that all members reach a 90% recall level.

Problem-based learning (PBL): A technique that asks students to select a problem and solve it. PBL is inquiry-centered and requires student groups to investigate a topic by focusing on a specific issue. For instance, in order to accomplish the curricular goal of enabling the students to understand how American continent was first settled, the teacher assigns the groups the task of imagining themselves to be the Europeans who were looking for a place that would provide religious freedom. The students are charged with solving the problem of finding and settling that place.

Project: An endeavor that students complete over time, either as members of a group or individually. Projects often result in a product such as a diorama, model, drama, cultural map, etc.

Proximity: A Teacher Expectations, Student Achievement (TESA) strategy that calls for the teacher to move next to or close to a student to elicit that student's attention. When this tactic is used to manage behavior, the teacher moves next to a disruptive student when making a correction. For low performing students, the teacher moves the students to sit close to him or her.

Response in turn: See round robin.

Right angle chart: A graphic organizer used to show how a concept and/or its supporting details may be transferred in one or more ways to related ideas.

Round robin: A tactic used for ensuring equal distribution of responses in a whole group or small group discussion. After asking the question and allowing wait time, the teacher selects one student to give the first response to the question. The teacher then designates the next responder to the right or left of the first. After that response, the teacher continues in the same direction around the class or group with each student responding in turn or saying, I pass. The teacher may ask for a summary of previous responses or change the question anytime during the activity.

Rubric: A scoring guide used as an assessment tool. The rubric identifies the benchmarks for a standard and sets a scale for determining the degree of quantity or quality of students' artifacts.

Signals: A tactic for managing cooperative group movement. The hands-up signal is the most ideal for cooperative classrooms. When students see the teacher raise his hand, they stop all interaction and raise their own. As others catch this signal, the class turns all attention to the teacher. The teacher uses wait time until all students are attending solely to him in silence.

Skinny question: A question taken from the first level of the three-story intellect that requires a yes, no, or other one word response. This type of question is convergent or close-ended.

Stems: A lead-in discussion tactic similar to three-story questions. The teacher provides the students with the stem that he or she wishes each student to complete. For example, a common stem is "Today, I learned . . .". Students may respond to the open-ended stem or lead-in question with a journal entry, a small group response, or a large group response. Stems are used regularly with equal response tactics.

Structured overview: A graphic organizer used to gather information about a topic. Most commonly used as a pre-reading strategy, it can also be used to gather information during a lecture, a film, or in a discussion. It is similar to a concept map.

That's a Good Idea: A formal group brainstorming strategy that makes use of round robin responses. Each member invents a way to improve a basic idea. The next person in turn must explain why the previous idea is "a good idea." This technique may be oral or written.

3-to-1 questions. A formal group strategy that jigsaws the level of question from the three-story intellect model. One student responds to the first-story question; a second student responds to the second-story question; the third responds to the third-story question. As a variation, all may respond to each of the three levels of questions and agree on a single best answer to each. This tactic is usually used at the end of a task.

2-4-8: A grouping and regrouping strategy usually used for informal cooperative groups. In the first round, a pair (2) completes a cooperative task; in the second round, that pair joins another pair (4) to share its results; in the third round, each foursome joins another foursome (8) to share results.

Venn diagram: A graphic organizer that uses overlapping circles to compare and contrast two or more concepts. It is based on set theory and answers the three questions: What fits the set? What does not? What fits both sets?

Wait time: The amount of time a teacher waits between posing question and asking a student to respond. The ideal time is three to five seconds. The usual time that rewards fast thinkers and punishes the careful thinkers is less than one second. This strategy is an essential Teacher Expectations, Student Achievement (TESA) component.

Web: A graphic organizer used to describe multiple features of a concept or topic through an analysis of attributes.

We bags: In this informal group strategy, a pair of students works with a brown paper bag. The pair writes or draws their answers to a sequence of questions on the bag. Questions may include names, schools, places of birth, favorite books or other items, aspirations, and so forth. For the second step, the teacher invites each pair to match with another pair and to share the bags.

Wraparound: See round robin.

Write-pair-share: In this informal cooperative strategy the teacher assigns each student to *write* his or her thoughts about a topic. After the writing segment, students form *pairs* and discuss what each wrote. After a brief discussion, the teacher invites different students to *share* common ideas with the class.

Blueprints for Achievement

FORMING

PERFORMING

APPENDIX B

FREQUENTLY ASKED QUESTIONS

NORMING

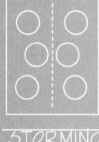

STORMING

CONFORMING

in the Cooperative Classroom

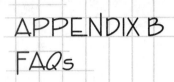

APPENDIX B
FAQs

FREQUENTLY ASKED QUESTIONS

WHEN DO I START USING COOPERATIVE GROUPS?

START USING COOPERATIVE GROUPS RIGHT AWAY.

It takes time to develop cooperative groups. The sooner you introduce your students to cooperative tasks, the sooner they will be skillful cooperative learners. Start with these steps:

1. Prepare your classroom to *signal* a cooperative atmosphere through bulletin boards, role cards, hand signals, room arrangement, and visible guidelines.

2. Take thirty to forty minutes to introduce the concept of cooperative learning and teach the basic procedures. See chapter 2 for informal lessons you can adapt to get your students started.

3. Expand the use of cooperative learning each day until 60 percent of students' time is spent working in cooperative groups.

CAN YOU GIVE A MODEL LESSON THAT ILLUSTRATES BUILD?

LET'S USE PORTMANTEAU AS A MODEL FOR A LESSON USING BUILD.

Portmanteau Defined

Literal: A large leather suitcase with two hinged compartments; coat carrier.

Literary: "A word . . . whose form and meaning are derived from a blending of two or more distinct forms (as smog from smoke and fog)" (Merriam-Webster 1998).

According to *Webster's Word Histories* (Merriam-Webster 1989), *portmanteau* as a literary concept has an interesting history:

	Analysis of BUILD strategies used in the Portmanteau lesson
B	1. drawing a definition (a creative thinking skill) 2. teaching others what you have learned 3. making connections to prior knowledge and experience
U	1. jigsawing (dividing the material among team members) 2. assigning roles for each team member 3. giving limited time (learn more as a team in short time than could be learned alone)
I	1. providing individual learning and teaching time 2. conducting a random oral quiz 3. checking in the teams
L	1. answering processing questions about how the team worked well together 2. teacher giving feedback and observations 3. discussing ways to improve team's effectiveness
D	1. keeping on task 2. encouraging team members during the task 3. checking the team for understanding

Figure B.1

A number of words originally coined or used as nonsense words have taken on specific meanings in subsequent use. Renowned among such words is *jabberwocky*, used by Lewis Carroll in *Through the Looking Glass* as the title of a nonsense poem about a fantastic monster called a *jabberwock*. A meaningless nonsense word itself, *jabberwocky* appropriately enough became a generic term for meaningless speech or writing.

Carroll was very fond of coining blends or, to use his term, "portmanteau" words, so called because blending words is like packing them into the same traveling bag. Thus Carroll not only added to the English language a number of blend words, he also gave us a new sense for *portmanteau*. We can now use it as an adjective to mean "combining more than one use or quality." Among the portmanteau words coined by Carroll which have become useful members of the language are *chortle* and *galumph*. *Chortle*, a blend of *chuckle* and s*nort*, means "to sing, chant, laugh, or chuckle exultantly." *Galumph*, probably an alteration of gallop, may also be influenced by some such word as *triumphant*. Today, it is used with the sense "to move with a clumsy heavy tread." (p. 246, italics in original)

For a summary of the BUILD strategies used in this lesson, see Figure B.1 or Blackline CB.1 in Appendix C.

Lesson Instructions:

1. Divide the class into groups of three. Assign the roles of worrier, encourager, and checker.

2. Distribute three different portmanteau words to each member in a group (see sample words in Figure B.2). Allow time for group members to study the definitions of their words and to draw a picture of each definition to serve as a memory and teaching aid.

3. When all students are ready, have each encourager teach the group the three words on his or her card using visual aids. Remind students that they will have a final quiz that will focus on *definitions*, not spellings. For the quiz, all members of the group are accountable to know the definitions of all nine words in the group.

4. After this first round of teaching, have the checkers check to see if their group members all understand.

5. Have the worriers lead the second round of teaching. And again, have the checkers check for understanding.

6. Then, ask the third and final member, the checker, to finish the round-robin teaching with his or her three words.

7. After all rounds are done, have checkers check for group members' understanding of all the words.

8. Pull the whole class back together. Instruct the teams to put away their definitions and pictures. Conduct a brief, random, oral quiz

Portmanteau Student Cards

CHATEAUINCINERADE
The very, very well done steak that was accidently left in the microwave for three hours

LINEBIND
When you go to the bank and are delighted that the line is short only to discover the person in front of you is depositing $500 in pennies

CUSTOMERANIA (or CUSTOMEPHRENIA)
The tendency of every salesperson in a store to ask "May I help you?" when you are just looking

MCLAG
Being at a fast-food hamburger joint and having to wait longer for your order than at a restaurant

AUSSIFICATION
What happens to most Americans who spend a long time in Australia

ACCELERYELLER
The person who thinks that when the stoplight changes to yellow it means to step on the gas

LEAFTOVER
The tiny piece of greenery stuck between someone's front teeth after eating spinach salad or soufflé

DEFIZZICATION
What happens to any opened carbonated drink after sitting around for three days

SOCDROOP
The tendency of socks which have lost their elastic to work their way down below the ankle

Figure B.2

with the groups choosing one member of each team to define one of the nine portmanteau words. Ask the rest of the class if the answer is correct.

9. After testing each team, encourage the teams to discuss their experiences of working together:

• What did we do to help each other in this lesson?

• What can we do next time to help each other even more?

10. Give the class your feedback and observations about how they worked together. Have team members shake hands and offer thanks for help with this lesson.

HOW DO I SELECT THE GROUPS?

SELECT GROUPS FIRST BY RANDOM CHOICES AND THEN BY MIXING ABILITY LEVELS.

In the first few lessons, use random mixes to signal to students that this is a cooperative classroom, with no cliques. Mark role cards for group membership and make a different mix for each cooperative task. In later lessons, consider dividing the class into thirds by ability or motivation and assign one student from each third to a group. (Three to a group is preferred.)

HOW DO I EVALUATE LEARNING IN COOPERATIVE GROUPS?

EVALUATE LEARNING IN COOPERATIVE GROUPS THE SAME WAY AS YOU ASSESS INDIVIDUAL AND COMPETITIVE LEARNING.

For the first year, use the same methods you now use to measure academic performance. If you grade *individual* quizzes, tests, projects, or essays, continue doing so. If you check mastery of each student's learning, continue doing so. Use *cooperative groups* for learning the material and for developing social skills (see chapters 2 and 3), but assess students individually. At least for the first year, *avoid group grades*. As you and the students become more comfortable and skilled with cooperative learning, you may introduce group grades when you think they are acceptable to use. Above all, ensure that your grading system is fair and equal (see chapter 10).

WHAT DO I DO WITH STUDENTS WHO WILL NOT COOPERATE?

WHEN STUDENTS DO NOT WANT TO PARTICIPATE IN A COOPERATIVE LEARNING GROUP, HONOR THEIR RIGHT TO WORK ALONE.

Start with the understanding that every student has a right to learn alone. It is a *privilege* to work together. When teachers honor students' right to work alone, they avoid needless power conflicts with the rare student who really does not want to work with peers.

HOW DOES COOPERATIVE LEARNING FIT WITH THE DIRECT INSTRUCTION LESSON DESIGN?

COOPERATIVE LEARNING CAN BE TAUGHT WITH A DIRECT INSTRUCTION MODEL.

A sample lesson follows that shows using cooperative learning with a thinking skill lesson on prioritizing.

Lesson Objective: To apply the thinking skill of *prioritizing*.

Anticipatory Set: Tell students, Turn to your neighbor and rank your three favorite subjects in school. Explain to your neighbor your priorities.

Input/Demo: Display and explain to students the menu of operations for prioritizing, a definition and synonyms for prioritizing, and appropriate times to use prioritizing (e.g., during a lecture while taking notes).

Check: Now, tell students, Turn to your neighbor and explain (a) the steps in prioritizing and (b) why ranking is an important thinking skill. Sample students' responses.

Guided Practice: Use a worksheet of sample items to rank. Have students agree on rankings and prepare explanations for each ranking.

Discussion and Check: Assign and discuss group reports.

Closure: Allow time for students to make journal entries.

HOW DOES COOPERATIVE LEARNING FIT WITH THE PROBLEM-BASED LEARNING (PBL) INQUIRY MODEL?

COOPERATIVE LEARNING CAN BE TAUGHT WITH THE PBL INQUIRY MODEL THAT FOCUSES ON CONTENT.

The following lesson shows cooperative learning with a content focus lesson.

Meet and Define the Problem: You are members of the historical society in your community. There is much interest in WWII as the 65th anniversary of Pearl Harbor approaches. What will your team do to properly honor the historical event?

Gather Facts: Students use the KND (**K**now, **N**eed to Know, and **D**o) chart to determine what they know, what they need to find out, and what they must do (Figure B.3 or Blackline CB.2 in Appendix C).

K N D Chart		
Know	**N**eed to Know	**D**o
1. Pearl Harbor attack	1. Who is still living as a WWII veteran?	1. Interview WWII vets
	2.	
2. Memorial		2.

Figure B.3

Research: Students in cooperative groups research various aspects of Pearl Harbor using books, journals, the Internet, interviews, films, and so forth.

Seek Alternatives and Advocate a Solution: Students in cooperative groups seek alternatives and decide on one to advocate as the best alternative. They present their ideas to others in an authentic performance.

HOW OFTEN SHOULD I USE COOPERATIVE GROUPS?

A GOOD GOAL IS TO USE COOPERATIVE GROUPS FOR AT LEAST 60 PERCENT OF STUDENTS' LEARNING TIME.

As you begin cooperative learning, you may wonder, How often should I use groups? or Will students tire with too much cooperation? However, research shows that to get the best achievement and social skill results, it is best to use cooperative learning at least 60 percent of the time. This means 60 percent of the students' time will be spent in learning together, not alone.

When just starting to use cooperative groups, consider this weekly plan:

- During the first week, use at least forty minutes to set up basic procedures, guidelines, and expectations for cooperative learning.

- During the second week, use *at least* two informal tasks each day for elementary students or one informal task per day for middle and high school students.

- During the third week, add formal task groups for guided practice (three cooperative practices of ten minutes each during the week), unit review, and vocabulary mastery.

- During the fourth week, start groups with a social skill hook lesson (see chapter 3) and daily social skill practices. In the elementary classroom, increase to three to five formal cooperative tasks blended with a variety of informal groups, base groups, discussions, and formal presentations. In the upper grades, plan to use task groups for more complex tasks throughout the week.

When teachers use variety in their design, students will not tire of cooperative group work. Figure B.4 illustrates a half-day model for an elementary cooperative learning session and Figure B.5 shows a week-long plan for an upper-grade English class.

A 60% Elementary Model
(1 Morning)

8:30	Sponge: Math homework, pair review	9:40	Reading
			a. Trios give play presentations
8:40	Base groups: Me Bag activity		b. Class feedback: What I liked about their play
9:00	Math	10:15	Recess
	a. All-class homework review	10:40	Reading
	b. New lesson lecture and board demo		a. Continue plays and feedback
	c. Guided practice: math trios with observer		b. Small-group processing
	d. Check and assign homework	11:15	Writing
			a. Individual journal entries
9:15	Reading		b. Journal sharing in trios
	a. Individual silent reading	11:45	Social skill practice
	b. Reading trios: read story and make a play		a. All-class discussion: Ways I encouraged
	c. Trios practice for play	12:00	Lunch
9:30	Nutrition break		

Figure B.4

A 60% Upper-Grade Model
(1 Week of a Freshman English Novel Unit)

Monday
- Introduce unit goals and agenda
- Base groups: goal setting
- All-class demonstration on selecting character traits with web organizer
- Check for understanding
- Homework reading assignment: chapter jigsaw

Tuesday
- Jigsaw task groups: prepare character web

Wednesday
- Character webs presented to class and wraparound: I learned . . .

Thursday
- Continue presentations and wraparound class for reactions
- Trios review with jigsaw

Friday
- Individual quiz on characters
- All-class summary discussion
- Base groups: assess members' performance in group

Figure B.5

WHAT SOCIAL SKILL AREAS NEED TO BE ADDRESSED FIRST?

FIRST CONCENTRATE ON COMMUNICATION, TRUST, LEADERSHIP, AND CONFLICT RESOLUTION SKILLS.

Communication: Skills in articulation and listening, expressive language and receptive language, verbal and non-verbal communication strategies

Trust building: Skills needed to enhance teamwork, maintain effective working relationships, and foster camaraderie

Leadership: Skills for accepting responsibility, encouraging others, problem solving, and decision making

Conflict resolution: Skills needed to challenge each other's ideas, reason, justify, seek consensus, and find solutions and alternatives

WHAT DO I DO IF MANY STUDENTS ARE NOT BEHAVING AFTER I HAVE TAUGHT THE SOCIAL SKILLS?

WHEN MANY STUDENTS ARE MISBEHAVING, TAKE MORE TIME TO WORK WITH THE WHOLE CLASS ON THEIR SOCIAL SKILLS.

First, spend more time working with the *whole* class on the cooperative social skills. Refocus and reteach the social skills to all students. (When only one or two students need more complex help in cooperating, goal redirection strategies will work best when the classroom *norm* is cooperation.)

Second, determine if students need to practice social skills using a simple model such as as think-pair-share. Go back to using pairs and make think-pair-share the core of your cooperative groups. Throughout a lesson (approximately every ten minutes), instruct students to: Turn to your partner and agree upon an answer to this question . . . . Then ask the pairs to share with the class. Seek several responses each time. Pair review, prediction pairs, and explain why exercises help students get used to working together. Be sure to stimulate reflection and then discuss the ideas.

HOW DO I DESIGN A COOPERATIVE LEARNING BULLETIN BOARD TO SUPPORT STUDENT LEARNING ABOUT TEAMWORK?

THE BULLETIN BOARD SHOULD COMMUNICATE THE SPIRIT OF COOPERATIVE LEARNING AS WELL AS THE KEY START-UP LOGISTICS. HERE ARE A FEW SUGGESTIONS:

Elementary—For younger students, cooperative story characters, cartoons, or other illustrations of cooperation work well. Post the tasks for the major group roles (e.g., checker, encourager, reader, recorder). Add a list of the key *norming* social behaviors expected during group work (e.g., stay in seats; one person speaks at a time; encourage each other; speak in six-inch, quiet voices). (See chapter 3 for *norming* behaviors.)

Middle—Build bulletin boards around sports figures and teamwork. Show samples of cooperative team play (e.g., football, basketball) and individualistic competition (e.g., tennis, swimming, golf). Discuss how they are alike (e.g., competition) and different (e.g., teams help each other, have roles, etc.).

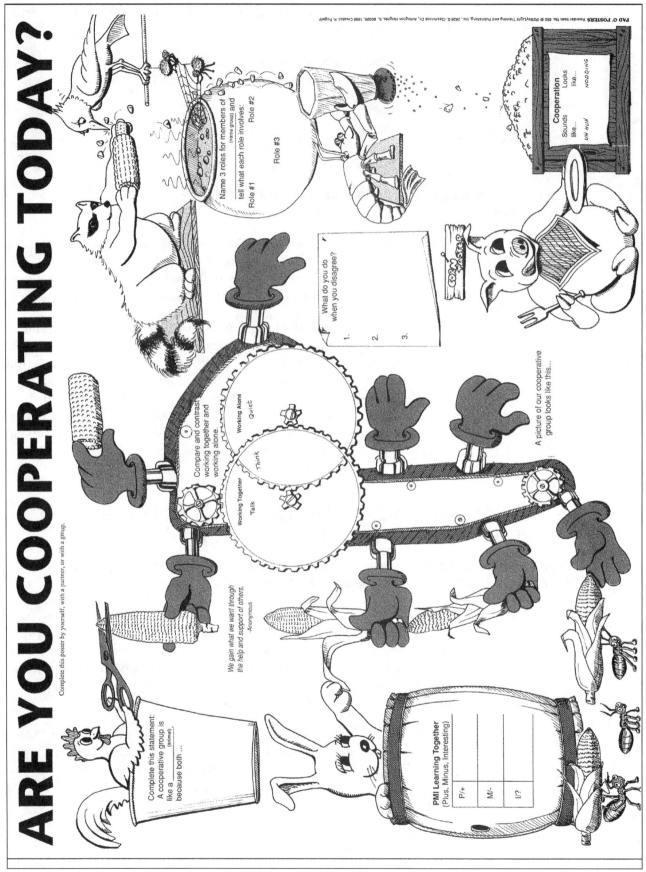

Figure B.6

Secondary—For older students, pictures of cooperation in the workplace, the athletic field, and interpersonal relationships are appropriate. Quotes—All for one, one for all or We sink or swim together—add another dimension.

If a bulletin board is not available, provide each student with a handout to keep in his or her handbook. Use as many graphic illustrations as possible. On the first days of class, use the bulletin board constantly for reference and reinforcement. Figure B.6 shows a bulletin board that worked for one class.

HOW DO I USE ROLE CARDS?

IT'S A GOOD IDEA FOR STUDENTS JUST STARTING WITH COOPERATIVE LEARNING TO HAVE ROLE CARDS OR A PRINTED WORKSHEET OF THE VARIOUS GROUP ROLES AND THEIR DUTIES.

Each role card describes the responsibilities of a group role. For cooperative tasks, each member of the group is assigned a role and receives the corresponding role card. When using role cards, give each group one set so group members can rotate jobs. To help with group assignments, use matching numbers, letters, or symbols for each set. (See examples in Figure B.7 or Blackline CB.3 in Appendix C)

Elementary Sample Role Cards

READER

Is everyone listening?
Is everything clear?
Shall I read any part again?

RECORDER

The main points are . . .
Should I write . . . ?
To summarize . . .

TRAVELER

Can you help us with . . . ?
Did your group understand . . . ?
My group thinks . . .

Figure B.7

(Adapted Marcus and McDonald, 1990.)

Three roles are particularly important: checker, worrier, and recorder.

The Checker. This role may be the most critical to cooperative learning. When a group completes an assigned task, it is the checker who checks that all members of the group can do the task, explain each answer, and tell why that answer was selected. When the checker does this job well, there is little need for more formal ways to gain *individual learning*. As the teacher, it is your job to act as the chief steward of learning and to ensure that each group task is set up for easy checking. In task assignments, teachers help checkers by structuring discussion questions to support the checker's role. To help the checker, share the *three-to-one technique:*

- Ask questions that allow at least *three* possible answers. In a trio, each student gives one possible answer for the recorder to write.

- Ask a follow-up question that challenges the students to agree on the *one* best answer from the list. They can rank or combine ideas.

- The checker checks to see if

  – all members agree (members signal thumbs up),

  – each member can explain the selected answer, and

  – each member can tell why that answer was selected.

Members should rehearse *explaining* and *telling why* before signing the group's worksheet to indicate I agree, I can explain, and I can tell why we decided on this. Figure B.8 shows samples of using the three-to-one technique.

Three-to-One

Elementary Example (for students who read "Three Billy Goats Gruff")

✓ List three ways the billy goats might have crossed the stream without meeting the troll.

✓ Agree which was the safest way to cross.

✓ Explain why you think your group's choice was the best it could make.

✓ Be sure all members can explain the group's choice.

Middle School Example (from a unit on drug abuse)

✓ List three illegal drugs that are available in this town.

✓ Agree on which drug has the worst effect on students your age.

✓ Explain the reasons for your group's choice.

✓ Be sure all members can explain the group's choice.

Secondary School Example (from a math problem-solving sample)

✓ Describe at least three ways to solve this problem.

✓ Solve it each way.

✓ Agree on which was the easiest and most accurate method to use.

✓ Explain the reasons for your choice.

✓ Be sure each member can explain the reason for the group's choice.

Figure B.8

The Worrier. The worrier has several responsibilities. First, the worrier checks with the group to be sure all members agree on the instructions that were given. If there is disagreement in the group, the worrier may ask for help. Second, the worrier sees that all members have an equal chance to participate. Third, the worrier keeps all members on task. In advanced groups, teach the worrier social skills for inviting on-task behavior.

The Recorder. Cooperative groups work best when there is a single recorder. Although each member is encouraged to keep his or her own notes, the recorder writes the official answers for more complex discussions. It is important that the recorder be encouraged to check what he or she writes against what the speaker wants to have written down. (The speaker has the final say.) The recorder's paper becomes the group's product, which is to be signed by each member and turned in to the teacher at the end of the lesson.

Using one pen and one sheet of paper contributes to *united teams*. This method enhances the feeling of one for all and all for one. When the task is done and all agree on the answers, each member in the group signs the worksheet. A signature means "this is my best work."

WHAT ARE THE EXAMPLES OF COOPERATIVE ROLES FOR VARIOUS SUBJECT AREAS?

ROLES DIFFER FOR EACH SUBJECT. BE CREATIVE!

Following are some roles that others have found useful:

The Materials Manager. (In primary grades, this role is called the Gopher.) This person gets all materials, returns materials to the bin, and sees that the group cleans up its area. The bin, located at the side or rear of the classroom, is where the necessary materials are placed for each assignment. (Some teachers assign a *storehouse manager* to hand out sets of materials to each materials manager.) During cooperative tasks, instruct materials managers to move quietly to the bin to get their groups' materials. A list on the board or a paper posted over the bin should detail what items are needed for each group. For example, a list for a lab in biology is shown in Figure B.9.

Today's Lab Materials

Earthworms
1 dissecting kit
1 worm bottle
1 observation sheet
1 instruction sheet
1 pencil
2 sheets of newsprint
1 cloth

Figure B.9

The Encourager. The more competitive a school climate, the more necessary it is to develop students' abilities to encourage. In the early grades, encouragement means a switch from putdowns (dumbbell, stupid, etc.) to encouragements (I like your idea and Keep it up). In the upper grades the switch is from jerk and nerd to that's a good idea, you're really trying hard, Great thinking, Atta boy, and Atta girl.

The encourager role develops this very important social skill among the students. A brief teaching of what encouraging looks like (e.g., smiles, pats on the back, high fives, etc.) and sounds like (e. g., Great idea, I like the energy you are using, Keep at it, etc.), followed by all students practicing the specific behaviors in group work and receiving focused feedback on their practice, goes a long way toward developing a positive classroom climate that is filled with encouraging statements.

Unlimited Roles. Many other roles are possible for groups. Which roles are integrated in an activity depends on the task assigned. For example, in a reading task, use a reader role. In mathematics, reader, calculator, and checker roles are appropriate. Combined roles are necessary in pairs and trios (e.g., recorder-checker). Pick and practice the roles that best fit the task and age levels of the students. See samples in Figure B.10.

Beyond the forming roles described here, a teacher can design roles specific to his/her subject matter. Here are samples:

Math Group
Calculator: Checks work on calculator
Analyst: Analyzes strategies
Bookkeeper: Checks answers; records time
Inventory controller: Keeps inventory on materials; controls supplies

Novel Group
Discussion leader: Prepares and leads questions
Vocabulary enricher: Selects enrichment questions
Literary illuminary: Reads favored passages
Agent: Gets materials

Science Group
Scientist: Observes progress; keeps time
Researcher: Provides guidelines to follow
Observer: Records information
Lab technician: Sets up materials and equipment

Writer's Group
Editor In Chief: Tracks progress; sets deadlines
Publisher: Sets guidelines
Scriber: Keeps notes
Author: Supplies materials

Social Studies Group
Presiding officer: Presides over the group
Parliamentarian: Observes group behavior
Secretary: Records information
Sergeant at arms: Keeps the time; gets materials

Primary Group
Captain: Encourages group
Umpire: Observes and reports
Scorekeeper: Writes down information
Runner: Gets what is needed

Figure B.10

HOW DO I INTRODUCE SOCIAL SKILLS?

START BY INTRODUCING THE BASIC SOCIAL SKILLS THAT STUDENTS NEED TO GET STARTED IN COOPERATIVE GROUPS.

(*Note*: Chapter 3 discusses this question in more detail). Select basic cooperative social skills that students need to learn. Predict which ones you want to emphasize during the first month or quarter. (See examples in Figure B.11). Post these on the bulletin board or give students a handout.

Examples of Forming Basic Social Skills

Elementary Example	Middle School Example	Secondary School Example
✓ Use 6″ voices.	✓ Use 6″ voices.	✓ Control your voice.
✓ Listen to your neighbor.	✓ It's ok to think.	✓ Think for yourself.
✓ Stay with the group.	✓ Don't interrupt others.	✓ Respect others' opinions.
✓ Look at the speaker.	✓ Help your neighbor.	✓ Carry your weight.
✓ Don't hurt feelings.	✓ Know and do your job.	✓ Help each other stay on task.
	✓ Listen to all ideas.	✓ Explore different points of view.
	✓ Use encouraging words.	✓ Include all members.

Figure B.11

During the first weeks of school, plan to use procedures that require face-to-face interactions. Model and then practice how the students should move desks in and out of groups, how students should sit close together in triangles or squares, and how students should listen to you.

Later in the first year, use a T-chart to clarify social skills such as listening, encouraging, carrying your weight, respecting, and including others (see Figure B.12). Before using each cooperative learning task, help the groups review the chart. After practicing the task, use the chart as a way to introduce simple processing: Which skills were practiced? Where was improvement?

T-Chart: Respecting

Looks Like	Sounds Like
eye contact	listening
nodding	questions

Figure B.12

HOW DO I ARRANGE MY ROOM FOR COOPERATIVE LEARNING?

THERE ARE MANY OPTIONS FOR ARRANGING YOUR CLASSROOM.

Plan the classroom arrangement for face-to-face cooperative learning. Arrange the classroom furniture differently from the traditional rows. Try for a permanent desk arrangement that encourages united groups in face-to-face interaction. As much as possible, provide aisles between student groups. This allows you to move easily among groups to listen, help, and monitor.

If the classroom cannot be arranged into a permanent design, spend twenty minutes of the first week teaching students how to move the desks in and out of the cooperative group arrangement. Do this in conjunction with the first cooperative lesson. Insist upon keeping the room in order and quiet as students practice how to get in and out of groups. Figures B.13–B.17 illustrate both permanent and moveable designs suitable for elementary, middle school, and high school arrangements.

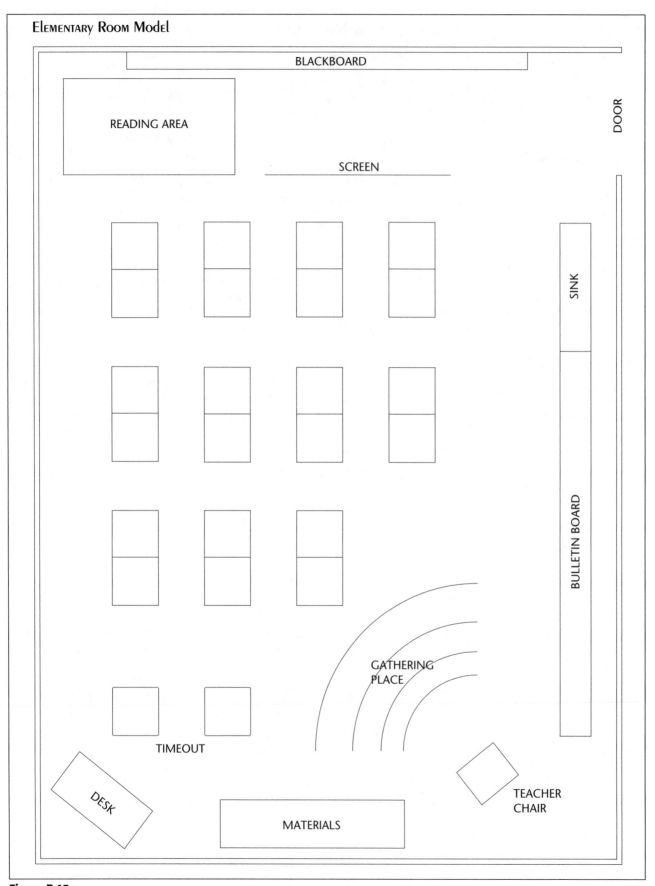

Figure B.13

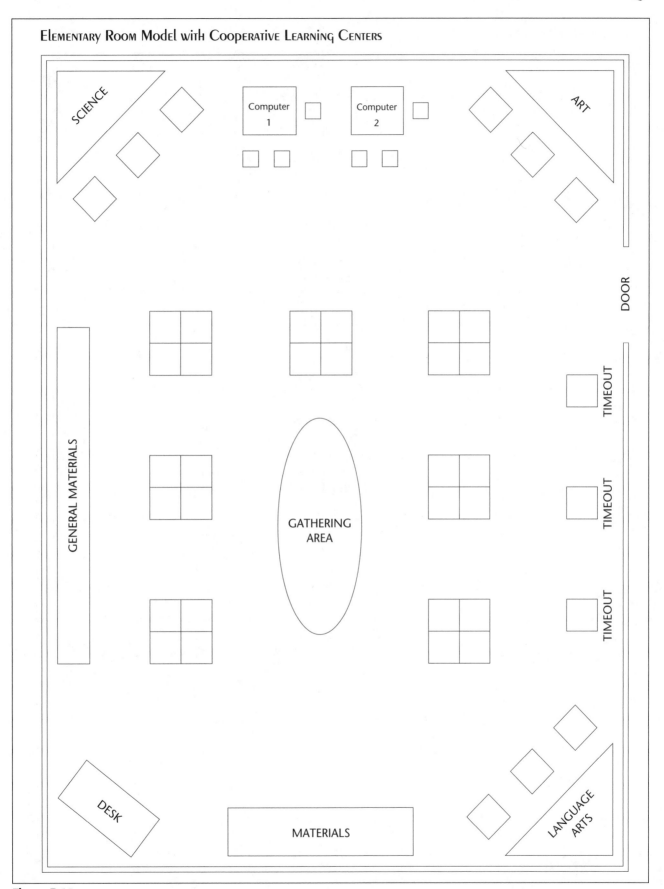

Elementary Room Model with Cooperative Learning Centers

Figure B.14

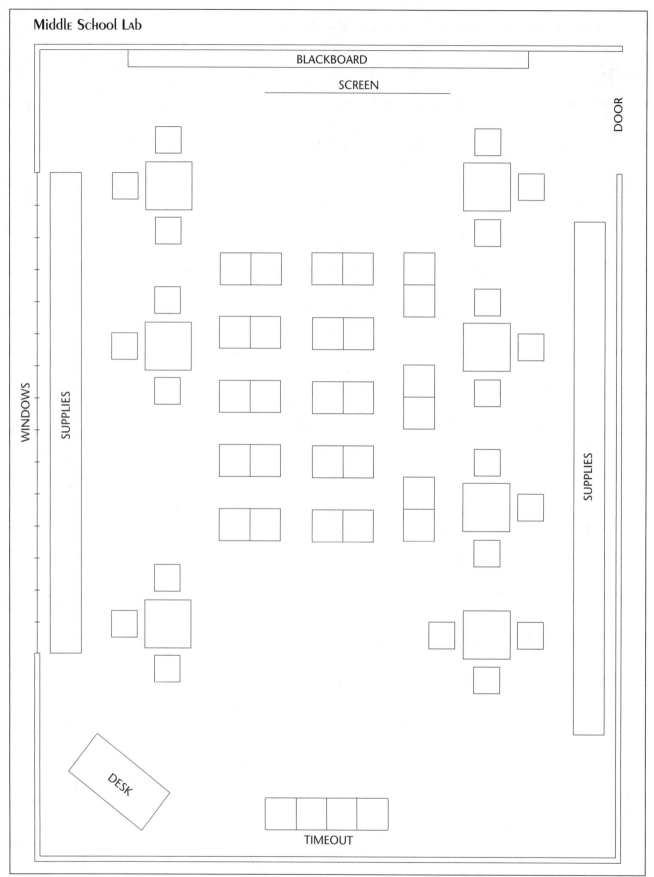

Middle School Lab

Figure B.15

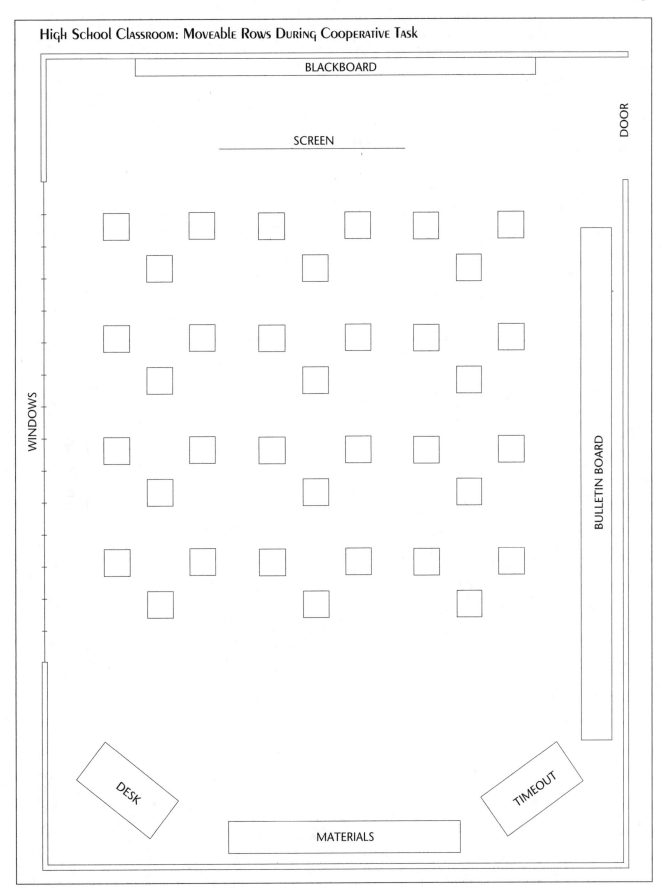

High School Classroom: Moveable Rows During Cooperative Task

BLACKBOARD

DOOR

SCREEN

WINDOWS

BULLETIN BOARD

DESK

TIMEOUT

MATERIALS

Figure B.16

High School Classroom: Moveable Rows During Lectures and Film

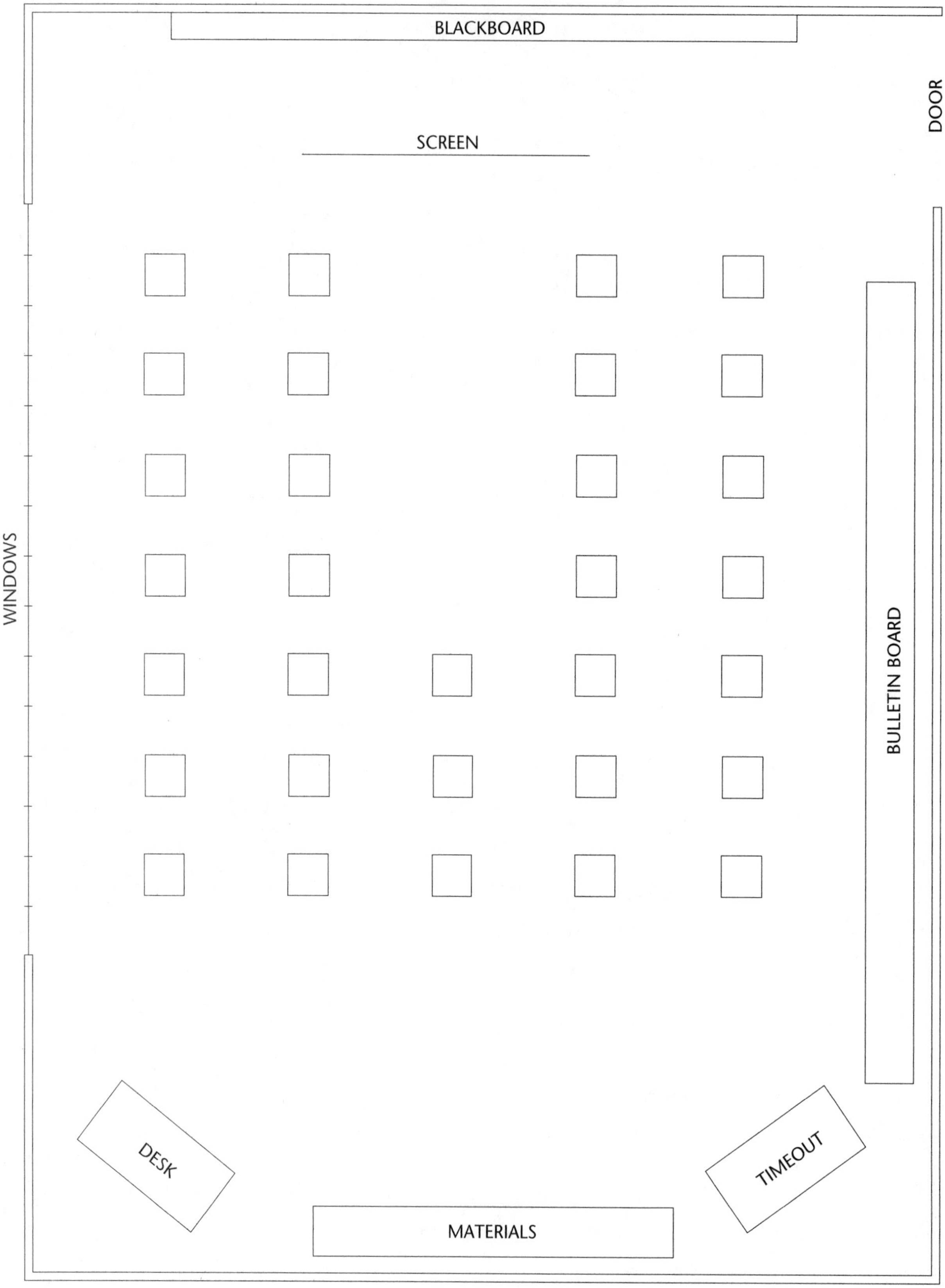

BLACKBOARD

DOOR

SCREEN

WINDOWS

BULLETIN BOARD

DESK

TIMEOUT

MATERIALS

Figure B.17

HOW DO I TEACH SIGNALS?

BEFORE STARTING GROUP WORK, TEACH EXPLICIT SIGNALS FOR DIFFERENT INSTRUCTIONS.

Getting students into groups to do a task is easy. Getting them to stop is more difficult. Shouting above students' concentrated conversation turns any teacher's voice sour. Instead of straining your voice, rely on a practiced signal.

For the most effective signal, use the time-tested hands up signal. Introduced in the early 1900s by the Girl Scouts, this signal works with students of any age.

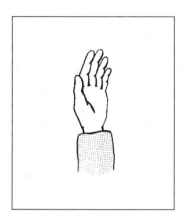

Introduce the signal by explaining to students what it is for; that is, this signal means the teacher wants the class' attention. Tell students: I'll hold up my hand when I want everyone to stop talking and pay attention to me. Let them know that this hands-up signal is your way of alerting them to listen for the next set of instructions. Explain to students that they are to do four things when they see the hand up signal:

- complete their thoughts,

- put their pencils down,

- put up their hands, and

- look at the teacher without talking.

When all students are silent, have put their pencils down, have raised their hands, and are looking at you, praise their attention (e.g., I appreciate your prompt cooperation) and give the next instruction.

After demonstrating the signal, conduct a short practice. Use wait time and support it with eye contact. If some students are slower to respond, use proximity: move next to the laggards and stand there with a raised hand.

After a week or two, some students may get sloppy in responding to the signal. For example, they may raise their hands when signaled, but forget to stop talking. To correct this, stand next to the offending group and either teach and repractice by having a strong group demonstrate the correct response followed by the class imitating the behavior, or give stronger recognition to the most responsive students. Never begin talking until all students are looking at you and are not talking or working. Keep your hand up until the moment of absolute silence.

There are several appropriate times to use the signal. Essentially, teachers use it to address the class. The three most common uses of the signal are when giving instruction to the class, when students' talking becomes too loud and controlled voice levels (i.e., 3", 6", 12" voices) are needed, and when a student or guest is to address the class.

The hands-up signal works in any class with any age of students, provided that the prompt response is consistently required. If all teachers in the school use the same signal, students benefit all the more.

It is not mandatory that every teacher use the same signal. Some prefer to flick the lights, ring a bell, or use the T hand signal to call for a timeout. Any signal is fine as long as the signal is taught, practiced, and used.

HOW DO I USE INCENTIVES?

USE INCENTIVES APPROPRIATELY.

Prepare incentives for cooperative learning. A classroom of *internally* motivated students is every teacher's dream. The reality is that external motivators may be a prerequisite for many students. To develop *internal* motivation, some of the most fundamental tools are *external* incentives and rewards. Incentives work best when teachers use a variety of motivators that help different students. Two external motivators that experienced practitioners of cooperative learning use are group rewards and lotteries. Note that the incentives are geared toward rewarding *the group* for accomplishments or rewarding individuals for contributions *to the group*.

Group Reward

Think about what to tell the students. Are the group rewards given to recognize the practice of specific social skills? How many times must the observer note each skill? Are groups expected to perform a fixed number of times? Is each group competing against itself to improve on its previous score, or is this an intergroup competition?

Intergroup. As long as students have the social skills to handle intergroup competition, consider giving the highest-scoring groups a group prize. For instance, if group A scores 79 on the task and groups B and C only score 65, then 79 wins. Teachers may discourage non-productive group behavior by first explaining the following rule to the class: If any member of the winning group makes negative remarks to the other groups, then his or her group may forfeit the prize. Encourage all groups to celebrate the top-achieving group.

Intragroup. A more appropriate form of recognition rewards groups that improve on their previous performances in using social skills. To encourage cooperation within each group, use a group improvement score without singling out any one member.

Individual. If individuals in the groups are identified, be sure the groups are not penalized. Focus on the team's improvement or give special recognition for individual improvement so the whole team benefits.

Lottery

To avoid inappropriate competition among teams, give each team a fair chance to earn the reward. One of the best ways to do this is by having a lottery. In a given task, each team can earn so many tickets for a team prize (e.g., one ticket per ten social skill points). Once a week have a drawing for a team prize that all members share. Here are some examples of appropriate prizes:

- ten minutes of free time for each member

- a certificate for each team member to hang on the wall

- a certificate for each member to buy a paperback book

- a grab bag of school supplies for each member

Some schools draw points at the end of a quarter or semester, usually with every class in the school eligible to win. All classroom points are placed in the schoolwide (draw, even if a team won in a classroom draw,) and the prizes are more significant. In one school, the prize was a field trip for each grade's winning team, with lunch paid by the PTA. In another, individual students who earned team contribution points were eligible for a bicycle. All students who earned fifty points a semester for team spirit received a special certificate. All who earned seventy-five points received a plaque and a T-shirt.

HOW DO I PLAN MY INTRODUCTORY COOPERATIVE LESSON?

THERE ARE A HOST OF STRATEGIES THAT INTRODUCE THE CLASS TO THE PURPOSE, METHODS, AND BENEFITS OF COOPERATIVE LEARNING. KEEP THE FIRST LESSON SHORT AND SIMPLE (THE KISS PRINCIPLE). TRY THE THREE-PART MODEL FROM *BLUEPRINTS* AS A FRAMEWORK FOR DESIGNING THE LESSON.

The three-part lesson design extends the architectural metaphor of the Blueprints title and consists of:

Part I: Setting Up the Scaffolding

Part II: Working the Crew

Part III: Reflecting on the Design

Part I, Setting Up the Scaffolding, pulls together all the preparation pieces needed *prior* to the lesson, including input information, handouts, and necessary materials. Typically, teachers use this getting ready section to identify the anticipatory set or focus activity, the objective, the instructions, and the cooperative and cognitive skills targeted in the lesson.

Use the key elements from the BUILD acronym as a tool to help plan a high-support, high-content, high-challenge lesson:

Build in high-order thinking for transfer

Unite teams in face-to-face interactions

Invite individual learning

Look over and discuss the interaction

Develop social skills of cooperation for life

Part II, Working the Crew, elaborates on the interactions that occur *during* the actual lesson. The activity includes a cooperative interaction structure and graphic organizer with which the students work. This activity section includes all aspects of working the crew as students get intensely involved in the cooperative task.

Part III, Reflecting on the Design, presents the metacognitive discussion questions that require students to reflect and assess their behaviors, their learning, and the lesson. In this part, evaluation focuses on four distinct areas—affective, social, cognitive, and metacognitive.

Affective processing focuses student thinking at the *feeling* level. Understanding how their feelings influence their learning is key to increasing students' learning.

Social skill processing highlights the expected cooperative behaviors. By targeting explicit social skills prior to the lesson and by discussing them immediately following the interaction, teachers help students track their progress in developing the social skills necessary for group work.

Cognitive processing follows a learning situation and consists of a typical classroom discussion in which students' answers are sampled, evaluated, and justified. This processing highlights *what* was learned.

Metacognitive processing asks students to think reflectively about *what* they have been doing and *how* they have been doing it. Metacognitive processing involves planning, monitoring, and evaluating one's thinking and behavior. It is like stepping outside the situation and looking in at what is going on inside the situation. This stage of thinking also fosters application and transfer of ideas as students reflect upon their thinking processes and their behavior in the groups.

The development of students' metacognitive dispositions starts with the teacher. What do you do to structure each student's learning to think about thinking? At the end of cooperative and thoughtful lessons, be sure to structure thoughtful "look-backs" at the quality of thinking used in the lesson. There is a plethora of options available to designers of cooperative and thoughtful lessons. The window of opportunity that cooperative lessons opens for thinking about thinking broadens when you take advantage of guidelines provided by experienced process facilitators:

- Invite students to write or sketch individual responses before sharing in small groups.

- Model sample responses.

- Use wraparounds rather than open volunteer responses. To help students listen to others, signal that several students will be asked to summarize the wraparound.

- Use "fat" prompts that allow multiple responses and extend them by asking: Why do you think so?

- Model acceptance (e.g., saying thank you, using eye contact, and smiles), drawing out (Tell me more, Give us an example), and encouragement (Take your time, You can do it, Great idea).

- Use wait time to encourage students to listen to each other.

- Use all-class reports from two or three small groups and avoid round robin reports from all groups on every task.

- Post products that show students' thinking about thinking.

Because many students may lack the strong social skills needed to do extended and whole-class processing, start with the KISS principle (keep it short and simple). Do the first processing in small groups only. When moving to whole-group processing, sample responses but do not ask every group to process. Later, as students learn to listen in a large group, extend the processing time.

Although all four levels of processing (affective, social skill, cognitive, and metacognitive) are important for each lesson, you may focus discussion on one or any combination of the three levels. By talking about thinking, you take advantage of the teachable moments and facilitate transfer.

There is no aspect of thinking in the cooperative classroom that is more difficult to do than inviting students to look back and review their learning. Nor is any element more important or more powerful. Skillful processing takes time, energy, and commitment. When a teacher provides the key to successful metacognition for each student, the results in learning and motivation are dramatic and powerful. As Ralph Waldo Emerson said, "What lies behind us and what lies before us are tiny matters compared to what lies within us."

WHAT ARE SOME WAYS TO PROMOTE REFLECTION IN COOPERATIVE GROUPS?

USE THOUGHTFUL LOOK-BACKS TO PROVIDE REFLECTION.

Blueprints offers numerous ways of looking back at the quality of students' thinking:

- *Media*—Student logs, newsprint, 3"x5" cards, videotapes, and art paper provide varied media on which students do their thinking.

- *Prompts*—Stem statements, PMI charts, Mrs. Potter's questions, cartoon strips, and other starter statements initiate students' thinking about thinking.

- *Focus*—Individual responses, small-group round robins, and whole-class reports provide a variety of focal points.

- *Means of expression*—Students can share ideas, write, sketch, and graph to express their multitude of ideas.

- *Extension*—When students have initiated this processing, the teacher can use different strategies to extend thinking:

  a. Ask for individual comments written in a thinking log or journal.

  b. Lead a class discussion using a graphic organizer, wait time, equal distribution of responses, fat questions, reinforcement of skillful thinking, and encouragement to help students explore thinking patterns.

WHAT ARE THE PREREQUISITES FOR INTRODUCING COOPERATIVE LEARNING?

THERE ARE TWO ESSENTIAL PREREQUISITES FOR INTRODUCING COOPERATIVE LEARNING. FIRST, TEACHERS MUST HOLD AND PRACTICE HIGH EXPECTATIONS FOR ALL STUDENTS. SECOND, TEACHERS MUST FEEL CONFIDENT IN THEIR BASIC CLASSROOM MANAGEMENT SKILLS.

The first prerequisite for introducing cooperative learning is high expectations. High expectations are both a belief about what is possible and a set of practices that reinforce to students and parents that the belief is real. When teachers doubt their ability to motivate any child to succeed and meet the learning standards, then their belief is false. When teachers excuse a child's performance, even with silent self-talk, because the child has a special need or comes from a family, religious, economic, or cultural group whose academic motivation or performance the teacher doubts, or when teachers tolerate unruly behavior with such self-talk statements as "the child has no discipline," "the parents don't help," or "this child lacks motivation," then those teachers are only mouthing the words "I have high expectations."

Teachers who hold high expectations practice what they preach. They communicate these expectations to their students and their students' parents. Their high expectations include that the child will meet daily homework standards, follow classroom procedures, work cooperatively with other students, stay on task, and meet all academic goals for challenging work. Challenging work includes tasks that challenge the child to understand grade level materials and to develop the thinking skills to transfer and apply new knowledge beyond tests.

After teachers have communicated high expectations to students and parents, they stubbornly insist that each child stay on track. Excuses are not accepted. If a child faces special difficulties, the teacher seeks out special remedies to overcome any and all barriers.

The second prerequisite for the introduction of cooperative learning is effective classroom management. Teachers' high expectations for all students must include high expectations for on-task behavior. These need to be communicated to students and parents in the form of classroom behavior standards, procedures, and consequences. Teachers must know how to apply corrective measures in a fair and equal manner to all students in that classroom. Where needed, they will teach social skills so that the classroom culture develops norms based on social responsibility and respect of others. As a consequence, students will respect the classroom regulations, follow procedures, and avoid disrupting any lesson.

Teachers who express high expectations (as evidenced by the high number of tasks assigned students) or demonstrate classroom management skills (as evidenced by the high number of students on-task at any moment of the day) are ready to take on cooperative learning.

Teachers who spend most of the day assigning low-level worksheet tasks or other nonproductive work and teachers who spend a good deal of time correcting misbehavior and pointing the finger of blame at the students are not ready for cooperative learning.

Blueprints for Achievement

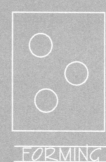

FORMING

PERFORMING

NORMING

APPENDIX C

BLACKLINES

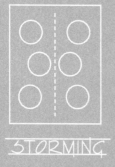

STORMING

CONFORMING

in the Cooperative Classroom

The SCANS Skills and Competencies

Foundation

1. *Basic skills:* Reads, writes, performs arithmetic and mathematical operations, listens, speaks.

2. *Thinking skills:* Thinks creatively, makes decisions, solves problems, visualizes, knows how to learn, and reasons.

3. *Personal qualities:* Displays responsibility, self-esteem, sociability, self-management, integrity, and honesty.

Workplace Competencies

1. *Resources:* Identifies, organizes, plans and allocates resources.
   - Time
   - Money
   - Materials and facilities
   - Human resources

2. *Interpersonal:* Works with others.
   - Participates as member of a team.
   - Teaches others new skills.
   - Exercises leadership.
   - Negotiates.
   - Works with diversity.

3. *Information:* Acquires and uses information.
   - Acquires and evaluates information.
   - Organizes and maintains information.
   - Interprets and communicates information.
   - Uses computers to process information.

4. Systems: Understands complex inter-relationships.
   - Understands systems.
   - Monitors and corrects performance.
   - Improves or designs systems

5. Technology: Works with a variety of technologies.
   - Selects technology.
   - Applies technology
   - Maintains and troubleshoots equipment.

(Adapted from Secretary's Commission on Achieving Necessary Skills, [SCANS] 1991.)

Categories of Instructional Strategies
that Affect Student Achievement

Category	Ave. Effect Size (ES)	Percentile Gain	No. of ESs	Standard Deviation (SD)
Identifying similarities and differences	1.61	45	31	.31
Summarizing and notetaking	1.00	34	179	.50
Reinforcing effort and providing recognition	.60	29	21	.35
Homework and practice	.77	28	134	.36
Nonlinguistic representations	.75	27	246	.40
Cooperative learning	.73	27	122	.40
Setting objectives and providing feedback	.61	23	408	.28
Generating and testing hypotheses	.61	23	63	.79
Questions , cues, and advance organizers	.59	22	1.251	.26

Blackline C1.2

The Normal Distribution

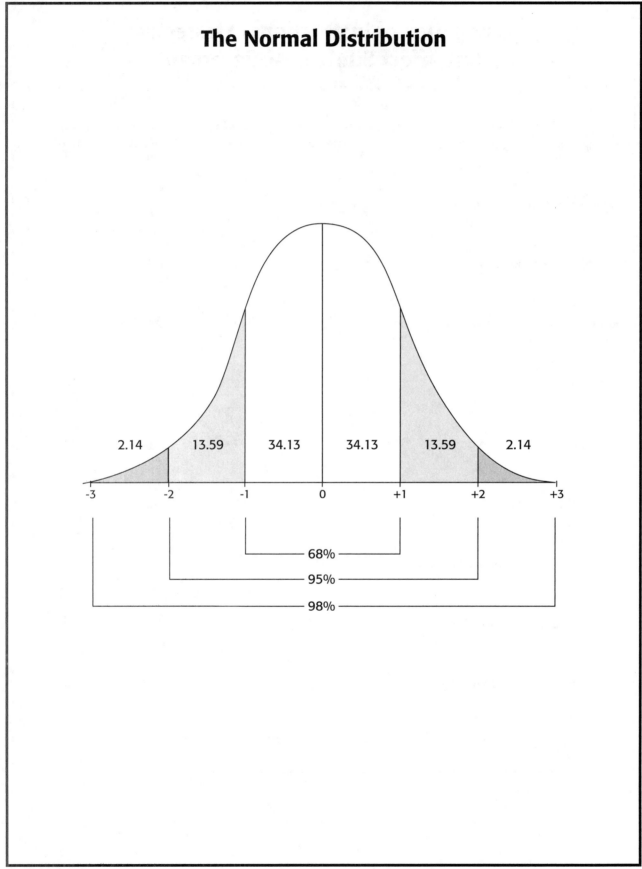

Rulers

Rulers were another example of the wide gulf separating my beliefs from those the children demonstrated whenever they were allowed to follow their ideas to logical conclusions. I had not realized that "rulers are not really real." We were about to act out "Jack and the Beanstalk" when Wally and Eddie disagreed about the relative size of our two rugs.

Wally:	The big rug is the giant's castle. The small one is Jack's house.
Eddie:	Both rugs are the same.
Wally:	They can't be the same. Watch me. I'll walk around the rug. Now watch—walk, walk, walk, walk, walk, walk, walk, walk, walk—count all these walks. Okay. Now count the other rug. Walk, walk, walk, walk, walk. See? That one has more walks.
Eddie:	No fair. You cheated. You walked faster.
Wally:	I don't have to walk. I can just look.
Eddie:	I can look too. But you have to measure it. You need a ruler. About six hundred inches or feet.
Wally:	We have a ruler.
Eddie:	Not that one. Not the short kind. You have to use the long kind that gets curled up in a box.
Wally:	Use people. People's bodies. Lying down in a row.
Eddie:	That's a great idea. I never thought of that.

Wally announces a try-out for "rug measurers." He adds one child at a time until both rugs are covered—four children end to end on one rug and three on the other. Everyone is satisfied, and the play continues with Wally as the giant on the rug henceforth known as the four-person rug. The next day Eddie measures the rugs again. He uses himself, Wally, and two other children. But this time they do not cover the rug.

Wally:	You're too short. I mean someone is too short. We need Warren. Where's Warren?
Teacher:	He's not here today.
Eddie:	Then we can't measure the rug.
Teacher:	You can only measure the rug when Warren is here?
Jill:	Because he's longer.
Deana:	Turn everyone around. Then it will fit.

(Eddie rearranges the measures so that each is now in a different position. Their total length is the same.)

Eddie:	No, it won't work. We have to wait for Warren.
Deana:	Let me have a turn. I can do it.
Jill:	You're too big, Deana. Look at your feet sticking out. Here's a rule. Nobody bigger than Warren can measure the rug.
Fred:	Wait. Just change Ellen and Deana because Ellen is shorter.
Jill:	She sticks out just the same. Wait for Warren.
Fred:	Now she's longer than before, that's why.
Teacher:	Is there a way to measure the rug so we don't have to worry about people's sizes?
Kenny:	Use short people.
Teacher:	And if the short people aren't in school?
Rose:	Use big people.
Eddie:	Some people are too big.
Teacher:	Maybe using people is a problem.
Fred:	Use three-year-olds.
Teacher:	There aren't any three-year-olds in our class.
Deana:	Use rulers. Get all the rulers in the room. I'll get a box of rulers.
Eddie:	That was *my* idea, you know.
Deanna:	This isn't enough rulers.
Eddie:	Put a short, short person after the rulers—Andy.
Andy:	I'm not short, short. And I'm not playing this game.
Wally:	Use the dolls.
Teacher:	So this rug is ten rulers and two dolls long? (Silence.) Here's something we can do. We can use one of the rulers over again, this way.
Eddie:	Now you made *another* empty space.
Teacher:	Eddie, you mentioned a tape measure before. I have one here.

(We stretch the tape along the edge of the rug, and I show the children that the rug is 156 inches long. The lesson is done. The next day Warren is back in school.)

Wally:	Here's Warren. Now we can really measure the rug.
Teacher:	Don't we really measure the rug with the ruler?
Wally:	Well, rulers aren't really real, are they?

Rulers are not real, but rug measurers are.

(From *Wally's Stories: Conversations in Kindergarten* [Daley 1981]).

Blackline C1.4

Business Card

_____	_____
learning goal	success you have had this week

_____
first name

_____
name of your school

_____	_____
title of your favorite book	benefit of doing your homework

K	W	L
What we Know	**What we Want to Know**	**What we Learned**

(Adapted from Ogle 1986.)

Blackline C2.2

MAIL-GRAM

To: _____

From: _____

Message: I Learned... _____

_____

_____

_____

Signed_____

MAIL-GRAM

To: _____

From: _____

Message: I Learned... _____

_____

_____

_____

Signed_____

MAIL-GRAM

To: _____

From: _____

Message: I Learned... _____

_____

_____

_____

Signed_____

Blackline C2.3

Jigsaw

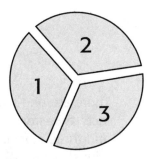

Base Group
(Members divide work.)

Individual Work
(Members decide what's
important and how to teach
their fellow group members.)

Base Group
(Members teach each other)

Two Decisions
#1 What to teach . . .
#2 How to teach it . . .

The Three-Story Intellect

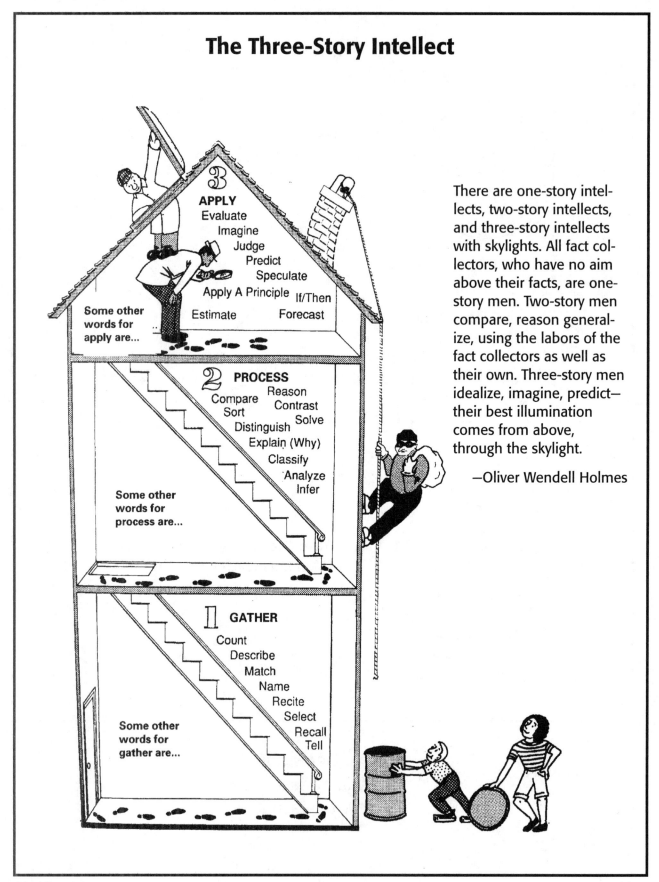

There are one-story intellects, two-story intellects, and three-story intellects with skylights. All fact collectors, who have no aim above their facts, are one-story men. Two-story men compare, reason generalize, using the labors of the fact collectors as well as their own. Three-story men idealize, imagine, predict—their best illumination comes from above, through the skylight.

—Oliver Wendell Holmes

B U I L D : Cooperative Lesson Planner

	B Build in High-Order Thinking	**U** Unite Teams	**I** Insist on Individual Learning	**L** Look Over Back and Debrief	**D** Develop Social Skills	
	Problem Solving Decision Making Creative Ideation	*Build Trust and Teamwork*	*Insure Individual Learning and Reponsibility*	*Plan, Monitor, and Evaluate*	*Communication, Leadership, Conflict Resolution*	
1	Critical and creative thinking	Bonding and group identity	Assigned roles	Goal setting	Paraphrase	I hear I see...
2	3-to-1 technique	Shared materials	Quiz	PMI	Affirm	That's a good idea
3	Problem solving	Single product	Random responses	Human graph	Clarify	Tell me more!
4	Decision making	Jigsaw	Individual application	Teacher observation sheet	Test options	What else?
5	Fat and Skinny Questions	Lottery	Individual grades	Student observer feedback	Sense tone	That feels ____
6	Application	Bonus points	Signature. I agree! I understand!	Success award	Encourage others	No put-downs!
7	Transfer within/across/into	Group grade	Round robin (Wraparound)	Log entry	Accept others' ideas	Set DOVE guidelines
8	Graphic organizers	Group reward	Homework	Individual transfer or application	T-chart	Looks like Sounds like
9	Metacognitive exercises	Consensus	Bonus points	Team ad	Disagree with ideas not people	Other point of view
10	Making metaphors	Extended projects	Expert jigsaw	Mrs. Potter's questions	Reach consensus	5 to fist

Blackline C2.6

BUILD Rubric

To what degree does this lesson:	1	2	3	4
Build in higher-order thinking.	All facts and recall	Implied thinking	Application of specific skill	High challenge thinking and reflecting
Unite the team.	Task can be done alone	Uses roles and guidelines	Has common goal structures	Supports common goal
Invite individual responsibility.	No reason to work together	Uses one strategy	Uses two strategies	Uses three or more strategies
Look back and review.	Not called for	Content review	Content and cooperation review	All three functions—content, cooperation, cognition—reviewed
Develop social skills.	Not done	Forced by structure	Encouraged by structure, taught and reviewed	Expectation integrated

T-Chart

Thinking Skill: Visualizing

Social Skill Target: _____

Cooperative

Looks Like	Sounds Like

Competitive

Looks Like	Sounds Like

Individualistic

Looks Like	Sounds Like

Blackline C2.8

Phases of Introduction of Social Skills

Phase	Social Skills Communication (C), Trust (T), Leadership (L), Conflict Resolution (CR)	
Forming to organize groups and establish behavior guidelines	Use a 6″ voice. (C) Listen to your neighbor. (C) Stay with the group. (C)	Heads together. (C) Do your job. (L) Help each other. (L)
Norming to complete assigned tasks and build effective relationships	Include all members. (L) Encourage others. (L) Listen with focus. (T)	Let all participate. (L) Respect each other's opinions. (T) Stay on task. (L)
Conforming to promote critical thinking and maximize the learning of all	Clarify. (C) Paraphrase ideas. (C) Give examples. (C)	Probe for differences. (CR) Generate alternatives. (CR) Seek consensus. (CR)
Storming to function effectively and enable the work of the team	Sense tone. (C) Disagree with idea not person. (CR) Keep an open mind. (T)	See all points of view. (CR) Try to agree. (CR) Contribute own ideas. (L)
Performing to foster higher-level thinking skills, creativity, and depth intuition	Elaborate on ideas. (C) Integrate ideas. (L) Justify ideas. (CR)	Extend ideas. (C) Synthesize. (L) Reach consensus. (CR)

Blackline C3.1

Assessing Your Class: The Forming Skills

Skill	Needed	Have	Comments
Move into a group.			
Move out of a group.			
One person talks at a time.			
Stay with group.			
Control volume of talk (3″, 6″, 12″).			
Practice all roles.			
Keep hands and feet to self.			

Blackline C3.2

Assessing Your Class: The Norming Skills

Skill	Needed	Have	Comments
Sincere compliments			
Respectful statements and actions			
Attentive listening			
Encouragement			
Taking turns to speak			
Applauding success			
Pride in role			

Encouragement

Looks Like	Sounds Like

Attentive Listening

Looks Like	Sounds Like

I A L A C

I A L A C

I A L A C

Blackline C3.6

Four Lobes of the Brain

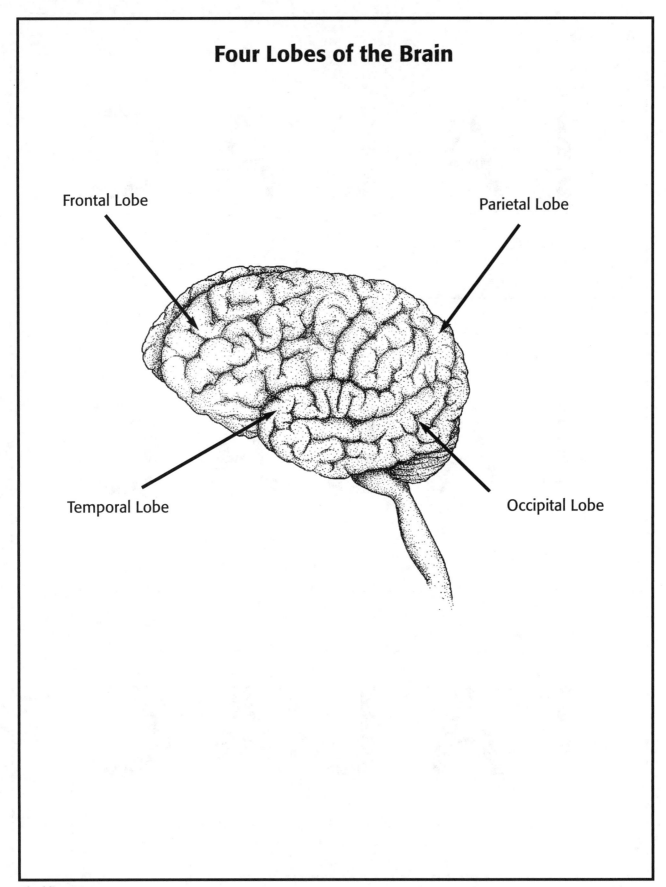

Frontal Lobe

Parietal Lobe

Temporal Lobe

Occipital Lobe

Brain Cell or Neuron

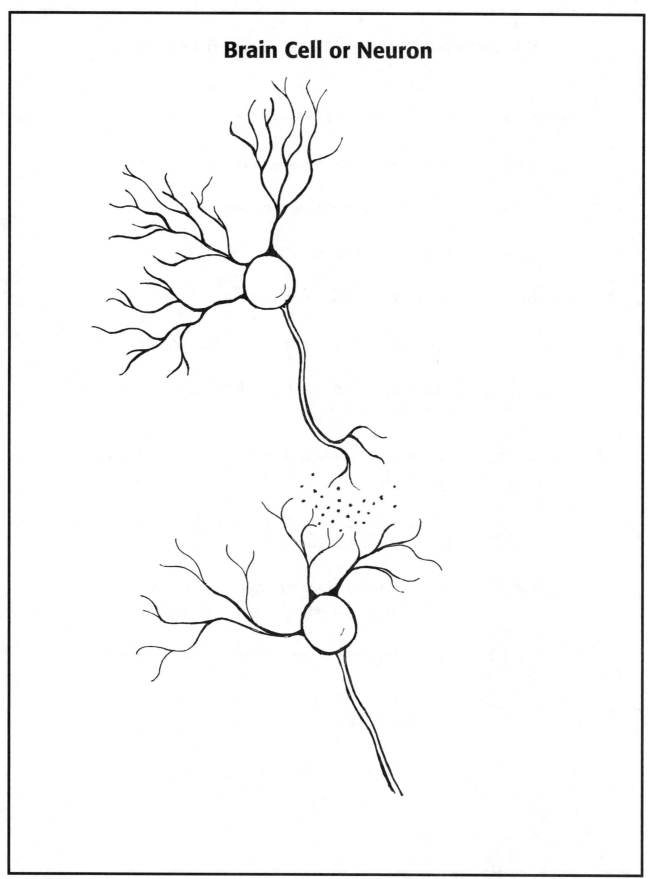

Blackline C4.2

Twelve Principles of Brain-Based Learning

Principle 1:   The brain is a parallel processor.

Principle 2:   Learning engages the entire physiology.

Principle 3:   The search for meaning is innate.

Principle 4:   The search for meaning occurs through patterning.

Principle 5:   Emotions are critical to patterning.

Principle 6:   The brain processes parts and wholes simultaneously.

Principle 7:   Learning involves both focused attention and peripheral perception.

Principle 8:   Learning always involves conscious and unconscious processes.

Principle 9:   We have at least two different types of memory: spatial (implicit) and rote (explicit).

Principle 10:   We understand and remember best when facts or skills are embedded in natural, spatial memory.

Principle 11:   Learning is enhanced by challenge and inhibited by threat.

Principle 12:   Each brain is unique.

(Adapted from Caine and Caine 1994)

Multiple Intelligences

Intelligence	Activities	Prodigies
Verbal/Linguistic	reading, writing, speaking, and listening	T. S. Elliot
Logical/Mathematical	inductive and deductive thinking, mathematical reasoning	Michael Polanyi
Visual/Spatial	visual/spatial arts, architecture, sciences	Van Gogh
Musical/Rhythmic	musical appreciation, skill, and performance	Mozart
Bodily/Kinesthetic	hand/eye coordination; physical abilities of athletes, dancers, surgeons	George Balanchine
Interpersonal	social, empathic, charismatic	Gandhi
Intrapersonal	introspective, reflective, philosophical	Socrates
Naturalist	classification of species, flora and fauna	Linnaeus

Blackline C4.4

Five Emotional Domains

1. awareness of feelings

2. control and self-regulation over emotions

3. sense of empathy for others

4. relationships with others

5. social skill repertoire

FAT and Skinny Questions

SKINNY QUESTIONS
Skinny questions
require simple
yes/no/maybe so
answers, a one-word
answer, or a nod or
shake of the head.
They take no space
or time.

FAT QUESTIONS
Fat questions
require a lot of
discussion and
explanation
with interesting
examples. Fat
questions take
time to think
through and
answer in depth.

Blackline C4.6

FAT and Skinny Questions Chart

FAT	Skinny	Questions

Mind Map

Thinking Skill: Brainstorming

Web

Mrs. Potter's Questions

1. What were you supposed to do?

2. What did you do well?

3. What would you do differently next time?

4. Do you need any help?

Create a Creature—Classification Lab

	A Body Symmetry	B Segmentation	C Form of Locomotion	D Sensory Organs	E Support Structures	F Body Covering
1						
2						
3						
4						
5						
6						

Graphic Organizers

Venn Diagram

Attribute Web

Mind Map

PMI

P+	
M−	
I?	

(deBono 1973)

T-Chart

Looks Like | Sounds Like

Ranking Ladder

1 _____
2 _____
3 _____
4 _____

Right Angle Thinking

A _____

B _____

Flow Chart

Fishbone

KWL

What We **K**now	What We **W**ant to Find Out	What We **L**earn

(Ogle 1986)

Hour Glass

Know/Recall

Topic

What If?

5 W Model

Thought Tree

Matrix

Blackline C5.1

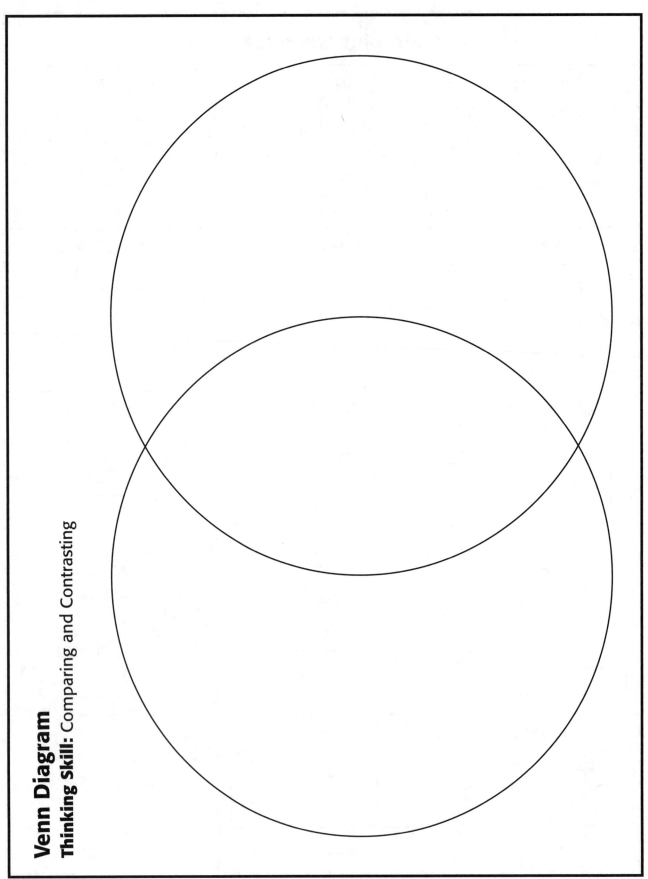

Venn Diagram
Thinking Skill: Comparing and Contrasting

Blackline C5.2

Attribute Web
Thinking Skill: Analyzing Attributes

Mind Map

Thinking Skill: Brainstorming

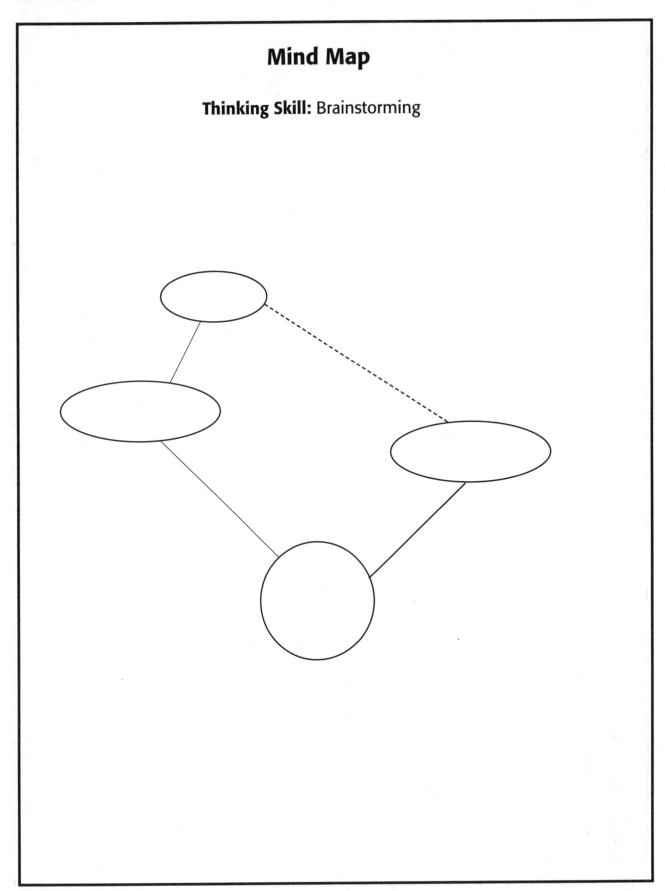

PMI
Thinking Skill: Evaluating

P+	M−	I?

(deBono 1973)

Blackline C5.5

T-Chart
Thinking Skill: Visualizing

Looks Like

Sounds Like

Ranking Ladder
Thinking Skill: Prioritizing

1.

2.

3.

4.

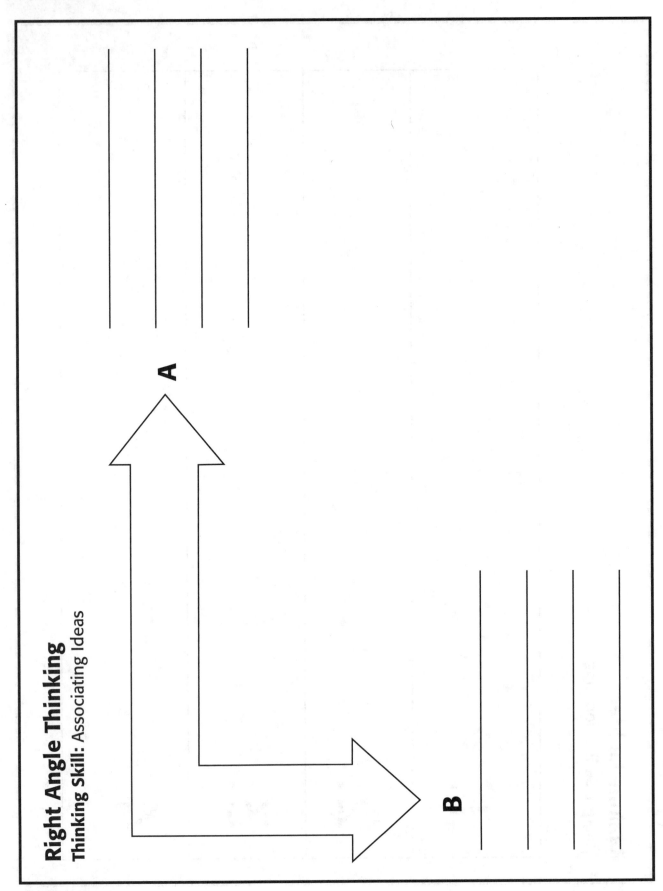

Right Angle Thinking
Thinking Skill: Associating Ideas

A

B

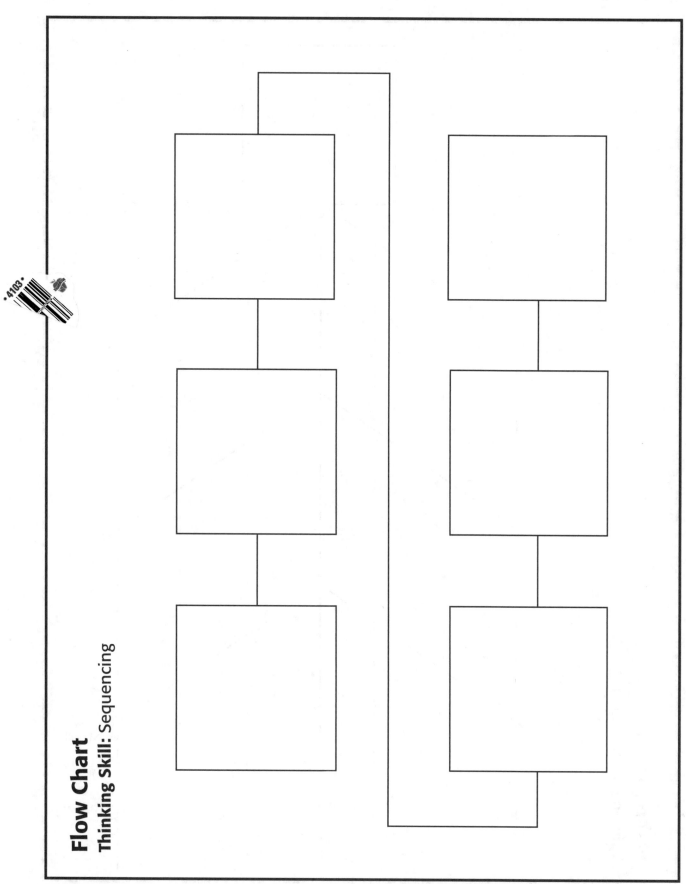

Flow Chart
Thinking Skill: Sequencing

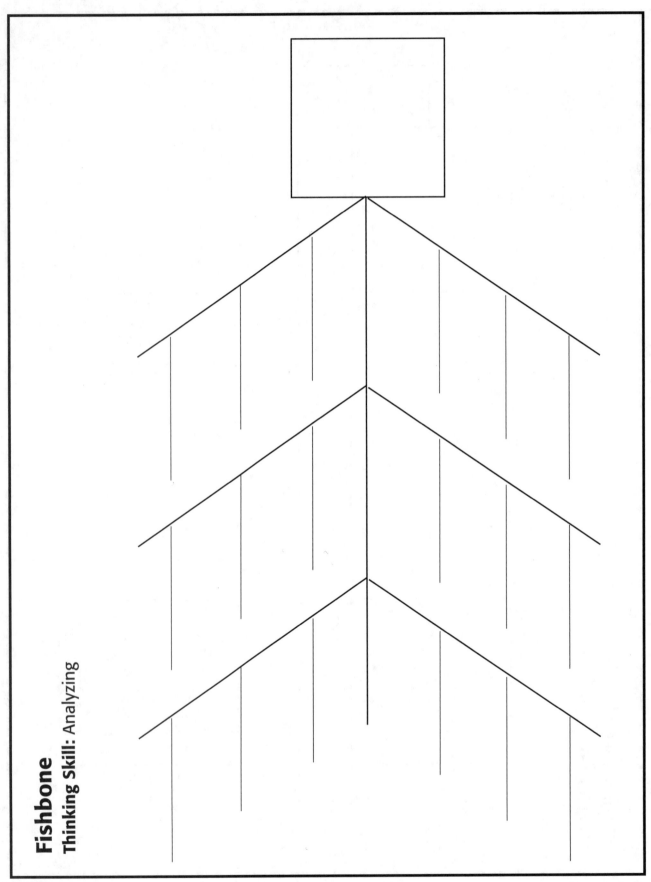

Fishbone
Thinking Skill: Analyzing

KWL
Thinking Skill: Predicting and Evaluating

What We **Know**	What We **Want** to Find Out	What We **Learned**

(Ogle 1986)

Blackline C5.11

Hour Glass

Thinking Skill: Hypothesizing

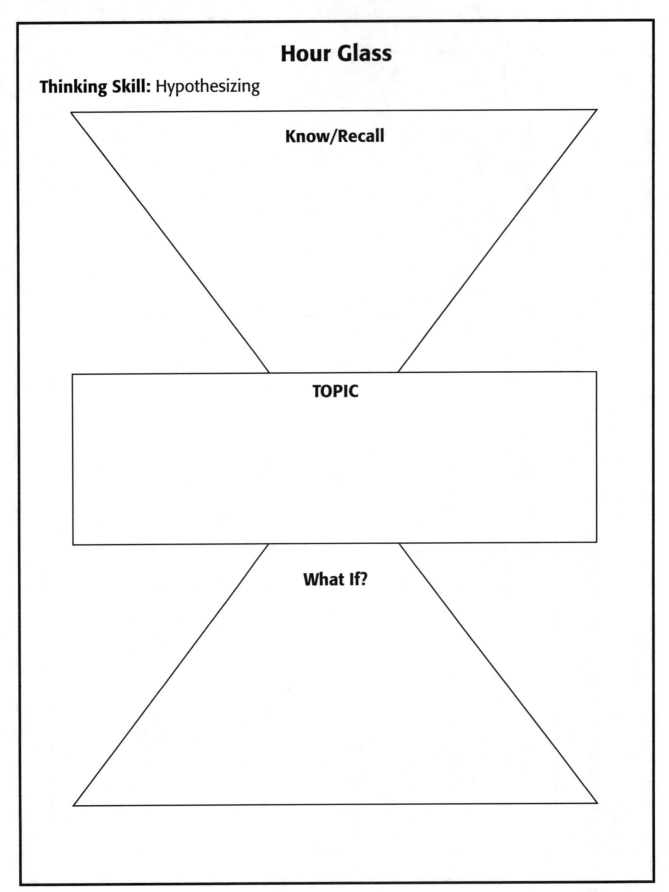

Know/Recall

TOPIC

What If?

5W Model

Thinking Skill: Classifying

Who	What	Where	Why	When

Summary

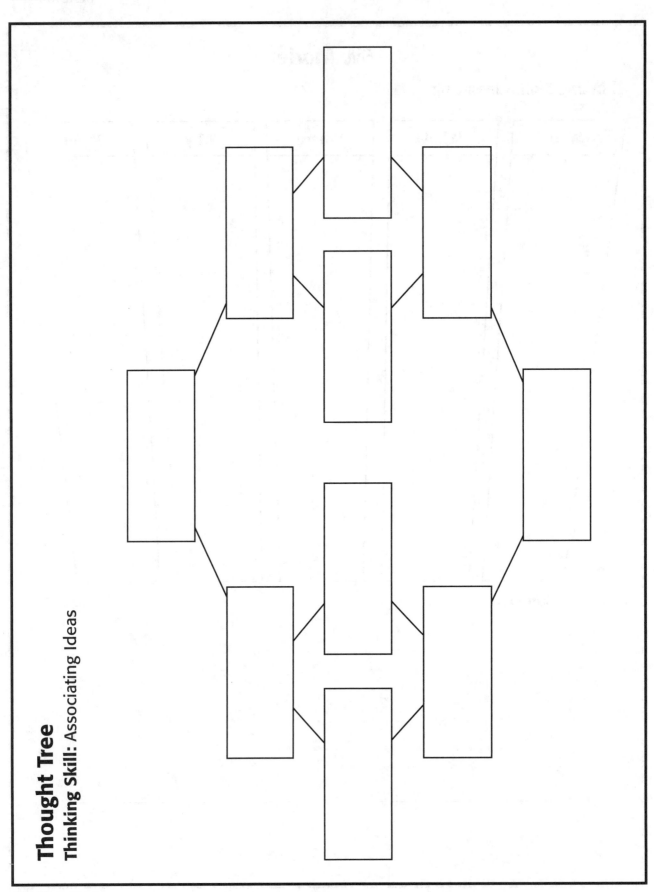

Thought Tree
Thinking Skill: Associating Ideas

Matrix
Thinking Skill: Classifying

Graphic Organizer Lesson Outline

Organizer:

Purpose of the Organizer:

Appropritate Use:

Timing:

Materials:

Content:

Instructions:

Cooperative Structure:

Mediation and Assessment:

African and Asian Elephants

Elephants are the largest of all land animals, and they are among the strangest looking animals in the world, with their long trunks, big ears, and pointed tusks. There are two basic kinds of elephants—African elephants and Asian (or Indian) elephants. It is rather easy to tell one kind from another.

Asian elephants have smaller ears than African elephants. They have a high forehead with two rather large "bumps" on it. The back of the Asian elephant bends up in the middle, and usually only the males have tusks.

African elephants have very large ears. Their foreheads don't have big bumps on them. The back of an African elephant bends down in the middle, and both the males and females have tusks.

African elephants are larger than Asian elephants, and the males of both kinds are larger than the females. The average Asian male is about 9 feet tall (2.74 meters) at the shoulder and weighs about 10,000 pounds (4,535 kilograms). African males average about 10 feet tall (3 meters) and weigh about 12,000 pounds (5,443 kilograms).

However, some elephants grow much larger than this. The largest African male on record was more than 12 $1/2$ feet tall (3.66 meters) and weighed about 22,000 (9,979 kilograms). The single elephant weighed as much as 150 average-sized people.

Male elephants are called bulls, and females are called cows. Young elephants are called calves. When an elephant calf is born, it is already a big animal. It is about three feet tall (1 meter) and weighs about 200 pounds (90 kilograms). Baby elephants are covered with hair, but as they grow they lose most of it.

Elephants can live a very long time. Asian elephants may live as along as 80 years, and African elephants may live for 60 years.

Stages of a Power Lesson

Stage 1:   Assess prior knowledge.

Stage 2:   Gather and understand
new information.

Stage 3:   Transfer new concepts.

Stage 4:   Assess learning.

Rubric for Evaluating Power Lessons for Lesson Power

provided *flexibility?*   1 2 3 4 5   _____

_____

engaged students with   1 2 3 4 5   _____
cognitive rehearsal?
_____

provided *variety?*   1 2 3 4 5   _____

_____

integrated

   content?   1 2 3 4 5   _____

_____

   cooperation?   1 2 3 4 5   _____

_____

   cognition?   1 2 3 4 5   _____

_____

   and developed prior knowledge?   1 2 3 4 5   _____

_____

   and generated new
   understanding?   1 2 3 4 5   _____

_____

   and facilitated transfer?   1 2 3 4 5   _____

_____

   and assessed process?   1 2 3 4 5   _____

_____

   and assessed results?   1 2 3 4 5   _____

_____

   and aligned with standards?   1 2 3 4 5   _____

_____

been *economical* (less is more)?   1 2 3 4 5   _____

_____

Blackline C6.2

BUILD : Cooperative Lesson Planner

	Build in High-Order Thinking	**U**nite Teams	**I**nsist on Individual Learning	**L**ook Over & Discuss	**D**evelop Social Skills
	Problem Solving, Decision Making, Creative Ideation	*Build Trust & Teamwork*	*Insure Individual Learning & Reponsibility*	*Plan, Monitor & Evaluate*	*Communication, Leadership, Conflict Resolution*
1					
2					
3					
4					
5					
6					
7					
8					
9					
10					

Blackline C6.3

Design a Decade

What do you do when you disagree?

Check the strategies you used.

❏ Argue – stand firm

❏ Persuade – justify, erason, appeal to

❏ Vote – majority rules

❏ Compromise – combine, modify

❏ Mediate – neutral party facilitator

❏ Arbitrate – agree to abide by decision of arbitrator

❏ Delay – table it, sleep on it, wait

❏ Reconceptualize – rethink, find new angles

❏ Negotiate – give and take

❏ Give in – give in, cave in, play martyr

❏ Seek Consensus – talk, cajole, juggle, adjust, modify

❏ Humor – veer away from confrontation

❏ Avoid – ignore or postpone indefinitely

What do you do when you disagree?

Check the strategies you used.

❏ Argue – stand firm

❏ Persuade – justify, erason, appeal to

❏ Vote – majority rules

❏ Compromise – combine, modify

❏ Mediate – neutral party facilitator

❏ Arbitrate – agree to abide by decision of arbitrator

❏ Delay – table it, sleep on it, wait

❏ Reconceptualize – rethink, find new angles

❏ Negotiate – give and take

❏ Give in – give in, cave in, play martyr

❏ Seek Consensus – talk, cajole, juggle, adjust, modify

❏ Humor – veer away from confrontation

❏ Avoid – ignore or postpone indefinitely

What do you do when you disagree?

Check the strategies you used.

❏ Argue – stand firm

❏ Persuade – justify, erason, appeal to

❏ Vote – majority rules

❏ Compromise – combine, modify

❏ Mediate – neutral party facilitator

❏ Arbitrate – agree to abide by decision of arbitrator

❏ Delay – table it, sleep on it, wait

❏ Reconceptualize – rethink, find new angles

❏ Negotiate – give and take

❏ Give in – give in, cave in, play martyr

❏ Seek Consensus – talk, cajole, juggle, adjust, modify

❏ Humor – veer away from confrontation

❏ Avoid – ignore or postpone indefinitely

Blackline C8.1

Tug O'War Thinking Creed

We pledge to . . .

Tug at ideas, not people.

Examine all sides of the issue.

Actively listen and clarify.

Modify our position when appropriate.

Seek the best decision,
not the winning position.

Blackline C8.2

PACTS

Paraphrase: Let me say what I think I heard from you . . . .

Am I on target?

Affirm: I appreciate that _____ is your (goal, belief, opinion, etc.).

I can see you are firm about your (goal, belief, opinion, etc.).

Clarify: I'm not clear on what you are saying. Could you clarify with an example?

Test Options: Let me state in different words what I think you are saying.

Summarize: Let me summarize the points you have made.

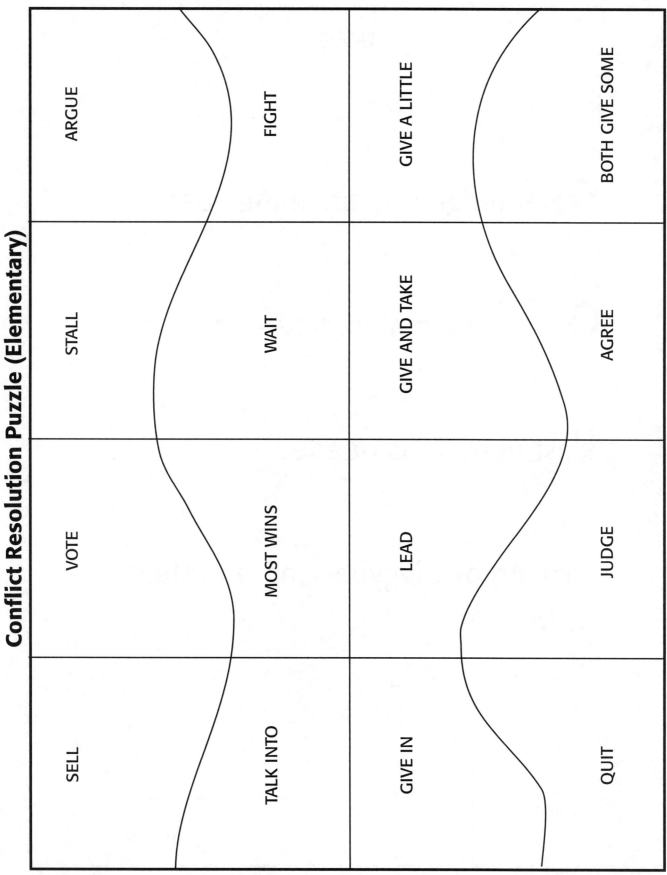

Conflict Resolution Puzzle (Elementary)

ARGUE	STALL	VOTE
FIGHT	WAIT	MOST WINS
GIVE A LITTLE	GIVE AND TAKE	LEAD
BOTH GIVE SOME	AGREE	JUDGE

SELL

TALK INTO

GIVE IN

QUIT

DOVE

Defer judgment; anything goes

Opt for original; different ideas

Vast number is needed

Expand by piggybacking on other's ideas

Human Graph

Conflict Resolution Puzzle (Middle School)

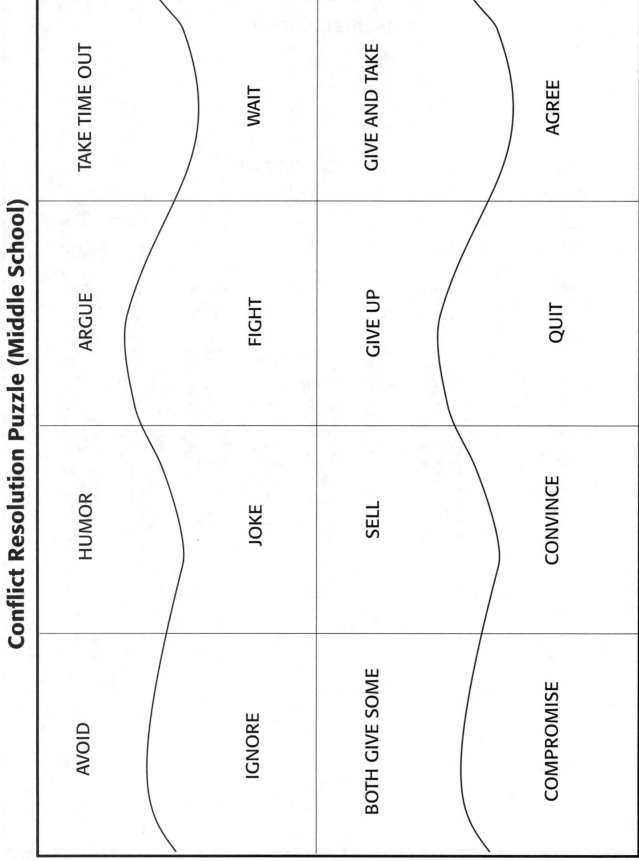

Conflict Resolution Puzzle (High School)

PERSUADE	MEDIATE	VOTE	RECONCEPTUALIZE
APPEAL TO	USE NEUTRAL FACILITATOR	MAJORITY RULES	RETHINK
HUMOR	ARGUE	NEGOTIATE	COMBINE
VEER FROM CONFRONTATION	STAND FIRM	GIVE AND TAKE	COMPROMISE

Blackline C8.8

A Continuum

FROM TRAINING TO TRANSFER: LEARNER SITUATIONAL DISPOSITIONS

Birds		Transfer Disposition	Teacher (Training) Transfer	Student (Classroom) Transfer
Ollie the Head-in-the Sand Ostrich		Overlooks	Does nothing; unaware of relevance and misses appropriate applications; overlooks intentionally or unintentionally. (resists) "Great session but this won't work with my kids or content"…or "I chose not to use…because…"	Misses appropriate opportunity; overlooks; persists in former way. "I get it right on the dittos, but I forget to use punctuation when I write an essay." (Doesn't connect appropriateness.)
Dan the Drilling Woodpecker		Duplicates	Drills and practices exactly as presented; Drill! Drill! Then stops; uses as an activity rather than as a strategy, duplicates. (copies) "Could I have a copy of that transparency?"	Performs the drill exactly as practiced; duplicates. "Yours is not to question why - just invert and multiply." (When dividing fractions) (No understanding of what she/he is doing.)
Laura the Look-Alike Penquin		Replicates	Tailors to kids and content, but applies in similar content; all look alike, does not transfer into new situations; replicates. (differentiates) "I use the web for every character analysis."	Tailors, but applies in similar situation; all look alike; replicates. "Paragraphing means I must have three 'indents' per page." (Tailors into own story or essay, but paragraphs inappropriately.)
Jonathan Livingston Seagull		Integrates	Raised consciousness; acute awareness; deliberate refinement; integrates subtly; with existing repertoire. (combines) "I haven't used any of your ideas, but I'm wording my questions carefully. I've always done this, but I'm doing more of it."	Is aware; integrates; combines with other ideas and situations. "I always try to guess (predict) what's gonna happen next on T.V. shows." (Connects to prior knowledge and experience.)
Cathy the Carrier Pigeon		Maps	Consciously transfers ideas to various situations, contents; carries strategy as part of available repertoire; maps. (associates) "I use the webbing strategy in everything."	Carries strategy to other content and situations. Associates and maps. Parent related story - "Tina suggested we brainstorm our vacation ideas and rank them to help us decide." (Carries new skills in life situations.)
Samantha the Soaring Eagle		Innovates	Innovates; flies with an idea; takes it into action beyond the initial conception; creates enhances, invents; risks. (diverges) "You have changed my teaching forever. I can never go back to what I used to do. I know too much. I'm too excited."	Innovates; takes idea beyond initial conception; risks; diverges. "After studying flow charts for computer class student constructs a Rube Goldberg type invention." (Innovates; invents; diverges; goes beyond and creates novel.)

Blackline C9.1

Transfer Cueing Questions

Overlooking
Think of an instance when the skill or strategy would be inappropriate.
I would not use _____ when _____.

Integrating
Think of an analogy for the skill or strategy.
_____ is like _____ because both _____.

Duplicating
Think of an opportunity passed when you could have used the skill or strategy.
I wish I'd known about _____ when _____.

Mapping
Think of an opportunity to use the new idea.
Next _____, I could use _____ when _____.

Replicating
Think of an adjustment that will make your application of _____ more relevant.
Next time I'm going to _____.

Innovating
Think of an application for a real-life setting.
I could use _____ when _____.

Blackline C9.2

Hitch a Ride for Transfer

"Somewheres"

Within Content

Across Discipline

Into Life

Bridging — Far & Wide — Scaffolding/Constructing

Bridging

1. Setting Expectations
2. Parallel Problem Solving
3. Cultivating Metacognition
4. Anticipating Applications
5. Generalizing Concepts
6. Unpacking Analogies

Hugging

1. Modeling Examples
2. Simulation
3. Matching
4. Problem-Based Learning
5. Varied Practice

Hugging — Near & Deep — Matching/Paralleling

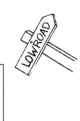

"Somethings"

Knowledge

Principles

Skills

Concepts

Attitudes

Dispositions

Stem Statements
A Starter List

Today, I learned . . .

From this lesson, an idea I had was . . .

Today, I discovered . . .

A problem I'm having is . . .

A connection I've made is . . .

I wonder . . .

What if . . .

Compared to . . .

Knowing _____, then _____.

If _____, then _____.

A surprise I had was. . .

Classifying

Cluster words that are alike.

Label the cluster.

Untangle subclusters.

Evaluate connections in the clusters.

Set the patterns.

The Dinner Party
By Mona Gardner

The country is India. A colonial official and his wife are giving a large dinner party. They are seated with their guests—army officers, government attachés and their wives, and a visiting American naturalist—in their spacious dining room, which has a bare marble floor, open rafters, and wide glass doors opening on to a veranda.

(BET what will happen next. Why do you think so? Find data to support your idea. Read to verify.)

A spirited discussion springs up between a young girl who insists that women have outgrown the jumping-on-a-chair-at-the-sight-of-a-mouse era and a Colonel who says that they haven't.

A woman's unfailing reaction in any crisis," the Colonel says, "is to scream. And while a man may feel like it, he has that ounce more of nerve control than a woman has. And that last ounce is what counts."

(Bet . . .)

The American does not join in the argument but watches the other guests. As he looks, he sees a strange expression come over the face of the hostess. She is staring straight ahead, her muscles contracting slightly. With a slight gesture she summons the native boy standing behind her chair and whispers to him. The boy's eyes widen and he quickly leaves the room.

Of the guests, none except the American notices this or sees the boy place a bowl of milk on the veranda just outside the open doors.

(Bet . . .)

The American comes to a start. In India, milk in a bowl means only one thing—bait for a snake. He realizes there must be a cobra in the room. He looks up at the rafters, the likeliest place, but they are bare. Three corners of the room are empty and the fourth the servants are waiting to serve the next course. There is only one place left—under the table.

His first impulse is to jump back and warn the others, but he knows the commotion would frighten the cobra into striking. He speaks quickly, the tone of his voice so arresting that it sobers everyone.

"I want know just what control everyone at this table has. I will count to three hundred—that's five minutes—and not one of you is to move a muscle. Those who move will forfeit fifty rupees. Ready!"

(Bet . . .)

The twenty people sit like stone images while he counts. He is saying ". . . two hundred and eighty . . ." when, out of the corner of his eye, he sees the cobra emerge and make for the bowl of milk. Screams ring out as he jumps to slam the veranda doors safely shut.

"You were right, Colonel," the host exclaims. "A man had just shown us an example of perfect control."

"Just a minute," the American says, turning to his hostess. "Mrs. Wynnes, how did you know that a cobra was in the room?"

A faint smile lights up the woman's face as she replies, "Because it was crawling across my foot."

Expert Jigsaw

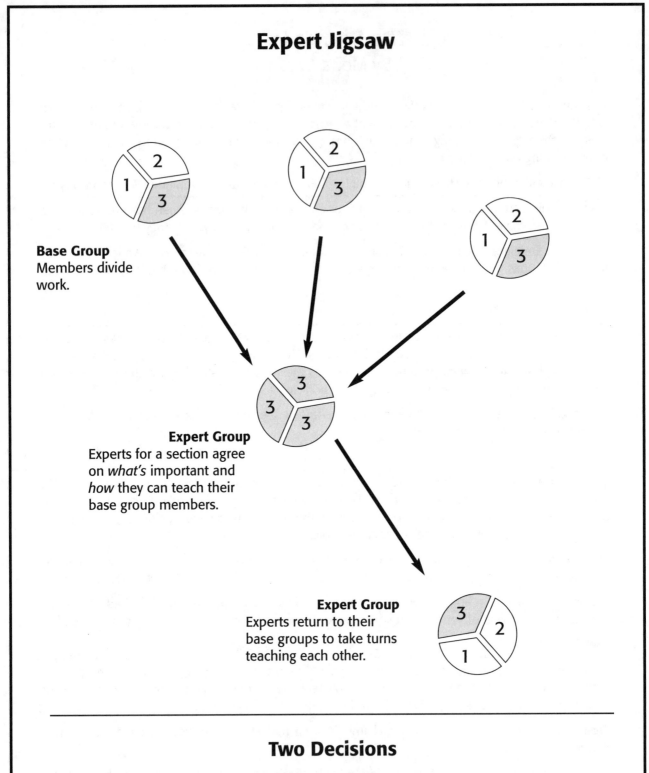

Base Group
Members divide work.

Expert Group
Experts for a section agree on *what's* important and *how* they can teach their base group members.

Expert Group
Experts return to their base groups to take turns teaching each other.

Two Decisions

#1 What to teach . . .

#2 How to teach . . .

The Sequence Chart

Name_____   Class_____

Problem:

Analysis of BUILD Strategies

Analysis of BUILD strategies used in the Portmanteau lesson

B
1. drawing a definition (a creative thinking skill)
2. teaching others what you have learned
3. making connections to prior knowledge and experience

U
1. jigsawing (dividing the material among team members)
2. assigning roles for each team member
3. giving limited time (learn more as a team in short time than could be learned alone)

I
1. providing individual learning and teaching time
2. conducting a random oral quiz
3. checking in the teams

L
1. answering processing questions about how the team worked well together
2. teacher giving feedback and observervations
3. discussing ways to improve team's effectiveness

D
1. keeping on task
2. encouraging team members during the task
3. checking the team for understanding

KND Chart

K	N	D
Know	Need to Find Out	Must Do

Elementary Sample Role Cards

READER

Is everyone listening?
Is everything clear?
Shall I read any part again?

RECORDER

The main points are . . .
Should I write . . . ?
To summarize . . .

TRAVELER

Can you help us with . . . ?
Did your group understand . . . ?
My group thinks . . .

(Adapted from Marcus and McDonald 1990.)

Blueprints for Achievement

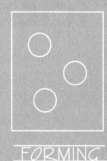

FORMING

PERFORMING

NORMING

BIBLIOGRAPHY

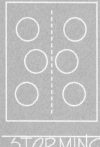

STORMING

CONFORMING

In the Cooperative Classroom

BIBLIOGRAPHY

Adler, M. J., and C. Van Doren. 1972. *How to read a book.* New York: Simon & Schuster.

Ambruster, B. B., and J. H. Anderson. 1980. *The effect of mapping on the free recall of expository texts* (Technical Report 160). Urbana-Champaign: Center for the Study of Reading, University of Illinois.

Anderson, R. C., E. H. Hiebert, J. H. Scott, and I. A. G. Wilkinson, eds. 1985. *Becoming a nation of readers: The report of the Commission on Reading.* Washington, DC: National Institute of Education.

Archibald, S., and J. Bellanca. 1988. *Early stars: Skills for saying "yes" to health.* Palatine, IL: IRI/SkyLight Training and Publishing.

Aronson, E. 1978. *The jigsaw classroom.* Beverly Hills, CA: Sage Publications.

Ausubel, D. 1978. *Educational psychology: A cognitive view,* 2nd ed. New York: Holt, Rinehart and Winston.

Barell, J. 1998. *Problem-based learning: An inquiry approach.* Arlington Heights, IL: SkyLight Training and Publishing.

Baron, F., B. Joan, and R. J. Sternberg, eds. 1987. *Teaching thinking skills: Theory and practice.* New York: W. H. Freeman.

Barron, F. 1969. *Creative person and creative process.* New York: Holt, Rinehart and Winston.

Bellanca, J. 1989. *Team stars.* Palatine, IL: IRI/SkyLight Training and Publishing.

———. 1990a. *The cooperative think tank.* Palatine, IL: IRI/SkyLight Training and Publishing.

———. 1990b. *Keep them thinking: Level III.* Palatine, IL: IRI/SkyLight Training and Publishing.

———. 1992. *The cooperative think tank II.* Palatine, IL: IRI/SkyLight Training and Publishing.

Bellanca, J., and R. Fogarty. 1986. *Catch them thinking: A handbook of classroom strategies.* Palatine, IL: IRI/SkyLight Training and Publishing.

Belonging. (16 mm film). 1980. Edina, MN: Interaction Book Company.

Berman, P., and M. McLaughlin. 1978. *Federal programs supporting educational change, Vol. VIII: Implementing and sustaining innovations.* Santa Monica, CA: Rand Corporation.

Beyer, B. K. 1983. Common sense about teaching thinking skills.

Educational Leadership 41(3): 44–49.

———. 1984a. Improving thinking skills—defining the problem. *Phi Delta Kappan* 65(7): 486–490.

———. 1984b. Improving thinking skills—a practical approach. *Phi Delta Kappan* 65(8): 556–560.

———. 1985a. Critical thinking: What is it? *Social Education* 49(4): 270–276.

———. 1985b. Teaching critical thinking: A direct approach. *Social Education* 49(4): 297–303.

———. 1985c. Teaching thinking skills: How the principal can know they are being taught. *NASSP Bulletin* 69(477): 70–83.

———. 1987. *Practical strategies for the teaching of thinking*. Boston: Allyn & Bacon.

———. 1988. *Developing a thinking skills program*. Boston: Allyn & Bacon

Beyer, B. K., and R. E. Charlton. 1986. Teaching thinking skills in biology. *The American Biology Teacher* 48(4): 207–212.

Black, H., and S. Black. 1987. *Building thinking skills: Books 1–3*. Pacific Grove, CA: Midwest Publications.

Blake, R., and J. Mouton. 1961. Comprehension of own and outgroup positions under intergroup competition. *Journal of Conflict Resolution* 5: 304–310.

Bloom, B. 1981. *All our children learning*. New York: McGraw-Hill.

Bloom, B.S., M. D. Engelhart, E. J. Furst, W. H. Hill, and D. R. Kratwohl. 1956. *Taxonomy of educational objectives: Cognitive domain, Handbook 1*. New York: David McKay.

Brandt, R. 1988. On teaching thinking: A conversation with Arthur Costa. *Educational Leadership* 45(7): 11.

———. 1999. Educators need to know about the human brain. *Phi Delta Kappan* 81(3): 235–238.

Brown, A. L. 1978. Knowing when, where, and how to remember: A problem of metacognition. In *Advances in instruction psychology, Vol. 1*, edited by R. Glaser. Hillsdale, NJ: Erlbaum.

———. 1982. Learning how to learn from reading. In *Reader meets author/bridging the gap: A psycholinguistic and sociolinguistic perspective*, edited by J.A. Langer and M.T. Smith-Burke. Newark, DE: International Reading Association.

Brown, A. L., J. C. Campione, and J. D. Day. 1981. Learning to learn: On training students to learn from texts. *Educational Researcher* 10 (2): 14–21.

Bruer, J. 1999. *The myth of the first three years*. New York: Free Press/Simon & Schuster.

Burke, K. 2000. *What to do with the kid who…: Developing cooperation, self-discipline, and responsibility in the classroom*, 2nd ed. Arlington Heights, IL: SkyLight Training and Publishing.

Bruner, J. 1960. *The process of education*. New York: Vintage Books.

Burns, M. 1976. *The book of think or how to solve a problem twice your size*. Boston: Little, Brown and Co.

Caine, R., and G. Caine. 1994. *Making connections: Teaching and the human brain.* New York: Addison-Wesley/Innovative Learning Publications.

Campbell, J. 1965. *The children's crusader: Colonel Francis W. Parker.* Doctoral dissertation, Teachers College, Columbia University.

Canfield, J. 1990. Improving students' self-esteem. *Educational Leadership* 48(1): 48–50.

Cawalti, G., ed. 1995. *Handbook of research on improving student achievement.* Arlington, VA: Educational Research Service.

Chase, L. 1975. *The other side of the report card.* Glenview, IL: Scott, Foresman.

Circles of Learning. (16 mm film). 1983. Edina, MN: Interaction Book Company.

Cohen, E. 1986. Designing groupwork. New York: Teachers College Press.

Coles, R. 1997. *The moral intelligence of children.* New York: Random House.

Costa, A. L. 1981. Teaching for intelligent behavior. *Educational Leadership* 39(1): 29–32.

———. 1984. Mediating the metacognitive. *Educational Leadership* 42(3): 57–62.

———, ed. 1985a. *Developing minds.* Alexandria, VA: Association for Supervision and Curriculum Development.

———. 1985b. *Teaching for intelligent behavior: A course syllabus.* Orangevale, CA: Search Models Unlimited.

———. 1988, Winter. What human beings do when they behave intelligently and how they can become more so. *California ASCD Journal* 1(1) (original title: *Search for Intelligent Life*).

———. 1991. *The school as a home for the mind.* Palatine, IL: IRI/Skylight Publishing.

———, ed. 2002. *Developing minds,* 3rd ed. Alexandria, VA: Association for Supervision and Curriculum Development.

Costa, A. L., and R. Garmston. 1985. The art of cognitive coaching: Supervision for intelligent teaching. Paper presented at the Annual Conference of the Association for Supervision and Curriculum Development, Chicago.

Costa, A., and L. Lowery. 1989. *Techniques for teaching thinking.* Pacific Grove, CA: Midwest Publications.

Costa, A. L., and B. Kallick. 2000. *Discovering and exploring habits of mind.* Alexandria, VA: Association for Supervision and Curriculum Development.

Csikszentmihalyi, M. 1990. *The psychology of optimal experience.* New York: Harper & Row.

Dansereau, D., et al. 1979. Development and evaluation of a learning strategy training program. *Journal of Educational Psychology* 71(1): 64–73.

Davidson, J. L. 1982. The group mapping activity for instruction in reading and thinking. *Journal of Reading* 26(1): 52–56.

de Bono, E. 1967. *New think.* New York: Basic Books.

———. 1973. *Lateral thinking: Creativity step by step.* New York: Harper & Row.

———. 1976. *Teaching thinking.* New York: Penguin Books.

Deutsch, M. 1949. An experimental study of the effects of cooperation and competition upon group processes. *Human Relations* 2: 199–232

———. 1973. *The resolution of conflict.* New Haven, CT: Yale University Press.

DeVries, D., and K. Edwards. 1973. Learning games and student teams: Their effects on classroom process. *American Journal of Educational Research* 10(4): 307–318.

DeVries, D., R. Slavin, G. Fennessey, K. Edwards, and M. Lombardo. 1980. *Teams-games-tournament.* Englewood Cliffs, NJ: Educational Technology.

Dewey, J. 1933. *How we think.* Boston: D.C. Heath & Co.

Dishon, D., and P. O'Leary. 1984. *A guidebook for cooperative learning.* Holmes Beach, FL: Learning Publications.

Durkin, D. 1978–79. What classroom observations reveal about reading comprehension instruction. *Reading Research Quarterly* 14(4): 481–533.

Edmonds, R., and J. R. Frederiksen. 1979. Search for effective schools: The identification and analysis of city schools that are instructionally effective for poor children. (ERIC ED170 396).

Eisner, E. W. 1983. The kind of schools we need. *Educational Leadership* 41(2): 48–55.

Elbow, P. 1973. *Writing without teachers.* New York: Oxford University Press.

———. 1981. *Writing with power.* New York: Oxford University Press.

Ferguson, M. 1980. *The aquarian conspiracy.* Los Angeles: J. P. Tarcher.

Feuerstein, R. 1979. *The dynamic assessment of retarded performance: The Learning Potential Assessment Device, theory, instruments, and technique.* Baltimore: University Park Press.

———. 1980. *Instrumental Enrichment.* Baltimore, MD: University Park Press.

Flavell, J. 1976. Metacognitive aspects of problem solving. In *The nature of intelligence,* edited by L. Resnick. Hillsdale, NJ: Erlbaum.

———. 1977. *Cognitive development.* Englewood Cliffs, NJ: Prentice-Hall.

Fogarty, R. 1989. From training to transfer: The role of creativity in the adult learner. Doctoral dissertation, Loyola University Chicago, IL.

———. 1990. *Keep them thinking: Level II.* Palatine, IL: IRI/SkyLight Training and Publishing.

———. 2001. *Differentiated learning: Different strokes for different folks.* Chicago, IL: Fogarty & Associates.

Fogarty, R., and J. Bellanca. 1986. *Planning for thinking: A guidebook for instructional leaders.* Palatine, IL: IRI Group.

———. 1986. *Teach them thinking.* Palatine, IL: IRI/SkyLight Training and Publishing.

———. 1989. *Patterns for thinking—Patterns for transfer.* Palatine, IL: IRI/SkyLight Training and Publishing.

Fogarty, R., and J. Haack. 1986. *The thinking log.* Palatine, IL: IRI/SkyLight Training and Publishing.

———. 1986. *The thinking/writing connection.* Palatine, IL: IRI/SkyLight Training and Publishing.

Fogarty, R., and K. Opeka. 1988. *Start them thinking.* Palatine, IL: IRI/SkyLight Training and Publishing.

Frankenstein, C. 1979. *They think again.* New York: Van Nostrand Rheinhold.

Fullan, M. 1982. *The meaning of educational change.* New York: Teachers College Press.

Gardner, H. 1983. *Frames of mind: The theory of multiple intelligences.* New York: Basic Books.

———. 1999. *Intelligence re-framed: Multiple intelligences for the 21st century.* New York: Basic Books.

Gibbs, J. 1987. *Tribes.* Santa Rosa, CA: Center Source Publications.

Glaser, R., ed. 1978. *Advanced instructional psychology.* 2 vols. Hillsdale, NJ: Erlbaum.

Glasser, W. 1986. *Control theory in the classroom.* New York: Harper & Row.

Goodlad, J. I. 1984. *A place called school, Prospects for the future.* New York: McGraw-Hill.

Goleman, D. 1995. *Emotional intelligence: Why it can matter more than IQ.* New York: Bantam Books.

Gordon, W. J. 1961. *Synectics: The development of creative capacity.* New York: Harper & Row.

Graves, D. H. 1983. *Writing: Teachers and children at work.* Portsmouth, NH: Heinemann Educational Books.

Guilford, J. P. 1977. *Way beyond IQ.* Buffalo, NY: Creative Education Foundation.

Hart, L. 1975. *How the brain works.* New York: Basic Books.

———. 1983. *Human brain and human learning.* White Plains, NY: Longman Publishing.

Haycock, K. 1998a. Good teaching matters . . . a lot. *OAH Magazine of History* 13(1): 61–63.

———. 1998b. *Good teaching matters: How well-qualified teachers can close the achievement gap.* Washington, DC: Education Trust.

Hord, S., and S. Loucks. 1979. *A concerns-based model for delivery of inservice.* Austin: University of Texas at Austin, Research and Development Center for Teacher Education, CBFM Project.

Hunter, M. 1971. *Transfer.* El Segundo, CA: Tip Publications.

———. 1982. *Teaching for transfer.* El Segundo, CA: Tip Publications.

Hyerle, D. 1996. *Visual tools for constructing knowledge.* Alexandria, VA: Association for Supervision and Curriculum Development.

Jensen, E. 1998. *Teaching with the brain in mind.* Alexandria, VA: Association for Supervision and Curriculum Development.

Jeroski, S., F. Brownlie, and L. Kaser. 1991. *Reading and responding: Network evaluation package.* Scarborough, Ontario, Canada: Nelson Canada.

Johnson, D. W. 1971. Role reversal: A summary and review of the research. *International Journal of Group Tensions* 1: 318–334.

————. 1975. Affective perspective-taking and cooperative predisposition. *Developmental Psychology* 11(6): 869–870.

————. 1980a. Constructive peer relationships, social development, and
cooperative learning experiences: Implications for the prevention of
drug abuse. *Journal of Drug Education* 10(1): 7–24.

————. 1980b. Group processes: Influences of student-student interactions on school outcomes. In *Social psychology of school learning*,
edited by J. McMillan. New York: Academic Press.

————. 1981. Student-student interaction: The neglected variable in
education. *Educational Researcher* 10(1): 5–10.

————. 1986. *Reaching out: Interpersonal effectiveness and self-
actualization*. Englewood Cliffs, NJ: Prentice-Hall.

————. 1987. *Human relations and your career: A guide to interpersonal
skills*, 2nd ed. Englewood Cliffs, NJ: Prentice-Hall.

Johnson, D. W., and R. Johnson. 1974. Instructional goal structure:
Cooperative, competitive, or individualistic. *Review of Educational
Research* 44(2): 213–240.

————. 1978a. Cooperative, competitive, and individualistic learning.
Journal of Research and Development in Education 12(1): 3–15.

————. 1978b. Social interdependence within instruction. *Journal of
Research and Development in Education* 12(1): 1–152.

————. 1979. Conflict in the classroom: Controversy and learning.
Review of Educational Research 49(1): 51–69.

————. 1982, October. Cooperation in learning: Ignored but powerful.
Lyceum.

————, eds. 1984. *Structuring cooperative learning: The 1984 handbook
of lesson plans for teachers*. Edina, MN: Interaction Book Company.

————. 1986. *Circles of learning: Cooperation in the classroom*.
Alexandria, VA: Association for Supervision and Curriculum
Development.

————. 1987. *Joining together: Group theory and group skills*, 3rd ed.
Englewood Cliffs, NJ: Prentice-Hall.

————. 1999a. *Learning together and alone: Cooperative, competitive
and individualistic learning*. Boston: Allyn & Bacon.

————. 1999b. *Methods of cooperative learning: What can we prove
works?* Edina, MN: Cooperative Learning Institute.

————. 2001. Cooperation, conflict, cognition, and metacognition. In
Developing minds: A resource book for teaching thinking, edited by A.
Costa. Alexandria, VA: Association for Supervision and Curriculum
Development.

Johnson, D., and R. Matross. 1977. The interpersonal influence of the
psychotherapist. In *The effective therapist: A handbook*, edited by A.
Gruman and A. Razin. Elmsford, NY: Pergamon Press.

Joyce, B. R. 1986. *Improving America's schools*. White Plains, NY:
Longman Publishing.

Joyce, B. R., and B. Showers. 1980. Improving inservice training: The
message of research. *Educational Leadership* 37(5): 379–385.

————. 1983. *Power in staff development through research and training*.
Alexandria, VA: Association for Supervision and Curriculum
Development.

Joyce, B. R., and M. Weil. 1985. *Models of learning*. Englewood Cliffs, NJ: Prentice-Hall.

Joyce, B. R., M. Weil, with E. Calhoun. 2000. *Models of teaching*, 6th ed. Boston: Allyn & Bacon.

Kagan, S. 1977. Social motives and behaviors of Mexican American and Anglo American children. In *Chicano psychology*, edited by J. L. Martinez. New York: Academic Press.

———. 1992. *Cooperative learning*. San Juan Capistrano, CA: Resources for Teachers.

Kagan, S., G. P. Knight, S. Martinez, and P. Espinoza Santana. 1981. Conflict resolution style among Mexican children: Examining urbanization and ecology effects. *Journal of Cross-Cultural Psychology* 12 (2): 222–232.

Kagan, S., and M. C. Madsen. 1972. Rivalry in Anglo American and Mexican children. *Journal of Personality and Social Psychology* 24: 214–220.

Kerman, S. 1979. Teacher expectations and student achievement. *Phi Delta Kappan* 60(10): 716–718.

Knowles, M. 1978. *The adult learner: A neglected species*, 2nd ed. Houston, TX: Gulf.

Kohlberg, L. 1981. *The meaning and measurement of moral development*. Worcester, MA: Clark University Press.

Krupp, J. A. 1981. *Adult development: Implications for staff development*. Connecticut, MA: Adult Learning and Development.

———. 1982. *The adult learner: A unique entity*. Connecticut, MA: Adult learning and development.

LeDoux, J. 1996. *The emotional brain*. New York: Simon & Schuster.

Lipman, M., A. Sharp, and F. Oscanyan. 1980. *Philosophy in the classroom*. 2nd ed. Philadelphia: Temple University Press.

Lochhead, J., and J. Clement, eds. 1979. *Cognitive process instruction*. Philadelphia: The Franklin Institute Press.

Luria, A. R. 1976. *Cognitive development: Its cultural and social foundations*. Cambridge, MA: Harvard University Press.

Lyman, F., and J. McTighe. 1988. Cueing thinking in the classroom: The promise of theory embedded tools. *Educational Leadership* 45(7): 18–24.

Machado, L.A. 1980. *The right to be intelligent*. New York: Pergamon Press.

MacKinnon, D. W. 1978. *In search of human effectiveness: Identifying and developing creativity*. Buffalo, NY: The Creative Educational Foundation, Inc., in association with Creative Synergetic Associates, Ltd.

Marcus, S. A., and P. McDonald. 1990. *Tools for the cooperative classroom*. Palatine, IL: IRI/SkyLight Training and Publishing.

Marzano, R. 1988. *Tactics for teaching thinking*. Alexandria, VA: Association for Supervision and Curriculum Development.

Marzano, R., and D. E. Arredondo. 1986. Restructuring schools through the teaching of thinking skills. *Educational Leadership* 43(8): 23.

Marzano, R., et al. 1988. *Dimensions of thinking: A framework for curriculum and instruction.* Alexandria, VA: Association for Supervision and Curriculum Development.

Marzano, R., D. Pickering, and J. Pollock. 2001. *Classroom instruction that works.* Alexandria, VA: Association for Supervision and Curriculum Development.

McCarthy, B. 1991. Using the 4MAT system to bring learning styles to schools. *Educational Leadership* 48(2): 31–37.

McTighe, J. 1987. Teaching for thinking, of thinking, and about thinking. In *Thinking skills instruction: Concepts and techniques,* edited by M. Heiman and J. Slomianko. Washington, D.C.: National Education Association.

Meeker, M. N. 1969. *The structure of intellect: Its interpretation and uses.* Columbus, OH: Charles E. Merrill.

Merriam-Webster. *Webster's Word Histories.* 1989. Springfield, MA: Author.

———. 1998. *Merriam-Webster Collegiate Dictionary,* 10th ed. Springfield, MA: Author.

Missouri Department of Elementary and Secondary Education. 1996. *Show-me standards.* Jefferson, MO: Author.

Moye, V. 1997. *Conditions that support transfer for change.* Arlington Heights, IL: SkyLight Training and Publishing.

Newman, F. M., A. S. Bryk, and J. K Nagaoka. 2001. *Authentic intellectual work and standardized test: Conflict or coexistence?* Improving Chicago schools series. Chicago: Consortium on Chicago School Research.

New York State Academy for Teaching and Learning. 2001. New York State learning standards. Available: http://www.nysart.nysed.gov/standards.html

Nickerson, R. S. 1983. Computer programming as a vehicle for teaching thinking skills. *Journal of Philosophy for Children* 4: 3–4.

———. 1985. Understanding understanding. *American Journal of Education* 93(2): 201–239.

Nickerson, R. S., D. N. Perkins, and E. E. Smith. 1984. *Teaching thinking* (BBN Report No. 5575).

———. 1985. *The teaching of thinking.* Hillsdale, NJ: Erlbaum.

Nickerson, R. S., W. S. Shepard, and J. Herrnstein.1984. *The teaching of learning strategies* (BBN Report No. 5578).

Noller, R. 1977. *Scratching the surface of creative problem solving: A bird's eye view of CPS.* Buffalo, NY: D.O.K.

Noller, R., S. Parnes, and A. Biondi. 1976. *Creative action book.* New York: Charles Scribner & Sons.

Noller, R., D. Treffinger, and E. Houseman. 1979. *It's a gas to be gifted or CPS for the gifted and talented.* Buffalo, NY: D.O.K.

Norris, S. P., and R. H. Ennis. *Evaluating critical thinking.* Pacific Grove, CA: Midwest Publications.

Ogle, D. 1986. K-W-L: A teaching model that develops active reading of expository text. *The Reading Teacher* 39(6): 564–570.

———. 1998. *Reading strategies: Meet the experts.* (Videocassette) Arlington Heights, IL: SkyLight Training and Publishing.

Opeka, K. 1990. *Keep them thinking: Level I.* Palatine, IL: IRI/SkyLight Training and Publishing.

Osborn, A. F. 1963. *Applied imagination.* New York: Charles Scribner & Sons.

Paley, V. G. 1981. *Wally's stories: Conversations in kindergarten.* Cambridge, MA: Harvard University Press.

Palincsar, A. 1984. The quest for meaning from expository text: A teacher guided journey. In *Comprehension instruction: Perspectives and suggestions,* edited by G. Duffy, L., Roehler, and J. Mason. White Plains, NY: Longman Publishing.

Parker, F. W. 1883. *Notes of talks on teaching.* New York: E. L. Kellogg.

———. 1894. *Talks on pedagogies: An outline of the theory of concentration.* New York and Chicago: E. L. Kellogg.

Parnes, S. 1972. *Creativity: Unlocking human potential.* Buffalo, NY: D.O.K.

———. 1975. *Aha! Insights into creative behavior.* Buffalo, NY: D.O.K.

Pearson, C. 1980, February. Can you keep quiet for three minutes? *Learning* 8: 40–43.

Pearson, P. D., R. Barr, M. L. Kamil, and P. Mosenthal, eds. 1984. *Handbook of reading research.* New York: Longman.

Perkins, D. N. 1983. *The mind's best work.* Cambridge, MA: Harvard University Press.

———, ed. 1986. *Knowledge as design.* Hillsdale, NJ: Erlbaum.

———. 1988. Thinking frames. Paper delivered at Association for Supervision and Curriculum Development Conference on Approaches to Thinking, Alexandria, VA.

———. 2001. The social side of thinking. In *Developing minds: A resource book for teaching thinking.* Alexandria, VA: Association for Supervision and Curriculum Development.

Perkins, D. N., R. Fogarty, and J. Barell. 1989. *The mindful school: How to teach for transfer.* Palatine, IL; SkyLight Training and Publishing.

Perkins, D. N., and B. Leondar, eds. 1977. *The arts and cognition.* Baltimore, MD: Johns Hopkins University Press.

Perkins, D. N., and G. Salomon. 1987. Transfer and teaching thinking. *Thinking: The second international conference,* edited by D.N. Perkins, J.C. Lochhead, and J.C. Bishop. Hillsdale, NJ: Erlbaum.

———. 1988. Teaching for transfer. *Educational Leadership* 46(1): 22–32.

———. 1989. Are cognitive skills context bound? *Educational Researcher* 47(1): 16–25.

Peters, T., and N. Austin. 1985. *Passion for excellence.* New York: Random House.

Peters, T., and R. Waterman, Jr. 1982. *In search of excellence.* New York: Warner Communications.

Piaget, J. 1972. *The psychology of intelligence.* Totowa, NJ: Littlefield Adams.

Polette, N. 1981. *Exploring books for gifted programs.* Metuchen, NJ: Scarecrow Press.

Polya, G. 1957. *How to solve it: A new aspect of mathematical method.* 2nd ed. Princeton, NJ: Princeton University Press.

Posner, G. J., K. A. Strike, P. W. Hewson, and W. A. Gertzog. 1982. Accommodation of a scientific conception: Toward a theory of conceptual change. *Science Education* 66(2): 211–227.

Posner, M. I., and S. W. Keele. 1973. Skill learning. In *Second handbook of research on teaching*, edited by R. M. W. Travers. Chicago: Rand McNally College Publishing Company.

Raths, L., S. Wassermann, A. Jones, and G. Rothstein. 1986. *Teaching for thinking: Theories, strategies and activities for the classroom*, 2nd ed. New York: Teachers College Press, Columbia University.

Rico, G. L. 1983. *Writing the natural way.* Los Angeles: J. P. Tarcher.

Rosenshine, B. V. 1986. Synthesis of research on explicit teaching. *Educational Leadership* 43(7): 60–69.

Rowe, M. B. 1996. Science silence, and sanctions. *Science and Children* 34(1): 35–37.

Rumelhart, D. E. 1981. Schemata: The building blocks of cognition. In *Comprehension and teaching: Research reviews,* edited by J. T. Guthrie. Newark, DE: International Reading Association.

Salomon, G. 1981. *Communication and education: Social and psychological interactions.* Beverly Hills, CA: Sage Publications.

Salomon, G. and D. Perkins. 1988. Rocky roads to transfer: Rethinking mechanisms of a neglected phenomenon. *Educational Psychologist* 24(2): 113–142.

Salovey, P., and J. D. Mayer. 1990. Emotional intelligence. *Imagination, Cognition, and Personality* 9: 185–211.

Schmuck, R., M. Chesler, and R. Lippit. 1966. *Problem solving to improve classroom learning.* Chicago: SRA.

Schmuck, R., and P. Schmuck. 1983. *Group processes in the classroom.* Dubuque, IA: Wm. C. Brown.

Schoenfeld, A. H. 1980. Teaching problem-solving skills. *American Mathematical Monthly* 87(10): 794–805.

———. 1983. Metacognitive and epistemological issues in mathematical understanding. In *Teaching and learning mathematical problem solving*, edited by E. A. Silver. Hillsdale, NJ: Erlbaum.

Secretary's Commission on Achieving Necessary Skills (SCANS). 1991. *What work requires of schools: A SCANS report for America 2000.* Washington, DC: US Department of Labor. Available: http://www.academicinnovations.com/report.html

Segal, J. W., S. E. Chipman, and R. Glaser, eds. 1985. *Thinking and learning skills.* 2 vols. Hillsdale, NJ: Erlbaum.

Sergiovanni, T. 1987. Will we ever have a true profession? *Educational Leadership* 44(9): 44–49.

———. 1994. *Building community in schools.* San Francisco: Jossey-Bass.

Sharan, S. 1980. Cooperative learning in small groups: Recent methods and effects on achievement, attitudes, and ethnic relations. *Review of Educational Research* 50(3): 241–271.

Sharan, S., R. Hertz-Lazarowitz, and Z. Ackerman. 1980. Academic achievement of elementary school children in small-group versus whole class instruction. *Journal of Experimental Education* 48(2): 125–129.

Sharan, S., and Y. Sharan. 1976. *Small-group teaching.* Englewood Cliffs, NJ: Educational Technology Publications.

Sigel, I. E. 1984. A constructivist perspective for teaching thinking. *Educational Leadership* 42(3): 18–21.

Simon, S. B. 1973. I am loveable and capable: A modern allegany of the classic put-down. Niles, IL: Argus Communications. (ERIC Do86582)

Slavin, R. E. 1977a. Classroom reward structure: An analytic and practical review. *Review of Educational Research* 47(4): 633–650

———. 1977b. Student team approach to teaching adolescents with special emotional and behavioral needs. *Psychology in the Schools* 14 (1): 77–83.

———. 1979. Effects of biracial learning teams on cross-racial friendships. *Journal of Educational Psychology* 71(3): 381–387.

———. 1980. *Using student team learning,* revised ed. Baltimore, MD: Center for Social Organization of Schools, Johns Hopkins University.

———. 1983a. *Cooperative learning.* New York: Longman.

———. 1983b. When does cooperative learning increase student achievement? *Psychology Bulletin* 94: 429–445.

Slavin, R. E., and S. Hansell. 1983. Cooperative learning and intergroup relations: Contact theory in the classroom. In *Friends in school,* edited by J. Epstein and N. Karweit. New York: Academic Press.

Slavin, R. E., and E. Oickle. 1981. Effects of cooperative learning teams on student achievement and race relations: Treatment by race interactions. *Sociology of Education* 54(3): 174–180.

Smith, F. 1986. *Insult to intelligence: The bureaucratic invasion of our classrooms.* New York: Arbor House.

Sousa, D. 2001. *How the brain learns,* 2nd ed. Thousand Oaks, CA: Corwin Press.

Sprenger, M. 1999. *Learning and memory: The brain in action.* Alexandria, VA: Association for Supervision and Curriculum Development.

Stauffer, R. 1969. *Reading as a thinking process.* New York: Harper & Row.

Sternberg, R. J. 1981. Intelligence as thinking and learning skills. *Educational Leadership* 39(10): 18–21.

———. 1984. How can we teach intelligence? *Educational Leadership* 42(1): 38–48.

———. 1985a. Critical thinking: Its nature, measurement and improvement. In *Essays on the intellect,* edited by F. R. Link. Alexandria, VA: Association for Supervision and Curriculum Development.

———. 1985b. Teaching critical thinking, Part I: Are we making critical mistakes? *Phi Delta Kappan* 67(3): 194–198.

———. 1986. *Intelligence applied: Understanding and increasing your intellectual skills.* New York: Harcourt Brace Javanovich.

Sternberg, R. J., and D. K. Detterman, eds. 1986. *What is intelligence?* Norwood, NJ: Ablex.

Swartz, R. J. 1986. Restructuring curriculum for critical thinking. *Educational Leadership* 43(8): 43–44.

————. 1987. Critical thinking attitudes and the transfer question. In *Thinking skills instruction: Concepts and techniques,* edited by M. Heiman and J. Slomianko. Washington, DC: National Education Association.

Swartz, R. J., and D. N. Perkins. 1987. Teaching for thinking: A developmental model for the infusion of thinking skills into mainstream instruction. In *Teaching thinking skills: Theory and practice*, edited by F. Baron and R. Sternberg. New York: W.H. Freeman and Co.

————. 1989. Structured teaching for critical thinking and reasoning in standard subject area instruction. In *Informal reasoning and education,* edited by D. Perkins, J. W. Segal, and J. F. Voss. Hillsdale, NJ: Erlbaum.

————. 1989. *Teaching thinking: Issues and approaches.* Pacific Grove, CA: Midwest Publications.

Sylwester, R. 1995. *A celebration of neurons: An educator's guide to the human brain.* Alexandria, VA: Association for Supervision and Curriculum Development.

Taba, H. 1942. The evaluation of critical thinking. In *Teaching critical thinking in the social studies,* edited by Howard Anderson. Washington, DC: National Council for the Social Studies.

————. 1965. The teaching of thinking. *Elementary English* 42: 534–542.

Thorndike, E. 1903. *Educational psychology.* New York: Lemke and Buechner.

Torrance, E. P. 1979. *The search for satori and creativity.* Buffalo and Great Neck, NY: Creative Education Foundation and Creative Synergetics Associates.

Tyler, R. W. 1986–87. The five most significant curriculum events in the twentieth century. *Educational Leadership* 44(4): 36–37.

Upton, R. 1985. *Strategic reasoning.* Bloomington, IN: Innovative Sciences, Inc.

US Department of Education. 1986. *What works: Research about teaching and learning.* Washington, DC: Author.

————. 1996. *Goals 2000: Increasing student achievement through state and local initiatives.* Washington, DC: Author. Available: http://www.ed.gov/G2K/GoalsRpt/intro.html/.

von Oech, R. 1983. *A whack on the side of the head.* New York: Warner Books.

————. 1986. *A kick in the seat of the pants.* New York: Harper & Row.

Vygotsky, L. S. 1962. *Thought and language.* Cambridge: Massachusetts Institute of Technology Press.

Walberg, F. 1980. *Puzzle thinking.* Philadelphia: Franklin Institute Press.

Warner, S. A. 1972. *Teacher.* New York: Vintage Books.

Wenglinsky, H. 2000. *How teaching matters: Bringing the classroom back into discussions of teacher quality.* Princeton, NJ: Educational Testing Service. Available at http://www.ets.org/research/pic.

Westwater, A., and P. Wolfe. 2000. The brain-compatible curriculum. *Educational Leadership* 49–52.

Whimbey, A. 1975. *Intelligence can be taught.* New York: Innovative Science.

———. 1977. Teaching sequential thought: The cognitive skills approach. *Phi Delta Kappan* 59(4): 255–259.

Whimbey, A., and J. Lochhead. 1982. *Problem solving and comprehension,* 3rd ed. Philadelphia: The Franklin Institute Press.

———. 1984. *Beyond problem solving and comprehension.* Philadelphia: Franklin Institute Press.

Williams, B. 2001. *Cooperative learning: A standard for high achievement.* Chicago, IL: Fogarty & Associates.

Winocur, S. 1983. *Project impact.* Costa Mesa, CA: Orange County School District.

Wittrock, M. C. 1967. Replacement and nonreplacement strategies in children's problem solving. *Journal of Educational Psychology,* 69–74.

INDEX